THE HISTORY OF THE SAINTS

The History of the Saints

or, AN EXPOSÉ OF JOE SMITH
AND MORMONISM

THIRD EDITION

John C. Bennett

Introduction by Andrew F. Smith

UNIVERSITY OF ILLINOIS PRESS
Urbana and Chicago

Introduction © 2000 by the Board of Trustees
of the University of Illinois
Manufactured in the United States of America
ⓒ This book is printed on acid-free paper.

Library of Congress Cataloging-in-Publication Data
Bennett, John Cook, 1804–1867.
The history of the saints, or, An exposé of Joe Smith and Mormonism /
John C. Bennett; introduction by Andrew F. Smith.
p.   cm.
Originally published: 3rd ed. Boston : Leland & Whiting, 1842.
With new introd.
Includes bibliographical references.
ISBN 0-252-02589-X (hardcover : alk. paper)
1. Mormons—Controversial literature.
2. Smith, Joseph, 1805–1844.
3. Mormons—Illinois—Nauvoo—History—19th century.
4. Nauvoo (Ill.)—Church history—19th century.
I. Title: History of the saints.
II. Title: Exposé of Joe Smith and Mormonism. III. Title.
BX8645.B45   2000
289.3—dc21   99-087027

C 5 4 3 2 1

CONTENTS

INTRODUCTION

Andrew F. Smith

In early September 1840, John Cook Bennett joined the Mormon church in Nauvoo, Illinois. His meteoric ascent to power was astounding. Within months of his arrival, he became mayor of the city, a major general in its militia, chancellor of its university, and the second most important person in the Mormon hierarchy. While his rise was phenomenal, his fall was even more extraordinary: less than two years after reaching the top leadership, Bennett left Nauvoo, publicly charging Mormonism's leader Joseph Smith with gross sexual improprieties, ethical degradation, financial misbehavior, theft, and murder.

Bennett presented his case for these charges in *The History of the Saints; or, An Exposé of Joe Smith and Mormonism*. In the preface to the book, Bennett apologizes for its defects in style and the odd arrangement of its pages caused by the haste in which it was compiled. It is indeed a disjointed compilation of private letters, legal documents, records, and excerpts from previously published articles and books—all bound together by Bennett's commentaries. Had Bennett used the material he collected to produce a well-developed argument, his book might have been more effective, but it would have required much more time to write, and for Bennett speed was essential. Bennett's notorious break with the Mormons had received extensive coverage in newspapers throughout the country. Knowing that the hype would soon subside, Bennett immediately launched a series of titillating anti-Mormon lectures that were sure to attract the press and add to his visibility. These lectures gave Bennett an opportunity to test potential material, and the hefty entrance fees paid by attendees were helpful to a man without any other known income. The prompt publication of *The History of the Saints* built on this notoriety, lent him legitimacy, and generated additional income through book sales. As the book was hastily assembled, its readers found it disorganized and difficult to understand at the time of its publication. It is even more so for today's readers, who may be even less aware of the specifics mentioned or the context of the events cited. However, as obscure as these matters may be to non-Mormons, the subjects and questions raised by this book have resonated through Mormon history.[1]

Mormon historians have generally dismissed John Cook Bennett as a true believer who sadly went astray or as an opportunist masquerading as a devout religious convert. As a consequence, Bennett's *History of the Saints* has been ignored or has served as a target of religious condemnation. However, while anti-Bennett cant may be useful as a tool of religious propaganda, historians have a different responsibility. Leaders of social institutions rarely represent themselves or their own actions accurately. They tend to give themselves a favorable gloss and cast an unfavorable light on those opposed to them. Sometimes misrepresentation is intentional, but mostly it is a reflection of the insiders' lack of understanding of their own motivations.

Exploring the exceptions often helps us to understand the real rules that govern an institution as opposed to those publicly promulgated by its leaders. Pariahs tell us much about the institutions from which they have been expelled. By examining closed or sensitive topics associated with the rejected, historians can better understand the true institutional norms and ways of operating. By examining Bennett's activities and the response of Mormon leaders, we can better understand early Mormonism and the mainstream response to the fledgling religion.

Bennett's Pre-Nauvoo Life

Although John Cook Bennett led a Barnumesque adult life, his early years were not particularly unusual. He was born in Fairhaven, Massachusetts, in 1804. A few years later his family moved to southeastern Ohio, where Bennett grew into adulthood. Little is known of his formal education. At the age of eighteen, Bennett decided to study medicine under the tutelage of his uncle, Dr. Samuel P. Hildreth, a skilled physician and renowned natural scientist. Bennett took full advantage of Hildreth's knowledge and ably served a three-year apprenticeship.[2] Bennett passed the exam required to practice medicine and was married in the Methodist church near Marietta in 1826. All evidence indicates that Bennett was a successful physician. In addition, he served as an itinerant Methodist minister and joined the Masons (10).

During this time, Bennett helped lobby Ohio legislators to incorporate a Methodist Episcopal Church. Subsequently, he supported a bill to create a Methodist university. However, when Bennett pleaded for support from the Ohio Annual Conference of the Methodist Associate Church, he was turned down. Bennett abruptly left the Methodist church and shifted his allegiance to the Christian Disciples, a sect founded by Thomas Campbell and his son Alexander Campbell. The Christian Disciples, or Campbellites, advocated Protestant reunion by discarding sectarian creeds and "restoring primitive Christianity." Bennett promptly proclaimed that his proposed university would be under the auspices of the Christian Disciples. As a result of this shift, Bennett secured the interest and backing of the leader of the denomination, Alexander Campbell, but lost support from Methodists in the Ohio legislature. The university bill was defeated. Bennett tried unsuccessfully to establish additional universities and medical colleges in Virginia and Ohio.

After these failures, Bennett wandered about the Midwest, settling in Indiana. In January 1833, he finally succeeded in incorporating Christian College in New Albany, Indiana. Unfortunately, Bennett had failed to consult with prominent Christian Disciples whose names he used in the incorporation bill. Campbell was upset and demanded that Bennett sever any connection between the college and the denomination. Bennett did so by changing the name of the institution to Indiana University.

The main problem Bennett confronted was how to finance the university. Bennett personally had few financial resources, and no assistance was forthcoming from other quarters. Bennett believed that many practicing physicians in the Midwest were highly skilled but did not possess medical degrees simply due to lack of money or opportunity. Although the new university neither offered classes nor possessed any equipment, Bennett conferred medical degrees upon anyone who purportedly passed examinations. He extended this practice to other academic areas, such as law, theology, and the arts and sciences. Bennett sold degrees throughout the Midwest and eventually in New York and New England. This antagonized degree-holding medical professionals, who pronounced his actions unethical and illegal. When the heat increased, Bennett quit Indiana and returned to Ohio, where he tried to lobby legislators to create another university. When Bennett's selling of diplomas was exposed, the Ohio senate unanimously voted the bill down.[3]

However, the Ohio legislature did incorporate Willoughby University of Lake Erie in Chagrin, a small community nineteen miles east of Cleveland on the turnpike to Buffalo. In July 1834, the trustees received a flattering letter from a "Dr. J. C. Bennett," who lived in South Bloomfield, Ohio. Bennett proclaimed that it was his duty to assist in building up the medical college. Some citizens of this community found him a "sober, moral man, scrupulously honest in all his dealings" (11). Without checking into his past, the Willoughby trustees appointed Bennett an agent for the university and elected him to the position of honorary member of the board (11). The trustees charged him with the responsibility of organizing the medical department and obtaining additional faculty. In a whirlwind of activity, Bennett recruited staff, prepared bylaws, solicited funds, and encouraged prospective students to enroll. The first term of the college commenced in November 1834. Several students were pleased enough with Bennett's instruction to sign a letter highly commending him (13).

Willoughby University had taken its name from Westel Willoughby, a prominent New York physician, in hopes that he might agree to serve as president of the struggling institution. To so encourage him, the town of Chagrin changed its name to Willoughby in late 1834. Bennett informed Westel Willoughby of the name change, but Willoughby was still unwilling to move from New York. He did recommend Bennett as a prospective president of the university (12).

Bennett's Itinerant Interludes

While still at Willoughby University, Bennett befriended William Smith, a faculty member who believed that tomatoes were a remedy for many diseases. In Bennett's first lecture he summarized Smith's beliefs, declaring that tomatoes successfully treated diarrhea, violent bilious attacks, and dyspepsia (indigestion), and urged all citizens to eat tomatoes as they were "the most healthy article of the Materia Alimentary." During the summer of 1835, he circulated an extract of his tomato lecture to newspapers and journals in Ohio. Bennett's praise of tomatoes was unusual, since many Americans still considered tomatoes to be inedible.[4] Even those Americans who ate tomatoes were not aware of their purported healthful qualities as claimed by Bennett. The immediate response to his ideas was sensational. Hundreds of newspapers, agricultural journals, and other works reprinted his claims, which continued to be published for years (31, 301).

Bennett entertained high hopes for his career at Willoughby University, but when his vending of diplomas from Indiana University surfaced, the trustees in Ohio removed him from his professorship and revoked his status as agent. While Bennett was upset with this turn of events, he remained charged with energy. He moved from Willoughby to Massillon, where he attempted to organize a "Grand Universal School." The purpose of the school was more than just the education of Massillon's youth. Bennett and Osee Welch, a Massillon resident, concluded that literary institutions also possessed banking powers. Welch, with Bennett's assistance, obtained a charter for the Universal School of Massillon from the Ohio General Assembly. Before the operation could go into effect, however, President Andrew Jackson's Specie Circular of July 1836 was issued. It required that government lands be purchased with gold or silver. A deflationary cycle ensued, ending in the Panic of 1837. Eight hundred banks nationwide suspended payments.[5]

From 1835 to 1838, Bennett continued to practice medicine and seek new opportunities (10–11, 13–14). He lived in at least six different localities in three states and traveled incessantly throughout the Midwest, eventually relocating to Hocking City, Ohio. While there, Bennett completed his first pamphlet, an obstetrical handbook entitled *The Accoucheur's Vade Mecum*. In addition to pursuing his medical profession, Bennett tried to incorporate a militia unit, named the Hocking Valley Dragoons, but the bill faltered in the Ohio legislature. Bennett left Hocking without his family, but with references from his uncle, the mayor of the city, and the local Methodist pastor (13–14).

Never one to be thwarted, Bennett moved to Fairfield, Illinois, and had a bill introduced into the Illinois legislature to incorporate another militia group, the Invincible Dragoons. The bill passed in early February 1839. Bennett's name was listed first among the petitioners.[6] As was customary, the militia chose its own officers, and Bennett was duly elected to the office of brigadier general (14).

While in Fairfield, Bennett also became interested in phrenology. Phrenology originated as an experimental "science" grounded in the assumption that anatomical and physiological characteristics have direct influence upon behavior. Today, it is remembered usually as the attempt to determine personality strengths and weaknesses based upon the contours of one's head. Phrenological societies sprung up in America during the 1830s. These societies propagated itinerant phrenologists, who exploited a growing interest in the subject by charging for developing charts. One such person was B. A. Parnell, who developed Bennett's phrenological chart during the late 1830s. As Bennett published his chart, he must have been satisfied with the findings (180–86).[7]

The Mormons

Bennett joined the Mormons in September 1840, but he had been in contact with them for eight years. In January 1832, Bennett encountered William McLellin, a recent convert to Mormonism. McLellin escorted Bennett to meet Joseph Smith and Sidney Rigdon, the leaders of the Mormon church in Hiram, Ohio. Joseph Smith Jr., prophet, seer, and revelator of the Mormon church, was born in Vermont in 1805. About 1823, by his account, he was visited by an angel named Moroni, who revealed the location of a record of the early inhabitants of North America. Smith asserted that the record had been inscribed in an unknown language on a set of plates of precious metal. He translated and published the discovery as the Book of Mormon. On April 6, 1830, Smith and others established a church at Manchester, New York. Subsequently, the denomination became known as the Church of Jesus Christ of Latter-day Saints, commonly called Mormons.

One important early Mormon convert was Sidney Rigdon, who had previously been a prominent Christian Disciple minister residing in Kirtland, Ohio.[8] Shortly after Rigdon joined the Mormons, Smith claimed to have received a revelation instructing him to move the church to Kirtland. Rigdon's conversion influenced others, including John Corrill, then living in Harpersville, Ohio. After Corrill's conversion, Smith sent him to Missouri, where Corrill was instrumental in establishing the Mormon church.[9]

While Bennett "talked considerable with Br Joseph" in 1832, no record of their conversations has been uncovered.[10] However, it is debatable if Bennett was impressed with either Smith or Mormonism. At the time, Bennett was a follower of Alexander Campbell, who was strongly opposed to the Mormons. Campbell published anti-Mormon articles in his publication, the *Millennial Harbinger.* These articles were compiled in the first anti-Mormon pamphlet, titled *Delusions: An Analysis of the Book of Mormon,* published in 1832.[11]

While at Willoughby, Bennett befriended Eber D. Howe, the publisher of the *Painesville Telegraph.* Howe printed several of Bennett's articles and promotions for the university. At this time, Howe also published *Mormonism Unvailed,* the first anti-Mormon book. The materials for the book were evidently collected by a Doctor Philastus Hurlbut. He was not a medical professional; his mother had given him the first name of Doctor.[12] Bennett later incorporated a total of thirty-one pages from *Mormonism Unvailed* in *The History of the Saints,* including many dispositions written by citizens who knew Joseph Smith and his family when they lived in New York (61–84). This he supplemented with other material regarding the plates Smith claimed to have found (174–75).

Bennett also included passages from *Mormonism Unvailed* concerning Solomon Spaulding's "Manuscript Found" and its relationship to the Book of Mormon. According to the affidavits, Solomon Spaulding was born in 1761 in Ashford, Connecticut. He attended Dartmouth College, where he studied for the ministry. He went into business in New York. In 1809 Spaulding moved to Conneaut, Ohio, where he began writing a book titled "Manuscript Found." Spaulding was proud of his work and read it to many Conneaut residents. In 1812, he moved to Pittsburgh, where he attempted unsuccessfully to publish his book. Subsequently, he moved to Amity, Pennsylvania, where he died in 1816.

According to Solomon's brother John Spaulding, "Manuscript Found" was "an historical romance of the first settlers of America, endeavoring to show that the American Indians" were "the descendants of the Jews, or the lost tribes." John Spaulding stated that his brother's work "gave a detailed account of their journey from Jerusalem, by land and sea, till they arrived in America, under the command of NEPHI and LEHI. They afterwards had quarrels and contentions, and separated into two distinct nations, one of which he denominated Nephites and the other Lamanites. Cruel and bloody wars ensued, in which great multitudes were slain. They buried their dead in large heaps, which caused the mounds so common in this country." John Spaulding compared the Book of Mormon with the content of his brother's manuscript as he recalled it and concluded that both contained the same historical matter and names, with the exception of the religious matter. John Spaulding had no idea how Joseph Smith Jr. had acquired his brother's manuscript.[13]

While conducting research for his work, Doctor Hurlbut tracked down

Conneaut's residents. Many remembered Spaulding's readings and willingly offered their testimony as to their recollections. As to be expected, there were differences among the affidavits, but most confirmed basic information consistent with John Spaulding's statements. Hurlbut then tried to locate the original manuscript. He tracked down Solomon Spaulding's wife, who had remarried and relocated first to New York and then to Massachusetts. She stated that Spaulding had a great many manuscripts, one of which was entitled "Manuscript Found," but she did not remember its contents. She believed that the manuscript was taken to the printing office of Patterson and Lambdin in Pittsburgh, but she did not recall what happened to it subsequently. However, she had left some of Spaulding's writings in a trunk in New York. Hurlbut examined the trunk but found only one manuscript in Spaulding's handwriting. This was an untitled romance, "purporting to have been translated from the Latin, found on 24 rolls of parchment in a cave, on the banks of Conneaut Creek, but written in modern style, and giving a fabulous account of a ship's being driven upon the American coast, while proceeding from Rome to Britain, a short time previous to the Christian era, this country then being inhabited by the Indians. This old M.S. has been shown to several of the foregoing witnesses, who recognise it as Spaulding's, he having told them that he had altered his first plan of writing, by going farther back with dates, and writing in the old scripture style, in order that it might appear more ancient. They say that it bears no resemblance to the '*Manuscript Found.*'"[14]

Seven years after the publication of *Mormonism Unvailed,* Benjamin Winchester, a Mormon living in Pennsylvania, tried to discredit Hurlbut and the Spaulding theory regarding the origin of the Book of Mormon. According to Winchester, Hurlbut had been a preacher in a Methodist church in Jamestown, New York, but had been "expelled for unvirtuous conduct with a young lady." Hurlbut joined the Mormons in 1832. In the spring of 1833, Hurlbut's "unvirtuous habits" were manifest; he was "cast off from the Church," and his Mormon license to preach was withdrawn. Hurlbut appealed the decision and his license was restored. But while visiting Thompson, Ohio, Hurlbut again attempted "to seduce a young female" and was "immediately expelled from the church." Hurlbut then set out "to demolish as far as practicable, what he had once endeavoured [*sic*] to build up," or so claimed Winchester. Hurlbut preached at several churches, spouting anti-Mormonism, and began writing the manuscript that subsequently provided the basis for *Mormonism Unvailed.* While lecturing, Hurlbut ran across a man who reported that Solomon Spaulding had written a manuscript in the form of a novel that "professed to give an account of a race of people who originated from the Romans, which Mr. S. said he had translated from a Latin parchment that he had found." Winchester concluded, without presenting any supporting evidence, that the manuscript that Hurlbut found was the only one that Spaulding had written.[15]

Mormonism Unvailed speculated that Sidney Rigdon had acquired Spaulding's "Manuscript Found" and passed it on to Joseph Smith, but this was clearly wrong. At that time, Rigdon was a follower of Alexander Campbell and had no known association with Smith. The supposed Rigdon connection with the Spaulding manuscript has been discredited subsequently by Mormon and non-Mormon historians, who have then concluded that the entire theory was wrong. Discrediting one speculation, however, does not demolish the theory.

According to Winchester, Hurlbut sold his manuscript along with the affidavits to E. D. Howe, who probably revised it and published it as *Mormonism Unvailed.* What precise influence Howe had in preparing the manuscript for publication is unclear. A number of affidavits appearing in the work were addressed to Howe; Hurlbut's name does not appear anywhere in the published work. According to Winchester, the reason for this was that Hurlbut's reputation "was too rotten."[16] Winchester clearly had religious motivation to attack Hurlbut and the Spaulding theory and he offered no outside evidence to support his accusations, yet subsequent observers have presented his allegations as fact.

There the matter rested until 1884, when a Spaulding manuscript was discovered by L. L. Rice, then living in Honolulu, Hawaii. Rice had purchased Howe's newspaper in the 1830s. Among Howe's papers was the untitled manuscript that Hurlbut had found in 1833. This was presumably the Spaulding romance that *Mormonism Unvailed* found to be unrelated to "Manuscript Found," described by those writing affidavits regarding Spaulding's manuscript. Rice donated the manuscript to the president of Oberlin College in Ohio. Beginning in 1885, Mormon sources proclaimed it to be "Manuscript Found."[17]

From this imbroglio, what clearly emerges is that Solomon Spaulding did not write the Book of Mormon. The existing Spaulding manuscript is not composed in the same style and has no religious content. Moreover, those supporting the Spaulding theory have offered no convincing connection between Joseph Smith and Spaulding's "Manuscript Found." If it were not for the affidavits of those who knew Spaulding when he wrote "Manuscript Found," the Spaulding theory could be dismissed. These affidavits, however, clearly attest that names and incidents in a Spaulding manuscript were similar to those in the Book of Mormon. Despite subsequent statements to the contrary, no evidence was offered at the time challenging the authenticity of the affidavits, which were widely circulated in newspapers and books (115–22). As none of those individuals who provided these affidavits are known to have retracted them, two possibilities emerge: either Hurlbut and Howe orchestrated a widespread anti-Mormon conspiracy among Solomon Spaulding's friends to discredit the Book of Mormon; or a Spaulding manuscript written about 1812 contained the names Nephi, Lehi, Lamanites, and portrayed incidents similar to those in the Book of Mormon. Based on the evidence currently available, either alternative is possible.

Anti-Mormon Agitation

Among the financial institutions that failed during the Panic of 1837 was the Kirtland Safety Anti-Banking Society, whose president was Sidney Rigdon and cashier was Joseph Smith. Local investors blamed Rigdon and Smith for the failure. An angry mob ran many Mormons out of Kirtland. A number of Mormons migrated to Missouri. Joseph Smith took the reins of power when he arrived in March 1838. Some Mormons became increasingly agitated concerning Smith's decisions. Dissent flared within the Missouri Mormon community as Smith attacked the dissenters. To enforce his will, Smith created the Daughter of Zion, or the Danites, a band of Mormon vigilantes who purportedly followed Smith's orders (324–26, 331–33).

This suppression of dissent internally contributed to the adoption of a "militant stance against potential foes outside the movement."[18] While difficulties had existed since the establishment of the first Mormon communities in Missouri, tension with non-Mormons rapidly increased as the Mormon presence expanded. During the summer of 1838 these matters exploded. Speaking at a Fourth of July celebration that year, Sidney Rigdon warned publicly that the "mob that comes on us to disturb us, it shall be between us and them a war of *extermination,* for we will follow them till the *last drop of their blood is spilled,* or else they will have to exterminate us. For we will carry the seat of *war* to their own *houses* and their own *families,* and one party or the other shall be utterly destroyed." Rigdon ended with a flourish: "Neither will we indulge any man, or set of men, in instituting vexatious lawsuits against us, to cheat us out of our rights; if they attempt it, we say woe be unto them. We this day, then, proclaim ourselves free, with a purpose and a determination, that can never be broken,—*No, Never!* No, NEVER!! NO, NEVER!!!" (141, 142).

Rigdon's speech received wide distribution, further inflaming non-Mormons throughout Missouri. An electoral altercation on August 6 pitted Mormons against non-Mormons throughout northwestern Missouri. Joseph Smith became more militant, and the Mormon militia plundered non-Mormon settlements on October 18.[19] Missouri governor Lilburn Boggs ordered the state militia, led by Generals John B. Clark (322–23), Samuel B. Lucas, and Alexander W. Doniphan, to expel the Mormons. Boggs maintained that "the Mormons must be treated as enemies, and must be exterminated, or driven from the State if necessary for the public peace." This was subsequently referred to as the "exterminating order."[20]

To avoid catastrophe, Joseph Smith asked Reed Peck and John Corrill, then the leader of the Mormon militia, to strike a deal with the state militia. The deal involved turning over Smith, Rigdon, and other Mormon leaders to the state militia; the Mormons agreed to leave Missouri, their property being given to the non-Mormons whose property had been destroyed in the "Mormon War."

Corrill claimed that Smith consented to this agreement; Smith blamed Corrill and the other dissenters for the entire fiasco, calling them ignorant men whose eyes were "full of adultery."[21]

The Mormon leaders surrendered and were imprisoned. Major General Lucas of the Missouri militia ordered General Doniphan to execute them. Doniphan refused to carry out the order as there had been no trial.[22] The grand jury of the circuit court in Daviess County indicted them for high treason against the state as well as for murder, burglary, arson, robbery, and larceny (324–28). Judge Austin A. King collected extensive testimony about the Mormon War (324–40), including statements from Sampson Avard (328–29), John Corrill (329–30), Reed Peck (331–33), John Whitmer (338–39), and George Hinkle (344–35). Their testimony was later published by the General Assembly of Missouri and by the United States Senate.[23]

Meanwhile, the majority of Mormons fled eastward toward the Mississippi River. When they crossed into Illinois, the citizens of Quincy welcomed them. Smith and Rigdon spent several months jailed in Missouri before they escaped to Illinois. Governor Boggs tried to extradite them. Illinois's Governor Thomas Carlin passed the extradition request down to the Hancock County sheriff, who returned it to the governor, claiming that the parties named had not been located.[24]

Beginning in May 1839, the Mormons began buying property in Lee County in Iowa Territory and in Commerce, Illinois, a small community within a horseshoe bend in the Mississippi River fifty-five miles north of Quincy. Smith renamed the community *Nauvoo,* which purportedly was a Hebrew word meaning "beautiful habitation for man" and connoting "the idea of rest" (188–93). The new community was founded upon the teachings of the developing Mormon religion. In 1840, the government of the Mormon church was structured into four major institutions: the First Presidency, consisting of Joseph Smith and two assistant presidents, Hyrum Smith, Joseph Smith's brother, and Sidney Rigdon; the Quorum of Twelve Apostles, who were effectively missionaries, headed by Brigham Young; the Nauvoo High Council, made up of twelve high priests, who formed the judicial arm of the church; and the Nauvoo stake presidency.[25]

Bennett Joins the Mormons

At the time of the Mormon expulsion, Bennett was thriving in southern Illinois. In 1840, the Illinois militia officers elected him to the unpaid position of quartermaster general of Illinois, responsible for the maintenance and distribution of arms and munitions throughout the state. Bennett attended a medical convention in Springfield in June (16–17), and while there he visited a Mormon meeting. Upon returning to Fairfield, Bennett commenced writing a series of flattery-filled letters to Joseph Smith and Sidney Rigdon. In the first letter, dated July 25, 1840, Bennett declared that he "should be much happier" with them and revealed his plans to move to Nauvoo the following spring. Two days later, a second letter from Bennett advised Smith and Rigdon to amass all Mormons in Nauvoo: "It would be my deliberate advice to you to concentrate all of your Church at one point. If Hancock county, with Commerce as its commercial emporium, is to be that point, well; fix upon it." Bennett declared that he was already with them in spirit and planned to be with them in person as soon as possible. He planned to practice his medical profession "but at the same time your people shall have all the benefits of my speaking powers, and my untiring energies in behalf of the good and holy faith." He hoped that time would "soon come when your people will become my people, your God my God." He suggested setting up a meeting in Springfield since he had "many things to communicate." Without waiting for a reply, Bennett wrote a third letter, reporting that only with difficulty could he "forgo the felicity of an immediate immersion into the true faith of your beloved people." Bennett wrote again on August 15, 1840, announcing his plans to relocate to Nauvoo immediately.[26] Bennett's friend N. N. Smith was upset with Bennett's move to Nauvoo, as his services were still "much required" in Fairfield (18).

The reason why Bennett went to Nauvoo was debated in 1842 and has been a topic of discussion ever since. *The History of the Saints* opens with Bennett's explanation of why he joined the Mormon church (5–10). Bennett avowed that he had "*never believed in them or their doctrines*" (5). According to Bennett, this was an undercover caper intended to acquire evidence of Mormon perfidy and to witness "the secret wires of the fabric, and likewise those who moved them" (7). His explanation was challenged by contemporaries. The editors of the *Alton Telegraph and Democratic Review,* for instance, reported that Bennett had offered "the most plausible excuse his ingenuity could invent for his conduct."[27] Bennett's rationalization has properly met with derision subsequently by most historians.

Some Mormon writers have postulated that Bennett genuinely believed in Mormonism when he went to Nauvoo but subsequently went astray. While there were many genuine cases of spontaneous conversion to Mormonism, religious fervor was not likely to have been central to Bennett's move to Nauvoo. The correspondence with Joseph Smith and Sidney Rigdon was presumably an effort to gain their confidence. The Mormons were rapidly growing and they promised an untapped political potential in Illinois. Bennett probably thought that he could exploit the Mormons for his own gain. He likely believed from the onset that Smith was a charlatan and Mormonism a fraud. Neither of these circumstances would have particularly mattered to him, for he pursued secular, not religious, goals (7).

Upon arrival in Nauvoo about September 1, 1840, Bennett immediately befriended Joseph Smith, who permitted him to board with the Smith family for several months. On September 21, Bennett received a patriarchal blessing from Hyrum Smith (42–44). Bennett became Joseph Smith's closest friend and confidant, later claiming to have known "Joseph *better than any other man living* for at least fourteen months!" William Law, who later became assistant president of the Mormon church, agreed with Bennett's assessment. According to Law, Bennett "was more in the secret confidence of Joseph than perhaps any other man in the city."[28]

Several factors contributed to Bennett's blossoming friendship with Smith. Shortly after Bennett's arrival, Joseph Smith's father died. He had been the patriarch of the Mormon church. This loss may have made Joseph Smith Jr. vulnerable, particularly because many other Mormon leaders were engaged in missionary work and were not in Nauvoo. Bennett had many positive qualities that might have been attractive to Joseph Smith. Bennett had been a preacher and therefore knew the Bible. As quartermaster general of Illinois, he ostensibly possessed a military background and controlled the distribution of the militia's arms and equipment. After a few months' trial, Smith offered Bennett his friendship.

Bennett actively participated in the general conference of the Mormon church held in early October 1840. Bennett "spoke at some length, on the oppression to which the Church had been subjected, and remarked that it was necessary for the brethren to stand by each other, and resist every unlawful attempt at persecution." On one morning, he was appointed to a committee "to draft a bill for the incorporation of the town of Nauvoo, and other purposes." He was also appointed the "delegate to urge the passage of the said bill through the legislature." In the afternoon, Bennett presented the outlines of its charter, which was approved without discussion.[29]

Bennett went to Springfield to lobby Illinois state legislators to incorporate the city of Nauvoo. Due to his previous productive lobbying activities, Bennett knew several political leaders in Springfield and he was the "boon companion" of the editor of the Democratic *Illinois Register*. To gain support, Bennett flattered both the Whigs and the Democrats and gained support from all legislators.[30] The Nauvoo charter was similar to other city charters, with the exception that it contained a provision for the creation of the Nauvoo Legion (194–99). The original legislation was subsequently expanded to permit any citizen of Hancock County to join the legion (201–2). Bennett also was responsible for the passage of a bill to incorporate the Nauvoo Agricultural and Manufacturing Association (202–4) and the Nauvoo House Association (204–5). Smith was elated with Bennett's role in lobbying for these bills (32). Smith characterized Bennett as a superior orator, "active and diligent, always employing himself in doing good to his fellow men." Two weeks later, Smith reported a revelation from God regarding Bennett (33).[31]

Thereafter, Bennett's rise to power in Nauvoo was spectacular. He was elected mayor of Nauvoo on February 1, 1841, and two days later gave his "Inaugural Address" (19–24, 31–32). As mayor, he served as executive of the city council and encouraged the passage of many ordinances (206–7). Bennett also served as the chancellor of the University of the City of Nauvoo, which had responsibility for the common schools in Nauvoo (24–25, 210–11). He was elected major general of the Nauvoo Legion (18, 31, 32–33, 34). He became an important religious leader at the general church conference in April 1841. Due to illness, Rigdon called upon Bennett to officiate at the conference in his stead. Joseph Smith appointed Bennett to replace the ailing assistant president until "Rigdon's health should be restored" (26).[32]

Joseph Smith was elected lieutenant general of the Nauvoo Legion, the highest military designation at that time in America. *The History of the Saints* includes an engraved illustration of Smith in his ornate lieutenant general's uniform, complete with epaulets, flashy embroidery, and a fancy hat decorated with stars and a plume (opp. 56). Despite Smith's senior rank, Bennett organized the legion, which included musicians, armorers, surgeons, heralds, and a host of high-ranking officers. The legion grew quickly, mainly because all able-bodied males in Nauvoo were required by law to join (211–14). As quartermaster general, Bennett shipped small arms and cannons from the state repository to Nauvoo. These transactions upset Governor Carlin, who fired Bennett from the quartermaster position, charging that Bennett had a conflict of interest. Bennett complained to an Illinois senator, who in turn asked Winfield Scott for an opinion (18–19), but it made no difference to Carlin. Bennett also courted newspaper editors, who published laudatory accounts of his activities, particularly when the cornerstone of the Nauvoo temple was laid (27–31). Bennett's views on slavery were also given prominence in Illinois newspapers (40).

The Rise of Anti-Mormonism in Illinois

When the Mormons fled Missouri, the citizens of Illinois welcomed them with open arms. With non-Mormon help, the Mormons were able to establish their community in Nauvoo. Within a short time, however, this support waned. One reason for the declining tolerance was the perceived criminal conduct of some Mormons. Issues related to theft were of particular concern, and non-Mormons accused Mormons of stealing. When these charges went to trial, non-Mormons believed that the Nauvoo courts failed to prosecute the offenders. Mormons denied such charges. William Law, one of Joseph Smith's councilors, asserted that there were no criminal charges lodged against Mormons in Illinois (87). However, cases were brought against Mormons for theft, murder, and rape, according to the records of Hancock, McDonough, and Adams counties and the City of Nauvoo (88–89). In letters to the Burlington *Hawk-Eye and Iowa Patriot,* David Kilbourn and Edward Kilbourn listed numerous alleged crimes committed by Mormons against non-Mormons. The Kilbourns specifically singled out Bennett for criticism in their letters. When Bennett published their letters in *The History of the Saints,* he expunged his own name (89–93).

The Kilbourns also reported that alcohol was sold in Nauvoo, and that drunkenness was not unknown. The Nauvoo City Council prohibited the sale of small amounts of spirits but permitted the wholesaling of alcoholic beverages and the retailing of beer and wine. Bennett and others claimed that Joseph Smith was an imbiber and that he was drunk occasionally (94). A few days before Bennett resigned as mayor of Nauvoo, he received a letter from Joseph Smith's secretary, William Clayton, complaining that several people retailed liquor in Nauvoo (95). While alcohol was undoubtedly sold in Nauvoo, the city council's ordinance eliminated legal bars and saloons so prevalent in other cities at the time.

On May 6, 1841, Judge Stephen A. Douglas appointed Bennett to the position of Master in Chancery for Hancock County (25). This position was an important one, as its holder often performed duties of a judge of the Supreme Court of Illinois. Bennett's appointment was made "over the application of several of the most reputable citizens of that county" and it met with considerable opposition among non-Mormons. Thomas Sharp, editor of the *Warsaw Signal* in Warsaw, Illinois, estimated that Bennett's appointment was "frowned on with indignity by nine-tenths of the substantial citizens of the county." Bennett called Sharp a liar for having insinuated that he was not sincere in his faith. The *Times and Seasons,* a Mormon newspaper in Nauvoo, responded by saying that Sharp opposed the appointment simply because Bennett was "a Mormon!" This was "the cause of the Editor's vile vituperation" (34).[33]

Yet, prior to this time, the *Warsaw Signal* was not particularly anti-Mormon. While there were many reasons why Sharp opposed the Mormons, his initial concern was their political power in Hancock County. Bennett's appointment, because he was a Mormon and appeared otherwise unqualified, deeply distressed Sharp. Bennett fueled the fire by telling Sharp that the Mormons would choose "always to make their power be felt at the ballot box."[34] Sharp promptly transformed the *Warsaw Signal* into an anti-Mormon newspaper. He also co-published William Harris's *Mormonism Portrayed.* Not much is known about Harris. He was born in 1803 in New Brunswick, Canada, and became a Mormon elder in 1834. Two years later, he received a patriarchal blessing from Joseph Smith Sr., in Kirtland, Ohio. Harris broke with Mormonism and published *Mormonism Portrayed* in Warsaw, Illinois. Sharp later announced that he had written the book based on materials supplied by Harris. Sharp particularly credited himself with writing the chapters on the Book of Mormon and the history of the Mormons. Bennett later incorporated most of this work into *The History of the Saints* (57–61, 109–14, 124–43).[35]

Mormonism Portrayed was not the first anti-Mormon book written by an insider. After Joseph Smith expelled him from the church, John Corrill published *Brief History of the Church of Christ of Latter Day Saints* in 1839. William Swartzell, a former deacon in the Mormon church, published his *Mormonism Exposed* in 1840.[36] Neither of these works appear to have had much distribution. Bennett did not quote from them in *The History of the Saints,* but he did reprint Corrill's testimony against the Mormons in Missouri in 1838 (329–30).

Many non-Mormons also weighed in against the Mormons. La Roy Sunderland, a Methodist minister and editor of *Zion's Watchman,* began a series of articles on Mormonism in January 1838. These were collected, edited, and published under the title of *Mormonism Exposed and Refuted.* The Mormon leader Parley P. Pratt responded to Sunderland's attacks with *Mormonism Unveiled: Zion's Watchman Unmasked, and its Editor, Mr. L. R. Sunderland, Exposed: Truth Vindicated: the Devil Mad, and Priestcraft in Danger!*[37] Bennett incorporated a small section of Sunderland's work into *The History of the Saints* (143–48, 161–62) but failed to mention Pratt's responses.

Jonathan B. Turner, a professor of the Illinois College in Jacksonville, Illinois, published *Mormonism in All Ages: or the Rise, Progress, and Causes of Mormonism* in 1842.[38] Among Turner's concerns was the origin of the Book of Mormon (103–9, 162–74). Outside of Illinois, writers in newspapers and periodicals attacked Mormonism. Bennett included some of this criticism, such as that conveyed by J. N. T. Tucker in the Millerite *Sign of the Times* (122–23). Mormon missionaries, proclaimed Tucker, engaged in performing fraudulent miracles (176–78).

Smith vs. Bennett; Bennett vs. Smith

Bennett sought to form a Masonic Lodge in Nauvoo. On October 15, 1841, Abraham Jonas, grand master of the Illinois Masonic Lodge, granted a dispensation to create the Nauvoo Lodge. Bennett was elected secretary of the lodge and assisted in writing its bylaws. However, shortly after the lodge was launched, Jonas received a letter from "a valued and esteemed Brother" stating that Bennett had been expelled from a lodge at Fairfield, Ohio. Jonas insisted on an immediate investigation. Jonas's letter that set forth the case concerning the reality of Bennett's expulsion was read at a special meeting of the lodge. Formal charges were filed against Bennett, who was requested to ad-

dress the accusations.[39] Bennett presented various documents that supported
his position, including a letter from his uncle Erastus Webb, a member of the
lodge from which Bennett had supposedly been expelled (48).

These charges were minor compared with those lodged by Joseph Smith.
The schism between Smith and Bennett that abruptly appeared in mid-1842
was likely a culmination of long-festering issues. Smith was impressed with
Bennett at first and made effective use of him in Nauvoo's secular realm.
However, Bennett's constant demand for attention was undoubtedly weari-
some. When Brigham Young and other apostles returned from England, Smith
could do without Bennett.

According to Joseph Smith, a short time after Bennett had arrived in Nauvoo, Smith reported that he had received a communication declaring that
Bennett "was a very mean man, and had a wife, and two or three children in
McConnelsville, Morgan county, Ohio." In February 1841, Smith sent George
Miller to McConnelsville to delve into Bennett's past. Miller interviewed several informants, who reported that Bennett's wife had "followed him from
place to place, with no suspicion of his unfaithfulness to her; at length however, he became so bold in his departures, that it was evident to all around that
he was a sore offender, and his wife left him under satisfactory evidence of
his adulterous connections; nor was this his only fault; he used her bad otherwise." Bennett wanted her to sue for divorce, but she had not agreed to do it.
He began to keep company with an unidentified young lady, who, "ignorant
of his having a wife living, gave way to his addresses, and became confident,
from his behavior towards her, that he intended to marry her." Bennett succeeded with this ploy and seduced "a respectable female by lying, and subjected her to public infamy and disgrace." Smith, "seeing the folly of such an
acquaintance, persuaded Bennett to desist; and, on account of his continuing
his course, finally threatened to expose him if he did not desist." But Bennett
was not, according to Smith, "contented with what he had already done, he
made the attempt on others, and by using the same language, seduced them
also."[40] Bennett was specifically accused of having had an adulterous relationship with Sarah Pratt, the wife of Orson Pratt. At the time, Pratt was one of
the Twelve Apostles engaged in missionary work in England. Bennett coun-
tered that Joseph Smith was attracted to Sarah Pratt. Bennett argued that Smith
intended to make Sarah Pratt one of his wives.[41]

These charges continued to spread about Nauvoo. Bennett resigned from
his position as mayor and voluntarily withdrew from the Mormon church on
May 17, 1842 (41–42). Joseph Smith penned a letter permitting Bennett to
do so "with the best of feelings" (40–41). At a special meeting of the city
council held two days later, Joseph Smith was elected mayor and Hyrum Smith
vice-mayor. According to Joseph Smith, "On account of the reports in circulation in the city this day, concerning the ex-Mayor, and to quiet the public

fraud. He subsequently joined the Episcopalians in Ohio. He indulged in a variety of nefarious activities, finally joining the Presbyterian church in Brooklyn, where he was charged with falsehood and drunkenness.[62]

The History of the Saints

While charges and countercharges reverberated around the country, Bennett announced that he intended to publish a tell-all book, titled "The History of the Saints," in which he planned to "tell most of the actings and doings at Nauvoo for the last two years, of most of their great men, and some of their great women, too."[63] When Bennett arrived in New York during early August 1842, he entered into discussions with the editor of the *New York Herald* for the publication of his Mormon exposé. After negotiations broke down, Bennett proclaimed the newspaper to be "the *Mormon official organ* in the eastern metropolis, and its ALIEN *editor* the *premonstration* of the *Prophet himself.*" He predicted that the *Herald*'s failure to obtain the publication contract for his exposé would generate "gratuitous vituperative editorial attacks of that '*Napoleon*' Editor on the author of this work" (159).

Unable to make a deal with the *Herald,* Bennett immediately concluded arrangements with Leland and Whiting in Boston. By mid-September he finished writing the manuscript, and a month later *The History of the Saints; or, an Exposé of Joe Smith and Mormonism* was published.

The work opens with a statement by the publishers, Emerson Leland and Willard J. Whiting, who believed that "the public needed to be informed of the true character of these pretended Mormon Saints, which we believe to be truly set forth in General Bennett's work, and in colors not heightened or exaggerated" (i–ii). Opposite the book's title page is an engraved portrait of John Cook Bennett dressed in his Nauvoo Legion uniform. The engraving is thought to be based on a painting by the Nauvoo artist Sutcliffe Maudsley. The engraving of Bennett is the only known surviving likeness of him.

The first section of the book, titled "Character of the Author," is one of the longest in the book and consists of forty-seven pages of testimonials, letters to Bennett, his "Inaugural Address," laws passed by the Nauvoo City Council, and newspaper articles that related to him in some way. Bennett inserted these because "of the violent and scurrilous attacks made upon me through the public papers by the Impostor and his emissaries" (4). Bennett's logic was that, if someone wrote him a letter or testimonial on a particular date, this proved that his character was unblemished up to that time. This reasoning was, of course, fallacious. People wrote letters and testimonials for many different reasons, none of which may have anything to do with Bennett's character. Also, the individuals writing testimonials may not have been aware of Bennett's nefarious activities. Alternately, a letter writer may well have been aware of Bennett's iniquitous schemes but simply wrote the letter to encourage Bennett to move elsewhere.

What Bennett did not mention in this section was also significant. For instance, he did not include any reference to his membership in the Christian Disciples. Neither did he refer to Christian College in New Albany and his selling of diplomas, nor did he admit to his abortive attempt to lobby Ohio legislators in 1833–34 or his removal from his position at Willoughby University. He did not write about his wife and family or his many extramarital affairs. Bennett's failure to mention these activities was itself evidence of imposture.

Contemporaries viewed the material in the "Character of the Author" section with some understanding. Simeon Francis of the *Sangamo Journal* wrote that "the attacks which have been made upon the character of Gen. Bennett, by the Mormon press, as well as by some others, since he abjured Mormonism, obviously rendered it necessary for him to sustain his reputation by the evidence of his standing among those with whom he had resided and associated for several of the past years, and by reference to the confidence which had been reposed in him by those who may have been supposed the best judges of his deserts." Subsequent commentators have been less charitable. The historian Hubert Howe Bancroft wrote that "when a man thrusts in your face three-score certificates of his good character, each signed by from one to a dozen persons, you may know that he is a very great rascal."[64]

Of the remaining three hundred pages of *The History of the Saints,* four-fifths consisted of material previously published in E. D. Howe's *Mormonism Unvailed,* the Burlington *Hawk-Eye and Iowa Patriot,* La Roy Sunderland's *Mormonism Exposed,* William Harris's *Mormonism Portrayed,* J. B. Turner's *Mormonism in All Ages,* Bennett's own articles, and many other sources.

Some contemporary observers were disturbed by Bennett's strong reliance on previously published material. The editor of the *New York Tribune* called the book "nothing more than a collection of all newspaper trash about the Mormons that has been published for the last few years." More than three-fourths of the book was deemed "too stupid and heavy ever to be read by any body." The remainder was "too disgusting, not so much from what is told as from the manner of telling it." *The History of the Saints* was "in every respect a wretched attempt at book making."[65]

To augment the large amount of previously published material, Bennett inserted some new disclosures that had not appeared in his earlier newspaper articles. Bennett wrote that a "temporal, as well as spiritual empire was the aim and expectation of the Prophet and his cabinet. The documents that will hereafter be introduced, will clearly show the existence of a vast and deep-laid scheme, upon their part, for conquering the states of Ohio, Indiana, Illinois, Iowa, and Missouri, and of erecting upon the ruin of their present governments a despotic military and religious empire" (5–6). The documents presented to support this allegation comprise ten pages of the book (293–302). Bennett claimed that the area between the Rocky Mountains and the Alleghenies was once a kingdom noted in the Book of Mormon, and he asserted that Smith "chiefly directed his schemes of aggrandizement" upon Missouri, Iowa, and Illinois. The "remaining states were to be licked up like salt, and fall into the immense labyrinth of glorious prophetic domination, like the defenceless lamb before the mighty king of the forest!" (293). This statement constituted the total of the proof of his allegation. The remaining pages of that section embraced a description of Missouri from Bradford's *Atlas,* a paragraph on hygiene and tomatoes, and a few lines on the Iowa Territory and Illinois. Bennett ended this section with a flourish: "As the GREAT PLOT AND LEAGUE is now fully before the nation . . . I will close this chapter with a single remark, that the public weal requires the vigilant eye of the body politic to LOOK WELL TO THE WEST!" (302).

Bennett left no infamy unclaimed in his attack on Mormonism and Joseph Smith: "It appears from the mass of evidence in this Exposé, that the Mormon Hierarchy are guilty of infidelity, deism, atheism; lying, deception, blasphemy; debauchery, lasciviousness, bestiality; madness, fraud, plunder; larceny, burglary, robbery, perjury; fornication, adultery, rape, incest; arson, treason, and murder; and they have out-heroded Herod, and out-deviled the devil, slandered God Almighty, Jesus Christ, and the holy angels, and even the devil himself, when they supposed him inimical to their plans and operations" (257). Based on these accusations, Bennett made "An Appeal to the Public" (302–7), urging "all good and religious men to unite their efforts for the purpose of checking and suppressing this Monster in his career of wickedness and blasphemy." Bennett predicted that as soon as the Mormons gained a majority, they "would proceed to exterminate, or convert forcibly, all those, whether Christian or Heathens, whom they style Gentiles, in distinction from their saintly selves" (302). This would have been a good place to end the book, but Bennett inserted thirty-three more pages of trial testimony and affidavits collected after the Mormons were expelled from Missouri in 1838 (307–40). Bennett finally concluded with "Remarks by Way of Addendum," briefly summarizing some points that he mentioned earlier in the book. With these closing comments, Bennett rested his case and "respectfully submitted" it to the public (340–41).

Copies of the book were promptly distributed to editors of newspapers on the East Coast and throughout the Midwest. Reviews of the book and summaries of its contents appeared in many papers across the nation.

As to be expected, the editor of the *New York Herald* did not think much of *The History of the Saints.* On October 21, 1842, the *Herald* announced that the book should "be classed under the obscene and licentious in the highest degree—neither can we believe half the filthy things it contains. It utterly disgraces its publisher." However, according to the publisher of the book, "at the time that the Herald's article was written—not a printed page of it had been out of the office." The *New York Tribune* explained this unusual circumstance "by the fact that Bennett of the Herald applied to Bennett of Nauvoo for the job of printing his book. The offer was rejected; and since that time Gen. B. and his forth coming book have been steadily abused. As every body knows, it would be strange if the Herald had taken any other course." Of course, the *New York Herald* accepted book promotions, noting that the work contained "interesting and astonishing disclosures [that] exhibited in their true colors the profligacy and wickedness of the Mormon leaders."[66]

The editor of the *Boston Post* was not impressed with Bennett's tale or his style of telling it. The editor hardly knew if it was right even to call attention to "this heap of monstrosities." Bennett's method was disgusting and betrayed "the catchpenny nature of the publication." The editor did believe that Bennett had not exaggerated the enormities of Mormon transgressions, for Mormonism was one of the most "humbug doctrines" then prevalent. As foolish as Mormonism was, reported the *Post,* it represented an extreme of the doctrinal spirit of the day. Mormonism differed not in quality but in degree from those things its neighbors were "quarrelling about in their churches. Ergo, the less said about belief of any kind the better, and the more said about good actions the better still."[67]

Other editors thought highly of the book and predicted it would sell well. The *Sign of the Times* said that the book gave "a full and minute history of the origin, rise and progress and designs of the Mormons, with the origin, claims and absurdities of the Book of Mormon." The editors believed that *The History of the Saints* contained "numerous statistics and disclosures which fully uphold the dark designs of the authors of this extended imposition." The *Boston Daily Mail* predicted that the book would "want with a rapid call." The editor of the *Hawk-Eye and Iowa Patriot* found the narrative of facts quite interesting, although many parts of it were "obnoxious to purity and delicacy of feeling." But, if just half of Bennett's statements were true—and the editor had no reason to doubt them—then Burlington was only thirty miles from "a class of individuals more diabolical, more dangerous and more deserving of destruction than any that can be found in the darkest dungeon in the land."[68]

As could be predicted, the *Sangamo Journal* reviewed the book in depth. It defended Bennett and assailed Joseph Smith and Mormonism. Other reviews attacked Bennett but agreed with his charges against Joseph Smith. The *Alton Telegraph and Democratic Review* found that Bennett showed "himself to have acted designedly towards the Mormons, both as a hypocrite and an ingrate." However, the editor believed Bennett's exposé, concluding that Joseph Smith was "a wicked designing, and corrupt man, possessing unlimited power and control, through the influence of a misguided religious fanaticism, over the minds and actions of a large and rapidly increasing number of unfortunate deluded fellow beings." The Alton editor believed that Smith should not be allowed "to indulge in his licentiousness, impositions, and blasphemy, unrebuked, and unpunished by the civil authorities of the land." Smith was denounced as "a disgrace to the American people." Likewise, the *Quincy Whig* declared that it was "a pity for the cause of truth and impartial history" that someone other than Bennett had not drawn up the work. Bennett's character was so questionable "that his statements will not go as far in convincing the public, as perhaps their truth and importance deserve." However, the *Whig* did not doubt the truth of Bennett's disclosures because there was "too much concurrent testimony to admit of a doubt."[69]

Needless to say, the Mormons were not overjoyed with the book. Joseph Smith prophesied "that whoever has any hand in the matter, will find themselves in a poor fix in relation to the money matters." While the book's financial earnings have not been uncovered, it is not likely that Smith's prediction was accurate. The book went through three editions in 1842. For two years, Bennett survived on the royalties of the book and fees for his lectures.[70]

George Joseph Lunt Colby, a non-Mormon, asked in the *Wasp* why the Boston authorities allowed its sale but acknowledged that "'tis fasshionable [*sic*], and fashion governs the world, together with the love of money." Colby believed that "any decent man who cares for the morals of his children, would refuse to have it in his house" and there were "places not so respectable, where it would be thrown out of doors." Yet, the book was "recommended to the Christian public! As bad as Mormonism may be—and we don't question but it is bad enough—it cannot be worse than the influence generated by such *trash*."[71]

Orson Pratt, who had been excommunicated from the Mormon church in August 1842 but readmitted in January 1843, stated that he had read Bennett's book "with the greatest disgust. No candid honest man can or will believe it." Pratt held that Bennett "disgraced himself in eyes of all civilized society who will dispise his very name." Orson Pratt's brother, Parley Pratt, stated that Bennett's book was "beneath contempt & would disgrace the society of *hell* & the *Devil*. But it will answer the end of its creation viz: to delude those who have rejected that pure & glorious record the Book of Mormon." Pratt continued that Bennett was "scarcely mentioned, & never except with a perfect disgust. His object was vengeance on those who exposed his iniquity."[72]

Bennett's exposé might have been forgotten had it not been for two major developments. First, the Mormons did in fact establish a theocratic empire in the West, although not where Bennett declared it would be. While the evidence was not presented by Bennett, statements made by Mormon leaders prior to his exposé lend credence to his claim that the Mormons intended to found their own empire. Bennett may have simply not had time to incorporate such statements into his book. More likely, he was familiar with the Mormon plans for territorial conquest, but his own role in fashioning them might have exposed him to a charge of treason.

Second, the polygamy charge accorded Bennett's exposé some longevity. Bennett was aware that Louisa Beaman was one of Smith's plural wives (256).[73] He correctly identified others who reportedly engaged in the secret wife system, and he described several categories of "spiritual wives." However, while other seceders mentioned the practice of polygamy in Nauvoo, none supported Bennett's exposition of it. If the categories described by Bennett did exist, it would be surprising that others did not refer to them.

The LDS Church acknowledged in 1852 that polygamy was indeed a fundamental tenet of their Mormon faith. They claimed that it had been established by Joseph Smith, who promulgated an undated revelation in 1843. However, the polygamy practiced in Utah was different than the "spiritual wife" doctrine described by Bennett. Three explanations have been proposed to account for this discrepancy. The first speculation holds that Bennett was not fully aware of the doctrine as practiced in Nauvoo and simply embellished what he knew. The second conjecture charged that Bennett was aware of the doctrine, but it evolved over time. The final speculation is that Bennett was the driving force behind the doctrine and that he had conceptualized it in this way. Bennett had led a promiscuous life prior to his becoming a Mormon. He had extramarital relations almost from his arrival in Nauvoo. It is extremely unlikely that Joseph Smith would have been unaware of them. That Smith waited so long to condemn Bennett publicly led some to suspect that Smith condoned his transgressions. Others claimed that both men were after the same women.

That Bennett might have influenced Joseph Smith to have a revelation regarding polygamy raises serious questions about Smith's divine connection. While it is easy to understand that the views expressed by Bennett might not have been precisely accurate, Joseph Smith might have honorably dealt with this by stating what he really believed about polygamy. The LDS church's subsequent public acceptance and then rejection of this doctrine of polygamy adds fuel to the fire. It does not seem likely that God would have changed perspective on a matter of this gravity, so many have asked: was the original "revelation" enunciated by Joseph Smith false?

Marketing and Reviews

Soon after *The History of the Saints* was published, Bennett was back on the lecture circuit, speaking in Buffalo, New York, and in Detroit, Kalamazoo, and Niles, Michigan. On December 30, 1842, Bennett began a lecture series in Illinois, first in Chicago, then in Peoria. Bennett charged fees for these presentations, usually from twelve and one-half to twenty-five cents per lecture, to help defray his "incidental" expenses. As his costs for the well-attended lectures were minimal and he also sold his book, Bennett did well financially in exposing the Mormons.[74]

Meanwhile, Lilburn W. Boggs, the former governor of Missouri, had sworn affidavits against Joseph Smith and Orrin Rockwell (151–52). Governor Reynolds of Missouri asked Governor Carlin of Illinois to extradite Joseph Smith. Carlin issued the warrant for Smith's arrest, and Smith was served on August 8, 1842. On that day, the Nauvoo City Council under the direction of Joseph Smith's brother passed the "Algerine Ordinance" granting the Nauvoo municipal court power to examine all warrants and to issue writs of habeas corpus (207–8). The Nauvoo municipal court, packed with Mormons, released Smith. Bennett referred to this ordinance as the one passed to protect "Mormon culprits and outlaws" (208). The governors of Illinois and Missouri were politically damaged by this development and offered a reward for the apprehension of Smith. Smith decided to leave Nauvoo (259–65), but he was arrested in Illinois. On a writ of habeas corpus, he was brought before Judge Nathaniel Pope of the United States district court in Springfield. The judge released Smith, maintaining that he "was not a fugitive from justice from the state of Missouri in the case of Gov. Boggs, he being in Illinois at the time of the perpetration of the felony."[75]

Whatever the truth or falsity of Bennett's accusations, the Mormon church was deeply affected by them. George Robinson, John Olney, C. L. Higbee, Francis Higbee, and William Allred supported Bennett and all eventually left the Mormon church (44–46). Joseph Smith's relationship with Sidney Rigdon never recovered. Mormons in other communities were in disarray due to Bennett's allegations.[76] However, relatively few abandoned the Mormon church. Those who left were promptly replaced by thousands of immigrants. Hence, the population of Nauvoo dramatically increased after Bennett's departure.

Most citizens of Nauvoo and most Mormons thought Bennett's allegations were wild exaggerations or entirely false. They believed that Bennett made his charges in retaliation for Smith's condemnation of Bennett's abominations and his subsequent expulsion from Nauvoo. Smith and other Mormon leaders fomented this anti-Bennett attitude to support their positions. They mobilized the elders of the Mormon church to campaign against Bennett. Smith and other Mormon leaders also were able to use Bennett as a scapegoat for other problems at Nauvoo.[77] Ironically, a likely consequence of Bennett's disclosures was to increase cohesion among most Mormons.

The outrageous manner and style of Bennett's exposé guaranteed extensive press coverage. In Illinois, Whig newspapers generally published Bennett's articles, while Democratic newspapers tended to disregard or scorn them. This was a consequence of Joseph Smith's public statements supporting Democratic candidates during the 1842 Illinois state election (35). Some newspapers published articles against Bennett, but most took hard positions against Mormonism.[78]

Despite the general anti-Mormon tone of the newspaper coverage, the Mormons were not necessarily hurt by it. On the contrary, several contemporary observers concluded that the publicity helped the Mormon cause. While many Americans undoubtedly opposed Mormonism, the vast majority had little or no knowledge of Mormons or their beliefs. Bennett's disclosures boosted Mormonism's national visibility and notoriety more than anything had before.[79] Some Mormon elders and other leaders campaigning against Bennett even reported conversions.

Epilogue

For the next two years, Bennett drifted around the Midwest and lectured on various topics. The financial bonanza that Bennett reaped on his anti-Mormon lecture circuit dwindled and the sales of his book declined. But events were underway in Nauvoo that gave new life to some of Bennett's accusations. Wilson Law, William Law, Charles Foster, Robert Foster—all of whom had been leaders in the Mormon church and all of whom had maligned Bennett—were expelled by Joseph Smith. Rather than leave Nauvoo as Bennett had done, they remained. On June 7, 1844, they published an issue of the *Nauvoo Expositor* intended to expose the evils of Joseph Smith and Mormonism. The city council declared it a public nuisance and directed the police to sack the newspaper office, confiscate all copies of the newspaper, and destroy the press and the type. The editors fled to Carthage and sought redress. The act of destroying the press incensed the citizens of Hancock County, and Joseph Smith, Hyrum Smith, John Taylor, and Willard Richards were jailed in Carthage. On June 27, 1844, an anti-Mormon mob assassinated Joseph Smith and Hyrum Smith.

Bennett appears not to have had any influence upon the events that unfolded in Carthage. He played no specific role in the anti-Mormon conventions held in Illinois during this time, and his influence was negligible by 1844. However, unlike previous anti-Mormon works, *The History of the Saints* was widely distributed. It served as the lens through which many Americans viewed the new Mormon church. Bennett's lectures and book bolstered anti-Mormon sentiments in and around Hancock County, but anti-Mormonism was on the rise before Bennett wrote his exposé and would likely have exploded even had he not published his book.

When Bennett heard about the murders of Hyrum and Joseph Smith, he headed for Illinois, arriving in Hancock County sometime in August 1844. Bennett attempted to influence the selection of the next Mormon leader to replace Joseph Smith by supporting Sidney Rigdon. Rigdon failed in his effort and was promptly excommunicated by the victor, Brigham Young. Bennett moved to Hampton, Illinois, where he met up with his old friend William McLellin, who had previously broken with the Mormons.[80] Bennett left Hampton sometime in early 1845 and settled in Cincinnati.

Still Bennett retained contact with many Mormons, such as Frederick Merryweather and his wife, who were friends of James Jesse Strang. Strang, born in New York in 1813, was a lawyer, newspaper editor, and excellent orator. At the age of thirty, Strang moved to Wisconsin Territory, where his wife's sister and her husband, Moses Smith, lived. Both were ardent Mormons. At the Smiths' insistence, Strang visited Nauvoo in February 1844. After receiving instruction by Joseph Smith and Hyrum Smith, Strang was baptized into the Mormon church and returned to Wisconsin to reconnoiter possible Mormon gathering sites. According to Strang, Joseph Smith sent him a letter appointing him successor nine days before Smith's death.[81] Some Mormons accepted the authenticity of the letter and followed Strang; Brigham Young and the majority of other Mormons dismissed it as a forgery.

Strang began purchasing property two miles west of Burlington, Wisconsin, proclaiming it the holy city of Voree, meaning "Garden of Peace." Bennett heard of Strang's activities and wrote to him, initiating a series of adulatory letters reminiscent of Bennett's earlier letters to Joseph Smith and Sidney Rigdon. Bennett moved to Voree about July 1, 1846. Shortly after his arrival, Bennett "was restored to the church by a perfectly unanimous vote of the whole congregation." Bennett brought his friend William McLellin into Strang's fold. In early August, Strang left Voree to visit midwestern and eastern cities and authorized Bennett to act as coadjutor until he returned.[82] Opposition to Bennett emerged within the community from the beginning, however, and increased throughout his tenure in Voree. As a result of many problems, Strang excommunicated Bennett in the spring of 1847.

Bennett moved to Plymouth, Massachusetts, where he established a new medical practice. He also embarked upon a major new venture raising poultry. By sheer accident, he crossbred the Cochin China fowl with the fawn-colored Dorking, the Great Malay, and the Wild Indian. Bennett called the result of this union the "Plymouth Rock" fowl.[83] He wrote a series of essays on poultry and announced his intention to exhibit his fowl in Boston's Quincy Market, challenging anyone to present a superior strain of fowl at the market for comparison. The resulting Exhibition of the New England Convention of Domestic Fowl Breeders and Fanciers, held in the autumn of 1849, was a success beyond anyone's expectations, with five to ten thousand people attending. Bennett pulled together his essays and published an encyclopedic work on domestic fowl, titled *The Poultry Book,* in 1850.[84]

Bennett did not bother to promote his poultry book for he was too busy making money marketing fowl. For the next three years, Bennett exhibited his fowl at exhibitions in Massachusetts. His activities promoting poultry produced a sensation throughout America. The newly termed "hen fever" quickly infected others in New England and promptly spread to the South and West. The *Massachusetts Ploughman* announced that "the fever of the season" was fowl. The *Boston Traveller* stated that hen fever was "now raging among our amateur farmers." In 1854, the *Northern Farmer* declared that "never in the history of the world, has there been so deep an interest felt in the gallinaceous races at present in this country."[85]

With hen fever sweeping the land, Bennett moved to Great Falls, New Hampshire, and significantly expanded his far-flung importing business to include other blood stock. In the summer of 1854, Bennett moved to Fort Des Moines, Iowa, taking his animals with him. By 1856, he had moved to Polk City, about fifteen miles north of Des Moines, where he remained for the rest of his life except for a few months in the Union Army. After a protracted illness, probably precipitated by a stroke, Bennett died in August 1867. His remains were interred in Polk City Cemetery. As to be expected, his grave has one of the largest markers in the cemetery.

Notes

1. Parenthetical numbers in text refer to pages in Bennett's book. For more information about Bennett's life, see Andrew F. Smith, *The Saintly Scoundrel: The Life and Times of John Cook Bennett* (Urbana: University of Illinois Press, 1997).

2. "An Account of BILIOUS REMITTENT FEVER," *Western Journal of the Medical and Physical Sciences* 3 (August–October 1829): 27–31.

3. *Journal of the Senate of the State of Ohio* (Columbus: Olmsted, Bailhache, 1833), 142–44.

4. *Painesville Telegraph,* November 21, 1834 (quote). For more information about tomato history, see Andrew F. Smith, *The Tomato in America: Early History, Culture and Cookery* (Columbia: University of South Carolina Press, 1994).

5. *Acts of a Local Nature, Passed at the First Session of the Thirty-Fourth General Assembly of the State of Ohio* (Columbus: James B. Gardener, 1836), 6; William Henry Perris, ed., *The History of Stark County, Ohio* (Chicago: Baskin and Battey, 1881), 459.

6. *Laws of Incorporation of the State of Illinois Passed by the Eleventh General Assembly* (Springfield: Wm. Walters, 1839), 45.

7. For more information about phrenology, see John D. Davies, *Phrenology: Fad and Science: A Nineteenth-Century Crusade* (New Haven: Yale University Press, 1955), 3–32.

8. For more information about Sidney Rigdon, see F. Mark McKiernan, *The Voice of One Crying in the Wilderness: Sidney Rigdon, Religious Reformer, 1793–1876* (1971; rpt., Independence, Mo.: Herald House, 1990), and Richard S. Van Wagoner, *Sidney Rigdon: A Portrait of Religious Excess* (Salt Lake City: Signature Books, 1994).

9. John Corrill, *Brief History of the Church of Christ of Latter Day Saints* (St. Louis: Printed for the Author, 1839). For more information about Corrill, see Kenneth H. Winn, "'Such Republicanism as This': John Corrill's Rejection of Prophetic Rule," in Roger Launius and Linda Thatcher, eds., *Differing Visions: Dissenters in Mormon History* (Urbana: University of Illinois Press, 1994), 45–75.

10. Jan Shipps and John W. Welch, eds., *The Journals of William E. McLellin* (Provo, Utah, and Urbana, Ill.: BYU Studies and the University of Illinois Press, 1994), 69 (quote); William E. McLellin to John C. Bennett, August 14, 1846, quoted in *Zion's Reveille* 2 (January 28, 1847): 65.

11. Alexander Campbell, *Delusions: An Analysis of the Book of Mormon* (Boston: B. H. Greene, 1832).

12. E. D. Howe, *Mormonism Unvailed* (Painesville, Ohio: By the Author, 1834); Rex C. Reeve Jr., "What Is 'Manuscript Found?'" in Kent P. Jackson, ed., *Manuscript Found: The Complete Original "Spaulding Manuscript"* (Provo, Utah: Religious Studies, Brigham Young University, 1996), vi–vii.

13. Howe, *Mormonism Unvailed,* 278–80.

14. Ibid., 288.

15. B. Winchester, *Spaulding Story, Concerning the Manuscript Found* (Philadelphia: Brown, Bicking and Guilpert, 1840), 5 (first quote), 6 (second, third, fourth, and fifth quotes), 8 (sixth quote).

16. Ibid., 11.

17. Solomon Spaulding, *The "Manuscript Found": A Verbatim Copy of the Original* (Lamoni, Iowa: Reorganized Church of Jesus Christ of Latter Day Saints, 1885); Jackson, *Manuscript Found.*

18. Winn, "'Such Republicanism as This,'" 65.

19. Joseph Smith's *History of the Church* proclaims that the non-Mormons really burned their townhouses down and in a diabolical scheme blamed it on the Mormons. See Joseph Smith, *History of the Church of Jesus Christ of the Latter-day Saints,* ed. B. H. Roberts, 6 vols., 2d ed., rev. (Salt Lake City: Deseret Book, 1976), 3:163–64. The early part of this work was written by Joseph Smith. By the time of his death in 1844, he had recorded the history only up to the year 1838. Willard Richards and others later completed it. Some sections that they added were taken directly from documents prepared by Smith, such as his diary, letters, and other records. To make matters even more confusing, the entire history was edited by others, including B. H. Roberts.

20. Corrill, *Brief History,* 41.

21. Scott H. Faulring, ed., *The Diaries and Journals of Joseph Smith* (Salt Lake City: Signature Books in Association with Smith Research Associates, 1989), 223 (quote); Winn, "'Such Republicanism as This,'" 45, 66.

22. Smith, *History of the Church,* 3:190–91.

23. U.S. Senate Document 189, "Testimony Given before the Judge of the Fifth Judicial Circuit of the State of Missouri, on the Trial of Joseph Smith Jr., and Others, for High Treason, and Other Crimes against that State," 26th Cong., 2d Sess., ordered to be printed February 15, 1841.

24. John Cook Bennett to the editor, January 7, 1843, quoted in the *Chicago Express,* January 11, 1843.

25. Robert Bruce Flanders, *Nauvoo: Kingdom on the Mississippi* (Urbana: University of Illinois Press, 1965), 45.

26. John C. Bennett to Joseph Smith, July 25, 1840, quoted in Joseph Smith's Letter Book 2, 109–10 (first quote); John C. Bennett to Joseph Smith, July 27, 1840, in Joseph Smith's Letter Book 2, 170–71 (second, third, fourth, and fifth quotes); John Cook Bennett to Joseph Smith, July 30, 1840, quoted in Joseph Smith's Letter Book 2, 109 (sixth quote); John Cook Bennett to Joseph Smith, August 15, 1840, quoted in Joseph Smith's Letter Book 2, 171–72, all MS 155, Reel 2, Joseph Smith Collection, LDS Church Archives, Salt Lake City.

27. *Alton Telegraph and Democratic Review,* November 19, 1842.

28. *The Return* 2 (June 1890): 285; Mary Audentia Smith Anderson and Bertha A. Helmer, *Joseph Smith III and the Restoration* (Independence, Mo.: Herald House, 1952), 57–59; Dr. W. Wyl (pseud. for Dr. Wilhelm Wymetal), *Mormon Portraits, or the Truth about the Mormon Leaders* (Salt Lake City: Tribune Printing and Publishing, 1886), 62; Smith, *History of the Church,* 5:156; John C. Bennett to James Jesse Strang, March [23], 1846, Western Americana MS 447, #33b, Coe Collection, Beinecke Library, Yale University, New Haven, Conn.; William Law to Thomas B. H. Stenhouse, November 24, 1871, quoted in Thomas B. H. Stenhouse, *The Rocky Mountain Saints* (New York: D. Appleton, 1873), 198.

29. Smith, *History of the Church,* 4:205–6 (all quotes); Flanders, *Nauvoo,* 95–96.

30. *The Return* 2 (June 1890): 285; *Times and Seasons* 3 (January 1, 1842): 651; *Alton Telegraph and Democratic Review,* July 23, 1842; Thomas Ford, *History of Illinois* (Chicago: S. C. Griggs, 1854), 263.

31. *Times and Seasons* 2 (January 15, 1841): 275; extract from William Clayton's Private Book, quoted in Andrew F. Ehat and Lyndon W. Cook, eds., *The Words of Joseph Smith* (Provo, Utah: Religious Study Center, Brigham Young University, 1981), 59 (quote); *Times and Seasons* 2 (June 1, 1841): 424.

32. *Times and Seasons* 2 (April 15, 1841): 386–87 (quote); Brigham Young's statement in the Minutes of the Meeting of the Church of Jesus Christ of Latter Day Saints on the trial of Sidney Rigdon, on September 8, 1844, quoted in the *Times and Seasons* 5 (September 15, 1844): 655; *New York Herald,* August 31, 1842.

33. *Alton Telegraph and Democratic Review,* May 22, 1841 (first quote); *Warsaw Signal,* as quoted in the *Quincy Whig,* May 29, 1841 (second quote); *Warsaw Signal,* July 14, 1841; *Times and Seasons* 2 (June 1, 1841): 431–32 (third quote).

34. *Warsaw Signal,* June 9, 1841.

35. William Harris, *Mormonism Portrayed: Its Errors and Absurdities Exposed* (Warsaw, Ill.: Sharp and Gamble, 1841), 14–18, 25; *Warsaw Signal,* September 11, 1844.

36. William Swartzell, *Mormonism Exposed, Being a Journal of a Residence in Missouri from the 28th of May to the 20th of August, 1838* (Pekin, Ohio: By the author, 1840).

37. *Zion's Watchman* 3 (January 13, 1838); La Roy Sunderland, *Mormonism Exposed and Refuted* (New York: Piercy and Reed, 1838); Parley P. Pratt, *Mormonism Unveiled: Zion's Watchman Unmasked, and its Editor, Mr. L. R. Sunderland, Exposed: Truth Vindicated: the Devil Mad, and Priestcraft in Danger!* (New York: For the Publisher, 1838).

38. J. B. Turner, *Mormonism in All Ages: or the Rise, Progress, and Causes of Mormonism* (New York: Platt and Peters, 1842). Turner was born in Templeton, Massachusetts, in 1805. He attended Yale and in May 1833 was offered a position at Illinois College, where he became professor of rhetoric. He was a supporter of public schools in Illinois and organized the Illinois State Teachers' Association in 1836. He strongly

condemned slavery and in 1847 resigned his professorship because of disagreement with the college on slavery and sectarian issues. Turner supported the creation of industrial universities. Largely due to Turner's efforts, the Illinois state legislature established an industrial university in Urbana in 1867, which later became the University of Illinois. It is interesting to note that when Turner's daughter wrote his biography, she completely omitted any mention of *Mormonism in All Ages*. See Mary Turner Carriel, *The Life of Jonathan Baldwin Turner* ([Jacksonville? Ill.]: n.p., 1911).

39. Abraham Jonas to George Miller, May 4, 1842, MS 751, #4, LDS Church Archives, Salt Lake City (quote); Joseph E. Morcombe, *History of the Grand Lodge of Iowa A. F. and A. M.* (Cedar Rapids: Torch Press, 1910), vol. 1, 145; Mervin B. Hogan, *The Official Minutes of Nauvoo Lodge* (Des Moines, Iowa: Research Lodge No. 2, A. F. and A. M., [April 4, 1974]), 3; idem, *The Founding Minutes of Nauvoo Lodge* (Des Moines, Iowa: Research Lodge No. 2, A. F. and A. M., [February 1971]), 3, 4, 11–13; idem, *The Official Minutes of Nauvoo Lodge* (Des Moines, Iowa: Research Lodge No. 2, A. F. and A. M., [April 4, 1974]), 11–12, 22–23; Richard H. Brown, quoted in Mervin B. Hogan, *Mormons and Freemasonry: The Illinois Episode* (Salt Lake City: Third Century Graphics, 1980), 272; Joseph King to Dr. M. Helm, May 17, 1842, MS 751, #5, LDS Church Archives, Salt Lake City; Mervin B. Hogan, "The Confrontation of Grand Master Abraham Jonas and John Cook Bennett at Nauvoo," paper presented before the Society of Blue Friars, Hotel Washington, Washington, D.C., February 22, 1976.

40. *Times and Seasons* 3 (July 1, 1842): 839, 842 (all quotes); Joseph Smith to Governor Thomas Carlin, June 24, 1842, quoted in Smith, *History of the Church,* 5:42.

41. Richard S. Van Wagoner, "Sarah M. Pratt: The Shaping of an Apostate," *Dialogue: A Journal of Mormon Thought* 19 (Summer 1986): 71; Wyl, *Mormon Portraits,* 61; "The Workings of Mormonism Related by Mrs. Orson Pratt, Salt Lake City, 1884," LDS Church Archives, cited by Breck England, *The Life and Thought of Orson Pratt* (Salt Lake City: University of Utah Press, 1985), 75; *Sangamo Journal,* July 15, 1842.

42. *Times and Seasons* 3 (July 1, 1842): 841.

43. *Wasp* 1 (May 21, 1842): 4.

44. *Sangamo Journal,* June 10, 1842; *Wasp* 1 (June 18, 1842): 2; *Times and Seasons* 3 (June 15, 1842): 830; Wilford Woodruff's Journal, typescript, 9 vols. (Midvale, Utah: Signature Books, 1983–85), 2:179; *Hawk-Eye and Iowa Patriot,* June 23, 1842 (quote); *Sangamo Journal,* July 8, 1842.

45. *Sangamo Journal,* July 15, 1842 (quote); *Times and Seasons* 3 (August 1, 1842): 872–73.

46. *Sangamo Journal,* July 8, 1842 (quote); ibid., July 15, 1842.

47. Ibid., July 15, 1842.

48. Ibid.

49. When Abraham Jonas, the Illinois Grand Master, found out about the violation of this regulation, he told the Mormons to hold meetings three times per day, such that nine persons could be admitted each day. This was done during late March and April 1842. *Sangamo Journal,* July 22, 1842.

50. Hogan, *Founding Minutes,* 10, 12–13; idem, *Official Minutes,* 19, 22–23; Minutes of the Nauvoo Lodge, MS 9115, LDS Church Archives, Salt Lake City.

51. *Sangamo Journal,* July 15, 1842.

52. Bennett was not the first person to state that Smith had prophesied Boggs's death by violent means. The *Quincy Whig* did so on May 21, 1842. Joseph Smith denied

making any such prediction. The *Quincy Whig*'s report and Smith's denial were reprinted in the *Wasp* 1 (May 28, 1842): 2. The issue was raised again in the *American Bulletin,* July 14, 1842, and *Northern Farmer,* 2d ser., 2 (July 1855): 304.

53. Anonymous letter to the editor, May 14, 1842, *Hawk-Eye and Iowa Patriot,* quoted in the *Wasp* 1 (May 28, 1842): 2; *American Bulletin,* July 14, 1842; *Northern Farmer,* 2d ser., 2 (July 1855): 304; *Wasp* 1 (May 14, 1842): 3; [George] Hinkle to Joseph Smith, June 12, 1842, MS 155, Reel 2, Joseph Smith Collection, LDS Church Archives, Salt Lake City.

54. A year after Bennett made these accusations, he announced through the *Hawk-Eye and Iowa Patriot* (October 28, 1843) that Governor Carlin believed that "MORE THAN TWENTY OF THE LEADING MORMONS WERE ENGAGED IN HIRING O. P. ROCKWELL TO SHOOT GOVERNOR BOGGS!" No evidence was offered to support this allegation, and Carlin made public no such statement.

55. *Sangamo Journal,* July 15, 1842 (quote); *American Bulletin,* July 14, 1842.

56. *American Bulletin,* July 16, 1842.

57. *Sangamo Journal,* July 15, 1842.

58. *Louisville Daily Journal,* August 6, 1842 (quote); *New York Herald,* September 4, 1842.

59. *Louisville Daily Journal,* August 6, 1842.

60. *Wasp* 1 (July 30, 1842): 3; *New York Herald,* August 12–13, 20, 1842; James Arlington Bennet to Joseph Smith, August 16, 1842, quoted in Smith, *History of the Church,* 5:112–14.

61. *New York Herald,* August 20, 1842; John Cook Bennett to James Arlington Bennet, August 27, 1842, quoted in *New York Herald,* August 30, 1842; *New York Sun,* August 30, 1842; Origin Bacheler, *Mormonism Exposed, Internally and Externally* (New York: [Watchman], 1838); *Baptist Advocate,* February 26, 1842.

62. *Bostonian,* June 15, 1842, quoted in *Times and Seasons* 3 (August 1, 1842): 362; *Letter to the Members of the Session of the Impostures and Calumnies of George Montgomery West* (Albany, N.Y.: Second Presbyterian Church, 1850); [Philander] Chase, *Bishop Chase's Defence against the Slanders of Rev. G. M. West* [1831].

63. *Sangamo Journal,* July 15, 1842.

64. *Sangamo Journal,* November 11, 1842; Hubert Howe Bancroft, *History of Utah* (San Francisco: The History Company, 1889), 150.

65. *Wasp* 1 (January 7, 1843): 2, 3.

66. *New York Herald,* October 21, 31, 1842; *New York Tribune,* October 27, 1842.

67. *Boston Post,* November 1, 1842.

68. *Sign of the Times* 4 (November 2, 1842): 56; *Boston Daily Mail,* October 27, 1842; *Hawk-Eye and Iowa Patriot,* November 10, 1842.

69. *Sangamo Journal,* November 11, 1842; *Alton Telegraph and Democratic Review,* November 19, 1842; *Quincy Whig,* November 19, 1842.

70. Smith, *History of the Church,* 5:156–57.

71. *Wasp* 1 (January 7, 1843): 2–3.

72. Orson Platt quoted in Parley Pratt to John Van Cott, May 7, 1843, quoted in Van Wagoner, "Sarah M. Pratt," 82.

73. Van Wagoner, "Sarah M. Pratt," 71.

74. *Buffalo Commercial Advertiser and Journal,* November 19, 21, 1842; *Illinois Register,* December 16, 1842; *Detroit Free Press,* December 7, 1842; *Detroit Daily Advertiser,* December 5, 1842; E. M. Webb to the editor, April 17, 1843, quoted in *Times*

and Seasons 4 (April 15, 1843): 166–67; *Niles Republican,* quoted in *Chicago Express,* January 14, 1843; *Niles Republican,* December 24, 1842; *Quincy Whig,* January 16, 1843; *Chicago Express,* December 31, 1842; *Chicago Democrat,* quoted in *Wasp* 1 (January 14, 1843): 1; *Peoria Register and North-Western Gazetteer,* January 6, 13, 1843; *Peoria Democratic Press,* January 11, 1843; *People's Advocate,* quoted in *Wasp* 1 (October 15, 1842): 1; *Illinois Register,* December 16, 1842; *Chicago Democrat,* December 14, 1842; *Davenport Gazette,* November 10, 1842, January 19, 1843.

75. John Cook Bennett to the editor, written January 7, 1843, *Chicago Express,* January 11, 1843.

76. John E. Page to Joseph Smith, August 8, 1842, quoted in Journal History of the Church, CR100/137, LDS Church Archives, Salt Lake City.

77. *Times and Seasons* 3 (September 1, 1842): 909; *Illinois Register,* July 14, 1843; *Quincy Herald,* July 23, 1843.

78. *New Orleans Daily Picayune,* September 21, 1842; *People's Advocate,* quoted in *Wasp* 1(October 15, 1842): 1; *Tennessee Telegraph,* quoted in *Wasp* 1 (November 12, 1842): 2; *Albany Argus,* August 1, 1842.

79. *Buffalo Commercial Advertiser and Journal,* November 21, 1842; *Baltimore Clipper,* quoted in *Times and Seasons* 4 (December 1, 1842): 27–28.

80. John C. Bennett's "Revelation Given to Joseph Smith" intended for Sidney Rigdon, from "Personal History of Warren Post 1867–1875," 75–78, copied from Stephen Post's Manuscript on July 4, 1874, typescript by John J. Hajicek, September 1994, personal collection of John Hajicek; *Alton Telegraph and Democratic Review,* September 21, 1844; *Daily People's Organ,* September 10, 1844; *The Prophet,* May 10, 1845. For more information about William E. McLellin, see Richard P. Howard, "William E. McLellin: 'Mormonism's Stormy Petrel,'" in Launius and Thatcher, *Differing Visions,* 76–101.

81. F. Merryweather to James Strang, February 8, 1847, quoted in *Zion's Reveille* 2 (February 25, 1847): 26; John C. Bennett to James Jesse Strang, March 31, 1846, Western Americana MS 447, #227, and John C. Bennett to James Jesse Strang, April 6, 1846, Western Americana MS 447, #228, Coe Collection, Beinecke Library, Yale University, New Haven, Conn.; John J. Hajicek, ed., *The Chronicles of Voree (1844–1849)* (Burlington, Wisc.: By the editor, 1991), 1, 6; Milo Milton Quaife, *The Kingdom of Saint James: A Narrative of the Mormons* (New Haven: Yale University Press, 1930), 1–13.

82. *Cincinnati Commercial,* February 24, 1846; John Cook Bennett to James Strang, February 24, 1846, Misc. Letters and Papers, P13, F66, RLDS Library-Archives, Independence, Mo.; *Zion's Reveille* 2 (November 25, 1847): 102; Hajicek, *Chronicles of Voree,* 54; *New Era and Herald of Zion's Watchman,* February 1847; *Saints' Herald,* December 29, 1888, 832.

83. *Boston Cultivator* 11 (September 15, 1849): 291. Bennett may have raised poultry as a youth. He claimed that his father, Captain John Bennett, had imported the first Black Poland fowl into the United States. See also the *Boston Cultivator* 11 (November 3, 1849): 348; John C. Bennett, *The Poultry Book* (Boston: Phillips, Sampson, 1850), 77, 199.

84. Bennett, *Poultry Book,* advertisement in book.

85. *Massachusetts Ploughman* 9 (March 23, 1850): n.p.; *Boston Traveller,* quoted in *The Northern Farmers' Almanac for 1851* (New York: A. B. Allen, 1850), n.p.; *Boston Cultivator* 13 (October 4, 1851): 316; *Northern Farmer* 2d ser., 1 (January 1854): 27.

THE HISTORY OF THE SAINTS

LIEUT. GEN. JOSEPH SMITH,
Mormon Prophet.

NOTE BY THE PUBLISHERS.

In offering the following work to the public, we think it not improper to make a few observations respecting the author and our connection with him.

We became aware, through the medium of the newspapers, that General Bennett was about to publish a work containing his disclosures respecting Joe Smith and the Mormons. Meeting him in New York, and being satisfied, from our intercourse with him, that he deserved our confidence, we made arrangements with him to publish the book he was preparing. During its preparation and passage through the press, we have been almost constantly in his society, and have seen him for a long time under a variety of circumstances. The result of our observations has been, that we place the most implicit reliance upon his veracity, and are perfectly convinced that he is a gentleman of strict honor, and of very considerable acquirements and information.

In regard to the statements he has made in the following pages, we cannot, of course, say any thing upon our personal knowledge; but we know, from our own inspection, that the documents, affidavits,

A

and certificates, he has inserted therein, are genuine ; and most of the letters, at least those of a recent date, came through the post-office into our hands, and were by us given to General Bennett, who invariably submitted them to our inspection.

We can also state that we have seen numerous letters from Nauvoo, written by respectable persons, who, we have learnt from the public papers, reside at Nauvoo, and who state things which corroborate, in all particulars, the disclosures of General Bennett.

Our motive in publishing this work is to let the public be informed of the true character of these pretended Mormon Saints, which we firmly and conscientiously believe to be truly set forth in General Bennett's work, and in colors not heightened or exaggerated.

As a true exposition, therefore, of Mormon Faith and Practice, we commend it to the serious and impartial attention of the public.

EMERSON LELAND,
WILLARD J. WHITING

THE

HISTORY OF THE SAINTS;

OR,

AN EXPOSÉ

OF

JOE SMITH AND MORMONISM.

BY

JOHN C. BENNETT.

BOSTON:
LELAND & WHITING, 71 WASHINGTON ST.
NEW YORK: BRADBURY, SODEN, & CO., 127 NASSAU STREET.
CINCINNATI: E. S. NORRIS & CO., 247 MAIN STREET.

1842.

A.Clark del.

O.Pelto.

John C. Bennett.

GEN. JOHN C. BENNETT,

Doctor of Medicine.

PREFACE.

I HAVE been induced to prepare and publish the following work by a desire to expose the enormous iniquities which have been perpetrated by one of the grossest and most infamous impostors that ever appeared upon the face of the earth, and by many of his minions, under the name and garb of Religion, and professedly by the direct will and command of Almighty God.

My facilities for doing what I have undertaken are as great as could possibly be desired. For eighteen months I was living with the Mormons at their chief city, and possessed the confidence of the Prophet himself, and of his councillors. I was, indeed, from an early period, one of their First Presidents, who, after the Prophet, are the rulers of the Church. This gave me access to all their secret lodges and societies, and enabled me to become perfectly familiar with the doings and designs of the whole Church.

This book contains a full and accurate account of my motives for joining them, and of the discoveries which I made among them, illustrated and confirmed by a variety of documents, both public and private.

I have not, I can fearlessly assert, exaggerated the facts I have here presented to the world, though I have, as they richly deserve, shown them up with an unsparing hand.

I have been obliged to insert much personal matter, and many testimonials respecting myself, in consequence of the violent and scurrilous attacks made upon me through the public papers by the Impostor and his emissaries. This, I trust, the reader will not impute to egotism, but to its real cause — a desire to strengthen my statements against the opposition which I am certain they will encounter.

In conclusion, I would commend to the candid and earnest attention of every patriotic and religious person the statement I have made; and, with the assurance that I have told the truth, and nothing but the truth, though by no means the whole truth, entreat them to use all their influence and exertions to arrest and quell the Mormon Monster in his career of imposture, iniquity, and treason.

The haste with which I have necessarily written my book will be my apology to the critics for its defects of style and arrangement. I have been more solicitous about the matter than the manner of it.

HISTORY OF THE SAINTS.

REASONS FOR JOINING THE MORMONS.

It is, of course, necessary for me to give some explanation of the reasons which led me to join the Mormons, and of my motives for remaining so long in connection with them. I am happy to have it in my power to do this easily and satisfactorily.

I find that it is almost universally the opinion of those who have heard of me in the eastern part of the United States, that I united myself to the Mormons from a conviction of the truth of their doctrines, and that I was, at least for some time, a convert to their pretended religion. This, however, is a very gross error. *I never believed in them or their doctrines.* This is, and indeed was, from the first, well known to my friends and acquaintances in the western country, who were well aware of my reasons for connecting myself with the Prophet; which reasons I will now proceed to state.

My attention had been long turned towards the movements and designs of the Mormons, with whom I had become pretty well acquainted, years before, in the state of Ohio; and after the formation of their establishment at Nauvoo, in 1839, the facts and reports respecting them, which I continually heard, led me to suspect, and, indeed, believe, that their leaders had formed, and were preparing to execute, a daring and colossal scheme of rebellion and usurpation throughout the North-Western States of the Union. It was to me evident that temporal, as well as spiritual, empire was the aim and expectation of the Prophet and

1 *

his cabinet. The documents that will hereafter be introduced, will clearly show the existence of a vast and deep-laid scheme, upon their part, for conquering the states of Ohio, Indiana, Illinois, Iowa, and Missouri, and of erecting upon the ruin of their present governments a despotic military and religious empire, the head of which, as emperor and pope, was to be Joseph Smith, the Prophet of the Lord, and his ministers and viceroys, the apostles, high-priests, elders, and bishops, of the Mormon church.

The fruition of this hopeful project would, of course, have been preceded by plunder, devastation, and bloodshed, and by all the countless horrors which invariably accompany civil war. American citizens could not be expected to stand quietly by, and suffer their governments to be overthrown, their religion subverted, their wives and children converted into instruments for a despot's lust and ambition, and their property forcibly appropriated to the use and furtherance of a base imposture. The Mormons would, of course, meet with resistance as soon as their intentions became evident; and so great was already their power, and so rapidly did their numbers increase, that the most frightful consequences might naturally be expected to ensue, from an armed collision between them and the citizens who still remained faithful to the God and the laws of their fathers.

These reflections continually occurred to me, as I observed the proceedings of the Mormons, and, at length, determined me to make an attempt to detect and expose the movers and machinery of the plot.

I perceived that it would be useless to undertake this by open opposition. So great and complete was the control that the Prophet had established over the souls of his followers, that very little of his vile proceedings could be made known from the confessions or testimony of his subordinates. Even if one or two did testify to any particular acts of wickedness, such were the address and influence of Smith, that he would, without difficulty, bring forward any required number of witnesses, who would perjure themselves in direct contradiction of his adversaries.

It at length occurred to me that the surest and speediest way to overthrow the Impostor, and expose his iniquity to the world, would be to profess myself a convert to his doctrines, and join him at the seat of his dominion. I felt confident that from my standing in society, and the offices I held under the state of Illinois, I should be received by the Mormons with open arms; and that the course I was resolved to pursue would enable me to get behind the curtain, and behold, at my leisure, the secret wires of the fabric, and likewise those who moved them.

I was quite aware of the danger I ran, should I be suspected or detected by the Mormons; and I also anticipated the probability of being received by many of my fellow-citizens with disbelief and obloquy, when the time came to throw off the mask, and proclaim to the world the discoveries I felt certain I should make. But none of these things deterred me. Impelled by a determination to save my country and my countrymen from the evils which menaced them through the machinations of the Prophet, I was rendered insensible to the risk I incurred. There was, it was evident, no other way of thwarting the Impostor and his myrmidons, and the plan I proposed to myself could not possibly, so far as I could foresee, fail of complete success.

I found in history a distinguished example of a somewhat parallel case, — that in which Napoleon, for the furtherance of the views of the French government upon Egypt and the East, had nominally adopted the Moslem creed. The following is the passage in his Life to which I refer : —

" Buonaparte entertained the strange idea of persuading the Moslems that he himself pertained in some sort to their religion, being an envoy of the Deity, sent on earth, not to take away, but to confirm and complete, the doctrines of the Koran, and the mission of Mahomet. He used, in executing this purpose, the inflated language of the East, the more easily that it corresponded, in its allegorical and amplified style, with his own natural tone of composition ; and he hesitated not to join in the external ceremonial of the Mahommedan religion, that his actions might seem to confirm his words. The French general celebrated the feast of the Prophet, as it recurred, with some Sheik of eminence, and joined in the litanies and worship enjoined by the Koran. He affected, too, the language of an inspired follower of the faith of Mecca, of which the following is a curious example : —

" On entering the sepulchral chamber in the pyramid of Cheops, ' Glory be to Allah,' said Buonaparte; ' there is no God but God, and Mahommed is his prophet;'—a confession of faith which is in itself a declaration of Islamism.

"'Thou hast spoken like the most learned of the prophets,' said the Mufti, who accompanied him.

"'I can command a car of fire to descend from heaven,' continued the French general, 'and I can guide and direct its course upon earth.'

"'Thou art the great chief to whom Mahommed gives power and victory,' said the Mufti.

"Napoleon closed the conversation with this not very pertinent Oriental proverb—'The bread which the wicked seizes upon by force, shall be turned to dust in his mouth.'"—*Life of Napoleon Buonaparte*, Vol. I., p. 416.

The motives which led Napoleon to profess Mohammedanism were undoubtedly a desire to advance the interests of his country, and to facilitate the operations of the army he commanded. But, if these motives justified him in the course he pursued, how much more had I to justify me in a similar line of conduct! His temporary profession of a false religion was by no means absolutely necessary under the circumstances; while, as I before observed, *mine* was indispensable to the end I had in view. And how much superior was my object to his! He merely wished to promote the ambitious views of his government; I, on the contrary, was endeavoring to save my country from the most dreadful evils — civil war, despotism, and the establishment of a false and persecuting religion.

"But how," inquires some cautious reader, "were you, as an honest man, justified in taking such a course? What confidence can I place in your statements, when I know, by your own confession, that you have once played the part of a hypocrite?"

These suspicions are very natural, and from the first I expected to incur them; but I think that a very little consideration of the extraordinary nature of my case will convince any candid person of the propriety, and indeed necessity, of the course of action I pursued.

Suppose for a moment, my dear reader, that you were located on our western frontier, in the vicinity of a large, powerful, and increasing tribe of savage Indians. Suppose it is apparent, from their movements, that they intend evil to the whites, your countrymen; that they are meditating murder, plunder, and devastation, and all the horrors that invariably attend an Indian war. Suppose that by going to them, and professing to be their friend, you knew that you would be received by them freely, and admitted into their councils, and could, by the intelligence you would thus gain, be enabled to frustrate their plans, and avert from your country the evils and dangers which these savages would otherwise bring upon it. Would you for a moment scruple to make such pretensions? especially if, as in the case of the Mormons, there were no other possible way to do what the safety of the west demanded, — viz., expose the imposture.

The fact that in joining the Mormons I was obliged to make a pretence of belief in their religion does not alter the case. That pretence was unavoidable in the part I was acting, and it should not be condemned like hypocrisy towards a Christian church. For so absurd are the doctrines of the Mormons that I regard them with no more reverence than I would the worship of Manitou or the Great Spirit of the Indians, and feel no more compunction at joining in the former than in the latter, to serve the same useful purpose.

I was perfectly satisfied, even before the Mormons went from Ohio, that it was the intention of Joe Smith and those who possessed his confidence, to destroy the sacred institutions of Christianity, and substitute, instead of its powerful restraints upon the unholy passions of the human heart, a frightfully-corrupt system, that would enable them to give free course to their lust, ambition, and cruelty — a system than which, one more abominable the arch-enemy of mankind himself could not have invented. Persons unacquainted with the subject can scarcely imagine the baseness and turpitude of Mormon principles, and the horrid practices to which these principles give rise. When they learn how habitually the Mormons sacrifice to their brutal propensities the virtue and happiness of young and innocent females, how they cruelly persecute those who refuse to join them, and how they murder those who attempt to expose them, they will look with indulgence upon almost any means employed to thwart their villanous designs and detect and disclose their infamy.

There was — I repeat it — no possible way for me to expose the enormous wickedness of the Mormon faith and conduct than to join them, profess my belief in their "religion," win their confidence, and take an active part, for a time, in carrying out their measures. This I did; and I appeal to every reader of this book whether, in view of the facts herein stated upon indubitable evidence, the course I took ought not to entitle me to the praise rather than the censure of honorable men.

Had I been actuated by selfish and dishonorable motives, I should have remained among the Mormons; for with them I possessed power, wealth, and the means to gratify every passion or desire that I might conceive. But I felt myself an humble instrument in the hands of God to expose the Impostor and his myrmidons, and to open the eyes of my countrymen to his dark and damnable designs. I have done my duty, and, whatever may be thought of my motives or my conduct, I am satisfied with the approval of my own conscience, and feel certain that I have acted rightly and honorably.

CHARACTER OF THE AUTHOR.

From S. P. Hildreth, M. D., President of the Medical Convention of the State of Ohio, January 1, A. D. 1838; and J. Cotton, M. D., President of the General Medical Society of the State of Ohio, January 5, A. D. 1829.

" MARIETTA, Ohio, *May* 25, 1831.

" To whom it may concern : —

" The undersigned with pleasure state, that they have for several years past been acquainted with Doctor J. C. Bennett, and have known him to be a very ingenious and successful practitioner of medicine and surgery, as well as an able writer in the Western Medical Journal. His moral character has ever been fair and unexceptionable.

" S. P. HILDRETH,
" JOHN COTTON."

From Thomas Burrell, Jr., M. D.; J. O. Masterson, A. M., of Trinity College, Dublin; and others, citizens of South Bloom-field.

"South Bloomfield, Ohio, *January* 1, 1835.

" We, the undersigned, citizens of South Bloomfield, Pickaway County, Ohio, do certify that we have been personally acquainted with Doctor John C. Bennett, for more than twelve months, (and several of us for a number of years,) during which time he sustained the character of a sober, moral man, scrupulously honest in all his dealings; and, in regard to his talents and professional acquirements, we believe them to be of the first order.

"Isaac Cade,
"Tho. Burrell, Jr.
"Benj. S. Olds,
"J. O. Masterson,
"Geo. R. Piper,
"William Pratt,
"C. R. Bye."

From the President and Secretary of the Board of Trustees of the Willoughby University.

"Chagrin, *August* 20, 1834.

"J. C. Bennett, M. D.

" Dear Sir, —
" A few days since, we, as officers of the Board of Trustees of the Willoughby University of Lake Erie, forwarded to you an appointment as agent for said Institution; since which time the Board have had a meeting, at which it was agreed that we should communicate with you on the subject of commencing our University by organizing the Medical Department first, or, in other words, by obtaining (if possible) two or more suitable persons to deliver a course of Lectures on Anatomy, Chemistry, &c., as soon as the necessary arrangements can be made. It was also proposed, at the meeting of the Board, to commence a select school, or preparatory department, as soon as a suitable person could be obtained to take charge of it, and circumstances justify the undertaking.

" The Board flatter themselves that yourself and your friend Mr. Masterson may yet feel it to be your duty to embark in this business, and assist in building up this Institution.

" We make the suggestion at this time for your consideration, and the Board would be happy to hear from you on the subject.

" On the lot which the trustees have purchased is a large two story dwelling-house, which could be fitted for a preparatory school, or for chemical and anatomical lectures, at a small expense.

" The Board feel thankful for the interest which you have taken in this *Embryo* Institution, and they flatter themselves that success will attend your efforts in its behalf, and that you may yet receive in some way a satisfactory reward.

"N. Allen, *President.*
"H. Graham, *Secretary.*"

From W. Willoughby, M. D., Professor of Midwifery in the College of Physicians and Surgeons in the Western District of New York.

"FAIRFIELD, *January* 20, 1835.

" My dear Sir, —

" Your communication of the 31st of December — mailed the 4th ultimo — has this day been received, for which you will receive my thankful acknowledgments.

" I feel under greater obligation than my feeble language can express, to my friends of the University located in your village, that they have honored me by naming their College after me ; and again, I am under renewed obligation to my much esteemed friends that they should deem my name worthy of designating their town. These testimonials of regard have made a deep impression upon my mind — never to be forgotten. Whatever I can do to insure the stability and prosperity of your school will be done with great cheerfulness and pleasure. If I cannot benefit your institution by personal services, I shall not fail of bestowing something toward its funds.

" The contemplated period for choosing your President had passed by ere I received your letter, so that I could not render the reasons why my name should not be among the candidates. The President should be one among you, live so contiguous as to be enabled to attend all your meetings of the trustees, and exercise a paternal care over the diversified interests of the University. These services could not be attended to by me. I am too far removed from the College to exercise the necessary supervision over its interests and its welfare. I hope, therefore, the honor has fallen upon yourself, or some other one, more able to serve you usefully than would be possible for me to do.

" I promise myself the pleasure of visiting my friends in your section of country — and the University — the ensuing summer, if my health and that of my wife will permit. Mrs. Willoughby's health is very bad, and I greatly fear will never be much improved. She is laboring under hydrathorax — from organic disease of the lungs.

" Receive, my dear sir, for yourself — for your colleagues and the Trustees of the University over whom you preside — my grateful acknowledgments for the honors conferred upon me, with my best wishes for your general and individual welfare. I am, my dear sir, with sentiments of high consideration, your obliged and very humble servant,

"WESTEL WILLOUGHBY.

"JOHN C. BENNETT, M. D.,
President of the Medical Faculty of the
  Willoughby University of Lake Erie."

From the Medical Class of the Willoughby University of Lake Erie.

"WILLOUGHBY, Ohio, *February* 21, A. D. 1835.

"At a meeting of the Medical Class of the Willoughby University of Lake Erie, convened at the College Edifice, on Saturday, the 21st inst., the following resolution was unanimously adopted:

"*Resolved*, That we, the members of the Medical Class of the Willoughby University of Lake Erie, present our thanks to John C. Bennett, M. D., President of our Medical Faculty, and Professor of the Principles and Practice of Midwifery, and the Diseases of Women and Children, for the very able, interesting, and scientific Course of Lectures, by him delivered, during the present session, and as a feeble testimonial of our high regard for the interest he has evinced in our welfare and improvement, and for his splendid talents as a teacher.

"JAMES WHEELER, *President.*

"T. F. ROBINSON,
"H. ROBINSON,
"RANSFORD ROGERS, } *Vice-Presidents.*
"DANIEL MEEKER,
"E. M. GLEESON,

"J. DWIGHT, } *Secretaries.*"
"R. H. HARDY,

From S. P. Hildreth, M. D., President of the Medical Convention of the State of Ohio, January 1, 1838, to Alfred Hobby, Esq., Mayor of Hocking City.

"MARIETTA, Ohio, *April* 11, A. D. 1838.

"To A. HOBBY, Esq., Mayor of Hocking City.
"Dear Sir, —
"In answer to your inquiries as to 'the acquirements and medical knowledge of Dr. John C. Bennett, as a physician and surgeon,' I with great pleasure answer, that I deem him to be well qualified in either branch, and that his opportunities for acquiring knowledge in the Practice of Medicine have been equal to those of any other in this portion of the State.
"Very respectfully,
"Your obedient servant,
"S. P. HILDRETH."

From the Rev. John Stewart, of the Methodist Episcopal Church.

"HOCKING CITY, Ohio, *April* 29, 1838.

"To whom it may concern: —
"This is to certify, that I have been for many years intimately acquainted with John C. Bennett, M. D., who was in 1825 my Family Physician; Dr. Bennett's advantages to acquire correct

2

medical knowledge have been very great, far superior to most physicians in this country; and I consider him one of our most able
and accomplished physicians and surgeons.

                                        " JOHN STEWART."

From Alfred Hobby, Esq., Mayor of Hocking City, Ohio.

                          " HOCKING CITY, Ohio, _June_ 9, 1838.

      " To whom it may concern : —

    " I with great pleasure state, that I have long had a very intimate
acquaintance with John C. Bennett, M. D., both as a medical man,
and private citizen. I have a personal knowledge of his skilful
and dexterous professional tact in some of the major operations in
surgery, such as the extirpation of the cancerous breast; and as a
citizen I deem him a gentleman of much moral and intellectual
worth.   ALFRED HOBBY."

    By perusing Mr. Stewart's certificate, and comparing
the foregoing dates and statements, it will be perceived
that they give a full account of my character and standing
from 1825, when I first commenced the practice of my
profession, up to June, 1838, when I removed from the
State of Ohio to the State of Illinois. On the 20th day
of February, 1839, I was unanimously elected Brigadier-
General of the Invincible Dragoons of the 2d Division
of Illinois Militia, and commissioned as follows : —

    "THOMAS CARLIN, Governor of the State of Illinois, to all to
        whom these presents shall come, greeting :

    " Know ye, That J. C. Bennett, having been duly elected to the
office of Brigadier-General of the Invincible Dragoons of the 2d
Division of the Militia of the State of Illinois, I, Thomas Carlin, Governor of said State, for and on behalf of the People of said State, do
commission him Brigadier-General of Invincible Dragoons of the Second Division of the Militia of the State of Illinois, to take rank from the
20th day of February, 1839. He is, therefore, carefully and diligently
to discharge the duties of said office, by doing and performing all manner of things thereunto belonging ; and I do strictly require all officers
and soldiers under his command to be obedient to his orders ; and
he is to obey such orders and directions as he shall receive from
time to time, from the Commander-in-Chief, or his superior officer.

    " In testimony whereof, I have hereunto set my hand and caused
the State Seal to be affixed. Done at Vandalia, this 25th of April,
in the year of our Lord one thousand eight hundred and thirty-nine,
and of the Independence of the United States the sixty-third.

                                        " THO. CARLIN.

    " By the Governor,
        " A. P. FIELD, _Secretary of State._"

On the 20th day of July, 1840, on the nomination of the principal military men of the State, I was appointed Quarter-Master-General of the State of Illinois, and commissioned as follows : —

" THOMAS CARLIN, Governor of the State of Illinois, to all to whom these presents shall come, greeting :

" Know ye, That J. C. Bennett having been duly appointed to the office of Quarter Master-General of the Militia of the State of Illinois, I, Thomas Carlin, Governor of said State, for and on behalf of the People of said State, do commission him Quarter-Master-General, to take rank from the 20th day of July, 1840. He is, therefore, carefully and diligently to discharge the duties of said office, by doing and performing all manner of things thereunto belonging ; and I do strictly require all officers and soldiers under his command to be obedient to his orders ; and he is to obey such orders and directions as he shall receive from time to time, from the Commander-in-Chief, or his superior officer.

" In testimony whereof, I have hereunto set my hand, and caused the Great Seal of State to be hereunto affixed. Done at Springfield, this 20th day of July, in the year of our Lord one thousand eight hundred and forty, and of the Independence of the United States the sixty-fifth.   THO. CARLIN.

" By the Governor,
            " A. P. FIELD, *Secretary of State.*"

———

" APPOINTMENT BY THE GOVERNOR. — Brigadier-General John C. Bennett to be Quarter-Master-General of the militia of the State of Illinois, from the 20th day of July.

" In making the above appointment, the Governor has selected an able, energetic and efficient officer. The duties that will devolve on him, perhaps no man in the State is better qualified to fill, and we have no doubt he will render due justice to the office which he has been selected to superintend. — *Wabash Republican,*" as quoted in *Times and Seasons,* No. 12, p. 190.

———

Official Documents, showing that I was in actual Service in the State, as a State Officer.

                              " ORDNANCE OFFICE,
                              " WASHINGTON, *October* 23, 1840.

" J. C. BENNETT, Esq. Qr. Master Genl. Illinois Ma. Nauvoo, Ill.
      " Sir, —
                " Capt. Wm. H. Bell, the officer in command of the St. Louis Arsenal, has been instructed to supply the artillery, small arms, &c., specified in your requisition of the 26th ult., received yesterday. The order will, no doubt, be filled immediately.
            " I am, respectfully,
                  " Your obedient servant,
                        " G. TALCOTT, *Lt. Col. Ord.*'

" To His Excellency THOMAS CARLIN.

" Sir, —

" The following Resolution has passed the House of Representatives.

" '*Resolved*, That the Governor be requested to furnish this House with a statement of the arms and accoutrements belonging to the State; the amount of the same, and where stationed, and how the companies bringing themselves under the regulation of the militia law, can be furnished with the same, and at what point, and that he report to this House as soon as suits his convenience.'

" Respectfully,

" JNO. CALHOUN,

"*Clerk of the House of Representatives.*

"*February* 16, 1841."

———

" DEPARTMENT OF STATE,
" SPRINGFIELD, Illinois, 16 *February*, 1841.

" To JOHN C. BENNETT, Quarter-Master-General of the Militia of the State of Illinois:

" Sir, —

" Enclosed I have the honor to send you a copy of a Resolution of the House of Representatives of the General Assembly of the State of Illinois, now in session, calling on me for information relative to the number and kind of arms, belonging to the State, their present location, as also the points where companies in this State can be furnished with the same.

" I have to request that you will report to me, so far as the information desired is in your possession, that I may lay the same before the House from which said Resolution emanated.

" I have the honor to be, sir,

" Your most obedient servant,

" THO. CARLIN."

———

" MEDICAL CONVENTION OF ILLINOIS.

"*To the Medical Profession of Illinois.*

" At a meeting of a number of the Physicians and Surgeons of the State of Illinois, convened in Springfield, on the 9th of June, 1840, for the purpose of making preliminary arrangements for the organization of a State Medical Society, the undersigned were appointed a committee of correspondence, and, as such, directed to address you on that subject. It was proposed that the medical men of the State of Illinois, should assemble in Convention, at Springfield, on the first Monday of December next, and then and there proceed to the complete organization of the Illinois State Medical Society — the Convention to be composed of one or more delegates from each County in the State. This proposition was unanimously adopted; and we now call upon you to coöperate with us in the consummation of so desirable a result. Hitherto we have been like a vessel cast upon a boisterous ocean, without compass or helm; we have acted solitary and alone, without harmony or concert; but when we see hundreds of our fellow-citizens and worthy friends, annually sacrificed by the empirical prescriptions of charlatan practitioners, on the altars of ignorance, erected within the very temple of Æsculapius, by rude and unskilful hands, is it not time for us to act? — We think so: not, however, by declaring war against mountebanks and uneducated pretenders to the art of healing within our borders; but by digesting a plan that shall be calculated in its legitimate operations to benefit the people, instruct the unlearned, improve ourselves, and elevate the entire profession above all mercenary considerations to a station of superior mental. moral and medical excellence. Already do our forests groan under the axeman's hand, and our prairies swarm with a busy, free and enterprising population; in Agriculture and Commerce, we are rapidly approximating to the level of the oldest States; our citizens are rearing Colleges and Universities for mental culture; our Divines and Lawyers have already attained a high rank and an elevated standing; and, shall medicine be wholly neglected? Is *law* of more consequence than *medicine*, or property more valuable than life? If not, let us not be behind our sister States in our efforts to improve our profession, and place it on a level with that of law. We ask not the protection of legal power, nor do we require the strong arm of legislative enactment to sustain us. We place ourselves before the public on our true merits, having a strong and abiding confidence in the wisdom of the people. All we require is a concerted effort, to enable us to diffuse true and useful medical knowledge — and this we ask. It is due to the profession and to humanity, now, and in all time to come. We hope then to see a general attendance on the day proposed.

"J. C. BENNETT, of Fairfield.
"C. V. DYER, of Chicago.
"A. W. BOWEN, of Juliet.
"M. HELM, of Springfield.
"E. H. MERRYMAN, do.
"F. A. McNEIL, do.
"J. TODD, do.
"W. S. WALLACE, do.
"D. TURNEY, of Fairfield.
"C. F. HUGHES, of Rochester.
"I. S. BERRY, of Vandalia.
"B. H. HART, of Alton."

Times and Seasons, Vol. I. No. 11, p. 174.

From Col. N. N. Smith.

"WABASH, *August* 27, A. D. 1840.

"GENERAL BENNETT:

"Dear Friend, —

"Yours of last week was duly received, and attended to. You speak of going to the north in a few days, but whether on business, or to change your residence, does not appear. I hope you do not intend leaving this county, as your business prospects are

2 *

good, and your professional services much required. I have heard that you intended winding up your business, and quitting our county, and this section of Illinois, but I supposed your visit to the north an official one, pertaining to your state appointment. Please write me before you start.

"Respectfully yours,
"N. N. Smith."

This gives an account of my standing up to the time of my removal to Nauvoo, in September, 1840. On the 5th day of February, 1841, I was unanimously elected Major-General of the Nauvoo Legion, and commissioned as follows : —

"Thomas Carlin, Governor of the State of Illinois, to all to whom these presents shall come, greeting:

"Know ye, That John C. Bennett having been duly elected to the office of Major-General of the Nauvoo Legion of the Militia of the State of Illinois, I, Thomas Carlin, Governor of said State, for and on behalf of the People of said State, do commission him Major-General of said Legion, to take rank from the 5th day of February, 1841. He is, therefore, carefully and diligently to discharge the duties of said office, by doing and performing all manner of things thereunto belonging; and I do strictly require all officers and soldiers under his command to be obedient to his orders; and he is to obey such orders and directions as he shall receive from time to time from the Commander-in-Chief, or his superior officer.

"In testimony whereof, I have hereunto set my hand, and caused the Great Seal of State to be hereunto affixed. Done at Springfield, this 16th day of February, in the year of our Lord one thousand eight hundred and forty-one, and of the Independence of the United States the sixty-fifth.
"Tho. Carlin.
"By the Governor,
"S. A. Douglass, Secretary of State."

The following letter from General Scott to Judge Young, one of the United States Senators from Illinois, shows clearly that I *could* legally officiate in the offices of Major-General and Quarter-Master-General of Illinois at the same time, and other official documents will show that I *did* so officiate.

"War Office, *August* 4, 1841.

"Dear Sir, —
"I hasten to reply to your letter of yesterday.
"You state this case ; — General J. C. Bennett, being the Quarter-Master-General of Illinois, (it is *presumed* with the *rank* of Brig-

adier-General,) he is elected, in a separate organization of a portion of the State, a Major-General, and commissioned accordingly.

" The professional question put to me, is — Are the two offices incompatible with each other? — in otner words, Does the acceptance of the second vacate the first?

" I answer — Not necessarily; — not unless there be something *express* to that effect in the constitution or laws of Illinois. The first office is in the general staff of the State; the second in the line of the militia *generally*, or in the line of the *separate* organization.

" For example; — General Jesup is the Quarter-Master-General of the United States army, which gives him, from the date of appointment, the rank of Brigadier-General under one act of Congress, and under another, for ten years' faithful services in that rank, he was made a Major-General by brevet. As Quarter-Master-General he serves as Brigadier-General: in all other situations, that is, *out of the staff*, his other commission makes him a Major-General.

" If the law of Illinois does not give the *rank* of Brigadier, or Major-General, to the officer appointed Quarter-Master-General, there is not even the show of incompatibility between the two commissions of General J. C. Bennett in the statement laid before me.

" It will be understood, of course, that, as Major-General of the army, I do not presume to have the least possible authority over questions arising in the militia, under the laws of the particular States. I venture merely to give, for what it may be worth, my professional opinion on a point submitted to me.

" I have the honor to remain, Sir,
" With great respect,
" Your most obedient servant,
" WINFIELD SCOTT.
" HON. R. M. YOUNG,
" *United States Senate.*"

On the 1st day of February, 1841, I was unanimously elected Mayor of the city of Nauvoo, and commissioned as follows : —

" THOMAS CARLIN, Governor of the State of Illinois, to all to whom these presents shall come, greeting :

" Know ye, that John C. Bennett having been duly elected to the office of Mayor of the city of Nauvoo, in the county of Hancock, I, Thomas Carlin, Governor of the State of Illinois, for and on behalf of the People of said State, do commission him Justice of the Peace for said city in said county, and do authorize and empower him to execute and fulfil the duties of that office according to law.

" And to have and to hold the said office, with all the rights and emoluments thereunto legally appertaining, until his successor shall be duly elected and qualified to office.

" In testimony whereof, I have hereunto set my hand, and caused the Great Seal of State to be hereunto affixed. Done at Spring-field, this 22d day of March, in the year of our Lord one thousand eight hundred and forty-one, and of the Independence of the United States the sixty-fifth.

" THO. CARLIN.
" By the Governor,
" LYMAN TRUMBULL, *Secretary of State.*"

On the 3d of February, 1841, I delivered to the City Council, in the presence of a large assembly, the following

INAUGURAL ADDRESS.

"CITY OF NAUVOO, Illinois, *February* 3, 1841.

" Gentlemen of the City Council ;
Aldermen and Councillors :

" Having been elected to the Mayoralty of this city by the unan-imous suffrages of all parties and interests, I now enter upon the duties devolving upon me as your Chief Magistrate under a deep sense of the responsibilities of the station.—I trust that the confi-dence reposed in me, by my fellow-citizens, has not been misplaced, and for the honor conferred they will accept my warmest sentiments of gratitude. By the munificence and wise legislation of noble, high-minded, and patriotic statesmen, and the grace of God, we have been blessed with one of the most liberal corporate acts ever granted by a legislative assembly. As the presiding officer of the law-making department of the municipal government, it will be expected that I communicate to you, from time to time, by oral or written messages, for your deliberative consideration and action, such matters as may suggest themselves to me in relation to the public weal ; and upon this occasion I beg leave to present the fol-lowing as matters of paramount importance.

" The 21st Sec. of the *addenda* to the 13th Sec. of the City Charter concedes to you plenary power ' to tax, restrain, prohibit and suppress, tippling-houses, dram-shops,' etc. etc., and I now recommend, in the strongest possible terms, that you take prompt, strong, and decisive measures to ' *prohibit and suppress* ' all such establishments. It is true you have the power ' to tax,' or *license and tolerate*, them, and thus add to the city finances ; but I consider it much better to raise revenue by an *ad valorem* tax on the property of sober men, than by licensing dram-shops, or taxing the signs of the inebriated worshippers at the shrine of Bacchus. The revels of bacchanalians in the houses of blasphemy and noise will always prove a disgrace to a moral people. *Public sentiment* will do *much* to suppress the vice of intemperance, and its concomitant evil results ; but ample experience has incontrovertibly proven that it cannot do *all* — the *law* must be brought to the rescue, and an effective prohibitory ordinance enacted. This cannot be done at a better time than the present. Let us *commence* correctly, and the great work of reform, at least so far as our peaceful city is concerned, can be summarily consummated. It would be difficult to calculate the vast amount of evil and crime that would be prevented, and the great good that would accrue to the public at large by fostering the cause of temperance; but suffice it to say that the one would be commensurate to the other. — No sales of spirituous liquors whatever, in a less quantity than a quart, except in cases of sickness, on the recommendation of a physician or surgeon duly accredited by the Chancellor and Regents of the University, should be tolerated. The liberty of selling the intoxicating cup is a *false* liberty — it enslaves, degrades, destroys, and wretchedness and want are attendant on every step, — its touch, like that of the *poison Upas*, is DEATH. Liberty to do good should be cheerfully and freely accorded to every man; but liberty to do evil, which is licentiousness, should be peremptorily prohibited. The public good imperiously demands it — and the cause of humanity pleads for help. The protecting ægis of the corporation should be thrown around every moral and religious institution of the day, which is in any way calculated to ennoble, or ameliorate the condition of the human family.

" The immediate organization of the University, as contemplated in the 24th Sec. of the act incorporating our city, cannot be too forcibly impressed upon you at this time. — As all matters in relation to mental culture, and public instruction, from common schools up to the highest branches of a full collegiate course in the Arts, Sciences, and Learned Professions, will devolve upon the Chancellor and Regents of the University, they should be speedily elected, and instructed to perfect their plan, and enter upon its execution with as little delay as possible. The wheels of education should never be clogged, or retrograde, but roll progressively from the *Alpha* to the *Omega* of a most perfect, liberal, and thorough course of university attainments. The following observations in relation to *false* education, from Alexander's Messenger, so perfectly accord with my feelings and views on this highly important subject, that I cannot do better than incorporate them in this message.

" ' Among the changes for the worse, which the world has witnessed within the last century, we include that specious, superficial, incomplete way of doing certain things, which were formerly thought to be deserving of care, labor, and attention. It would seem that appearance is now considered of more moment than reality. The modern mode of education is an example in point. Children are so instructed as to acquire a smattering of every thing; and, as a matter of consequence, they know nothing properly. Seminaries and academies deal out their moral and natural philosophy, their geometry, trigonometry, and astronomy, their chemistry, botany, and mineralogy, until the mind of the pupil becomes a chaos; and, like the stomach when it is overloaded with a variety of food, it digests nothing, but converts the superabundant nutriment to poison. This mode of education answers one purpose : — it enables people to *seem learned*; and seemingly, by a great many, is thought all-sufficient. Thus we are schooled in quackery, and are early taught to regard showy and superficial attainments as most desirable. Every boarding school Miss is a Plato in petticoats, without an ounce of that genuine knowledge, that true philosophy, which would enable her to be useful in the world, and to escape those perils with which she must necessarily be encompassed. Young people are taught to use a variety of hard terms, which they understand but imperfectly ; — to repeat lessons which they are unable to apply ; — to astonish their grandmothers with a display of their parrot-like acquisitions ; — but their mental energies are clogged and torpified with a variety of learned lumber, most of which is discarded from the brain long before its possessor knows how to use it. This is the quackery of education.

" 'The effects of the erring system are not easily obliterated. The habit of using words without thought, sticks to the unfortunate student through life, and should he ever learn to think, he cannot express his ideas without the most tedious and perplexing verbosity. This is, more or less, the fault of every writer in the nineteenth century. The sense is encumbered with sound. The scribbler appears to imagine that if he puts a sufficient number of words together he has done his part; and, alas! how many books are written on this principle. Thus literature, and even science itself, is overloaded with froth and flummery. Verbalizing has become fashionable and indispensable, and one line from an ancient author will furnish the materials for a modern treatise.'

" Our University should be a '*utilitarian*' institution — and competent, industrious, teachers, and professors, should be immediately elected for the several departments. ' Knowledge is power,'—foster education and we are forever *free !* Nothing can be done which is more certainly calculated to perpetuate the free institutions of our common country, for which our progenitors ' fought and bled, and died,' than the general diffusion of useful knowledge amongst the people. Education should always be of a purely *practical* character, for such, and such alone, is calculated to perfect the happiness, and prosperity, of our fellow-citizens — ignorance, impudence, and false knowledge, are equally detestable, — shame and confusion follow in their train. As you now possess the power, afford the most ample facilities to the Regents to make their plan complete ; and thus enable them to set a glorious example to the world at large. The most liberal policy should attend the organization of the University, and equal honors and privileges should be extended to all classes of the community.

" In order to carry out the provisions of the 25th Sec. of the act incorporating our city, I would recommend the immediate organization of the Legion. Comprising, as it does, the entire military power of our city, with a provision allowing any citizen of Hancock county to unite by voluntary enrolment, early facilities should be afforded the Court Martial for perfecting their plan of drill, rules, and regulations. Nothing is more necessary to the preservation of order, and the supremacy of the laws, than the perfect organization of our military forces, under a uniform and rigid discipline, and approved judicious drill; and to this end I desire to see all the departments, and cohorts of the Legion put in immediate requisition. The Legion should be all powerful, panoplied with justice and equity, to consummate the designs of its projectors — at all times ready, as minute men, to serve the state in such way and manner as may, from time to time, be pointed out by the Governor. You have long sought an opportunity of showing your attachment to the state government of Illinois — it is now afforded: the Legion should maintain the constitution and the laws, and be ready at all times for the public defence. The winged warrior of the air perches upon the pole of American liberty, and the beast that has the temerity to ruffle her feathers should be made to feel the power of her talons; and until she ceases to be our proud national emblem we should not cease to show our attachment to Illinois. Should the tocsin of alarm ever be sounded, and the Legion called to the tented field by our Executive, I hope to see it able, under one of the proudest mottos that ever blazed upon a warrior's shield — *Sicut patribus sit Deus nobis;* as God was with our fathers, so may he be with us — to fight the battles of our country, as victors, and as freemen : the juice of the uva, or the spirit of insubordination should never enter our camp, — but we should stand, ever stand, as a united people — one and indivisible.

" I would earnestly recommend the construction of a wing-dam in the Mississippi, at the mouth of the ravine at or near the head of Main Street, and the excavation of a ship-canal from that point to a point terminating in a *grand reservoir* on the bank of said river, east of the foot of said street a distance of about two miles. This would afford, at the various outlets, the most ample water power for propelling any amount of machinery for mill and manufacturing purposes, so essentially necessary to the building up of a great commercial city in the heart of one of the most productive and delightful countries on earth. I would advise that an agent be immediately appointed on behalf of the city corporation, to negotiate with eastern capitalists for the completion of this great work, on the most advantageous terms, even to the conveyance of the privilege for a term of years. This work finished, and the future greatness of this city is placed upon an imperishable basis. In addition to the great advantages that will otherwise accrue to the city and country by the construction of this noble work, it would afford the best harbor for steam-boats, for winter quarters, on this magnificent stream.

" The public health requires that the low lands, bordering on the Mississippi, should be immediately drained, and the entire timber removed. This can and will be one of the most healthy cities in the west, provided you take prompt and decisive action in the premises. ' A Board of Health should be appointed and vested with the usual powers and prerogatives.

" The Governor, Council of Revision, and Legislature of Illinois, should be held in everlasting remembrance by our people — they burst the chains of slavery and proclaimed us forever free ! A vote of thanks, couched in the strongest language possible, should be tendered them in our corporate capacity; and, when this is done,

Quincy, our first noble city of refuge, when you came from the
slaughter in Missouri with your garments stained with blood, should
not be forgotten.

" As the Chief Magistrate of your city I am determined to execute all state laws, and city ordinances passed in pursuance to law,
to the very letter, should it require the strong arm of military power
to enable me to do so. As an officer I know no man ; the peaceful
unoffending citizen *shall* be protected in the full exercise of all his
civil, political, and religious rights, and the guilty violator of law
shall be punished without respect to persons.

" All of which is respectfully submitted.

" JOHN C. BENNETT."

Times and Seasons, Vol. II., No. 8, p. 316.

On the 3d day of February, 1841, I was unanimously
elected Chancellor of the University of the City of Nauvoo,
as will hereafter appear.

" We are glad to see the action of the Council on the subject of
education ; and that they have chosen a Board of Regents, and
appointed a Chancellor and Registrar for the ' University of the City
of Nauvoo.' The appointment, we think, does great credit to the
Council, and, we have no doubt but that the board will assiduously
engage in the great and all-important work of education "

Times and Seasons, Vol. II., No. 8, p. 319.

" AN ORDINANCE, ORGANIZING THE ' UNIVERSITY OF THE
CITY OF NAUVOO.'

" Sec. 1.   Be it ordained by the City Council of the City of Nau-
voo, That the ' University of the City of Nauvoo,' be, and the same
is hereby organized, by the appointment of the following Board of
Trustees, to wit : John C. Bennett, Chancellor, William Law, Regis-
trar, and Joseph Smith, Sidney Rigdon, Hyrum Smith, William
Marks, Samuel H. Smith, Daniel H. Wells, N. K. Whitney, Charles
C. Rich, John T. Barnett, Wilson Law, Don C. Smith, John P.
Greene, Vinson Knight, Isaac Galland, Elias Higbee, Robert D.
Foster, James Adams, Robert B. Thompson, Samuel Bennett,
Ebenezer Robinson, John Snider, George Miller, and Lenos M.
Knight, Regents ; who shall hereafter constitute the ' Chancellor
and Regents of the University of the City of Nauvoo,' as contem-
plated in the 24th section of ' An act to incorporate the City of
Nauvoo,' approved December 16, 1840.

" Sec. 2.   The Board named in the 1st section of this ordinance
shall hold its first meeting at the office of Joseph Smith, on Tuesday,
the 9th day of February, 1841, at 2 o'clock, P. M.

" Sec. 3.   This ordinance shall take effect, and be in force, from
and after its passage.

" Passed, Feb. 3d, A. D. 1841.

" JOHN C. BENNETT, *Mayor*

" JAMES SLOAN, *Recorder*."

"COMMON SCHOOL BOOKS ADOPTED.

" *Extract from the Minutes of the Board of Regents.*

"UNIVERSITY OF THE CITY OF NAUVOO,
Illinois, *December* 18, A. D. 1841.

" *Gentlemen of the Board of Regents:*

"Permit me to present for your ADOPTION, the following series of books for Common Schools, which I have carefully selected and *approved*, to wit: — Town's Spelling Book; Town's Introduction to Analysis; Town's Analysis; M'Vickar's Political Economy for Schools; Help to Young Writers; Girl's Reading Book, by Mrs. Sigourney; Boy's Reading Book, by Mrs. Sigourney; Bennett's Arithmetic; Bennett's Book Keeping; Kirkham's English Grammar; Olney's Geography.

" JOHN C. BENNETT, *Chancellor.*

" Adopted as follows, to wit: —

" Yeas — Joseph Smith, Hyrum Smith, Charles C. Rich, Heber C. Kimball, John Taylor, N. K. Whitney, Samuel H. Smith, John Snider, Wm. Marks, Ebenezer Robinson, Elias Higbee, (Regents,) William Law, (Registrar,) John C. Bennett, (Chancellor,) 13.

" Nays — None.

" Absent — Sidney Rigdon, Daniel H. Wells, John T. Barnett, Wilson Law, John P. Green, Vinson Knight, Isaac Galland, Robert D. Foster, James Adams, Samuel Bennett, George Miller, Lenos M. Knight, (Regents,) 12."

Times and Seasons, Vol. III., No. 5, p. 652.

On the 6th day of May, A. D. 1841, I was appointed Master in Chancery for Hancock County, as follows: —

"Know all men by these presents, That I, Stephen A. Douglass, Justice of the Supreme Court, and presiding Judge of the Fifth Judicial Circuit of the State of Illinois, do constitute and appoint John C. Bennett, Esq., Master in Chancery, in and for the County of Hancock, in said State, and do authorize and impower him to have, exercise and enjoy, all the rights, privileges and emoluments pertaining to said office of Master in Chancery.

"Given under my hand and seal, this 6th day of May, A. D. 1841.

"S. A. DOUGLASS, [seal.]"

"STATE OF ILLINOIS,
Hancock County.

"This day, personally appeared before the undersigned, Judge of the Fifth Judicial Circuit of the State of Illinois, John C. Bennett, Esq., who, being first duly sworn, declared that he would faithfully support the Constitution of the United States and of this State, and that he would faithfully discharge his duties as Master in Chancery, according to the best of his knowledge, skill and understanding.

"Given under my hand and seal, this 6th day of May, A. D. 1841.

"S. A. DOUGLASS, [seal.]"

On the 7th day of April, 1841, I was elected to the
First Presidency of the Mormon Church, as will be seen
by reference to the conference minutes, published in the
"Times and Seasons," (the official Mormon paper, edited
by Joe Smith, the Prophet, assisted by John Taylor, the
Apostle,) Vol. II., No. 12, page 387, from which I extract
the following : —

"Gen. J. C. Bennett was presented with the First Presidency, as
Assistant President, until President Rigdon's health should be restored."

----◆----

MORMON TESTIMONY, UP TO THE TIME OF, AND
SUBSEQUENT TO, MY WITHDRAWAL FROM THE
CHURCH.

"'The Quarter-Master-General of Illinois, (Dr. J. C. Bennett) has
joined the Mormons and been baptized according to their faith.
Under such a leader they will no doubt be able to whip the Missourians in the next campaign.' — *Louisville Journal.*

"*Very liberal,* MR. EDITOR : But the '*next campaign*' belongs to
the PEOPLE, and unless they arise with one voice and avenge the
wrongs of an innocent and much injured community — farewell to
LIBERTY — she has fled forever, and *mobocrats* bear rule."— *Times
and Seasons,* Vol. II., No. 3, p. 234.

" ☞ GREAT MORAL VICTORY ! — The high grouñds taken by
our Mayor, General Bennett, in relation to the great work of temperance reform, have been fully sustained by the City Council.
President Joseph Smith, chairman of the committee to whom was
referred that part of the inaugural address of His Honor, the Mayor,
which relates to *Temperance,* reported the following Ordinance to
the City Council on the 15th instant, which was elaborately discussed by Aldermen Wells and Whitney, and Councillors J. Smith,
H. Smith, Rigdon, Law, and Greene, and in Committee of the
Whole, by His Honor, and after dispensing with the rules, read
three several times, and passed UNANIMOUSLY.

" This ordinance passed by ayes and noes, on the call of Coun-
cillor Barnett, as follows : —

" Yeas — Aldermen Wells, Smith, Marks and Whitney — Coun-
cillors Joseph Smith, Hyrum Smith, Don C. Smith, Rigdon, Law,
Rich, Barnett, Greene, and Knight — and the Mayor — 14. (Full
Council.)

" Nays — None !

" Thus has the City of Nauvoo set a glorious example to the
world — sustained by *principle,* and the GREAT GOD ; to wit ·-

"AN ORDINANCE IN RELATION TO TEMPERANCE.

"Sec. 1. Be it ordained by the City Council of the City of Nauvoo, That all persons and establishments whatever, in this City, are prohibited from vending whisky in a less quantity than a gallon, or other spirituous liquors in a less quantity than a quart, to any person whatever, excepting on the recommendation of a Physician duly accredited, in writing, by the 'Chancellor and Regents of the University of the City of Nauvoo,' and any person guilty of any act contrary to the prohibition contained in this ordinance, shall, on conviction thereof before the Mayor, or Municipal Court, be fined in any sum not exceeding twenty-five dollars, at the discretion of said Mayor, or Court; and any person or persons who shall attempt to evade this ordinance by giving away liquor, or by any other means, shall be considered alike amenable, and fined as aforesaid.

"Sec. 2. This ordinance, to take effect, and be in force, from and after its passage.

"Passed, Feb. 15th, A. D. 1841.

"JOHN C. BENNETT, *Mayor.*

"JAMES SLOAN, *Recorder.*"

"'Gen. J. C. Bennett, a very popular and deserving man, has been elected Mayor of Nauvoo, Hancock county.' — *Chicago Democrat.*

"We cheerfully respond to the above statement respecting our worthy Mayor, and we are indeed glad that any of our friends of the press, can nobly come forward and award to faithfulness and integrity their due, even if found in a Mormon.

"We would say, that if untiring diligence to aid the afflicted and the oppressed, zeal for the promotion of literature and intelligence, AND A VIRTUOUS AND CONSISTENT CONDUCT, are evidences of popularity, &c., we venture to say that no man deserves the appellations of 'popular and deserving' more than Gen. J. C. Bennett."
Times and Seasons, Vol. II., No. 10, p. 351.

"LAYING THE CORNER STONE OF THE TEMPLE.
GENERAL CONFERENCE.

"'Oh! that I could paint the scenes
Which on my heart are sketch'd.'

"The general conference of the Church, together with the laying of the corner stones of the Temple of our God, now building in this city, have long been anticipated by the saints of the Most High, both far and near, with great pleasure, when they should once more behold the foundation of a house laid, in which they might worship the God of their fathers.

"It frequently happens, that our anticipations of pleasure and delight, are raised to such a height that even exceeds the enjoyment itself, but we are happy to say, this was not the case with the immense multitude who witnessed the proceedings of the sixth of April, and subsequent days of conference. The scenes were of such a character, the enjoyment so intense, that left anticipation far behind.

" However anxious we are to portray the grandeur and majesty of the celebrations, the union and order which every way prevailed, we are confident, we shall come very far short of doing them justice.

"For some days prior to the sixth, the accession of strangers to our city was great, and on the wide-spread prairie, which bounds our city, might be seen various kinds of vehicles wending their way from different points of the compass to the city of Nauvoo, while the ferry-boats on the Mississippi were constantly employed in wafting travellers across its rolling and extensive bosom.

" Among the citizens, all was bustle and preparation, anxious to accommodate their friends who flocked in from distant parts, and who they expected to share with them the festivity of the day, and the pleasures of the scene.

" At length the long-expected morn arrived, and before the king of day had tipped the eastern horizon with his rays, were preparations for the celebration of the day going on. Shortly after sunrise, the loud peals from the artillery were heard, calling the various companies of the Legion to the field, who were appointed to take a conspicuous part in the day's proceedings.

" The citizens from the vicinity, now began to pour in from all quarters, a continuous train, for about three hours, and continued to swell the vast assembly.

" At eight o'clock, A. M., Major-General Bennett left his quarters to organize and prepare the Legion for the duties of the day, which consisted of about fourteen companies, several in uniform, besides several companies from Iowa, and other parts of the county, which joined them on the occasion.

" At half past nine, Lieut. General Smith was informed that the Legion was organized and ready for review, and immediately accompanied by his staff, consisting of four Aids-de-camp, and twelve guards, nearly all in splendid uniforms, took his march to the parade ground. On their approach, they were met by the band, beautifully equipped, who received them with a flourish of trumpets and a regular salute, and then struck up a lively air, marching in front to the stand of the Lieut. General. On his approach to the parade ground the artillery was again fired, and the Legion gave an appropriate salute while passing. This was indeed a glorious sight, such as we never saw, nor did we ever expect to see such a one in the west. The several companies, presented a beautiful and interesting spectacle, several of them being uniformed and equipped, while the rich and costly dresses of the officers, would have become a Bonaparte or a Washington.

" After the arrival of Lieut. General Smith, the ladies who had made a beautiful silk flag, drove up in a carriage to present it to the Legion. Maj. General Bennett, very politely attended on them, and conducted them in front of Lieut. General Smith, who immediately alighted from his charger, and walked up to the ladies, who presented the flag, making an appropriate address. Lieut. General Smith, acknowledged the honor conferred upon the Legion, and stated that as long as he had the command, it should never be disgraced; and then politely bowing to the ladies gave it into the hands of Maj. General Bennett, who placed it in possession of Cornet Robinson, and it was soon seen gracefully waving in front of the Legion. During the time of presentation, the band struck up a lively air and another salute was fired from the artillery.

"After the presentation of the flag, Lieut. General Smith, accompanied by his suite, reviewed the Legion, which presented a very imposing appearance, the different officers saluting as he passed. Lieut. General Smith then took his former stand and the whole Legion by companies passed before him in review.

THE PROCESSION.

"Immediately after the review, Gen. Bennett organized the procession, to march to the foundation of the Temple, in the following order; to wit:

Lieut. Gen. Smith,
Brig. Generals Law and Smith,
Aids-de-Camp, and conspicuous
strangers,
General Staff,
Band,
2nd Cohort, (foot troops,)
Ladies eight abreast,
Gentlemen, eight abreast,
1st Cohort, (horse troops.)

"Owing to the vast numbers who joined in the procession, it was a considerable length of time before the whole could be organized.

"The procession then began to move forward in order, and on their arrival at the Temple block, the Generals with their staffs and the distinguished strangers present, took their position inside of the foundation, the ladies formed on the outside immediately next the walls, the gentlemen and infantry behind, and the cavalry in the rear.

"The assembly being stationed, the choristers, under the superintendence of B. S. Wilber, sung an appropriate hymn.

"Prest. Rigdon, then ascended the platform, which had been prepared for the purpose, and delivered a suitable

ORATION,

which was listened to with the most profound attention by the assembly. From the long affliction and weakness of body we hardly expected the speaker to have made himself heard by the congregation, but he succeeded beyond our most sanguine expectations, and being impressed with the greatness and solemnities of the occasion, he rose superior to his afflictions and weakness, and for more than an hour occupied the attention of the assembly.

"It was an address worthy a man of God, and a messenger of salvation. We have heard the speaker on other occasions when he has been more eloquent, when there has been more harmony and beauty in the construction of his sentences, and when the refined

3 *

ear has been more delighted; but never did we hear him pour out such pious effusions; in short it was full to overflowing, of Christian feeling and high-toned piety.

"He called to review the scenes of tribulation and anguish through which the Saints had passed, the barbarous cruelties inflicted upon them for their faith and attachment to the cause of their God, and for the testimony of Jesus, which, they endured with patience, knowing that they had in heaven a more enduring substance, a crown of eternal glory.

"In obedience to the commandments of their Heavenly Father, and because that Jesus had again spoken from the heavens, were they engaged in laying the foundation of the Temple that the Most High might have a habitation, and where the Saints might assemble to pay their devotions to his holy name.

"He rejoiced at the glorious prospect which presented itself of soon completing the edifice, as there were no mobs to hinder them in their labors, consequently their circumstances were very different than before.

"After the address, the choir sung a hymn. Prest. Rigdon then invoked the blessings of Almighty God upon the assembly, and upon those who should labor on the building.

"The First Presidency superintended the laying of the

CHIEF CORNER STONE,

on the south-east corner of the building, which done, Prest. J. Smith arose and said, that the first corner stone of the Temple of Almighty God was laid, and prayed that the building might soon be completed, that the Saints might have an habitation to worship the God of their fathers.

"Prest. D. C. Smith and his Councillors, of the High Priests' Quorum, then repaired to the south west corner, and laid the corner stone thereof.

"The High Council, representing the Twelve laid the north-west corner stone.

"The Bishops with their Councillors laid the north-east corner stone with due solemnities.

"The ceremony of laying the corner stones being over, the Legion marched to the parade ground, and formed a hollow square for an address. Maj. General Bennett addressed the Legion at some length, applauding them for their soldierlike appearance, and for the attention which both officers and men had given to the orders.

"Lieutenant-General Smith likewise expressed his entire approbation of the conduct of the Legion and all present.

"The assembly then separated with cheerful hearts, and thanking God for the great blessings of peace and prosperity by which they were surrounded, and hearts burning with affection for their favorite and adopted state.

"It was indeed a gladsome sight, and extremely affecting, to see the old revolutionary patriots, who had been driven from their homes in Missouri, strike hands and rejoice together, in a land where they knew they would be protected from mobs, and where they could again enjoy the liberty for which they had fought many a hard battle.

"The day was indeed propitious — heaven and earth combined to make the scene as glorious as possible, and long, very long, will the 6th of April, A. D. 1841, be remembered by the many thousands who were present.

"The whole passed off with perfect harmony and good feeling. The people were truly of one heart and mind, no contention or discord; even persons unconnected with the Church forgot their prejudices, and for once took pleasure in the society of the Saints, admired their order and unanimity, and undoubtedly received favorable impressions by their visit.

"Too much praise cannot be given to Maj. General Bennett for his active services on the occasion: he has labored diligently for the prosperity of the city, and particularly for the Legion, and it must have been a proud day for him, and entirely satisfactory, to see his efforts crowned with success, and his labor so well bestowed.

"R. B. THOMPSON."

Times and Seasons, Vol. II., No. 12, p. 380.

"IMPORTANT.

"Dr. Bennett is of the opinion that most of the bilious affections to which our citizens are subjected during the hot season, can be prevented by the free use of the Tomato — we are of the same opinion, and as health is essential to our happiness and prosperity as a people, we would earnestly recommend its culture to our fellow-citizens, and its general use for culinary purposes. Do not neglect it."

Times and Seasons, Vol. II., No. 13, p. 404.

"It is well known, that Gen. Bennett has for some time been striving to organize the militia of this state, on a plan which would make them more effective in the time of emergency. The example of his skill and ability, to effect that object, so necessary for the public weal, is now fairly before the public; and as lovers of our country we hope that it will be satisfactory and be adopted by the citizens of this state.

"In time of peace, it is necessary to prepare for war; the following remarks of Gen. Washington to both houses of Congress, in 1793, are so appropriate, that we cheerfully give them a place.

"'I am pressing upon you the necessity of placing ourselves in a condition of complete defence, and exact the fulfilment of duties towards us. The people ought not to indulge a persuasion contrary to the order of human events. There is a rank due to the nation, which will be withheld, if not lost, by the known weakness and absolute neglect to improve our system of defence. *If we desire to avoid insult, we must be ready to repel it.*'"

Times and Seasons, Vol. II., No. 14, p. 416.

"*From the Belleville Advocate.*

"'Mr. BOYD: I have read with much interest, the 'Inaugural Address' of Dr. John C. Bennett, of the city of Nauvoo, which was delivered to the City Council on the 3d of February last, as published in the 'Times and Seasons.'

" ' It is a document which, I think, is entitled to the particular notice of our respectable fellow-citizens : and if it should meet your views, as it does mine, diffusing a will to promote morality and science, I would be proud to see it in its *verbatim* character, portrayed in the columns of your widely circulating paper, the " Belleville Advocate."

" ' I am and have been long acquainted with Dr. Bennett, and his present character in the military department of this State is not inferior to any in the Union.

" ' With this communication, you will receive the Address.

" ' With sentiments of respect,

" ' I have the honor to be

" ' Yours, respectfully, &c.

" ' W. G. GOFORTH, M. D.

" ' BELLEVILLE, Illinois, *March* 22, 1841.' "

" We should be happy to comply with the request of our worthy and esteemed M. D. friend, ' Old Pills,' to publish the ' Address,' entire, which he was kind enough to furnish us; but the press of other matter prevents. We have given it an attentive perusal ; and heartily concur with the sentiments contained therein. Certainly, they ought to be the guide of those who are placed in immediate authority over the morals of community, and Mayor Bennett clearly understands his duties. We shall make some extracts from his speech, and earnestly commend them to our readers. We think, our ' town' Trustees might profit by the example that is set them, by the Mayor of Nauvoo."

Times and Seasons, Vol. II., No. 14, p. 419.

———

" Not only has the Lord given us favor in the eyes of the community, who are happy to see us in the enjoyment of all the rights and privileges of freemen, but we are happy to state, that several of the principal men of Illinois, who have listened to the doctrines we promulge, have become obedient to the faith, and are rejoicing in the same; among whom is John C. Bennett, M. D., Quarter-Master-General of Illinois." — *Times and Seasons*, Vol. II., No. 6, p. 275.

———

" *For the Times and Seasons.*

"THE NAUVOO LEGION.

" The firm heart of the Sage and the Patriot is warm'd
By the grand ' Nauvoo Legion: ' The ' Legion ' is form'd
To oppose vile oppression, and nobly to stand
In defence of the honor, and laws of the land.
Base, illegal proscribers may tremble — 'tis right
That the lawless aggressor should shrink with affright,
From a band that's united fell mobbers to chase,
And protect our lov'd country from utter disgrace.

"Fair Columbia! rejoice! look away to the West,
To thy own Illinois, where the saints have found rest:
See a phœnix come forth from the graves of the just,
Whom Missouri's oppressors laid low in the dust:
See a phœnix — a ' Legion ' — a warm-hearted band,
Who, unmov'd, to thy basis of freedom will stand.

" When the day of vexation rolls fearfully on —
When thy children turn traitors — when safety is gone —
When peace in thy borders no longer is found —
When the fierce battles rage, and the war-trumpets sound;
Here, here are thy warriors — a true-hearted band,
To their country's best int'rest forever will stand;
For *then* to thy standard, the ' Legion ' will be
A strong bulwark of Freedom — of pure Liberty.

" Here's the silver-hair'd vet'ran, who suffer'd to gain
That Freedom he now volunteers to maintain :
The brave, gallant young soldier — the patriot is here
With his sword and his buckler, his helmet and spear ;
And the horseman whose steed proudly steps to the sound
Of the soul-stirring music that's moving around ;
And here, too, is the orphan, whose spirit grows brave
At the mention of ' Boggs,' and his own father's grave ;
Yes, and bold-hearted Chieftains as ever drew breath,
Who are fearless of danger — regardless of death ;
Who've decreed in the name of the Ruler on high
That the Laws *shall be honor'd* — that treason *shall die.*

" Should they need reënforcements, those rights to secure,
Which our forefathers purchas'd ; and Freedom ensure,
There is still in reserve a strong Cohort above ;
' *Lo! the chariots of Israel, and horsemen thereof.*'
                                                " ELIZA.
" CITY OF NAUVOO, *June* 2, 1841."
                    Times and Seasons, Vol. II., No. 17, p. 467.

" EXTRACT

" *From a Revelation given to Joseph Smith, Jr., Jan.* 19, 1841.

" Again, let my servant, John C. Bennett, help you in your labor,
in sending my word to the Kings and people of the earth, and stand
by you, even you my servant Joseph Smith in the hour of affliction,
and his reward shall not fail if he receive counsel ; and for his love,
he shall be great; for he shall be mine if he does this, saith the
Lord. I have seen the work he hath done, which I accept, if he
continue ; and will crown him with blessings and great glory."
                    Times and Seasons, Vol. II., No. 15, p. 425.

"THE WARSAW SIGNAL.

"We can hardly find language to express our surprise and disapprobation at the conduct of the Editor of the 'Signal,' as manifested in that paper of the 19th ult. We had fondly hoped that the sentiments there expressed, would never have dared to be uttered by any individual, in the community in which we reside, whose friendship we esteem, and whose virtuous and honorable conduct, have secured them the approval of every patriotic and benevolent mind. We are, however, anxious to know the real feelings of individuals, and are glad that the latent feelings of the Editor of the Signal, have at last, manifested themselves, clearly and distinctly.

"And, we would ask the Editor of the Signal, what is the cause of his hostility — of this sudden and unexpected ebullition of feeling —this spirit of opposition and animosity? Whose rights have been trampled upon? Whose peace have we disturbed? General Bennett has been appointed Master in Chancery, by Judge Douglass, and General Bennett is a Mormon! This is the atrocious act — this is the cause of the Editor's vile vituperation. It will not require the gift of discernment to tell what spirit the Editor was possessed of, when he wrote the following: —

"'Bennett has but recently become an inhabitant of this State — he joins a sect and advocates a creed in which no one believes he has any faith.'

"It is obvious, that the intention is to make the community believe, that General Bennett is a mere renegado — hypocrite — and all that is base in humanity. But General Bennett's character as a gentleman, an officer, a scholar, and physician, stands too high to need defending by us; suffice it to say, that he is in the confidence of the Executive, holds the office of Quarter-Master-General of this State, and is well known to a large number of persons of the first respectability throughout the State. He has, likewise, been favorably known for upwards of eight years by some of the authorities of the Church, and has resided three years in this State. But being a Mormon, HIS VIRTUES ARE CONSTRUED INTO DEFECTS, and is thought a proper object of the base, cowardly, and ungentlemanly attack of the Editor of the 'Signal.'"

Times and Seasons, Vol. II., No. 15, pp. 431, 432.

"Generals Joseph Smith, John C. Bennett, and Hyrum Smith, and some other citizens of Nauvoo, attended the military parade, at Montrose, on the 14th, as visitors, on the special invitation of General Swazey, and Colonel Fuller of Iowa, the officers in command. Generals Joseph and Hyrum Smith attended, attired in plain citizen's garb, as citizens, without the least military appearance about them. General Bennett, and some of his staff officers, it is true, appeared in the 'splendid and brilliant uniform of the Nauvoo Legion,' as the Editor of the Signal is pleased to term it. All passed off with perfect good feeling, and in a highly creditable manner."

Times and Seasons, Vol. II., No. 23, p. 563.

"STATE GUBERNATORIAL CONVENTION.

"CITY OF NAUVOO, Illinois, }
December 20, A. D. 1841. }

"To my friends in Illinois: —

"The Gubernatorial Convention of the State of Illinois have nominated COLONEL ADAM W. SNYDER for GOVERNOR, and COLONEL JOHN MOORE for LIEUTENANT-GOVERNOR of the *State of Illinois* — election to take place in August next. COLONEL MOORE, like JUDGE DOUGLASS, and ESQ. WARREN, was an intimate friend of GENERAL BENNETT, long before that gentleman became a member of our community; and General Bennett informs us that no men were more efficient in assisting him to procure our *great chartered privileges* than were *Colonel Snyder*, and *Colonel Moore*. They are sterling men, and friends of equal rights — opposed to the oppressor's grasp, and the tyrant's rod. With such men at the head of our State Government, we have nothing to fear. In the next canvass we shall be influenced by no *party* consideration — and no Carthaginian coalescence or collusion, with our people, will be suffered to affect, or operate against, *General Bennett or any other of our tried friends already semi-officially in the field;* so the partisans in this county who expect to divide the friends of humanity and equal rights, will find themselves mistaken — we care not a fig for *Whig* or *Democrat:* they are both alike to us; but we shall go for our *friends,* our TRIED FRIENDS, and the cause of *human liberty,* which is the cause of God. We are aware that ' *divide and conquer,*' is the watch word with many, but with us it cannot be done — we love liberty too well — we have suffered too much to be easily duped — we have no cat's-paws amongst us. We voted for GENERAL HARRISON, because we *loved* him — he was a *gallant officer,* and a *tried statesman;* but this is no reason why we should always be governed by his *friends* — he is now DEAD, and all of *his* friends are not *ours.* We claim the privileges of freemen, and shall act accordingly. DOUGLASS is a *Master Spirit,* and *his friends are our friends* — we are willing to cast our banners on the air, and fight by his side in the cause of humanity, and equal rights — the cause of liberty and the law. SNYDER, and MOORE, are *his* friends — they are *ours.* These men are free from the prejudices and superstitions of the age, and such men we *love,* and such men will ever receive our support, be their *political predilections* what they may. Snyder, and Moore, are *known* to be our friends; their friendship is *vouched* for by those whom we have tried. We will never be justly charged with the sin of ingratitude — they *have* served us, and we *will* serve them.   "JOSEPH SMITH,

"*Lieutenant-General of the Nauvoo Legion.*"

Times and Seasons, Vol. III., No. 5, p. 651.

"RULES OF ORDER OF THE CITY COUNCIL.

"*Extracts from the Minutes of the City Council.*

"The Council then received the following communication from the Mayor, to wit:

"MAYOR'S OFFICE, CITY OF NAUVOO, Illinois, *January* 22, A. D. 1842.

" Gentlemen of the City Council ;
        " Aldermen and Councillors : —

" I have carefully selected and prepared the following 'Rules of Order of the City Council of the City of Nauvoo,' and present them for your adoption, to wit : —

" *Rules of Order of the City Council of the City of Nauvoo.*

" DUTIES OF THE MAYOR.

" 1st. The Mayor, or President *pro tempore*, shall take the chair and organize the Council, within thirty minutes after the arrival of the hour to which it shall have been adjourned, and, while presiding, shall restrain all conversation irrelevant to the business then under consideration.

" 2d. The Mayor having taken the chair, and a quorum (which shall consist of a majority of the entire Council) being present, the Council shall be opened by prayer, after which the journal of the preceding meeting shall be read by the Recorder, to the end that any mistake may be corrected that shall have been made in the entries ; after which no alteration of the journal shall be permitted, without the unanimous consent of the members present.

" 3d. The Mayor shall decide all questions of order — subject, nevertheless, to an appeal to the Council, by any member.

" 4th. When the question is taken on any subject under consideration, the Mayor shall call on the members in the affirmative to say, *ay*, — those in the negative to say, *no* — and he shall declare the result. When doubts arise on the decision, he may call on the members voting to rise, or take the yeas and nays — the yeas and nays, likewise, may be taken on the call of any four members.

" 5th. The Mayor shall have a right to vote on all occasions ; and when his vote renders the division equal, the question shall be lost.

" 6th. The Mayor shall sign his name to all acts, addresses, and resolutions of the Council.

" OF THE VICE-MAYOR.

" 7th. The Council shall elect a Vice-Mayor, to serve as President *pro tempore*, who shall preside during the absence of the Mayor, and who shall be chosen by ballot — and a majority of the votes of the members present shall be necessary to a choice.

" 8th. If at any meeting when a majority shall be assembled, neither the Mayor, nor the President *pro tempore*, shall be present, the Council shall proceed to the election of a President for that meeting.

" OF THE RECORDER.

" 9th. The Recorder shall keep a journal of the proceedings of the Council, and shall enter therein whatever a majority of the members shall order ; and, in all cases, the yeas and nays, or dissent of any member, when required to do so.

" 10th. The Recorder shall read whatever is laid before the Council for the consideration of the members, and shall countersign every act, address, or resolution, passed by the Council, noting the date of its passage.

" 11th. When the yeas and nays are called upon any question, the Recorder shall read over distinctly, first, the names of the members who voted in the affirmative, and next, the names of those who voted in the negative.

" OF THE MARSHAL.

" 12th. The Marshal shall serve as Door-Keeper, and Sergeant-at-Arms, to the Council.

" ORDER OF BUSINESS.

" 13th. After the reading of the journal of the preceding meeting, the Mayor shall call for petitions, and no petition shall be received thereafter, unless by unanimous consent.

" 14th. Petitions having been called for and disposed of, reports of Standing Committees shall next be received, then reports of Select Committees, and then any miscellaneous business shall be in order.

" DECORUM.

" 15th. The Mayor shall always be at liberty to deliver his sentiments in debate, on any question before the Council; but when the Mayor speaks, it shall be from his chair.

" 16th. In cases of disorderly conduct in spectators, the Mayor may either order the persons out, committing the disorder; have the room cleared; or fine or commit the offenders to prison for contempt.

" OF ORDER AND DEBATE.

" 17th. When any member is about to speak in debate, or offer any matter to the Council, he shall rise from his seat, and address the Mayor as 'Mr. President,' and avoid personalities.

" 18th. When two members rise at the same time, the Mayor shall name the person to speak, but in all other cases, the member first rising shall speak first. No member shall speak more than three times to the same question without leave of the Council, nor speak more than twice without leave, until every person choosing to speak shall have spoken.

" 19th. Any member may call another to order, and when a member is so called to order, he shall immediately desist speaking, until the Mayor decide whether he is in order, or not; and every question of order shall be decided without debate; but any member may appeal from his decision to the Council; if the decision be in favor of the member called to order, he shall be at liberty to proceed; if otherwise, the Council shall determine upon the propriety of his proceeding with his observations.

" 20th. When a question has been taken and carried in the affirmative, or negative, it shall be in order for any member of the majority to move for the reconsideration thereof; but no motion for the reconsideration of any vote shall be in order, after the paper

4

upon which the same shall have been taken, shall have gone out of the possession of the Council.

"21st. No motion, or proposition, shall be received as an amendment which shall be a substitute for the proposition before the Council; but nothing shall be considered a substitute which shall have relation to the subject matter under consideration.

"22d. When the yeas and nays are called, every member shall vote, unless specially excused; and in voting by yeas and nays, the Counsellors shall be called first, the Aldermen next, and the Mayor last.

"23d. When a motion is made and seconded, it shall be reduced to writing, and shall be first read aloud before any order be taken thereon; but the question, 'Will the Council now consider it,' shall not be put, unless called for by a member, or is deemed necessary by the Mayor: and on motions to amend, the question of consideration shall in no case be put.

"24th. Any motion may be withdrawn or modified by the mover, at any time before a final decision or amendment.

"25th. When a question is under debate, no motion shall be received but to adjourn, to lie on the table, for the previous question, to postpone indefinitely, to postpone to a day certain, to commit, or to amend; which several motions shall have precedence in the order they stand arranged. A motion to strike out the enacting words of a bill, shall have precedence of a motion to amend, and, if carried, shall be considered a rejection.— And a motion to refer to a Standing Committee, shall have precedence of one to refer to a Select Committee. A motion to adjourn shall always be in order; that, and a motion to lie on the table, shall be taken without debate.

"26th. The previous question shall be in this form, 'Shall the main question be now put?' It shall only be admitted when demanded by a majority of the members present; until it is decided, shall preclude all amendment and further debate of the main question, and upon said question there shall be no debate.

"27th. Any member may call for the division of a question where the sense will admit of it, but a question to strike out and insert shall be indivisible.

"28th. When a question is carried in the affirmative by yeas and nays, any member may enter on the journal his reasons for dissenting.

"29th. It shall not be in order to introduce a bill, unless by way of report from committee, or leave be previously asked and obtained.

"30th. Every bill or resolution requiring the signature of the Mayor and Recorder, shall receive three several readings previous to its passage.

"31st. The first reading of a bill shall be for information, and if opposition be made to it, the question shall be, 'Shall this bill be rejected?' If no opposition be made it shall go to the second reading without a question, when it shall be open for discussion and amendment, or such order as the Council may think proper to take, except the question on the passage thereof, which can only be taken, on the day of the introduction of the bill, by the consent of two thirds of the members present.

" 32nd. Before any bill or resolution requiring the signature of the Mayor and Recorder, shall be read a third time, the question shall be put, ' Shall this bill be read a third time?' and if a majority of the members present shall not vote in the affirmative, the same shall be declared to be rejected.

" 33rd. On the third reading of a bill, the question shall be on its passage, but it may be committed at any time previous to its passage.

" 34th. When a blank is to be filled, and different sums or dates are proposed, the question shall be first taken on the highest sum or longest date, and thence downwards.

" 35th. The Council may at any time suspend any of its rules by a majority of three fourths of the members present.

" 36th. After the arrival of the hour to which the Council may stand adjourned, no member who may have appeared, shall absent himself without leave of those present, or of the Council when formed.

" Of Committees.

" 37th. All Standing and Select Committees shall be appointed by the Mayor, unless otherwise directed, and the first named member shall be the Chairman. The following Standing Committees shall be appointed, to wit :

A Committee of Ways and Means, to consist of one member from each ward, to whom shall be referred all subjects of taxation and revenue.

A Committee of Improvement, to consist of one member from each ward, to whom shall be referred all subjects relative to repairs and opening of roads and streets, and other subjects of a similar nature.

A Committee of Claims, to consist of three members, to whom shall be referred all matters of claims against the city, and applications for remission of penalties.

A Committee of Unfinished Business, to consist of two members, who shall examine the journal of the preceding Council, and report such business as may have remained unfinished.

A Committee of Elections, to consist of three members.

A Committee of Police, to consist of one member from each ward, who are empowered to call upon any officer of the Corporation, for any information, report, paper or other matter relative to the police.

A Committee of Municipal Laws, to consist of five members, to whom shall be referred all bills for ordinances presented to the Council.

A Committee of Public Grounds, to consist of one member from each ward.

A Committee of Public Works, to consist of three members.

" Of Amendment to Rules.

" 38th. All motions for amendment of the rules, shall be submitted one month previous to a final determination thereof, unless three fourths of the members present shall assent that it shall be finally acted on the day on which it is submitted.

"Of Balloting.

"39th. In balloting for committees, a plurality of votes shall be sufficient to make a choice, but in other cases a majority of the whole number of votes shall be required to decide.

" All of which is respectfully submitted.
"John C. Bennett, *Mayor.*

" The above communication was read by the Recorder to the City Council, on the 22d January, 1842, and referred to a Select Committee, consisting of Joseph Smith and Orson Pratt, — the Committee reported back the Communication and recommended its adoption, which was carried."

Times and Seasons, Vol. III., No. 7, pp. 683—686.

" In regard to the correspondence between Dr. C. V. Dyer and Gen. Bennett, referred to by Gov. Duncan, his statements are foul perversions of truth; the correspondence does not show either myself or Gen. Bennett to be abolitionists, but the friends of *equal rights and privileges to all men.*" —*Times and Seasons*, Vol. III., No. 15, p. 808.

From Sidney Rigdon, Esq., Attorney at Law, to Major-Gen. James Arlington Bennet, LL. D., of Arlington House, L. I.

"Post-Office, Nauvoo, Illinois, *April* 23, 1842.

" Sir, —

" A letter has appeared in the New York Herald, giving a description of certain individuals in this city. I take the liberty of addressing this letter to you, that I may answer my part and show my opinion. The subject of this address is General J. C. Bennett. General Bennett is five feet five inches high, one hundred and forty-two pounds' weight, and thirty-seven years of age. He is at once Major-General in the Nauvoo Legion, Quarter-Master-General of the State, Mayor of the City of Nauvoo, and Master in Chancery for the County of Hancock. He is a Physician of great celebrity, and a successful practitioner; of great versatility of talent; of refined education, and accomplished manners; discharges the duties of his respective offices with honor to himself, and credit to the people. He possesses much decision of character; honorable in his intercourse with his fellows, and a most agreeable companion; possessing much vivacity and animation of spirit, and every way qualified to be a useful citizen, in this or any other city.

" Very respectfully, your obedient servant,
"Sidney Rigdon, *Post-Master.*

" J. A. Bennet, Esq."

Official Withdrawal from the Mormon Church.

" *May* 17, 1842.

" Brother James Sloan, —

" You will be so good as to permit General Bennett to withdraw his name from the Church record, if he desires to do so, and this with the best of feelings towards you and General Bennett.
"Joseph Smith."

" In accordance with the above I have permitted General Bennett to withdraw his membership from the Church of Jesus Christ of Latter Day Saints, this 17th day of May, 1842 ; the best of feelings subsisting between all parties.   JAMES SLOAN,
" *General Church Clerk and Recorder.*

"CITY OF NAUVOO, *May* 17, 1842.
" The above is a true copy from the original.
ORSON PRATT."

After my *withdrawal* from the Church, the Prophet and his minions withdrew from me the hand of fellowship, and ANTE-DATED the MORMON BULL OF EXCOMMUNICATION, and presented it to Professor Orson Pratt, A. M., one of the twelve Mormon Apostles, for his signature, *some days after I showed him my official withdrawal,* and Mr. Pratt REFUSED *to sign it* — stating as his reason THAT HE KNEW NOTHING AGAINST ME. This BULL was signed by the Mormon Hierarchy, who *forged* the names of Lyman Wight, who was then in Tennessee; William Smith, who was in Pennsylvania; and John E. Page, who was in Pittsburgh! — These are three of the Mormon Apostles.

Prentice and Weissinger, the able editors of the Louisville Journal, in their paper of July 23, 1842, in speaking on this subject, say, —

" Here Gen. Bennett publishes a copy of a highly honorable dismission from the Mormon Church, given him by the general church clerk and recorder, at Bennett's own request, and in accordance with Joe Smith's written instructions.   Subsequently to this withdrawal and honorable dismission of Gen. B., Joe Smith, in anticipation of an attempt on the part of the General to expose his villanies, undertook to blast Bennett's character, and destroy his credibility, by publishing a pretended copy of a withdrawal of the fellowship of the Church from him, giving this withdrawal of fellowship a date prior to that of the honorable dismission, and appending to it the names of men, who, at the date of the document, were more than a thousand miles off.   This fraud and forgery, on the part of the Prophet, is rendered so perfectly palpable, that even he himself cannot pretend to deny it."

New Election of Mayor and Vice-Mayor of the City of Nauvoo, on the Resignation of General Bennett.

" On the 17th instant, General John C. Bennett resigned the office of Mayor of the City of Nauvoo, and on the 19th, General Joseph Smith, the former Vice-Mayor, was duly elected to fill the
4 *

vacancy; and on the same day, General Hyrum Smith was elected Vice-Mayor in place of General Joseph Smith, elected Mayor.

" The following vote of thanks was then unanimously voted to the Ex-Mayor, General Bennett, by the City Council, to wit: Resolved by the City Council of the City of Nauvoo, that this Council tender a vote of thanks to General John C. Bennett, for his great zeal in having good and wholesome laws adopted for the government of this city, and for the faithful discharge of his duty while Mayor of the same.

"Passed May 19, 1842.   JOSEPH SMITH, *Mayor.*
" JAMES SLOAN, *Recorder.*"
From "*The (Nauvoo) Wasp,*" *of May* 21, 1842, Vol. I., No. 6.

It will be seen by the foregoing documents, that I was in perfectly good odor with the saints and their rulers, in the Holy City, up to the time of my withdrawal from the Church, and even afterwards. So it appears, from the Prophet's own showing, that the Lord was remarkably well pleased with his servant John C. Bennett so long as he was an advocate of the Mormon creed; but when he came out on the pretended man of God, the Lord's Anointed Old White Hat Prophet, Joe contended that he always knew Bennett was a scoundrel. It appears, therefore, that either the Lord, or Joe, was mistaken. Which do you think it was, Christian reader?

I will now conclude by giving my Patriarchal Blessing, from the Holy Hyrum Smith, the Patriarch of the whole Mormon Church, and *Heir-Apparent* to the THRONE.

A Blessing pronounced on the Head of J. C. Bennett, son of J. and N. Bennett, born in the Town of Fair Haven, Bristol County, Massachusetts, August 3, A. D. 1804, *by Hyrum Smith, Patriarch of the Church of Jesus Christ of Latter Day Saints, September* 21, 1840.

" John C. Bennett — I lay my hands upon your head in the name of Jesus Christ, and inasmuch as thou art a son of Abraham, I bless you with the holy priesthood, with all its graces, and gifts, and with wisdom in all the mysteries of God. Thou shalt have knowledge given thee, and shalt understand the keys by which all mysteries shall be unlocked. Thou shalt have great power among the children of men, and shalt have influence among the great and the noble, even to prevail on many, and bring them to the knowledge of the truth. Thou shalt prevail over thy enemies; and shalt know when thou hast gained power over them, and in this thine heart shall rejoice. Many souls shall believe, because of the proclamation which thou shalt make. The Holy Spirit shall rest upon thee, insomuch, that thy voice shall make the foundation on which thou standest to shake, — so great shall be the power of God.

"His favor shall rest upon thee in dreams and visions, which shall manifest the glory of God. Beloved brother, if thou art faithful, thou shalt have power to heal the sick ; cause the lame to leap like an hart; the deaf to hear; and the dumb to speak, and their voice shall salute thine ears; thy soul shall be made glad and thy heart shall rejoice in God. Thou shalt be like unto Paul, who, according to his own words, was like ' one born out of due time,' and shalt have the visions of heaven open, even as they were to him.

"Thy name shall be known in many nations, and thy voice shall be heard among many people. Yea, unto many of the remnants of Israel shalt thou be known, and when they shall hear of thy coming they shall rejoice, and thou shalt proclaim the gospel unto many tribes of the house of Israel.

"If thou shouldst step aside from the path of rectitude at any time because of temptation, the Lord shall call after thee, because of the integrity of thine heart, and thou shalt return to the path from whence thou hast strayed, for God shall illume the path by the light of his everlasting covenant, and with its light thou shalt keep the way.

"God is with thee, and has wrought upon thy heart to come up to this place, that thou mayest be satisfied that the servants of God dwell here. God shall reward thee for thy kindness, and thou shalt be fully satisfied hereafter. Thy soul shall be enlarged, thy mind shall be clear, and thy judgment informed, and the knowledge of all these things shall be made clear to thy understanding. Thou wilt have to pass through tribulation, but thou shalt remember the promises of the Lord, and shalt be comforted, and shalt have the greater manifestations of the power of God.

"Thou must travel and labor for Zion, for this is the mind and will of God. Let thy voice be heard, and thy prayers and supplications and thy rejoicings be known. Turn not aside from the truth for the popularity of the world; but be like Paul. Let God be thy shield and buckler, and *he shall shield thee forever.* Angels shall guide thee, and shall lift thee out of many dangers, and difficulties ; and after thou art delivered, thou shalt know they have done it, and thy heart shall be comforted.

"Thou shalt have power over many of thy friends, and relations, and shalt prevail with them, and when thou shalt reason with them, it shall be like Paul reasoning with Felix, and they shall tremble when they hear thy words. Thou shalt be blessed with the blessings of Abraham, Isaac, and Jacob, and if thou art faithful, thou shalt yet be a Patriarch, and the blessings thou shalt pronounce shall be sealed in heaven. Thou shalt have an inheritance among the Saints in time and in eternity, for this is the will of God. If thou continue faithful and steadfast in the Everlasting Covenant, thou shalt have power over the winds and the waves, and they shall obey thy voice when thou shalt speak in the name of Jesus Christ.

"The power of God shall shield thee while thou art laboring for

Zion. Thou shalt outride the storm of adversity with patience, and shalt be crowned with immortality in the Celestial Kingdom, when Christ shall descend. Even so, Amen.
" R. B. THOMPSON, Scribe."

CORRESPONDENCE.

" LA HARPE, Hancock County, Illinois, }
" June 18, 1842.   }

" To MAJOR-GENERAL J. C. BENNETT :

" Sir, —

" By your solicitation, I raised the 3d Company of Cavalry of the 2d Regiment and 1st Cohort, of the Nauvoo Legion, and accepted the office of Captain. It is now rumored, that you are about to resign the command of the Legion, which induces me to tender to you my resignation.
" Yours, respectfully,
" JOHN F. OLNEY,
" Capt. 3d C. 2d R. 1st C. N. L.

" Accepted, June 20, A. D. 1842.
" JOHN C. BENNETT, Major-General.'

" NAUVOO, June 20, A. D. 1842.

" MAJOR-GENERAL BENNETT :

" Dear Sir, —

" I would respectfully tender you my resignation of the offices of Brevet Major-General, and Cornet of the Nauvoo Legion, which offices I was pleased to accept at your instance, and <i>yours only</i>, believing then, as I now do, that you were the only man in our city, capable and qualified to hold the office of Major-General in, or to command, said Legion. Be assured, sir, that nothing more or less would tempt me to resign, than the fact of your intention of doing the same.
" Very respectfully, yours, &c.
" GEO. W. ROBINSON,
" Brevet Maj. Gen. and Cor. N. L.

" Accepted, July 1, A. D. 1842.
" JOHN C. BENNETT, Major-General."

" NAUVOO, July 3, A. D. 1842.

" GENERAL BENNETT :

" Sir, —

" The Sangamo Journal came in to-day. I expected something from you, but was disappointed; but presumed you knew nothing of the new arrangement of the mails. I just saw Col. C. L. Higbee, and saw the affidavit of Mrs. Schindle. <i>Good!</i> The letter to N——, [Nancy,— Miss Nancy Rigdon,] C. L. H. [Col. Chauncy L. Higbee,] will get. F. M. H. [Col. Francis M. Higbee] has it, and I told him to get it. I will leave this for the present, and await the return of our folks from meeting, before I seal it, unless the mail should come before they return.

"2 o'clock. Our folks have returned from meeting, and the way Joe took back what he said about us, was a caution. He said he had agreed to take back what was said, but, on thinking it over, he could not do it, for any man that would suffer *Bennett* to come into their houses, was just as bad as he; and he would, however, say this much, that one continued course of rascality in Mr. Rigdon and myself, for some time back, was the cause of his coming out on us, and if that would be any satisfactory confession, we could have that much, and do what we pleased. He said, that whenever he exposed iniquity, the persons chastised would turn round and endeavor to injure him. 'Now,' says he, '*look out!* LOOK OUT!!! These men, I will venture to say, will come out on me, with all their power, and say and do all they can to put me down ; but do not believe one word of their CURSED LIES, FOR I KNOW I AM A PROPHET!!!' Joe soaped over Messrs. Ivins, Hunter, and Pierce, and I think some have already *consecrated*, and quite likely the balance will. Joe did not say much about Higbee. He stated that a young man came down to see him the other day, and wanted to know why he came out on him; but, says he, 'I have settled all matters with him, and shall not mention his name, for he confessed his sins to me, and begged I would not mention him.' *Francis will roar.* Yours, respectfully,

"GEO. W. ROBINSON."

_____

"NAUVOO, *July* 4, A. D. 1842.

"GENERAL JOHN C. BENNETT:
"Dear Sir,—
"I received your favor by Mr. Hamilton, to-day, and have done all in my power to accomplish your business, according to your request. * * * * * * * * * I have talked with Mrs. G**, and labored hard to show her the necessity of coming out to befriend the innocent, and defend her own character from Joe's foul aspersions; but she says that she will not give her affidavit now, but thinks that she will in the course of two or three days. She wants to have a talk with O. Pratt before she gives it. I have seen Pratt, and he says, if she comes to talk with him, he will tell her, that if she knows any thing, to tell it, let it hit where it will. There were a great many out to meeting yesterday. Smith preached—said considerable against you, and stated that Messrs. Robinson and Rigdon had requested him to recall what he had said against them; but instead of doing it, according to promise, he vilified them worse than ever, if it were possible to do it—no other names mentioned ; but he insinuated very hard on Francis in the forenoon, and on myself in the afternoon, by saying that those who had resigned, were no better than yourself, after placing you at the lowest grade he possibly could, in his awkward way of doing it. I have seen Nancy, [Nancy Rigdon,]—she told me to say to you, '*go ahead*, and make of her name as much as you please, in relating the circumstance which happened between Smith and herself.' Mr. Pratt and his wife say, that if ever Smith renews the attack on them, they will come out against him. and stand it no longer.
"Yours, with respect,
"C. L. HIGBEE."

"Nauvoo, *July* 6, 1842.

" General John C. Bennett :

" Dear Sir, —

" Joseph Smith is yet thrashing about, tearing up the D****, and slandering every body. He has not lit on Rigdon and Robinson very severely as yet, but touched them slightly on Sunday, also myself; and we must keep things right side up. Mrs. Schindle's affidavit is a good one, and Mrs. G**, I have understood, was going to give hers. Mrs. Pratt, I think, will also give hers — also, Miss Nancy Rigdon. Joe is operating with Mrs. White, and it is reported, that he is to settle upon her a fine sum soon, or return the money he and Sherman took from Bill White some time ago. You ought to see Mrs. White, and labor with her, as soon as possible, and secure her testimony, *because it would be great.* As it respects my affidavit, sir, for God's sake, my sake, and the sake of my people, do not show it to any one on earth, *as yet*, never, until I give you liberty. Stiles has seen it, and you must swear him that he will keep dark as h***. I am yet true as death, and intend to stick or die, but you must keep my name back, because I am not ready as yet to leave ; *and as soon as you bring my name out, they are certain to take my life* — they go it like h***, yet. I am likely to sell my property here, and as soon as I do, I will emigrate like lightning. Scorch them with the Missouri writ — that is what scares them like the d****, Porter not excepted.

" Your dear friend,
FRANCIS M. HIGBEE.

" P. S. I think I will be out to Carthage to see you soon : come in as soon as you can, but do not stay here long, or over night. Pratt is true — Rigdon is good.   F. M. H."

"Nauvoo, *July* 5, 1842.

" Doctor Bennett :

" Dear Friend, —

" Orissa's health is yet in a very critical situation, and we are very anxious to have your professional advice, *for we do not know what to do without it.* I will give you as accurate a description of the case as possible. * * * * * * * * * *. We wish you to write your prescription in full, and send it to Sarah's, [Prof. Orson Pratt's, — Sarah M. Pratt being the sister of Mrs. Orissa A. Allred,] where we shall remain until Orissa recovers. *We. all, with one accord, send you our best respects.* Mr. Pratt would write, but he is *afraid to.* He wishes to be *perfectly still*, until your second letter comes out — then you may hear.

" Yours, respectfully,
" WILLIAM M. ALLRED."

" *From W. F. Parrish, Esq., Attorney at Law.*

" Massillon, *July* 31, 1842.

" Dear Sir, —

" Prof. Wm. M. Smith, M. D., informed me, that you passed through this place on Friday last, on your way to New York, to make an exposition of that infamous scoundrel, *Joe Smith*, and others connected with him, in their piracy upon the human family. I am exceedingly sorry, sir, that I could not have had an interview with you upon this subject, for, be assured, I consider any means which can be adopted to bring such a ruthless ruffian to justice, as most laudable, and not only worthy the attention, but imperatively demanded at the hands of him who may be in possession of facts that will enable him to accomplish that object. I am, however, aware, that the man who attempts it, puts his life in competition with a secret influence of the most dangerous, dark, and damning kind, that may be brought to bear upon him, at times and places, and under circumstances least anticipated, — an influence that can be known only by those who have had the means of knowing that we have, and which it is hard to make others believe exists in an enlightened community.

"I have known you by reputation for some time, but have not the pleasure of your acquaintance personally; have said but little upon the subject of your connection with the *Prophet*, but have thought much, and am not disappointed in the issue.

"You, no doubt, have learned, in your close connection with Joe, the position I occupied in his cabinet; and let me inquire what his present feelings are toward me? My life was sought for a time; how is it now? I was once a peculiar favorite of the Prophet and rulers in Israel, called to be his scribe by revelation, wrote his early history, kept his daily journal, superintended his mercantile, land, and banking speculations, under his directions.

"I joined the Church in 1833, and withdrew in 1837, at the head of some forty others, and shortly after was excommunicated by a *Bull* from his *Holiness*; and not long after that, I made Kirtland, the stake of Zion, so exceedingly unpleasant to him, that he got a revelation to leave between two days, and has not been there since.

"I lectured against them in the Temple, twice a week, during the season; once his *lickskillets* attempted to expel me by force from the *sanctum sanctorum*, but did not succeed. At about that time, their printing-office fell into our hands, which, if they had not consumed by fire, would soon have been speaking the truth as an atonement for an ill-spent life. Before I left them, those that were disaffected, met frequently, and consulted upon the matter, and many of the first in official stations of the Church, were convinced of the abominations of our leader, as well as myself, and so expressed themselves in our private councils, to wit, Bishop Whitney, Orson Hyde, Parley P. Pratt, Orson Pratt, Doctor Williams, Cahoon, and others, but had not the moral courage to come out publicly. By the by, have Orson Pratt and Rigdon left them, as you intimated in your communications? Please write me who among the leaders have left, and what the prospects are for breaking them up. Can it be done? Be assured, sir, I would most cheerfully assist you in this laudable undertaking, were I situated so that I could. But I do not see how I can possibly, at this time, come to New York.

"My professional business, I suppose, I might leave, as I have a partner in Canton; but I am concerned in a mercantile establishment in this place also, and my partner is absent, and will be for a month at least.

"At the time I left the Church, I wrote, by way of exposition, several newspaper articles; and the expectations of the public were highly raised, in anticipation that I intended to publish a book, although I did not so pledge myself, but intended to publish a weekly periodical of that character, and should have done so, had not our printing-office been burnt.

"I am, no doubt, in possession of some facts that you are not; and were I so situated that I could, I would join you in New York, and assist in your publication.

"Your obedient servant,
"W. F. PARRISH.

"GENERAL J. C. BENNETT, New York."

From Erastus Webb, M. D., of Circleville, Ohio.

"CIRCLEVILLE, June 23, 1842.

"DR. BENNETT:

"Dear Sir,—

"Your letter of the 7th ult. was duly received. I have conversed with the Master and Secretary of Pickaway Lodge. The Secretary is at this moment making out a certificate under the seal of this Lodge, in answer to a letter received some time ago, from your Deputy-Grand-Master, making inquiries respecting your standing in this Lodge. The result will be FAVORABLE, it appearing on record that you were a member of this Lodge about fourteen years ago, and left it in *peace and friendship*. This will, of course, satisfy your calumniators.

"Dear sir,

"I remain, very respectfully,

"Your friend,
"E. WEBB."

From S. Francis, Esq., Editor of the Sangamo Journal.

"SPRINGFIELD, Illinois, July 6, 1842.

"MAJOR-GENERAL BENNETT:

"Dear Sir,—

"Yours of the 2d came safe to hand last night. Your first number appears in our paper sent to you by the mail which brings you this. These publications must produce intense excitement, and, notwithstanding every effort will be made to discredit them by Smith and his friends, the *people will believe them.* You certainly have undertaken an arduous duty; but, judging from your success so far, the friends of morality, of truth, of true religion, have strong confidence that you will succeed in tearing away the veil that has hitherto concealed the 'polluted' Monster, who styles himself the Prophet of God.

"Go on with the good work. You will have the best wishes of the good. Obtain all the *documentary evidence* possible. *Affidavits* from Miss Rigdon, and other ladies mentioned, would produce mighty results. We hope to hear from you, in reference to the

Boggs affair, more fully, before next paper. Should you succeed in strangling the Monster with whom you are now grappled, you will have high claims to rank with those who have achieved the highest good for their species.

" Respectfully yours,

" S. FRANCIS."

"SPRINGFIELD, *July* 10, 1842

" Dear Sir, —

* * * * * * * * * * *

" We will give all your letters designed for publication. Joe flounders, but *your statements are believed by all* — rest assured of this fact.

" I wrote you four or five days since. Furnish all the documentary evidence possible, all the affidavits possible, and send us your *disclosures* at St. Louis. Every body is now looking to the Journal for your publications. We should be glad to have from your own pen an account of the *Danites*, their obligations to each other, and the design of their society. Joe must come down. Governor Reynolds will be obliged to demand him, and innocent individuals must not be implicated with him. This last matter is important. A hair of the heads of those who were employed by him should not be injured, provided they will sustain you and tell the truth.

" I have been writing to my friend Mr. Chambers, the editor of the St. Louis Republican, this evening, and I introduced your name, the object of your visit to St. Louis, and solicited for you his kindness, and all the assistance and counsel you may wish. Please call upon him, and mention your name — if not in his office, leave your address.

" Let me hear from you promptly, and I am respectfully, &c.

" S. FRANCIS.

" GENERAL J. C. BENNETT.'

OPINIONS OF THE NEWSPAPER PRESS.

From the Sangamo Journal of July 8, 1842 — *a leading western paper, published at Springfield, the seat of government of the State of Illinois, by S. Francis, Esq., Editor.*

" The public will be astounded at the statements made by General Bennett in the article which follows from under his own hand. — That in this day of light and intelligence such a man as Joe Smith should be able to collect around him a mass of people, and make them believe in his shallow and miserable scheme of imposture, is matter of astonishment now, and will be more so in after times.

" General Bennett is the individual appointed by Judge Douglass Master in Chancery for Hancock County — a most important and responsible office, from the fact that the Master in Chancery, in

5

many cases, performs the duty of a Judge of the Supreme Court.
We have, therefore, the official endorsement of Judge Douglass,
(which, however, is not needed,) in support of the character of
General Bennett for truth, and all those qualities required of one
who fills an office of high responsibility.

"We state these facts, that the public may duly appreciate the
attacks of those men upon General Bennett, who are acting with
Joe Smith, to decry and to destroy him."

————

*From the Louisville Journal of July 23, 1842 — a periodical second
to none in America, edited by George D. Prentice, Esq. and
—— Weisinger.*

" General John C. Bennett was lately, next to Joe Smith, the
most distinguished member of the Mormon Church. He was commander of the Mormon Legion; and he was, and still is, Master in
Chancery for Hancock. County — a county peopled principally by
the Mormons. Some time ago a quarrel broke out between him
and Joe Smith, which resulted in his abandoning the Mormon
Church, and laying before the world an exposition of Smith's character and conduct. This exposition, as far as we have read it, is
one of the most startling things of the kind we ever saw. Moreover, it is deeply interesting to the public. Joe Smith is generally
regarded as a mere miserable fanatic; but, although he may be a
fanatic, he is something more; he is the Prophet and the Commander-in-Chief of thirty thousand Mormons, all of whom regard
him as a leader sent from Heaven, and look upon his commands as
emanating from the Most High. Backed by his multitudinous and
deluded host, he already attempts to control the politics of Illinois,
and defies both the civil and military authorities of that State to call
him to account for any thing that he has done or may do."

————

From the Sangamo Journal of July 15, 1842.

" The publications made by General Bennett are *believed* by
all men."

————

*From the Warsaw Signal of July 9, 1842 — a paper printed in
Hancock County, (the place of Smith's residence,) and edited by
Thomas C. Sharp, Esq., Attorney at Law.*

" We understand that General Bennett has commenced writing
for the Sangamo Journal a series of communications, going to show
the rascality of Joe Smith and his clan, and the dangerous designs
which he is capable of forming and executing. The General asks
not to be believed on his own assertions, but proves matters as he
goes; he is a man of great energy and perseverance, and we should
not be surprised if he made the Mormons feel like stuck hogs for a
few months to come."

From the Cleveland Herald of July 19, 1842 — a paper edited by J. A. Harris, Esq.

" By the Sangamo Journal we have a portion of the promised disclosures touching the infamous conduct of the Prophet Joseph Smith, promised by General Bennett, but recently a Mormon high in office and enjoying Smith's unbounded confidence. The disclosures show corruption such as had rarely been developed before the days of the Latter Day Saints; and if the half Bennett states be true, Joe richly deserves the penitentiary instead of reverence and obedience from his deluded followers. Bennett gives names freely, and calls upon many witnesses to sustain the truth of his statements."

From the Chicago American of July 28, 1842 — a paper edited by William W. Brackett, Esq.

" FROM NAUVOO.

" Two gentlemen, who passed through holy Joe's city on Thursday of last week, state, that soon after their arrival Joe made a speech in front of the Temple. The subject of his speech was — Bennett — the Sangamo Journal — Mrs. Pratt — and other matters. Joe swore like a pirate, and used the most obscene language. He appeared to be much excited, and it would be an act of charity to suppose that the holy debauchee was drunk as well as mad.

" Joe, it is said, anticipates a requisition for his person from the Governor of Missouri. He has the utmost horror of the idea of being given up. Joe thinks that Judge Ford will not give him up if he should be elected Governor.

" Joe, it is further said, is laboring to make up the breach with Rigdon, Pratt, and others, by offers of special favor. We trust that in this effort he will not succeed. Joe cannot now harm these men. He will not injure them. He dare not fulfil his threats, and his promises are not to be relied on. — We again call upon Messrs. Rigdon and Pratt, as they regard virtue, honor, and the reputation of their families, to come out from this Nauvoo ' *Babylon, and Mother of Harlots*,' the home of ' the whoremonger and the adulterer,' and ' be not a partaker of her plagues.' The developments which have been made, must sink Joe Smith to the lowest depths of infamy in the eyes of all honest men. He must fall so certain as God punishes vice and rewards virtue.

" Miss Martha H. Brotherton has done herself honor, and the cause of virtue is greatly indebted to her for the publication she has made. We trust her example will be followed by Mrs. Pratt and Miss Rigdon. The holy cause of insulted virtue — of wronged innocence — of the honor and character of families — demand that THE IMPOSTOR BE UNVEILED AND EXHIBITED TO THE WORLD IN ALL HIS DEFORMITY. — *Sangamo Journal*."

From the Chicago American of August 1, 1842.

" ORSON PRATT. — We learn from the Warsaw Signal that this gentleman has gone from Nauvoo. He left a communication with his friends which stated that he had been induced to take this course on account of the treatment of his wife by Smith, and of the general management of the Church by him.

" We further learn from other sources that Smith, finding his attempts on Mrs. Pratt were matters of notoriety, went to her husband with a manufactured story that his wife was a base woman, and that the fact was well known to him. This communication had such an effect upon Mr. Pratt — at once blasting his happiness and the reputation of a virtuous woman — that the wretched husband left the city.

" It will be recollected that Mrs. Schindle, in her affidavit detailing the attempt of Smith upon her, said — ' He told her she must never tell his propositions to her, for he had *all* the influence in that place, and if she told *he would ruin her character, and she would be under the necessity of leaving.*'

" This same scheme has been carried out in reference to Mrs. Pratt. She ' told' on the Impostor, and was marked by him for destruction. In a public speech in Nauvoo on the 14th, Joe spoke of this lady — a woman whose reputation had been as fair as virtue could make it until she came in contact with him — in a manner only befitting the lowest and most degraded vagabond in existence.

" The reader can hence learn the state of society at Nauvoo. The facts furnished are presented by the holy Joe himself.

" We do not know what course will be pursued by Mr. Pratt. If he sinks under the denunciations and schemes of Joe Smith — if he fails to defend the reputation of himself and of the woman he has vowed before high Heaven to protect — he will fix a stain upon his character which he can never wash out, and carry to the grave the pangs caused by ' the gnawings of the worm that never dies.'

" We trust that he will secure for himself a more honorable position in life, and will come to the rescue of the fame of his lady, and expose the infamous course of the Prophet, as becomes a *man*, an honorable *citizen*, and a *sincere Christian. — Sangamo Journal.*"

" ☞ Joe Smith, in a speech in Nauvoo on Thursday the 14th inst., (and which was heard by two gentlemen of our city,) said — ' *He wished Bennett was in Hell!* — he had given him more trouble than any man he ever had to do with.' Joe was undoubtedly sincere in this expression of his wishes.

" In the same speech he declared that Mrs. Pratt, the wife of Mr. O. Pratt, ' had been a ——— from her mother's breast.' This was the lady whom Bennett says Joe attempted to seduce, and who resisted all his efforts with the heroism of insulted virtue.'

" In what a horrid and depraved condition society must be in Nauvoo! — *Sangamo Journal.*"

Mr. Pratt returned to Nauvoo the day after he left, and

has since been nobly bearding the lion in his den. His
voice is lifted like ten thousand thunders against the iniquities of the Mormon Prophet and his minions. Pratt
is an honest man.

---

*From the Cincinnati Republican of July 26, 1842 — a paper edited
by C. C. Waller, Esq.*

" ☞ General BENNETT, the distinguished seceder from the Mormon faith, was in town on Sunday, and stopped at the Broadway
Hotel. He has made so many startling disclosures of the iniquities
practised by Joe Smith on the noodles congregated at Nauvoo that
his life is considered in danger of the assassin's steel. He left
yesterday morning on the Robert T. Lytle, for the east."

---

*From the Circleville Herald of July 29, 1842 — a paper edited by
T. J. Davis, Esq.*

" But, from his intimate and confidential relationship, J. C.
Bennett, a Mormon leader, had so far become acquainted with the
atrocious criminality of Smith's practices, and was known to stand
so high in Smith's confidence, that the latter, in order to compel
him to observe secrecy himself, and at the same time hush up the
whisperings and murmurings of some of his deluded followers, who
could not surrender all sense of virtue and propriety to his wicked
and impious requisitions under the plea of revelations from heaven,
compelled Bennett to make an affidavit, and make it public in the
congregation, to the effect that Smith was not guilty of what had
been charged against him in his intercourse with members of the
society. Bennett subsequently withdrew from the *Church.* And
now, disregarding the oath he had been compelled to take or die,
as neither legally nor morally binding upon him, he has published
a detailed exposure of Mormonism as now constituted."

---

*From the Cincinnati Gazette of July 27, 1842 — a paper edited by
the Hon. Judge John C. Wright and J. C. Vaughan, Esq.*

" MORMONISM.

" The facts developed with regard to the conduct of Joe Smith,
the leader and first of the sect, are startling in the extreme.
" The details are too disgusting almost for publication. They
show Smith to be a monster who is using the power he possesses to
gratify a brutal lust. The proof on this point is conclusive. Leading western papers speak of the fair character of the witnesses,
and regard their testimony as conclusive. To give some idea of
the conduct of Joe Smith, and of the manner in which he attempts
to carry his points, we give the testimony of Mrs. Pratt."

5 *

From the Louisville Journal of July 25, 1842.

" ☞ We copy below, from the Sangamo Journal, the second letter of General Bennett, portraying the character and detailing the horrible and revolting conduct of Joe Smith, the Prophet and leader of the Mormons. The exposition, as our readers will see, does not rest at all upon the personal veracity of General Bennett himself, but is sustained by the affidavits of men and women who cannot be mistaken as to the facts stated, and who have no motive for misrepresenting them. Those facts are proved by testimony strong enough to send any man on earth, prophet or no prophet, to the penitentiary or the gallows."

From the Buffalo Patriot and Journal of July 18, 1842.

" THE MORMONS.—We have copied into another column the Mormon disclosures of General BENNETT. The Sangamo Journal, in a postscript, says, —

" ' We have another communication from General Bennett. Its disclosures are horrible. We shall publish it in an extra as soon as possible.'

" Gen. B. evidently writes under high excitement, but there is much in his communication that deserves attention. He shows up, as we believe, in its true colors, one of the most stupendous schemes of villany and religious fraud and imposture that the world ever saw. ' Errors of opinion,' said JEFFERSON, ' may be safely tolerated, so long as reason is left free to combat them.' The remark is true in its general sense, but the Mormons form an exception. Their errors of opinion may be tolerated, but to their religious errors they have superadded a military and political organization dangerous in the extreme, when wielded as it is by one so unscrupulous as *Joe Smith*."

From the New York Herald of August 12, 1842 — a rich and racy paper, edited by General James Gordon Bennett, LL. D.

" ARRIVAL EXTRAORDINARY. — The celebrated General John Cooke Bennett arrived in this city yesterday. He is preparing to publish a book, which is to be a full and complete history of the Mormons, public and private — the secrets of their religion — their mode of life at Nauvoo — the celebrated Prophet Joe Smith's secret system of wives — their mode of warfare — tactics — civil and religious government — with various other curious and perfectly original matters. It will be one of the richest *brochures* that ever emanated from the press of any country."

From the Wabash Express — a paper published at Terre Haute.

" MORMON TROUBLES — EXPOSE.

" We publish a very singular document from Gen. JOHN C. BENNETT, a distinguished Mormon, dated at Nauvoo, June 27. It appears that himself and the Prophet, JOE SMITH, have had a regular separation. If half what Gen. BENNETT states be true, the new teacher is a most hardened sinner, deserving a place in the Alton penitentiary, instead of a high rank in the community of Latter Day Saints.

"The writer speaks with great freedom, and in a spirit of daring bravery. BENNETT has held a high rank in the Nauvoo Legion — a body of troops well disciplined; and he is spoken of, in some of the eastern papers, as a man of eminent military talents."

From the New York Sun of August 5, 1842 — a paper of very extensive circulation and great usefulness.

"THE MORMON REVELATIONS. — We watch the further move ments of the Mormon expounded, and the Anti-Mormon expounder, with some degree of anxiety, as affording a thorough explanation to the philosophy of fanaticism, whose victims we so frequently find recorded in the history of civilization. This pretty family quarrel between the Mormon chiefs, whether it originated in motives of purity or in pitiable incentives to gain, will carry its salutary effects throughout the controversy. We doubt not that Joe Smith is a shrewd and cunning man, but John C. Bennett is more than a match for him even in these qualities of modern science. There was an almost inconceivable moral courage in a man of our age, who, uneducated in political sciences, could call together a mighty host of uncivilized human beings, and finally adopt the holy privileges of the ancient prophetic race.

"The rule of our male Cassandra, our modern Jacob — a combined prophet and patriarch — could not last forever. He has degenerated from the religious moralist and priest into the lowest grade of chicanery and vice; he stands before us a swindler of his community, an impious dictator over free will, and now in his most glaring, and even hideous, aspect — a libertine, unequalled in civilized life — a Giovanni of some dozens of mistresses, and these acquired under the garb of prophetic zeal. However unworthy may be the instrument of this exposition, he is deserving of thanks, and may be absolved from some taints of immorality by becoming an evidence for the moral commonwealth. The state of these revelations, although not contained in the ' Book of Mormon,' or viewed by the divine inspiration of Joe's stone spectacles, will soon assume the settled principles of truth, and must bear conviction to the misled and ill-treated sect.

"Bennett now has blasted the spiritual and temporal Joseph Smith with a charge of horrid crimes; and Joe, in return for these favors, will attempt to blast the temporal and mortal John C. Bennett with a charge of still more horrid gunpowder. Both explosions will make a noise in the world: the moral one from the mouth of fame, the igneous one from the mouth of a pistol. At all events, both combatants appear booked on the calendar of fate — one for punishment in the next world, the other for a still less agreeable infliction in this small sphere. Up to this time, however, the only murder committed, is that of the ' King's English.'

" We firmly trust that the punishment of Smith will be heavy in the extreme : his fate should be a warning to those itinerant mongers of religion, who, in every guise and form, infest the community ; who steal away the dearest gifts of God, and render desolate firesides by their obscenity and lust. We have now an exponent of the modern philosophy of religious fanaticism ; the rise of Mahomet is no longer a problem ; his effigy of the nineteenth century has been destroyed. We have long expected this discovery, and now it comes ; the wires are withdrawn from the animated puppet, and the excited Fantoceini twist and turn, without harmony or concord. The ruler and the sceptre have passed away ; hypocrisy and error can no longer bear the powerful test of sincerity, truth, and morality.

" ' Error,' observed a scholiast, ' begets a legion of followers,' and the Mormon fanaticism has fulfilled this prediction. It has conquered the Nauvoo Legion, but soon it will exist in name alone ; its numbers are fast diminishing. Combination of societies, founded on religious and social basis, will be henceforth regarded with distrust, as weapons of misrule — instruments placed in the hands of designing oligarchs. Charity, benevolence, sympathy, and pure religion, require no associations to forward their plans ; they are the ingredients of every well-formed, cultivated mind."

From the St. Louis Bulletin of July 14, 1842 — *a useful paper, edited by Vespasian Ellis, Esq. and Wm. T. Yeomans, Esq.*

" MORMONISM. — The disclosures being made by Gen. Bennett in relation to this sect, are far from being void of interest. We publish to-day some matters from Bennett in relation to the attempted assassination of Gov. Boggs, which are at least of sufficient importance to be inquired into. One of their own papers, the Nauvoo Wasp, while defending Smith from any participation in the matter, gloried in the act, for it says, ' *It remains to be known who did the noble deed.*' Apart from the act of which he is accessory, there are now pending against him in this State indictments for crimes sufficient not only to predicate a demand upon, but to induce the Governor of Illinois to give him up."

From the New York Tattler of September 5, 1842 — *an interesting and influential periodical issued by Dillon and Hooper.*

" The exposures which General J. C. Bennett is making of the Mormon humbug in the west, are unique, rich, astonishing, and comical beyond precedent. It seems that there is a systematic course of carnal delight, for the especial behalf of Joe Smith and his favored few.

" We think the effect of making these scandalous things public will be to deter people from giving any credence to the Mormon fanatics."

From the New York Tribune of September 1, 1842 — a very popular and influential paper edited by Horace Greeley, Esq. and —— McElrath.

"FROM NAUVOO. — We were yesterday favored with the perusal of several private letters from this metropolis of the modern False Prophet. All is in confusion there. Joe Smith and O. P. Rockwell were in hiding at the last accounts — of course, within or about the city — to avoid obeying the process from Missouri. It was given out that Joe would appear and stand a trial before the Nauvoo Court! but would not be carried off to Missouri. Every effort was being made to counteract the revelations of Gen. J. C. Bennett, and to induce those to whom he appeals in his published statements to come out against them. Thus far the success has been trifling. Several are preparing to leave Nauvoo and Mormonism; some of them will come out with statements sustaining Bennett. Among the females there is a very natural reluctance to publishing statements at all. We suspect the Prophet's 'spiritual' race is nearly run."

From the foregoing documents and extracts, the public can judge of the character and standing of the author of this work, and of the opinion entertained of his disclosures by many of the principal leading journals of the country.

JOE SMITH — HIS CLAIMS AND CHARACTER.

Under this head, I shall make free extracts from " Mormonism Portrayed," by Rev. William Harris; and " Mormonism Unveiled," by E. D. Howe, Esq.; and wind up with some original affidavits, or statements.

From " Mormonism Portrayed," by Rev. William Harris.

"The great noise which Smith has made, and the influence which he now sways in the world, is a striking illustration of what a man may attain through impudence. The scheme of Mormonism is too deep ever to admit the supposition that he is the dupe of his own imposture. His claims are such that they must be admitted as true, or he must be branded as a consummate knave — for his works plainly show that he is neither a fool, nor a fanatic, but a deliberate designer, who intends the whole scheme which he has set in operation, for the gratification of his own vanity and selfishness.   In order to show this, I design to set forth, first, the claims which Smith makes for himself, and secondly, his real character.

"On page 177 of the Book of Covenants, you have the titles of Smith, in the following language : — ' Behold there shall be a record kept amongst you, and in it thou (Smith) shalt be called a seer, a translator, a prophet, an Apostle of Jesus Christ, and an elder of the Church.'   And on page 88, ' a revelator, like unto Moses, having all the gifts of God, which he bestows upon the *head of the Church.*'

"On page 126, Book of Covenants, it appears that he is the only one to receive revelations for the Church.   ' And this ye shall know assuredly, that there is none other appointed unto you to receive commandments and revelations, until he is taken, if he abide in me.'

"On page 177, Book of Covenants, you have his power over the Church.   ' Wherefore, (meaning the Church,) thou shalt give heed unto all his words and commandments, which he shall give unto you, AND HIS WORDS YE SHALL RECEIVE AS IF FROM MY OWN MOUTH. Mark this revelation, for it is important in a *political* point of view. By this we are told that the Church is to obey all the words and commands of Smith, as though they were from the MOUTH OF THE LORD, both in things *spiritual* and *temporal.*   Now, I ask the community, while men are duped, as we know that they are, is not Mormonism inimical to the institutions of our country ?   Cannot Smith, at any time, set himself up as superior to the civil law ?   Can he not commit any act of depredation, and screen himself from punishment ?   Can he, ah ! does he, not control the votes of his followers ?   Let the ballot-box, at every election where they have voted, answer, and it will be found that they have voted, almost to a man, with Smith.   Is not this contrary to the spirit of our free institutions ?   Is it not an imposition on the rights of the other citizens, who enter into the civil compact only on the condition that all shall think and act for themselves ?   Carry out the principle.   Suppose that the Mormons should become a majority of the citizens of the State of Illinois, where they are now concentrating their numbers ; would it be right that such a majority, controlled by *one man,* should rule ?   Would not such a state of things be a total subversion of Republicanism, and the establishment, in effect, of a despotism ?   If so, the principle is the same while they are in the minority.   But I digress.

"On page 112, Book of Covenants, he claims exemption from temporal labor.   ' And in temporal labor thou shalt not have strength, for this is not thy calling ; attend to thy calling, and thou shalt have wherewith to magnify thy office.   And again I say unto you, that if ye desire the mysteries of the kingdom, provide for him food and raiment, and whatsoever thing he needeth, to accomplish the work.' Now, every one who has any knowledge of Smith, knows that the averment in this revelation is not true ; for he is a large, portly man, remarkable for physical strength.   It was, then, evidently designed merely to excuse his laziness, and enable him to suck a livelihood from his followers.

[His age is 37 years — his height, 6 feet — and his weight, 212 pounds.]

"On page 180, Book of Covenants, Smith claims to have been

ordained by John the Baptist, in the presence of our ancient fathers, Joseph, Jacob, Isaac, Abraham and Adam, to the Aaronic priesthood; and also, on the same page, is an account of his ordination to the Melchisedec priesthood, by Peter, James, and John.   Now, what better evidence can be adduced, of the total ignorance of this man, respecting the nature of the priesthood, than is here afforded? What is the office and calling of a priest? St. Paul says, it is to 'offer gifts and sacrifices for sins.'   A priesthood cannot, therefore, exist in the Christian church — Christ having been offered as a complete sacrifice for all.   And St. Paul, in Heb. vii. 18, speaking of the priesthood, says, 'For there is verily a disannulling of the commandments going before, for the *weakness* and *unprofitableness* thereof;' and in the 17th verse, he says, 'For he, (the Father,) testifieth, thou, (Christ,) art a priest forever, after the order of Melchisedec.'   Now here, as by the whole tenor of the apostle's argument, it appears that the Aaronic and Levitical priesthoods were done away, and Christ created sole priest, *forever,* after the order of Melchisedec.   He, then, is the only priest known to the Christian religion.   But this Latter Day Prophet has risen up to tell the world that God has annulled his former decrees, and revived the old priesthood which was abolished for its weakness and unprofitableness; and that Christ is stripped of the office which was given him *forever,* and he, Smith, made successor to him — claiming, thereby, to be equal in official dignity to the Mediator; and that too, when Christ, according to the apostles, was made a priest after the order of Melchisedec, because the priesthood would be in him unchangeable.   Was there ever more abominable blasphemy?

"By reference to page 181, Book of Covenants, it will appear that Smith is at the head of the Mormon Church. 'And thou shalt not command him who is at the *head of the Church.*'   And, in the Book of Mormon, page 66: 'And he shall be great, like unto Moses.'

"Search the annals of infallible Rome!   Read the history of her most aspiring pretenders, and where was there ever assumed higher titles, greater authority, or more immaculate holiness, than is now assumed by this image of the beast, arisen in these latter days!

"In reviewing these claims of Smith, what a striking contrast is presented between him and the apostles!   They acknowledged no head but Christ; they sought no titles but those of apostles, servants, or ministers of the New Covenant.   All were permitted to receive revelations for the church — all were on a level, as regards their authority.   But Smith, not satisfied with calling himself a seer, a prophet, and a revelator, claims to be 'great like unto Moses.'   It almost seems like blasphemy; but, as thousands profess to believe in the claims of this empty pretender, it becomes a duty to expose their weakness in the most effectual manner possible.

"Let us, then, ask, where is the least point of analogy between these men?   We read of Moses being sent by God, from the burning bush to deliver the Israelites from under the tyranny of Pharaoh, of the signs and wonders that attested his mission, of his leading the people out, of their journeying through the wilderness, of the division of the Red Sea, of the cloudy and fiery pillar that went before to

guide them in the way, of angel's food and quails for their subsist-
ence, of rivers of water flowing from the flinty rock to satiate their
thirst, of the miraculous durability of their clothing, of their glorious
reception of the lively oracles, the cloud overshadowing, the mountain shaking, the trump of God waxing louder and louder, the voice
of Nature's Author heard, his glory manifested, the people quaking,
and all this in attestation of the divinity of the mission of Moses,
and the laws of Jehovah.

"Now, what is there in the history of your Latter Day Prophet,
that can compare with this? Where was the power of this pretender
to work miracles, when his followers, fainting with hunger, were
famished on the way? Where was he, when their enemies pressed
sore upon them, threatening destruction? Did he then give even
the slightest assistance to his people? No! on the contrary, he led
the flight. Give us, then, at least, one well-authenticated and incontestable instance of the miraculous power of this man, before he
is claimed to be great like unto Moses.

"But where is there any analogy in the character of the two men?
Moses was said to be the meekest and one of the most benevolent
and upright of men. Now, is there any of this meekness in the
character of Smith? Let his harangues to his people speak, let his
own writings speak, and they will show him to be one of the most
vindictive men that can be produced. And what evidence is there
of his benevolence? At the very time that the widows of the Church,
and, indeed, the poorer class, were suffering for want of the common necessaries of life, Smith demanded at the hands of the people,
twelve hundred dollars per year, in order to aggrandize himself, and
enable him to live in luxury. And when some complained that
this would be a violation of the rules of the Church, he remarked,
that if he could not obtain his demand, his people might go to hell,
and he would go to the Rocky Mountains! And this, too, when
the Bishop is appointed by revelation, to deal out to every man
according to his wants. Here, then, is a beautiful specimen of his
benevolence — he must have his enormous demands satisfied, though
his people starve, even by breaking through the laws of the Church.
Where was there any thing like Moses in this? But look at his
example before his people. At the very time that their enemies
were pressing them, he was found, like a giddy boy, or an abandoned
renegado, wrestling for amusement, on the Sabbath day; and when
reproved, said, 'Never mind, it is a time of war.' Those who were
with Smith at the periods referred to, know that these things are
true. And what do they show? Any thing but a Moses.

"Having now shown the emptiness of Smith's claims, let us, for
a moment, inquire into his real origin and character. The following
remark is from the Rev. John A. Clark, of the city of Philadelphia,
but formerly of Palmyra, New York: —

"'Joe Smith, who has since been the chief Prophet of the Mormons, and was one of the most prominent ostensible actors in the
first scenes of this drama, belonged to a very shiftless family near
Palmyra. They lived a sort of vagrant life, and were principally
known as *Money-Diggers*. Joe, from a boy, appeared dull, and ut-

terly destitute of genius; but his father claimed for him a sort of second sight, a power to look into the depths of the earth, and discover where its precious treasures were hid. Consequently, long before the idea of a GOLDEN BIBLE entered their minds, in their excursions for money-digging, which, I believe, usually occurred in the night, that they might conceal from others the knowledge of the place where they struck upon treasures, Joe used to be usually their guide, putting into a hat a peculiar stone he had, through which he looked to decide where they should begin to dig.' "

From Mormonism Unveiled, by E. D. Howe, Esq.

" We next present to the reader, a few, among the many depositions which have been obtained from the neighborhood of the Smith family, and the scene where the far-famed Gold Bible had its pretended origin.

" The divine authenticity of the Gold Bible, or the Book of Mormon, is established by three special and eight collateral witnesses, making in the whole eleven, without whom there is no pretension to testimony; and if their testimony is probable and consistent with truth, and unimpeached, according to the common rules of jurisprudence, we are bound to believe them.

" Upon the principles of common law, we are prepared to meet them; and they are offered to us in no other light. Under all circumstances, in civil and ecclesiastical tribunals, witnesses may be impeached, and after a fair hearing, on both sides, the veracity and credibility may be adjudged.

" If the eleven witnesses are considered, from what has already been said, unimpeached, we will offer the depositions of some of the most respectable citizens of our country, who solemnly declare upon their oaths that no credit can be given to any one member of the Smith family. Many witnesses declare that they are in the possession of the means of knowing the Smiths for truth and veracity, and that they are not upon a par with mankind in general. Then, according to the common rules of weighing testimony, the eleven witnesses stand impeached before the public; and, until rebutting testimony can be produced which shall go to invalidate the respectable host which are here offered, we claim that no credit can or ought to be given to the witnesses to the Book of Mormon.

" We have not only testimony impeaching the moral characters of the Smith family, but we show, by the witnesses, that they told contradictory stories, from time to time, in relation to their finding the plates, and other circumstances attending it, which go clearly to show that none of them had the fear of God before their eyes, but were moved and instigated by the devil.

" PALMYRA, Wayne County, N. Y., *Dec.* 2, 1833.

" I, Peter Ingersoll, first became acquainted with the family of Joseph Smith, Sen. in the year of our Lord, 1822. I lived in the neighborhood of said family, until about 1830; during which time the following facts came under my observation.

" The general employment of the family, was digging for money. I had frequent invitations to join the company, but always declined being one of their number. They used various arguments to induce me to accept of their invitations. I was once ploughing near the house of Joseph Smith, Sen., about noon, he requested me to walk with him a short distance from his house, for the purpose of seeing whether a mineral rod would work in my hand, saying, at the same time, he was confident it would. As my oxen were eating, and being myself at leisure, I accepted the invitation. When we arrived near the place at which he thought there was money, he cut a small witch-hazel bush, and gave me direction how to hold it. He then went off some rods, and told me to say to the rod, ' Work to the money,' which I did, in an audible voice. He rebuked me severely for speaking it loud, and said it must be spoken in a whisper. This was rare sport for me. While the old man was standing off some rods, throwing himself into various shapes, I told him the rod did not work. He seemed much surprised at this, and said he thought he saw it move in my hand. It was now time for me to return to my labor. On my return, I picked up a small stone and was carelessly tossing it from one hand to the other. Said he, (looking very earnestly,) ' What are you going to do with that stone?' ' Throw it at the birds,' I replied. ' No,' said the old man, ' it is of great worth;' and upon this, I gave it to him. ' Now,' says he, ' if you only knew the value there is back of my house,' and pointing to a place near, ' there,' exclaimed he, ' is one chest of gold, and another of silver.' He then put the stone which I had given him, into his hat, and stooping forward, he bowed and made sundry manœuvres, quite similar to those of a stool-pigeon. At length, he took down his hat, and, being very much exhausted, said, in a faint voice, ' If you knew what I had seen, you would believe.' To see the old man thus try to impose upon me, I confess, rather had a tendency to excite contempt than pity. Yet I thought it best to conceal my feelings, preferring to appear the dupe of my credulity, than to expose myself to his resentment. His son Alvin then went through with the same performance, which was equally disgusting.

" Another time, the said Joseph, Sen., told me that the best time for digging money, was in the heat of summer, when the heat of the sun caused the chests of money to rise near the top of the ground. ' You notice,' said he, ' the large stones on the top of the ground — we call them rocks, and they truly appear so, but they are, in fact, most of them chests of money raised by the heat of the sun.'

" At another time, he told me that the ancient inhabitants of this country used camels instead of horses. For proof of this fact, he stated that in a certain hill, on the farm of Mr. Cuyler, there was a cave containing an immense value of gold and silver, stands of arms, also, a saddle for a camel, hanging on a peg, at one side of the cave. I asked him of what kind of wood the peg was. He could not tell, but said it had become similar to stone or iron.

" The old man, at last, laid a plan which he thought would accomplish his design. His cows and mine had been gone for some time, and were not to be found, notwithstanding our diligent search for them. Day after day was spent in fruitless search, until, at length, he proposed to find them by his art of divination. So he took his stand near the corner of his house, with a small stick in his hand, and made several strange and peculiar motions, and then said he could go directly to the cows. So he started off, and went into the woods, about one hundred rods distant, and found the lost cows. But, on finding out the secret of the mystery, Harrison had found the cows, and drove them to the above-named place, and milked them. So that this stratagem turned out rather more to his profit than it did to my edification. The old man, finding that all his efforts to make me a money-digger had proved abortive, at length ceased his importunities. One circumstance, however, I will mention, before leaving him. Some time before young Joseph found, or pretended to find, the gold plates, the old man told me that in Canada, there had been a book found, in a hollow tree, that gave an account of the first settlement of this country, before it was discovered by Columbus.

"In the month of August, 1827, I was hired by Joseph Smith, Jr., to go to Pennsylvania, to move his wife's household furniture up to Manchester, where his wife then was. When we arrived at Mr. Hale's, in Harmony, Pa., from which place he had taken his wife, a scene presented itself, truly affecting. His father-in-law (Mr. Hale,) addressed Joseph, in a flood of tears: 'You have stolen my daughter, and married her. I had much rather have followed her to her grave. You spend your time in digging for money — pretend to see in a stone, and thus try to deceive people.' Joseph wept, and acknowledged *he could not see in a stone now*, NOR NEVER COULD; and that his former pretensions in that respect, were all false. He then promised to give up his old habits of digging for money and looking into stones. Mr. Hale told Joseph, if he would move to Pennsylvania and work for a living, he would assist him in getting into business. Joseph acceded to this proposition. I then returned with Joseph and his wife to Manchester. One circumstance occurred, on the road, worthy of notice, and I believe this is the only instance where Joe ever exhibited true Yankee wit. On our journey to Pennsylvania, we could not make the exact change at the toll gate near Ithaca. Joseph told the gate tender that he would 'hand' him the toll on his return, as he was coming back in a few days. On our return, Joseph tendered to him 25 cents, the toll being 12½. He did not recognize Smith, so he accordingly gave him back the 12½ cents. After we had passed the gate, I asked him if he did not agree to pay double gatage on our return? 'No,' said he, 'I agreed to *hand* it to him, and I did, but he handed it back again.'

"Joseph told me, on his return, that he intended to keep the promise which he had made to his father-in-law; 'but,' said he, 'it will be hard for me, for they will all oppose, as they want me to look in the stone for them to dig money.' And, in fact, it was as he predicted. They urged him, day after day, to resume his old practice of looking in the stone. He seemed much perplexed as to the course he should pursue. In this dilemma, he made me his confidant, and told me what daily transpired in the family of Smiths. One day he came and greeted me, with a joyful countenance

Upon asking the cause of his unusual happiness, he replied in the following language : ' As I was passing, yesterday, across the woods, after a heavy shower of rain, I found, in a hollow, some beautiful white sand, that had been washed up by the water. I took off my frock, and tied up several quarts of it, and then went home. On my entering the house, I found the family at the table, eating dinner. They were all anxious to know the contents of my frock. At that moment, I happened to think of what I had heard about a history found in Canada, called the golden Bible ; so I very gravely told them it was the golden Bible. To my surprise, they were credulous enough to believe what I said. Accordingly I told them that I had received a commandment to let no one see it ; for, says I, no man can see it with the naked eye and live. However, I offered to take out the book and show it to them, but they refused to see it, and left the room. Now,' said Joe, ' I have got the damned fools fixed, and will carry out the fun.' Notwithstanding, he told me he had no such book, and believed there never was any such book, yet, he told me that he actually went to Willard Chase, to get him to make a chest, in which he might deposit his golden Bible. But, as Chase would not do it, he made a box himself, of clapboards, and put it into a pillow-case, and allowed people only to lift it, and feel of it through the case.

" In the fall of 1827, Joseph wanted to go to Pennsylvania. His brother-in-law had come to assist him in moving, but he himself was out of money. He wished to borrow the money of me, and he presented Mr. Hale as security. I told him in case he could obtain assistance from no other source, I would let him have some money. Joseph then went to Palmyra ; and said he, ' I there met that damn fool Martin Harris, and told him that I had a command to ask the first *honest man* I met with for fifty dollars in money, and he would let me have it. I saw at once,' said Joe, ' that it took his notion, for he promptly gave me the fifty.'

" Joseph thought this sum was sufficient to bear his expenses to Pennsylvania ; so he immediately started off, and since that time I have not been much in his society. While the Smiths were living at Waterloo, William visited my neighborhood ; and, upon my inquiry how they came on, he replied, ' We do better there than here ; we were too well known here to do much.' PETER INGERSOLL.

" STATE OF NEW YORK, } ss.
    Wayne County, }

" I certify, that on this 9th day of December, 1833, personally appeared before me the above-named Peter Ingersoll, to me known, and made oath, according to law, to the truth of the above statement. " TH. P. BALDWIN,
                        " *Judge of Wayne County Court.*"

" Testimony of William Stafford.

" MANCHESTER, Ontario County, N. Y. *December* 8, 1833.

" I, William Stafford, having been called upon to give a true statement of my knowledge, concerning the character and conduct of the family of Smiths, known to the world as the founders of the Mormon sect, do say, that I first became acquainted with Joseph, Sen., and his family, in the year 1820. They lived, at that time, in Palmyra, about one mile and a half from my residence. A great part of their time was devoted to digging for money : especially in the night time, when they said the money could be most easily obtained. I have heard them tell marvellous tales, respecting the discoveries they had made in their peculiar occupation of money digging. They would say, for instance, that in such a place, in such a hill, on a certain man's farm, there were deposited keys, barrels and hogsheads of coined silver and gold — bars of gold, golden images, brass kettles filled with gold and silver — gold candlesticks, swords, &c. &c. They would say, also, that nearly all the hills in this part of New York, were thrown up by human hands, and in them were large caves, which Joseph, Jr., could see, by placing a stone of singular appearance in his hat, in such a manner as to exclude all light; at which time they pretended he could see all things within and under the earth, — that he could see within the above-mentioned caves, large gold bars and silver plates, — that he could also discover the spirits in whose charge these treasures were, clothed in ancient dress. At certain times, these treasures could be obtained very easily; at others, the obtaining of them was difficult. The facility of approaching them, depended, in a great measure, on the state of the moon. New moon and good Friday, I believe, were regarded as the most favorable times for obtaining these treasures These tales I regarded as visionary. However, being prompted by curiosity, I at length accepted of their invitations, to join them in their nocturnal excursions. I will now relate a few incidents attending these excursions.

"Joseph Smith, Sen., came to me one night, and told me, that Joseph, Jr., had been looking in his glass, and had seen, not many rods from his house, two or three kegs of gold and silver, some feet under the surface of the earth ; and that none others but the elder Joseph and myself could get them. I accordingly consented to go, and early in the evening repaired to the place of deposit. Joseph, Sen., first made a circle, twelve or fourteen feet in diameter. This circle, said he, contains the treasure. He then stuck in the ground a row of witch-hazel sticks, around the said circle, for the purpose of keeping off the evil spirits. Within this circle he made another, of about eight or ten feet in diameter. He walked around three times on the periphery of this last circle, muttering to himself something which I could not understand. He next stuck a steel rod in the centre of the circles, and then enjoined profound silence upon us, lest we should arouse the evil spirit who had the charge of these treasures. After we had dug a trench about five feet in depth around the rod, the old man, by signs and motions, asked leave of absence, and went to the house to inquire of young Joseph the cause of our disappointment. He soon returned, and said, that Joseph had remained all this time in the house, looking in his stone and watching the motions of the evil spirit — that he saw the spirit come up to the ring, and as soon as it beheld the cone which we had

6 *

formed around the rod, it caused the money to sink. We then went into the house, and the old man observed, that we had made a mistake in the commencement of the operation; if it had not been for that, said he, we should have got the money.

"At another time, they devised a scheme, by which they might satiate their hunger with the mutton of one of my sheep. They had seen in my flock of sheep, a large, fat, black wether. Old Joseph and one of the boys came to me one day, and said that Joseph, Jr., had discovered some very remarkable and valuable treasures, which could be procured only in one way. That way was as follows: — That a black sheep should be taken on to the ground where the treasures were concealed — that after cutting its throat, it should be led around a circle while bleeding. This being done, the wrath of the evil spirit would be appeased: the treasures could then be obtained, and my share of them was to be four-fold. To gratify my curiosity, I let them have a large fat sheep. They afterwards informed me that the sheep was killed pursuant to commandment; but as there was some mistake in the process, it did not have the desired effect. This, I believe, is the only time they ever made money-digging a profitable business. They, however, had around them constantly a worthless gang, whose employment it was to dig money nights, and who, day times, had more to do with mutton than money.

"When they found that the people of this vicinity would no longer put any faith in their schemes for digging money, they then pretended to find a Gold Bible, of which, they said, the Book of Mormon was only an introduction. This latter book was at length fitted for the press. No means were taken by any individual to suppress its publication: no one apprehended any danger from a book, originating with individuals who had neither influence, honesty or honor. The two Josephs and Hiram, promised to show me the plates, after the Book of Mormon was translated. But, afterwards, they pretended to have received an express commandment, forbidding them to show the plates. Respecting the manner of receiving and translating the Book of Mormon, their statements were always discordant. The elder Joseph would say that he had seen the plates, and that he knew them to be gold; at other times he would say that they looked like gold; and other times he would say he had not seen the plates at all. I have thus briefly stated a few of the facts, in relation to the conduct and character of this family of Smiths; probably sufficient has been stated without my going into detail.

"WILLIAM STAFFORD.

"STATE OF NEW YORK, }
  Wayne County,   } ss.

"I certify, that on this 9th day of December, 1833, personally appeared before me William Stafford, to me known, and made oath to the truth of the above statement, and signed the same.
"TH. P. BALDWIN,
"Judge of Wayne County Court."

"*Testimony of Willard Chase.*

"Manchester, Ontario County, New York, 1833.

"I became acquainted with the Smith family, known as the authors of the Mormon Bible, in the year 1820. At that time, they were engaged in the money-digging business, which they followed until the latter part of the season of 1827. In the year 1822 I was engaged in digging a well. I employed Alvin and Joseph Smith to assist me; the latter of whom is now known as the Mormon Prophet. After digging about twenty feet below the surface of the earth, we discovered a singularly appearing stone, which excited my curiosity. I brought it to the top of the well, and as we were examining it, Joseph put it into his hat, and then his face into the top of his hat. It has been said by Smith, that *he* brought the stone from the well; but this is false. There was no one in the well but myself. The next morning he came to me, and wished to obtain the stone, alleging that he could see in it; but I told him I did not wish to part with it, on account of its being a curiosity, but would lend it. After obtaining the stone, he began to publish abroad what wonders he could discover by looking in it, and made so much disturbance among the credulous part of community, that I ordered the stone to be returned to me again. He had it in his possession about two years. I believe, some time in 1825, Hiram Smith, (brother of Joseph Smith,) came to me, and wished to borrow the same stone, alleging that they wanted to accomplish some business of importance, which could not very well be done without the aid of the stone. I told him it was of no particular worth to me, but merely wished to keep it as a curiosity, and if he would pledge me his word and honor that I should have it when called for, he might take it; which he did, and took the stone. I thought I could rely on his word at this time, as he had made a profession of religion. But in this I was disappointed, for he disregarded both his word and honor.

"In the fall of 1826, a friend called upon me, and wished to see that stone, about which so much had been said; and I told him, if he would go with me to Smith's, (a distance of about half a mile,) he might see it. But, to my surprise, on going to Smith's, and asking him for the stone, he said, 'You cannot have it;' I told him it belonged to me, repeated to him the promise he made me, at the time of obtaining the stone: upon which he faced me with a malignant look, and said, 'I don't care who in the Devil it belongs to, *you* shall not have it.'

"In the month of June, 1827, Joseph Smith, Sen., related to me the following story: 'That some years ago, a spirit had appeared to Joseph his son, in a vision, and informed him that in a certain place there was a record on plates of gold, and that he was the person that must obtain them, and this he must do in the following manner: On the 22d of September, he must repair to the place where was deposited this manuscript, dressed in black clothes, and riding a black horse, with a switch tail, and demand the book in a certain name, and after obtaining it he must go directly away, and neither lay it down nor look behind him. They accordingly fitted out Joseph with a suit of black clothes and borrowed a black horse. He repaired to the place of deposit and demanded the book, which was in a stone box, unsealed, and so near the top of the ground that he could see one end of it, and raising it up, took out the book of gold; but fearing some one might discover where he got it, he laid it down to place back the top stone, as he found it; and turning round, to his surprise there was no book in sight. He again opened the box, and in it saw the book, and attempted to take it out, but was hindered. He saw in the box something like a toad, which soon assumed the appearance of a man, and struck him on the side of his head. Not being discouraged at trifles, he again stooped down and strove to take the book, when the spirit struck him again, and knocked him three or four rods, and hurt him prodigiously. After recovering from his fright, he inquired why he could not obtain the plates; to which the spirit made reply, because you have not obeyed your orders. He then inquired when he *could* have them, and was answered thus: Come one year from this day, and bring with you your oldest brother, and you shall have them. This spirit, he said, was the spirit of the prophet who wrote this book, and who was sent to Joseph Smith, to make known these things to him. Before the expiration of the year, his oldest brother died; which the old man said was an *accidental providence!*

"Joseph went one year from that day, to demand the book, and the spirit inquired for his brother, and he said that he was dead. The spirit then commanded him to come again, in just one year, and bring a man with him. On asking who might be the man, he was answered that he would know him when he saw him.

"Joseph believed that one Samuel T. Lawrence was the man alluded to by the spirit, and went with him to a singular looking hill, in Manchester, and showed him where the treasure was. Lawrence asked him if he had ever discovered any thing with the plates of gold; he said no; he then asked him to look in his stone, to see if there was any thing with them. He looked, and said there was nothing; he told him to look again, and see if there was not a large pair of specs with the plates; he looked and soon saw a pair of spectacles, the same with which Joseph says he translated the Book of Mormon. Lawrence told him it would not be prudent to let these plates be seen for about two years, as it would make a great disturbance in the neighborhood. Not long after this Joseph altered his mind, and said L. was not the right man, nor had he told him the right place. About this time he went to Harmony in Pennsylvania, and formed an acquaintance with a young lady by the name of Emma Hale, whom he wished to marry. In the fall of 1826 he wanted to go to Pennsylvania to be married; but being destitute of means, he now set his wits to work how he should raise money, and get recommendations, to procure the fair one of his choice. He went to Lawrence with the following story, as related to me by Lawrence himself. That he had discovered in Pennsylvania, on the bank of the Susquehannah River, a very rich mine of silver, and if he would go there with him, he might have a share in the profits; that it was near high-water mark, and that they could load it into boats and take it down the river to Philadelphia, to market. Lawrence then asked Joseph if he was not deceiving him; no, said he, for I have been there and seen it with my own eyes, and if you do not find it so when we get there, I will bind myself to be your servant for three years. By these grave and fair promises Lawrence was induced to believe something in it, and agreed to go with him. L. soon found that Joseph was out of money, and had to bear his expenses on the way. When they got to Pennsylvania, Joseph wanted L. to recommend him to Miss H., which he did, although he was asked to do it; but could not well get rid of it as he was in his company. L. then wished to see the silver mine, and he and Joseph went to the river, and made search, but found nothing. Thus Lawrence had his trouble for his pains, and returned home lighter than he went, while Joseph had got his expenses borne, and a recommendation to his girl.

"Joseph's next move was to get married; the girl's parents being opposed to the match: as they happened to be from home, he took advantage of the opportunity, and went off with her and was married.

"Now, being still destitute of money, he set his wits at work how he should get back to Manchester, his place of residence; he hit upon the following plan, which succeeded very well. He went to an honest old Dutchman, by the name of Stowel, and told him that he had discovered on the bank of Black River, in the village of Watertown, Jefferson County, N. Y., a cave, in which he had found a bar of gold, as big as his leg, and about three or four feet long. That he could not get it out alone, on account of its being fast at one end; and if he would move him to Manchester, N. Y., they would go together, and take a chisel and mallet, and get it, and Stowel should share the prize with him. Stowel moved him.

"A short time after their arrival at Manchester, Stowel reminded Joseph of his promise; but he calmly replied, that he would not go, because his wife was now among strangers, and would be very lonesome if he went away. Mr. Stowel was then obliged to return without any gold, and with less money than he came.

"In the fore part of September, (I believe,) 1827, the Prophet requested me to make him a chest, informing me that he designed to move back to Pennsylvania, and expecting soon to get his gold book, he wanted a chest to lock it up, giving me to understand at the same time, that if I would make the chest he would give me a share in the book. I told him my business was such that I could not make it; but if he would bring the book to me, I would lock it up for him. He said that would not do, as he was commanded to keep it two years, without letting it come to the eye of any one but himself. This commandment, however, he did not keep; for in less than two years, twelve men said they had seen it. I told him to get it and convince me of its existence, and I would make him a chest; but he said, that would not do, as he must have a chest to lock the book in, as soon as he took it out of the ground. I saw him a few days after, when he told me that I must make the chest. I told him plainly that I could not, upon which he told me that I could have no share in the book.

" A few weeks after this conversation he came to my house, and related the following story : That on the 22d of September, he arose early in the morning, and took a one horse wagon, of some one that had staid over night at their house, without leave or license ; and, together with his wife, repaired to the hill which contained the book. He left his wife in the wagon, by the road, and went alone to the hill, a distance of thirty or forty rods from the road ; he said he then took the book out of the ground and hid it in a tree top, and returned home. He then went to the town of Macedon to work. After about ten days, it having been suggested that some one had got his book, his wife went after him ; he hired a horse, and went home in the afternoon, staid long enough to drink one cup of tea, and then went for his book, found it safe, took off his frock, wrapt it round it, put it under his arm and ran all the way home, a distance of about two miles. He said he should think it would weigh sixty pounds, and was sure it would weigh forty. On his return home, he said he was attacked by two men in the woods, and knocked them both down and made his escape, arrived safe and secured his treasure. He then observed that if it had not been for that stone, (which he acknowledged belonged to me,) he would not have obtained the book. A few days afterwards, he told one of my neighbors that he had not got any such book, nor never had such an one ; but that he had told the story to deceive the d——d fool, (meaning me,) to get him to make a chest. His neighbors having become disgusted with his foolish stories, he determined to go back to Pennsylvania, to avoid what he called persecution. His wits were now put to the task to contrive how he should get money to bear his expenses. He met one day in the streets of Palmyra a rich man, whose name was Martin Harris, and addressed him thus : 'I have a commandment from God to ask the first man I meet in the street to give me fifty dollars, to assist me in doing the work of the Lord by translating the Golden Bible.' Martin being naturally a credulous man, hands Joseph the money. In the spring of 1829 Harris went to Pennsylvania, and on his return to Palmyra, reported that the Prophet's wife, in the month of June following, would be delivered of a male child that would be able when two years old to translate the Gold Bible. Then, said he, you will see Joseph Smith, Jr., walking through the streets of Palmyra with a Gold Bible under his arm, and having a gold breastplate on, and a gold sword hanging by his side. This, however, by the by, proved false.

" In April, 1830, I again asked Hiram for the stone which he had borrowed of me ; he told me I should not have it, for Joseph made use of it in translating his Bible. I reminded him of his promise, and that he had pledged his honor to return it ; but he gave me the lie, saying the stone was not mine nor never was. Harris at the same time flew in a rage, took me by the collar and said I was a liar, and he could prove it by twelve witnesses. After I had extricated myself from him, Hiram in a rage shook his fist at me, and abused me in a most scandalous manner. Thus I might proceed in describing the character of these High Priests, by relating one transaction after another, which would all tend to set them in the same light in

which they were regarded by their neighbors, viz.: as a pest to society. I have regarded Joseph Smith, Jr., from the time I first became acquainted with him until he left this part of the country, as a man whose word could not be depended upon. Hiram's character was but very little better. What I have said respecting the characters of these men, will apply to the whole family. What I have stated relative to the characters of these individuals, thus far, is wholly true. After they became thorough Mormons, their conduct was more disgraceful than before. They did not hesitate to abuse any man, no matter how fair his character, provided he did not embrace their creed. Their tongues were continually employed in spreading scandal and abuse. Although they left this part of the country without paying their just debts, yet their creditors were glad to have them do so, rather than to have them stay, disturbing the neighborhood.
"WILLARD CHASE.

"On the 11th December, 1833, the said Willard Chase appeared before me, and made oath that the foregoing statement to which he has subscribed his name, is true, according to his best recollection and belief.
FRED'K SMITH,
"*Justice of the Peace of Wayne County.*"

"*The Testimony of Parley Chase.*

"MANCHESTER, *December* 2, 1833.
"I was acquainted with the family of Joseph Smith, Sen., both before and since they became Mormons, and feel free to state that not one of the male members of the Smith family was entitled to any credit whatsoever. They were lazy, intemperate, and worthless men, very much addicted to lying. In this they frequently boasted of their skill. Digging for money was their principal employment. In regard to their Gold Bible speculation, they scarcely ever told two stories alike. The Mormon Bible is said to be a revelation from God, through Joseph Smith, Jr., his Prophet, and this same Joseph Smith, Jr., to my knowledge, bore the reputation among his neighbors of being a liar. The foregoing statement can be corroborated by all his former neighbors. PARLEY CHASE."

"PALMYRA, *December* 13, 1833.
"I certify that I have been personally acquainted with Peter Ingersoll for a number of years, and believe him to be a man of strict integrity, truth and veracity. DURFEY CHASE."

"PALMYRA, *December* 4, 1833.
"I am acquainted with William Stafford and Peter Ingersoll, and believe them to be men of truth and veracity. J. S. COLT."

"PALMYRA, *December* 4, 1833.

"We, the undersigned, are personally acquainted with William Stafford, Willard Chase and Peter Ingersoll, and believe them to be men of truth and veracity   "GEORGE BECKWITH,

"NATH'L H. BECKWITH,

"THOMAS ROGERS, 2d,

"MARTIN W. WILCOX."

"*The Testimony of David Stafford.*

"MANCHESTER, *December* 5, 1833.

"I have been acquainted with the family of Joseph Smith, Sen., for several years, and I know him to be a drunkard and a liar, and to be much in the habit of gambling. He and his boys were truly a lazy set of fellows, and more particularly Joseph, who very aptly followed his father's example, and in some respects was worse. When intoxicated he was very quarrelsome. Previous to his going to Pennsylvania to get married, we worked together making a coal-pit. While at work at one time, a dispute arose between us, (he having drinked a little too freely,) and some hard words passed between us, and as usual with him at such times, was for fighting. He got the advantage of me in the scuffle, and a gentleman by the name of Ford interfered, when Joseph turned to fighting him. We both entered a complaint against him and he was fined for the breach of the peace. It is well known, that the general employment of the Smith family was money-digging and fortune-telling. They kept around them, constantly, a gang of worthless fellows who dug for money nights, and were idle in the daytime. It was a mystery to their neighbors how they got their living. I will mention some circumstances and the public may judge for themselves. At different times I have seen them come from the woods early in the morning, bringing meat which looked like mutton. I went into the woods one morning very early, shooting partridges, and found Joseph Smith, Sen., in company with two other men, with hoes, shovels, and meat that looked like mutton. On seeing me they run like wild men to get out of sight. Seeing the old man a few days afterwards, I asked him why he run so the other day in the woods ; ' Ah,' said he, ' you know that circumstances alter cases ; it will not do to be seen at all times.'

"I can also state, that Oliver Cowdery proved himself to be a worthless person, and not to be trusted or believed when he taught school in this neighborhood. After his going into the ministry, while officiating in performing the ordinance of baptism in a brook, William Smith, (brother of Joseph Smith,) seeing a young man writing down what was said, on a piece of board, was quite offended and attempted to take it from him, kicked at him, and clinched for a scuffle. Such was the conduct of these pretended Disciples of the Lord.   DAVID STAFFORD.

"On the 12th day of December, 1833, the said David Stafford appeared before me, and made oath that the foregoing statement, by him subscribed, is true.   FRED'K SMITH,

"*Justice of the Peace of Wayne County, New York.*"

" *The Testimony of Barton Stafford.*

" MANCHESTER, Ontario County, New York, *November* 3, 1833

" Being called upon to give a statement of the character of the family of Joseph Smith, Sen., as far as I know, I can state that I became acquainted with them in 1820, and knew them until 1831, when they left this neighborhood. Joseph Smith, Sen., was a noted drunkard and most of the family followed his example, and Joseph, Jr., especially, who was very much addicted to intemperance. In short, not one of the family had the least claims to respectability. Even since he professed to be inspired of the Lord to translate the Book of Mormon, he one day, while at work in my father's field, got quite drunk on a composition of cider, molasses and water. Finding his legs to refuse their office, he leaned upon the fence and hung for some time ; at length recovering again, he fell to scuffling with one of the workmen, who tore his shirt nearly off from him. His wife, who was at our house on a visit, appeared very much grieved at his conduct, and to protect his back from the rays of the sun, and conceal his nakedness, threw her shawl over his shoulders, and in that plight escorted the Prophet home. As an evidence of his piety and devotion, when intoxicated, he frequently made his religion the topic of conversation ! !

" BARTON STAFFORD.

" STATE OF NEW YORK, ⎱ ss.
  Wayne County, ⎰

" I certify that on the 9th day of December, 1833, personally appeared before me, the above-named Barton Stafford, to me known, and solemnly affirmed according to law, to the truth of the above statement and subscribed the same.

" THOS. P. BALDWIN,
A Judge of Wayne County Court.'

" I, Henry Harris, do state that I became acquainted with the family of Joseph Smith, Sen., about the year 1820, in the town of Manchester, New York. They were a family that labored very little — the chief they did, was to dig for money. Joseph Smith, Jr., the pretended Prophet, used to pretend to tell fortunes ; he had a stone which he used to put in his hat, by means of which he professed to tell people's fortunes.

" Joseph Smith, Jr., Martin Harris, and others, used to meet together in private, a while before the gold plates were found, and were familiarly known by the name of the ' Gold Bible Company.' They were regarded by the community in which they lived, as a lying and indolent set of men, and no confidence could be placed in them.

" The character of Joseph Smith, Jr., for truth and veracity was such, that I would not believe him under oath. I was once on a jury before a Justice's Court, and the jury could not, and did not, believe his testimony to be true. After he pretended to have found the gold plates, I had a conversation with him, and asked him where he found them and how he come to know where they were.

7

He said he had a revelation from God that told him they were hid in a certain hill, and he looked in his stone and saw them in the place of deposit; that an angel appeared, and told him he could not get the plates until he was married, and that when he saw the woman that was to be his wife, he should know her, and she would know him. He then went to Pennsylvania, got his wife, and they both went together and got the gold plates — he said it was revealed to him, that no one must see the plates but himself and wife.

" I then asked him what letters were engraved on them, he said italic letters written in an unknown language, and that he had copied some of the words and sent them to Dr. Mitchell and Professor Anthon of New York. By looking on the plates he said he could not understand the words, but it was made known to him that he was the person that must translate them, and on looking through the stone was enabled to translate.

" After the book was published, I frequently bantered him for a copy. He asked fourteen shillings a piece for them; I told him I would not give so much; he told me he had had a revelation that they must be sold at that price.

" Some time afterwards I talked with Martin Harris about buying one of the books, and he told me they had had a new revelation, that they might be sold at ten shillings a piece.
                                                                  " HENRY HARRIS."

"STATE OF OHIO,   } ss.
   Cuyahoga County, }

" Personally appeared before me, Henry Harris, and made oath in due form of law, that the foregoing statements subscribed by him are true.   " JONATHAN LAPHAM,
                                                 "*Justice of the Peace.*"

" PALMYRA, Wayne County, New York, 11*th mo*. 28*th*, 1833.

" In the early part of the winter in 1828, I made a visit to Martin Harris's, and was joined in company by Jos. Smith, Sen., and his wife. The Gold Bible business, so called, was the topic of conversation, to which I paid particular attention, that I might learn the truth of the whole matter. They told me that the report that Joseph, Jr., had found golden plates, was true, and that he was in Harmony, Pennsylvania, translating them — that such plates were in existence, and that Joseph, Jr., was to obtain them, was revealed to him by the spirit of one of the Saints that was on this continent, previous to its being discovered by Columbus. Old Mrs. Smith observed that she thought he must be a Quaker, as he was dressed very plain. They said that the plates he then had in possession were but an introduction to the Gold Bible — that all of them upon which the Bible was written, were so heavy, that it would take four stout men to load them into a cart — that Joseph had also discovered by looking through his stone, the vessel in which the gold was melted from which the plates were made, and also the machine with which they were rolled; he also discovered in the bottom of the vessel three balls of gold, each as large as his fist. The old lady said also, that after the book was translated, the plates were to be publicly exhibited — admittance twenty-five cents. She calculated it would bring in annually an enormous sum of money — that money would then be very plenty, and the book would also sell for a great price, as it was something entirely new — that they had been commanded to obtain all the money they could borrow for present necessity, and to repay with gold. The remainder was to be kept in store for the benefit of their family and children. This and the like conversation detained me until about eleven o'clock. Early the next morning, the mystery of the spirit being like myself (one of the order called Friends) was revealed by the following circumstance : The old lady took me into another room, and after closing the door, she said, ' Have you four or five dollars in money that you can lend until our business is brought to a close ? the spirit has said you shall receive fourfold.' I told her that when I gave, I did it not expecting to receive again — as for money I had none to lend. I then asked her what her particular want of money was ; to which she replied, ' Joseph wants to take the stage and come home from Pennsylvania to see what we are all about.' To which I replied, he might look in his stone and save his time and money. The old lady seemed confused, and left the room, and thus ended the visit.

" In the second month following, Martin Harris and his wife were at my house. In conversation about Mormonites, she observed, that she wished her husband would quit them, as she believed it was all false and a delusion. To which I heard Mr. Harris reply : ' *What if it is a lie; if you will let me alone I will make money out of it !* ' I was both an eye and an ear witness of what has been stated above, which is now fresh in my memory, and I give it to the world for the good of mankind. I speak the truth and lie not, God bearing me witness. ABIGAIL HARRIS."

" PALMYRA, *November* 29, 1833.

" Being called upon to give a statement to the world of what I know respecting the Gold Bible speculation, and also of the conduct of Martin Harris, my husband, who is a leading character among the Mormons, I do it free from prejudice, realizing that I must give an account at the bar of God for what I say. Martin Harris was once industrious, attentive to his domestic concerns, and thought to be worth about ten thousand dollars. He is naturally quick in his temper, and in his mad-fits frequently abuses all who may dare to oppose him in his wishes. However strange it may seem, I have been a great sufferer by his unreasonable conduct. At different times while I lived with him, he has whipped, kicked, and turned me out of the house. About a year previous to the report being raised that Smith had found gold plates, he became very intimate with the Smith family, and said he believed Joseph could see in his stone any thing he wished. After this he apparently became very sanguine in his belief, and frequently said he would have no one in his house that did not believe in Mormonism ; and because I would not give credit to the report he made about the gold plates, he became more austere towards me. In one of his fits of rage he struck me with the butt-end of a whip, which I think had been used for driving oxen, and was about the size of my thumb, and three or four feet long. He beat me on the head four or five times, and the next day turned me out of doors twice, and beat me in a shameful manner. The next day I went to the town of Marion, and while there my flesh was black and blue in many places. His main complaint against me was, that I was always trying to hinder his making money.

"When he found out that I was going to Mr. Putnam's, in Marion, he said he was going too, that they had sent for him to pay them a visit. On arriving at Mr. Putnam's, I asked them if they had sent for Mr. Harris; they replied, they knew nothing about it; he, however, came in the evening. Mrs. Putnam told him never to strike or abuse me any more; he then denied ever striking me; she was however convinced that he lied, as the marks of his beating me were plain to be seen, and remained more than two weeks. Whether the Mormon religion be true or false, I leave the world to judge, for its effects upon Martin Harris have been to make him more cross, turbulent and abusive to me. His whole object was to make money by it. I will give one circumstance in proof of it. One day, while at Peter Harris's house, I told him he had better leave the company of the Smiths, as their religion was false; to which he replied, ' If you would let me alone, I could make money by it.'

" It is in vain for the Mormons to deny these facts; for they are all well known to most of his former neighbors. The man has now become rather an object of pity; he has spent most of his property, and lost the confidence of his former friends. If he had labored as hard on his farm as he has to make Mormons, he might now be one of the wealthiest farmers in the country. He now spends his time in travelling through the country spreading the delusion of Mormonism, and has no regard whatever for his family.

" With regard to Mr. Harris's being intimate with Mrs. Haggard, as has been reported, it is but justice to myself to state what facts have come within my own observation, to show whether I had any grounds for jealousy or not. Mr. Harris was very intimate with this family, for some time previous to their going to Ohio. They lived a while in a house which he had built for their accommodation, and here he spent the most of his leisure hours; and made her presents of articles from the store and house. He carried these presents in a private manner, and frequently when he went there, he would pretend to be going to some of the neighbors, on an errand, or to be going into the fields. After getting out of sight of the house, he would steer a straight course for Haggard's house, especially if Haggard was from home. At times when Haggard was from home, he would go there in the manner above described, and stay till twelve or one o'clock at night, and sometimes until daylight.

" If his intentions were evil, the Lord will judge him accordingly, but if good, he did not mean to let his left hand know what his right hand did. The above statement of facts, I affirm to be true.   LUCY HARRIS."

"MANCHESTER, Ontario County, *December* 1, 1833.

"I, Roswell Nichols, first became acquainted with the family of Joseph Smith, Sen., nearly five years ago, and I lived a neighbor to the said family about two years. My acquaintance with the family has enabled me to know something of its character for good citizenship, probity and veracity — For breach of contracts, for the non-payment of debts and borrowed money, and for duplicity with their neighbors, the family was notorious. Once, since the Gold Bible speculation commenced, the old man was sued; and while the sheriff was at his house, he lied to him and was detected in the falsehood. Before he left the house, he confessed that it was sometimes necessary for him to tell an honest lie, in order to live. At another time, he told me that he had received an express command for me to repent and believe as he did, or I must be damned. I refused to comply, and at the same time told him of the various impositions of his family. He then stated their digging was not for money, but it was for the obtaining of a Gold Bible. Thus contradicting what he had told me before : for he had often said, that the hills in our neighborhood were nearly all erected by human hands — that they were all full of gold and silver. And one time, when we were talking on the subject, he pointed to a small hill on my farm, and said, 'In that hill there is a stone which is full of gold and silver. I know it to be so, for I have been to the hole, and God said unto me, *Go not in now, but at a future day you shall go in and find the book open, and then you shall have the treasures.*' He said that gold and silver was once as plenty as the stones in the field are now — that the ancients, half of them melted the ore and made the gold and silver, while the other half buried it deeper in the earth, which accounted for these hills. Upon my inquiring who furnished the food for the whole, he flew into a passion, and called me a sinner, and said he, 'You must be eternally damned."

"I mention these facts, not because of their intrinsic importance, but simply to show the weak-mindedness and low character of the man.   ROSWELL NICHOLS."

"MANCHESTER, Ontario County, *November* 15, 1833.

"I, Joshua Stafford, became acquainted with the family of Joseph Smith, Sen., about the year 1819 or '20. They then were laboring people, in low circumstances. A short time after this, they commenced digging for hidden treasures, and soon after they became indolent, and told marvellous stories about ghosts, hobgoblins, caverns, and various other mysterious matters. Joseph once showed me a piece of wood which he said he took from a box of money, and the reason he gave for not obtaining the box, was, that it *moved*. At another time, he, (Joseph, Jr.,) at a husking, called on me to become security for a horse, and said he would reward me handsomely, for he had found a box of watches, and they were as large

7 *

as his fist, and he put one of them to his ear, and he could hear it
' tick forty rods.' Since he could not dispose of them profitably at
Canandaigua or Palmyra, he wished to go east with them. He
said if he did not return with the horse, I might take his life. I
replied, that he knew I would not do that. ' Well,' said he, ' I did not
suppose you would, yet I would be willing that you should.' He
was nearly intoxicated at the time of the above conversation.

JOSHUA STAFFORD.''

" MANCHESTER, Ontario County, November 8, 1833.

"I, Joseph Capron, became acquainted with Joseph Smith, Sen.,
in the year of our Lord, 1827. They have, since then, been really
a peculiar people — fond of the foolish and the marvellous — at one
time addicted to vice and the grossest immoralities — at another
time making the highest pretensions to piety and holy intercourse
with Almighty God. The family of Smiths held Joseph, Jr., in high
estimation on account of some supernatural power, which he was
supposed to possess. This power he pretended to have received
through the medium of a stone of peculiar quality. The stone was
placed in a hat, in such a manner as to exclude all light, except that
which emanated from the stone itself. This light of the stone, he
pretended, enabled him to see any thing he wished. Accordingly
he discovered ghosts, infernal spirits, mountains of gold and silver,
and many other invaluable treasures deposited in the earth. He
would often tell his neighbors of his wonderful discoveries, and urge
them to embark in the money-digging business. Luxury and wealth
were to be given to all who would adhere to his counsel. A gang
was soon assembled. Some of them were influenced by curiosity,
others were sanguine in their expectations of immediate gain. I
will mention one circumstance, by which the uninitiated may know
how the company dug for treasures. The sapient Joseph discovered, north-west of my house, a chest of gold watches ; but, as they
were in the possession of the evil spirit, it required skill and stratagem to obtain them. Accordingly, orders were given to stick a
parcel of large stakes in the ground, several rods around, in a circular form. This was to be done directly over the spot where the
treasures were deposited. A messenger was then sent to Palmyra
to procure a polished sword : after which, Samuel F. Lawrence, with
a drawn sword in his hand, marched around to guard any assault
which his Satanic majesty might be disposed to make. Meantime,
the rest of the company were busily employed in digging for the
watches. They worked as usual till quite exhausted. But, in spite
of their brave defender, Lawrence, and their bulwark of stakes, the
devil came off victorious, and carried away the watches. I might
mention numerous schemes which this young visionary and impostor had recourse to for the purpose of obtaining a livelihood.
He, and indeed the whole of the family of Smiths, were notorious
for indolence, foolery and falsehood. Their great object appeared
to be, to live without work. While they were digging for money,
they were daily harassed by the demands of creditors, which they
never were able to pay. At length, Joseph pretended to find the

gold plates. This scheme, he believed, would relieve the family from all pecuniary embarrassment. His father told me, that when the book was published, they would be enabled, from the profits of the work, to carry into successful operation the money-digging business. He gave me no intimation, at that time, that the book was to be of a religious character, or that it had any thing to do with revelation. He declared it to be a speculation, and said he, ' When it is completed, my family will be placed *on a level* above the generality of mankind !! ' JOSEPH CAPRON."

" PALMYRA, *November* 28, 1833.

" Having been called on to state a few facts which are material to the characters of some of the leaders of the Mormon sect, I will do so in a concise and plain manner. I have been acquainted with Martin Harris, about thirty years. As a farmer, he was industrious and enterprising, so much so, that he had (previous to his going into the Gold Bible speculation) accumulated, in real estate, some eight or ten thousand dollars. Although he possessed wealth, his moral and religious character was such, as not to entitle him to respect among his neighbors. He was fretful, peevish and quarrelsome, not only in the neighborhood, but in his family. He was known to frequently abuse his wife, by whipping her, kicking her out of bed, and turning her out of doors, &c. Yet he was a public professor of some religion. He was first an orthodox Quaker, then a Universalist, next a Restorationer, then a Baptist, next a Presbyterian, and then a Mormon. By his willingness to become all things unto all men, he has attained a high standing among his Mormon brethren. The Smith family never made any pretensions to respectability. G. W. STODARD.

" I hereby concur in the above statement. RICHARD H. FORD."

" PALMYRA, *December* 4, 1833.

" We, the undersigned, have been acquainted with the Smith family, for a number of years, while they resided near this place, and we have no hesitation in saying, that we consider them destitute of that moral character, which ought to entitle them to the confidence of any community. They were particularly famous for visionary projects, spent much of their time in digging for money which they pretended was hid in the earth ; and to this day, large excavations may be seen in the earth, not far from their residence, where they used to spend their time in digging for hidden treasures. Joseph Smith, Senior, and his son Joseph, were in particular considered entirely destitute of *moral character, and addicted to vicious habits.*

" Martin Harris was a man who had acquired a handsome property, and in matters of business his word was considered good ; but on moral and religious subjects, he was perfectly visionary, — sometimes advocating one sentiment, and sometimes another. And in reference to all with whom we were acquainted, that have embraced Mormonism from this neighborhood, we are compelled to say, were very visionary, and most of them destitute of moral character, and without influence in this community; and this may account why they were permitted to go on with their impositions undisturbed. It was not supposed that any of them were possessed of sufficient character or influence to make any one believe their book or their sentiments, and we know not of a single individual in this vicinity that puts the least confidence in their pretended revelations.

" Geo. N. Williams,   Wells Anderson,
" Clark Robinson,   N. H. Beckwith,
" Lemuel Durfee,   Philo Durfee,
" E. S. Townsend,   Giles S. Ely,
" Henry P. Alger,   R. W. Smith,
" C. E. Thayer,   Pelatiah West,
" G. W. Anderson,   Henry Jessup,
" H. P. Thayer,   Linus North,
" L. Williams,   Thos. Rogers, 2d.
" Geo. W. Crosby,   Wm. Parke,
" Levi Thayer,   Josiah Francis,
" R. S. Williams,   Amos Hollister,
" P. Sexton,   G. A. Hathaway,
" M. Butterfield,   David G. Ely,
" S. P. Seymour,   H. K. Jerome,
" D. S. Jackways,   G. Beckwith,
" John Hurlbut,   Lewis Foster,
" H. Linnell,   Hiram Payne,
" Jas. Jenner,   P. Grandin,
" S. Ackley,   L. Hurd,
" Josiah Rice,   Joel Thayer,
" Jesse Townsend,   E. D. Robinson,
" Rich'd. D. Clark,   Asahel Millard,
" Th. P. Baldwin,   A. Ensworth,
" John Sothington,   Israel F. Chilson."
" Durfey Chase,

" Manchester, *November* 3, 1833.

" We, the undersigned, being personally acquainted with the family of Joseph Smith, Sen., with whom the celebrated Gold Bible, so called, originated, state : that they were not only a lazy, indolent set of men, but also intemperate ; and their word was not to be depended upon ; and that we are truly glad to dispense with their society.

" Pardon Butts,   A. H. Wentworth,
" Warden A. Reed,   Moses C. Smith,
" Hiram Smith,   Joseph Fish,
" Alfred Stafford,   Horace N. Barnes,
" James Gee,   Silvester Worden."
" Abel Chase,

" Harmony, Pa., *March* 20, 1834.

" I first became acquainted with Joseph Smith, Jr., in November, 1825. He was at that time in the employ of a set of men who were called 'money-diggers;' and his occupation was that of seeing, or pretending to see by means of a stone placed in his hat, and his hat closed over his face. In this way he pretended to discover minerals and hidden treasure. His appearance at this time, was that of a careless young man — not very well educated, and very saucy and insolent to his father. Smith, and his father, with several other 'money-diggers,' boarded at my house while they were employed in digging for a mine that they supposed had been opened and worked by the Spaniards, many years since. Young Smith gave the 'money-diggers' great encouragement, at first, but when they had arrived in digging, to near the place where he had stated an immense treasure would be found — he said the enchantment was so powerful that he could not see. They then became discouraged, and soon after dispersed. This took place about the 17th of November, 1825; and one of the company gave me his note for $12 68 for his board, which is still unpaid.

" After these occurrences, young Smith made several visits at my house, and at length asked my consent to his marrying my daughter Emma. This I refused, and gave my reasons for so doing; some of which were, that he was a stranger, and followed a business that I could not approve; he then left the place. Not long after this, he returned, and while I was absent from home, carried off my daughter, into the state of New York, where they were married without my approbation or consent. After they had arrived at Palmyra, N. Y., Emma wrote to me inquiring whether she could take her property, consisting of clothing, furniture, cows, &c. I replied that her property was safe, and at her disposal. In a short time they returned, bringing with them a Peter Ingersoll, and subsequently came to the conclusion that they would move out, and reside upon a place near my residence.

" Smith stated to me, that he had given up what he called 'glass-looking,' and that he expected to work hard for a living, and was willing to do so. He also made arrangements with my son Alva Hale, to go to Palmyra, and move his (Smith's) furniture, &c., to this place. He then returned to Palmyra, and soon after, Alva, agreeable to the arrangement, went up and returned with Smith and his family. Soon after this, I was informed they had brought a wonderful Book of Plates down with them. I was shown a box in which it is said they were contained, which had, to all appearances, been used as a glass box of the common window glass. I was allowed to feel the weight of the box, and they gave me to understand, that the Book of Plates was then in the box — into which, however, I was not allowed to look.

" I inquired of Joseph Smith, Jr., who was to be the first who would be allowed to see the Book of Plates? He said it was a young child. After this, I became dissatisfied, and informed him that if there was any thing in my house of that description, which I could not be allowed to see, he must take it away; if he did not, I was determined to see it. After that, the plates were said to be hid in the woods.

" About this time, Martin Harris made his appearance upon the stage ; and Smith began to interpret the characters or hieroglyphics which he said were engraven upon the plates, while Harris wrote down the interpretation.   It was said, that Harris wrote down one hundred and sixteen pages, and lost them.   Soon after this happened, Martin Harris informed me that he must have a *greater witness*, and said that he had talked with Joseph about it — Joseph informed him that he could not, or durst not show him the plates, but that he (Joseph) would go into the woods where the Book of Plates was, and that after he came back, Harris should follow his track in the snow, and find the Book, and examine it for himself. Harris informed me afterwards, that he followed Smith's directions, and could not find the plates, and was still dissatisfied.

" The next day after this happened, I went to the house where Joseph Smith, Jr., lived, and where he and Harris were engaged in their translation of the book.   Each of them had a written piece of paper which they were comparing, and some of the words were ' *my servant seeketh a greater witness, but no greater witness can be given him.*'   There was also something said about ' *three that were to see the thing* ' — meaning, I supposed, the Book of Plates, and that ' *if the three did not go exactly according to the orders, the thing would be taken from them.*'   I inquired whose words they were, and was informed by Joseph or Emma, (I rather think it was the former,) that they were the words of Jesus Christ.   I told them, that I considered the whole of it a delusion, and advised them to abandon it.   The manner in which he pretended to read and interpret, was the same as when he looked for the money-diggers, with the stone in his hat, and his hat over his face, while the Book of Plates was at the same time hid in the woods !

" After this, Martin Harris went away, and Oliver Cowdery came and wrote for Smith, while he interpreted as above described.   This is the same Oliver Cowdery, whose name may be found in the Book of Mormon.   Cowdery continued a scribe for Smith until the Book of Mormon was completed, as I supposed and understood.

" Joseph Smith, Jr., resided near me for some time after this, and I had a good opportunity of becoming acquainted with him, and somewhat acquainted with his associates, and I conscientiously believe from the facts I have detailed, and from many other circumstances, which I do not deem it necessary to relate, that the whole ' Book of Mormon ' (so called) is a silly fabrication of falsehood and wickedness, got up for speculation, and with a design to dupe the credulous and unwary — and in order that its fabricators may live upon the spoils of those who swallow the deception.

"ISAAC HALE.

" Affirmed to and subscribed before me, March 20, 1834.

"CHARLES DIMON,
" J. Peace."

" STATE OF PENNSYLVANIA, *Susquehannah County*, ss.

" We, the subscribers, associate Judges of the Court of Common Pleas, in and for said county, do certify that we have been many

years personally acquainted with Isaac Hale, of Harmony township
in this county, who has attested the foregoing statement; and that
he is a man of excellent moral character, and of undoubted veracity.
Witness our hands.   " WILLIAM THOMPSON.
                                      " DAVIS DIMOCK.
" *March* 21, 1834."

" Elder Lewis also certifies and affirms in relation to Smith as
follows :—

" ' I have been acquainted with Joseph Smith, Jr., for some time :
being a relation of his wife, and residing near him, I have had frequent opportunities of conversation with him, and of knowing his
opinions and pursuits. From my standing in the Methodist Episcopal church, I suppose he was careful how he conducted or expressed himself before me. At one time, however, he came to my
house, and asked my advice, whether he should proceed to translate
the Book of Plates (referred to by Mr. Hale) or not. He said that
God had commanded him to translate it, but he was afraid of the
people · he remarked, that he was to exhibit the plates to the world,
at a certain time, which was then about eighteen months distant.
I told him I was not qualified to give advice in such cases. Smith
frequently said to me that I should see the plates at the time
appointed.

" ' After the time stipulated had passed away, Smith being at my
house was asked why he did not fulfil his promise, show the Golden
Plates and prove himself an honest man ? He replied that he himself was deceived, but that I should see them if I were where they
were. I reminded him then, that I stated at the time he made the
promise, I was fearful " the enchantment would be so powerful " as
to remove the plates, when the time came in which they were to be
revealed.

" ' These circumstances, and many others of a similar tenor, im-
bolden me to say that Joseph Smith, Jr., is not a man of truth and
veracity ; and that his general character in this part of the country,
is that of an impostor, hypocrite and liar.
                                      ' NATHANIEL C. LEWIS.'

" Affirmed and subscribed, before me, March 20, 1834.
                                      " CHARLES DIMON,
                                        " *J. Peace.*"

" We subjoin the substance of several affidavits, all taken and
made before Charles Dimon, Esq. by credible individuals, who have
resided near to, and been well acquainted with Joseph Smith, Jr. —
illustrative of his character and conduct.

" Joshua McKune states, that he ' was acquainted with Joseph
Smith, Jr., and Martin Harris, during their residence in Harmony,

Pa., and knew them to be artful seducers;' — that they informed him that ' Smith had found a sword, breastplate, and a pair of spectacles, at the time he found the gold plates ' — that these were to be ' shown to all the world as evidence of the truth of what was contained in those plates,' and that ' he (McKune) and others should see them at a specified time.' He also states, that ' the time for the exhibition of the plates, &c., has gone by, and he has not seen them.' ' Joseph Smith, Jr., told him that his (Smith's) first-born child was to translate the characters, and hieroglyphics upon the plates, into our language at the age of three years; but this child was not permitted to live, to verify the prediction.' He also states that, ' he has been intimately acquainted with Isaac Hale twenty-four years, and has always found him to be a man of truth, and good morals.'

" Hezekiah McKune states that, ' in conversation with Joseph Smith, Jr., he (Smith) said he was nearly equal to Jesus Christ; that he was a prophet sent by God to bring in the Jews, and that he was the greatest prophet that had ever arisen.'

" Alva Hale, son of Isaac Hale, states, that Joseph Smith, Jr., told him, that ' his (Smith's) gift in seeing with a stone and hat, was a gift from God,' — but also states, ' that Smith told him at another time that this " *peeping* " was all d——d nonsense. He (Smith) was deceived himself, but did not intend to deceive others; — that he intended to quit the business, (of peeping,) and labor for his livelihood.' That afterwards, ' Smith told him, he should see the plates from which he translated the Book of Mormon,' and accordingly at the time specified by Smith, he (Hale) ' called to see the plates, but Smith did not show them, but appeared angry.' He further states, that he knows Joseph Smith, Jr. to be an impostor, and a liar, and knows Martin Harris to be a liar likewise.

" Levi Lewis states that, he has ' been acquainted with Joseph Smith, Jr., and Martin Harris, and that he has heard them both say, adultery was no crime. Harris said he did not blame Smith, for his (Smith's) attempt to seduce Eliza Winters,' &c.; — Mr. Lewis says that, he ' knows Smith to be a liar; — that he saw him (Smith) intoxicated at three different times while he was composing the Book of Mormon, and also that he has heard Smith, when driving oxen, use language of the greatest profanity. Mr. Lewis also testifies that he heard Smith say, he (Smith) was as good as Jesus Christ; — that it was as bad to injure him as it was to injure Jesus Christ.' ' With regard to the plates, Smith said God had deceived him — which was the reason he (Smith) did not show them.'

" Sophia Lewis certifies that, she ' heard a conversation between Joseph Smith, Jr., and the Rev. James B. Roach, in which Smith called Mr. R. a d——d fool. Smith also said, in the same conversation, that, he (Smith) was as good as Jesus Christ;' and that she ' has frequently heard Smith use profane language.' She states that she heard Smith say, ' the Book of Plates could not be opened under penalty of death by any other person but his (Smith's) first-born, which was to be a male.' She says she ' was present at the birth of this child, and that it was still-born, and very much deformed.' "

Testimony of Fanny Brewer, of Boston.

"Boston, *September* 13, 1842.

" To the Public : — I have long desired that some one who had a *certain knowledge* of the hidden practices and abominations at Nauvoo, would have the moral courage to come out with a full development; and my desires have been realized in General Bennett's disclosures. As the ice is now broken, I, too, have a tale to tell. In the spring of 1837, I left Boston for Kirtland, in all good faith, to assemble with the Saints, as I thought, and worship God more perfectly. On my arrival, I found brother going to law with brother, *drunkenness* prevailing to a great extent, and every species of wickedness. *Joseph Smith, a Prophet of God,* (*as he called himself,*) *was under arrest for* EMPLOYING TWO OF THE ELDERS TO KILL A MAN BY THE NAME OF GRANDISON NEWELL, belonging to Mentor; but was acquitted, AS THE MOST MATERIAL WITNESS DID NOT APPEAR!!! I am personally acquainted with one of the employees, Davis by name, and he frankly acknowledged to me, that *he was prepared to do the deed under the direction of the Prophet,* and was only prevented from so doing by the entreaties of his wife. There was much excitement against the Prophet, on another account, likewise, — AN UNLAWFUL INTERCOURSE BETWEEN HIMSELF AND A YOUNG ORPHAN GIRL RESIDING IN HIS FAMILY, AND UNDER HIS PROTECTION!!! Mr. Martin Harris told me that the Prophet was most notorious for *lying* and LICENTIOUSNESS!! In the fall of 1837, the Smith family all left Kirtland, by REVELATION, (or *necessity,*) for Missouri. The Prophet left between two days. I carried from this place to Kirtland, goods to the amount of about fourteen hundred dollars, as I was told I could make ready sales to the Saints; but I was disappointed. I accordingly sent them to Missouri to be sold by H. Redfield. There they were stored in a private room. Smith, the Prophet, hearing that they were there, took out a warrant, under pretence of searching for stolen goods, and got them into his possession. They were then, by a sham court, which he held, adjudged to him, and the boxes were opened. As the goods were taken out, piece by piece, HYRUM SMITH,* *who stood by, said,* IN THE MOST POSITIVE MANNER, *that he could swear to every piece, and tell where they had been bought,* although a Mr. Robbins, who was present, told them that *he knew the boxes, and that the goods were mine,* for I had charged him to take care of them. *Dr. Williams, likewise, told them that they were my goods,* AND THAT HYRUM NEVER SAW A PIECE OF THEM!! They, however, refused to give them up, but, in defiance of law and justice, kept them for their own profit. The Prophet has told many stories about this matter, but the above is the true one. *I know that many of the Mormons will make any statements that their Prophet desires them to,* and have *no hesitation* in resorting to the MOST BAREFACED PERJURY to accomplish their purposes — save their friends, or destroy their enemies.

" I had strong intimations of the truth of all the matters disclosed

* [It appears from this testimony, and that of Willard Chase and others, that the beloved HYRUM *is a prince of liars, scoundrels, cut-throats, and ruffians,* under the garb of religious sanctity ; NOT TO BE BELIEVED UNDER OATH.]

8

by General Bennett, some months before they came to the public eye, by persons high in the confidence of the Prophet, and who had every opportunity of knowing.

"These are facts not to be contradicted, and are but a few out of the many I am acquainted with about the Prophet and his friends. Nothing could induce me to have my name appear before the public, but a hope that the united testimony of those who, by the mercy of God, have been delivered from the snares of the villains, may be the means of redeeming some of my fellow-beings, and especially my own sex, from the destruction that would fall upon them if they continued under the influence of the vile impostor.

" FANNY BREWER.

—

"SUFFOLK, ss. September 13, 1842.

"Then personally appeared the above-named Fanny Brewer, and made oath, that the foregoing affidavit, by her subscribed, is true.

"Before me,

" BRADFORD SUMNER,
" Justice of the Peace."

———

" BOSTON, September 19, 1842.

"On or about the middle of June, 1837, I rode with Joseph Smith, Jr., from Fairport, Ohio, to Kirtland. When we left Fairport, we had been drinking pretty freely; I drank brandy, he brandy and cider, both together; and when we arrived at Painsville, we drank again; and when we arrived at Kirtland, we were very drunk.

"In July, William Smith, one of the twelve Apostles, arrived at Kirtland, from Chicago, drunk, with his face pretty well bunged up; he had black eyes and bunged nose, and told John Johnson that he had been MILKING THE GENTILES to his satisfaction, for that time.

"About the last of August, 1837, Joseph Smith, Brigham Young, and others, were drunk at Joseph Smith, Jr.'s house, all together; and a man, by the name of Vinson Knight, supplied them with rum, brandy, gin, and port wine, from the cash store; and I worked in the loft, over head. He, Joseph, told Knight not to sell any of the rum, brandy, gin, or port wine, for he wanted it for his own use. They were drunk, and drinking, for more than a week.

"Joseph Smith said that the Bank was got up on his having a revelation from God, and said it was to go into circulation to MILK THE GENTILES. I asked Joseph about the money. He said he could not redeem it; he was paid for signing the bills, as any other man would be paid for it, — so he told me, — and they must do the best they could about it.

"October 13. — Hyrum Smith's wife was sick, and Brigham Young prayed with her, and laid on hands, and said she would get well; but she died at six o'clock at night.

"Joseph Smith, Jr., and others, went to Canada, in September. Said he, Joseph, had as good a right to go out and get money, as any of the brethren. He took money, in Canada, from a man by the name of Lawrence, and promised him a farm, when he arrived at Kirtland; but when he arrived, Joseph was among the missing, and no farm for him. (He took nine hundred dollars from Lawrence.)

" William Smith told Joseph if he did not give him some money he would tell where the Book of Mormon came from ; and Joseph accordingly gave him what he wanted.   G. B. FROST.

" SUFFOLK, ss. *September* 19, 1842.

" Then personally appeared the aforenamed G. B. Frost, and made oath that the foregoing affidavit, by him subscribed, is true.

"Before me,   BRADFORD SUMNER,
                                "*Justice of the Peace.*"

From Rev. George Montgomery West, A. M., D. D., the able Defender of the Christian Faith.

"BOSTON, *September* 19, 1842.

" The undersigned is personally acquainted with Miss Fanny Brewer, and has no hesitation in saying that she sustains an unblemished character for truth and moral worth in the city of Boston.

" The undersigned is also personally acquainted with Mr. George B. Frost, of the same city ; and hereby certifies, that he is perfectly worthy of belief, and he now is, and has been, for a length of time past, a perfectly temperate man, and an accredited member of the Temperance Society.   G. M. WEST."

CHARACTER OF JOE SMITH, AND TWO OF HIS AC-COMPLICES—WILLIAM LAW AND JOHN TAYLOR—FOR TRUTH AND HONESTY.

An article appeared in the (Nauvoo) Times and Seasons, of July 1, 1842, from the pen of General William Law, (one of Joe's Councillors of the First Presidency, selected by *special revelation* from Heaven, through Joe, as he boasts, for his *great piety* and *unquestioned veracity!*) dated June 17, 1842, and headed, "MUCH ADO ABOUT NOTHING ! ! " as follows : —

" Where is there a record against any of *our people* for a *penitentiary* crime ? NOT IN THE STATE ! ! Where is there a record of *fine, or county imprisonment,* (for ANY breach of law,) against *any of the Latter Day Saints ?* I know of none in the State ! If then they have broken no law, they consequently have taken away no man's rights, they have infringed upon no man's liberties."

Joseph Smith, the Prophet, and John Taylor, the Apostle, (the senior and junior editors of the Times and Seasons,) *endorse* the statement in an editorial, as follows : —

" The *above are plain matters of fact* that every one may become

acquainted with by reference to the COUNTY OR STATE RECORDS!
We might add that in regard to MORAL PRINCIPLES *there is no city
in the State or in the United States*, that can compare with the *city
of Nauvoo!!!* You may live in our city for a month, and not hear
an oath sworn — you may be here as long and not see one person
intoxicated; so notorious are we for sobriety, that at the time the
Washingtonian Convention PASSED THROUGH our city, a meeting
was called for them," etc. etc.

What unblushing impudence, and barefaced lying, in
the face of *recorded* truth! These are a trio of the most
Heaven-daring liars the world ever saw, as will appear from
the RECORDS and *facts* following : —

" THE PEOPLE OF THE STATE OF ILLINOIS *vs.* TIMOTHY LEWIS,
(Mormon.)

" Indicted for *larceny*, October 2, 1840. Sentenced to four years'
imprisonment *in the penitentiary* — thirty days' solitary confinement,
— for stealing horses."

———

" THE PEOPLE OF THE STATE OF ILLINOIS *vs.* SALLY CASTILE
AND FRANCIS CASTILE, (Mormons.)

" Indicted for stealing a log-chain, October 5, 1841. These defendants were convicted by a jury of Hancock county for the above
theft, — new trial granted — the venue changed to McDonough,
where no witnesses appeared, and they were discharged."

———

" THE PEOPLE OF THE STATE OF ILLINOIS *vs.* ——— JOHNSON,
(Mormon.)

" Arrested for stealing, and escaped from the officers."

———

" THE PEOPLE OF THE STATE OF ILLINOIS *vs.* ALANSON BROWN,
(Mormon, Danite.)

" In jail under process from McDonough county for stealing, and
for murdering a man, by stabbing, in Hancock."

———

" THE PEOPLE OF THE STATE OF ILLINOIS *vs.* ——— GEAR,
(Mormon.)

" In jail for *incest* and *rape* on HIS OWN DAUGHTER !!!"

———

" THE PEOPLE OF THE STATE OF ILLINOIS *vs.* WILLIAM WOOD,
(Mormon.)

" Change of venue from Hancock county to McDonough, and
sentenced to the *penitentiary* for two years, for stealing horses."

———

" THE PEOPLE OF THE STATE OF ILLINOIS *vs.* ——— LINDSAY,
(Mormon.)

" Sent to the *penitentiary* from Adams county, for stealing a saddle from B. F. Marsh, Esq., in Hancock county."

The above cases are from the records of Hancock, McDonough, and Adams counties.

From the City Records.

"STATE OF ILLINOIS,   } scilicet.
 Hancock County,   }

"Before me, John C. Bennett, Mayor of the city of Nauvoo, in said county, personally came H. G. Sherwood, Marshal of said city, who being duly sworn according to law, deposeth and saith: That on, or about, the twenty-second day of April, 1841, in the county of Hancock, there was stolen from his premises, or near thereto, one one-horse wagon, in his custody as the property of said city, and this deponent verily believes that Eleazer King, Alonzo F. King, and Enoch M. King, are guilty of the fact charged; and further this deponent saith not.   H. G. SHERWOOD.

"Sworn to, and subscribed, before me, at my office, this twenty-third day of April, 1841.   JOHN C. BENNETT,
                                        "*Mayor of the City of Nauvoo.*"

From the (Burlington) Hawk-Eye and Iowa Patriot — a paper edited by James G. Edwards, Esq.

"MR. EDITOR: It is with extreme reluctance that the undersigned are induced to intrude upon the public what will probably, by many of your readers, be considered merely as private grievances. But the indignities and injuries which we have suffered at the hands of the deluded followers of that wretched Impostor, Joe Smith, have been so many and frequent, that ' forbearance long since ceased to be a virtue ;' and a sense of duty to ourselves and others impels us to make the following statements, which may be the means of preventing some individuals from making shipwreck of their fortunes and character, by embracing this miserable scheme of humbug and delusion.

"It may be proper here to remark, that we shall state *facts* — facts that can be neither gainsaid or denied; and, if half the truth is told, it will convince the world that ' truth is stranger than fiction,' and will act like the spear of Ithuriel, in exposing, in all their deformity, some of the atrocious features of an imposture, as ridiculous and silly as the designs of its authors are dangerous and treasonable.

"That there are not *some* worthy men and good citizens who *sincerely* believe in the mission of Joe Smith as a Prophet, we should be sorry to believe ; but in speaking of a community like this, we speak of them collectively, and of the general features of their system.

"They have now been in our midst for more than two years. They came among us in a destitute and suffering condition ; a condition that called into lively exercise all the benevolent feelings of our natures ; we believed that they had been *persecuted* on account of their *religious!* sentiments, that a majority of them were honest, and

8 *

we were disposed to give them an opportunity to live down — if false — the evil reports that have followed them, whenever they have been compelled to make a removal. In proof that a kindly disposition has been exercised, we may point to the fact, that until very recently, not a newspaper in their vicinity has published a harsh remark in reference to them or their Prophet. How has the kindness thus extended been requited? they have rung the changes on their 'persecutions in Missouri,' till it no longer possesses the power to bind together the discordant elements of *Mormonism*, and abuse of the men that have opened their doors to them, and ever treated them kindly, has become the order of the day. The events of the past year have forced the conviction upon us, that, in relation to their troubles in Missouri, there are 'two sides to the story.'

"Three years since, we could retire at night without that painful feeling of insecurity which now exists; then it was unnecessary to lock our buildings to secure our property from robbers; now, nothing is safe, however strongly secured by bolts and bars.

"The undersigned, having been somewhat in the way of the fulfilment of a pretended revelation relative to the building up a city at Montrose, — which, being interpreted into the unknown tongue of Mormonism, meaneth 'Zarahemla,' — have been the greatest sufferers by these depredations ; no less than *thirteen Robberies*, amounting in value to more than *One Thousand Dollars*, having been committed on our property since the Mormons came here, and though we have offered rewards for the detection of the thieves and the recovery of the property, we have never, in a single instance, succeeded in accomplishing either. A case in which we made an attempt to ferret out the thieves, and were thwarted by the direct interference of Joe Smith, will presently be mentioned.

" We subjoin an account of the various robberies : —

" Robbery 1st.— Store robbed of a general assortment of goods, a Mormon Bishop (Vinson Knight) at the time living overhead, with only a thin floor between.

" Robbery 2nd. — Warehouse broken open, and robbed of one barrel of pork, two barrels sugar, and five kegs lard.

" Robbery 3rd. — Smoke-house entered by breaking lock, and robbed of 33 hams and 11 shoulders.

" Robbery 4th. — 1½ barrels salt stolen from the building where it was stored.

" Robbery 5th. — 1 barrel salt.

" Robbery 6th. — 1 saddle, bridle, and martingal, stolen from stable.

" Robbery 7th. — 4 wagon wheels stolen from the wagon standing in front of the house.

" Robbery 8th. — 3 saddles, bridles, and martingals stolen from stable.

" Robbery 9th. — 60 bushels wheat, in sacks, stolen from granary.

" Robbery 10th. — Warehouse *again* entered by breaking lock, and robbed of 6 boxes glass, 150 pounds bacon, (together with 2 boxes axes belonging to C. Peck, Esq.)

" Robbery 11th. — 6 barrels salt, *the salt taken from the barrels, and the barrels left.*

" Robbery 12th. — 300 to 400 bushels of corn stolen from the crib during the past summer, at various times.

" Robbery 13th. — 1 wheel stolen from a chariotee standing in the enclosure of the undersigned. — These are the principal robberies, to say nothing of petty, every day stealing of trifles, which is annoying enough. The character of the articles stolen precludes the idea that they were taken to any considerable distance from Montrose, *or Nauvoo!* The robbery last mentioned must have been from sheer malice, as one wheel of a carriage could be of no benefit to any one.

" The premises from which our conclusions are drawn, that the greater part of this mischief is done by Mormons, are, that in every case of robbery, the silly story is at once raised by them, and circulated with the greatest industry, that we have secreted our own property for the sake of raising an excitement against the Mormons ; or the robbery is justified, and surprise expressed that we don't lose more than we do, *because* we oppose the swindling schemes of their Prophet. As before stated, the stand taken by us to prevent the building up of Montrose by the ' Latter Days,' had rather thwarted their plans ; the Prophet himself proclaimed that ' he did not care how much was stolen from the K————s,' thus giving full license to his followers to go on and plunder as much as they pleased, often, indeed, in his discourses justifying theft, by citing the example of Christ while passing through the cornfield. On one occasion he said the world owed him a good living, and if he could not get it without, he would *steal* it — ' and *catch* me at it,' said he, ' if you can.' This is the doctrine that is taught — not to be *caught* stealing — and it has for months been the common talk among the understrappers of Joe Smith that we should be driven from the place ; — the various robberies of which we have given a history show the *means* by which such a result is to be brought about.

" We come now to a circumstance which goes clearly to show the hollow-hearted character of the scoundrel Prophet and the other leading Mormons, and which convinces us that all their pretended zeal for the detection of villany and the punishment of offenders is a mere *ruse* to give persons abroad a favorable opinion of their morals, and is of a piece with the farce exhibited in the enactment of a law by the City Council of Nauvoo, that no ardent spirits should be sold within the corporate limits of Nauvoo, under severe penalties, yet winking at the establishment of a *drunkery* at the very portals of the Temple, and in full view of the Mayor's office. The morning after robbery No. 10, convinced by traces in the sand on the bank of the river, that the property stolen had been taken *across* the river, — with a view to obtain, if possible, a further clew to the robbers, one of the undersigned, accompanied by a young man from Ohio, went to one of the leaders of the society (Stephen Markham) at Nauvoo, and solicited his aid in ferreting out the thieves, which he appeared quite willing to render ; we examined several skiffs along the river bank, and at length came to one belonging to J. C. Annis, an *Elder.* Markham observed that he believed James Dunn (a son-in-law of Annis) was the thief, and added, ' Old Annis is, in

my opinion, no better.' Pointing to the skiff, he continued, 'If
that skiff could speak, it would tell you where your goods are.'
Some further conversation was had, as to the best plan of making
some discoveries of the robbers, and he (Markham) gave the names
of James Dunn, an Elder; D. B. Smith, a relative of the Prophet
Joe; O. P. Rockwell; —— Stevens; J. D. Parker, Elder and Capt.
Nauvoo Legion; H. G. Sherwood, City Marshal and Elder, as
being very suspicious characters, at the same time remarking that
he did not believe Sherwood would be concerned in committing
any of the robberies himself, but that he would probably be willing
to share the plunder.

  " The young man that accompanied the writer observed that he
formerly knew D. B. Smith in Ohio, and he thought he could gain
his confidence, and, by stratagem, obtain information of the place of
concealment of the stolen goods; this, by the advice of a magistrate
and a legal gentleman, he undertook. To gain their confidence he
found an easy matter, and he soon had an interview with Dunn,
Smith, and Rockwell, who, he avers, proposed to him to aid them in
robbing the store of the undersigned. To this he assented, and the
arrangements were made on their part to commit the robbery, and on
ours to take them in the act. It is believed that up to this moment
Markham was desirous that the guilty should be caught; but he,
with the other leaders, found the *matter was going too far* — that, if
we succeeded in catching so many of their elders, it would raise an
excitement against them, and show the world their true character.
Here, too, was a fine opportunity for the gratification of those
vindictive feelings by which it is well known Joe Smith is ever
actuated; the Prophet therefore caused the young man to be arrested, ordered him to give up every thing he had on his person,
cocked and presented his rifle, and threatened to shoot — to use his
own language on the occasion — ' QUICKER THAN HELL CAN SCORCH
A FEATHER.' The young man was taken before the Mayor's Court;
the six individuals above named were then called as witnesses; and,
though they appeared to rejoice at their narrow escape through the
kindness of their leaders, they showed a spirit of vindictiveness
towards the young man who, from a sincere desire that justice might
be done, consented to watch their movements; — they testified that he
had counterfeit coin in his possession. On the part of the defence,
it was proved that the coin was loaned to him by the Magistrate,
before alluded to, and the writer, — for the purpose of showing it, to
induce them to believe that he could supply any quantity, and to
inspire them with confidence in him. Yet, with all this testimony
going to show his good intentions, that the coin was given to him
for a specific purpose, and that he was engaged in a laudable endeavor to bring the guilty to justice, *this Mormon Court Martial
bound him over for his appearance at Court;* and where was Stephen
Markham, the Mormon leader, who could in one moment have set
the matter in its true light? The moment the young man was
arrested, he mounted his horse and started for Quincy, and thus
avoided giving testimony that would at once have set the young
man at liberty.

" With this matter is closely connected the conspiracy, as the Mormons please to call it. A young man living with Joe, a relative of the Elect Lady, (Joe's wife,) by the name of Lorenzo D. Wasson, and O. P. Rockwell, complained that the undersigned had conspired, &c., to unlawfully procure an indictment.

" The same six witnesses that appeared in the former case were sworn on the part of the prosecutor. The undersigned, viewing the whole proceedings with that contempt which they merited, asked the witnesses no questions, and introduced no witnesses themselves ; yet, with all their efforts, the complaint was unsustained by a shadow of truth. To have done any thing with us under *such* circumstances would have been too barefaced even for a *Mormon* Court Martial, and we were, of course, immediately discharged by General Bennett, the Chief Justice of the Mayor's Court. That this malicious prosecution was instigated and set on foot by Joe Smith, it is useless for him to deny ; he said previously that he would have us arrested, and afterwards boasted that he had. As for his tool, Lorenzo D. Wasson, we have only to say, that he did not even make his appearance in Court ; it was sufficient for him that, to please the 'money-digger,' he had *perjured* himself for the purpose of injuring one who never saw him or heard of him before.

" The evening that these proceedings took place, and during our absence, a valuable horse was poisoned, and the evening subsequently another was poisoned. These two horses were standing in a stable, with their heads to open windows ; three other horses, not thus exposed, escaped.

" Would it be taxing our credulity too much to believe that a man who could conceive a murderous plot to assassinate a man (Mr. Grandison Newell of Ohio) that opposed his designs, and that *has* a 'DANITE BAND' 'to haul his enemies into the brush,' and a 'DESTROYING ANGEL,' commissioned to kill their cattle, burn their buildings, poison their wells, and destroy their lives, if necessary to the accomplishment of his infamous designs, — would not for a moment hesitate to employ desperadoes to commit any, or all, of the acts of outrage with which we have been visited ?

" Allusion has been made to a pretended revelation, which conflicts with the interests of the undersigned and others. Our object being to strip from this Impostor the 'silver veil' that covers his hideousness, we shall, in a future article, give a full history of the revelation, and the interest with which it conflicts. It may appear to some that our remarks about this bold Blasphemer are harsh in the extreme ; but a moment's reflection will convince any one, that *he is either what he claims to be, a Prophet of the Lord, or a scoundrel without one redeeming quality, and capable of doing any deed of darkness.*   " D. W. KILBOURN.,
                                        " EDWARD KILBOURN.

" MONTROSE, IOWA, }
September 20, 1841." }

Hundreds of such cases might be enumerated, but the above will suffice.

Few can doubt the profanity of many of the citizens of
Nauvoo, and the Prophet Joe, in particular.   Mr. Benjamin Avise, of Carthage, said that the first time he ever saw
Joe and heard him speak, *he swore an oath!*   Joe is notoriously profane, but he says God will not notice him in
cursing the damned Gentiles !

All who are acquainted with the Prophet know that he
gets most gloriously drunk, occasionally ; but he says he
only does this to try the faith of the Saints, and show them
that he is fallible, like other men.

I recollect once that I was taking tea at Joe's house,
when there were present, besides myself, Mrs. Merrick
and several gentlemen.   Joe was in a very glorious state ;
so intoxicated, indeed, that he could scarcely hold up his
head.   The Elect Lady, Emma, having left the room in
disgust at her husband's beastly state, the Prophet began to
fancy that we were all suspiciously observing him ; and I
shall never forget the ludicrous gravity in which he leaned
forward over the table, and addressing Mrs. Merrick,
hiccoughed out, *" Sister — Merrick — do — you — feel*
ruined ? "   Joe took the bowl of Bacchus that day with
a *perfect looseness !*

I recollect, upon another occasion, when the female portion of Doctor O'Harra's family were on a visit at old Mrs.
Smith's, Joe happened in, tolerably drunk, and commenced
discoursing in a very low and vulgar manner, much to the
annoyance of the ladies.   After he had taken his exit,
Miss Margaret O'Harra observed, " What ruffian is
that, pray ? "   To which the old lady replied, " O, I perceive you are not acquainted with our folks ; that is our
son, Joseph, the Prophet."   I thank Miss O'Harra for the
suggestion.   " The Ruffian Prophet " is quite an appropriate name for the beast.   The reader will perceive that
Joe has not that regard for *temperance* that his vote on the
city temperance ordinance, which I wrote and procured
him to present to the Council, would seem to indicate.   His
advocacy of that wholesome measure was a mere ruse
for *foreign consumption.*

It would appear, likewise, from the following complaint,
taken from the city records, that there is some *spirit sold,*
and consequently *drank,* in the Holy City.

"To John C. Bennett, Mayor of the City of Nauvoo.

"Respected Sir, —
"I have complaints to make, against the following individuals, for selling *spirituous liquors*, contrary to the laws of this city, viz. : — John McIlwrick and Ebenezer Jennings.
"John McIlwrick, for retailing whisky to Margaret Robinson, on the twenty-first of April, 1842. Witnesses, — Alice Martin and Lucy Clayton.
"Ebenezer Jennings, for retailing whisky, on the seventeenth of March, 1842. Witness, — Mary Hardman.
"*I am sorry to see the* DRUNKENNESS *that has* of late manifested itself *in our city*, and for one would rejoice to see it put to an end. *Cases are almost daily occurring ;* but, *for want of time*, I am not able to obtain the necessary evidence. The above cases are collected, merely to show to the individuals concerned, that people are aware of their transgression of the laws; and if the law is put in force upon them, I am in hopes that it will serve as a warning and restraint for the future.   Yours, with respect,
                                   "William Clayton.
"Nauvoo City, *May* 9, 1842."

When liars, black-hearted liars, — such as the holy trio, Smith, Law, and Taylor, — are so barefaced as to challenge the records, their refuge of lies shall not cover them.

"Because ye have said, We have made a covenant with death, and with hell are we at agreement : when the overflowing scourge shall pass through, it shall not come unto us : for we have made lies our refuge, and under falsehood have we hid ourselves." — *Isaiah* 28 : 15.
"And your covenant with death shall be annulled, and your agreement with hell shall not stand; when the overflowing scourge shall pass through, then shall ye be trodden down by it." — *Isaiah* 28 : 18.

It is very evident, from the above, that these pretended men of God, who speak as they are " moved by the Holy Ghost," are not in all cases to be depended upon, even when they make careful and deliberate statements through their public newspaper, the acknowledged organ of their Church, and the frequent medium of their inspired communications to the world. Is it not plain, that even the Prophet can sometimes be *mistaken* in his assertions, even if we acquit him of the guilt of lying, by supposing that he is ignorant of the notorious facts we have quoted?
It would also seem that the Holy City of Nauvoo is not quite so pure and inoffensive a place as has been represented; but that, on the contrary, whatever may be the moral

professions made, the practice does not altogether conform thereto ; and that there is almost as much depravity as is commonly found in a Gentile city of the same size.

JOE'S BANKRUPT APPLICATION.

The Bankrupt law, section 2, provides that no conveyances of property shall be made in contemplation of bankruptcy, subsequent to the 1st of January, 1841; and an Act concerning Religious Societies, under which the Mormon Church was incorporated, provides for the appointment of TRUSTEES, not a SOLE TRUSTEE IN TRUST, who are authorized "to purchase a quantity of land not exceeding five acres," &c. &c.   See act approved Feb. 6, 1835.

From a Book of Mortgages and Bonds, page 95.

" CITY OF NAUVOO, Hancock Co., Illinois, }
                        February 2, A. D. 1842. }
    " To the County Recorder of the county of Hancock :
" Dear Sir, —
        " At a meeting of the ' Church of Latter Day Saints ' at this place, on Saturday the 30th day of January, A. D. 1841, I was elected *sole Trustee* for said Church, to hold my office *during life,* (my successor to be the First Presidency of said Church,) and vested with *plenary powers* as *sole Trustee* in Trust for the Church of Jesus Christ of Latter Day Saints, to receive, acquire, manage and convey property, real, personal, or mixed, for the sole use and benefit of said Church, agreeable to the provisions of an act entitled 'An Act concerning Religious Societies,' approved February 6, 1835.
                        " JOSEPH SMITH, [L. S.] "

" STATE OF ILLINOIS, } ss.
    Hancock County, }
        " This day personally appeared before me, Daniel H. Wells, a justice of the peace, within and for the county of Hancock aforesaid, Isaac Galland, Robert B. Thompson, and John C. Bennett, who, being duly sworn, depose and say that the foregoing certificate of Joseph Smith is true.
                        " ISAAC GALLAND,
                        " R. B. THOMPSON,
                        " JOHN C. BENNETT.

" Sworn to and subscribed this third day of February, in the year of our Lord one thousand eight hundred and forty-one, before me,
            " DANIEL H WELLS, *Justice of the Peace.*"

Compendious Extracts from the Records of Hancock County.

"In book R, page 21, there is a deed from Joseph Smith and wife to Julia M. Smith, Joseph Smith, Jr., F. G. W. Smith, and Alexander Smith, (the first an adopted daughter, and the remainder all small children of Joseph and Emma Smith,) executed December 21, 1841, and recorded January 1, 1842, for lots 1, 2, 3, and 4, block 12, in the city of Nauvoo, — for the consideration of ' *one hundred dollars* to them in hand paid,'— property worth about three thousand dollars.

"Another in the same book, p. 151, from the same to the same, (Joseph Smith and wife to their children,) executed March 17, 1842, and recorded April 9, 1842, for the east half of south-east 31, 5 north, 8 west; and west half of north-west 5, and east half of north-east 6, 4 north, 8 west — for the consideration of two thousand dollars.

"Another in the same book, (R,) pages 159, 160, and 161, from Joseph Smith and wife to Joseph Smith, *as sole Trustee in trust for the Church of Jesus Christ of Latter Day Saints,* executed October 5, 1841, and recorded April 18, 1842, (*the same day he visited Carthage to file his schedule for — bankruptcy,* and I have no doubt the deed was executed on the 16th, 17th, 18th, or 19th of April, 1842, and ante-dated to October 5, 1841, for so Joe informed me, and Dr. Marshall, Esquire Sherman, and others, of Carthage, stated that the writing was *fresh,* and *changed materially in appearance soon after ;* and on the 7th of July, 1842, Calvin A. Warren, Esq., one of Joe's Attorneys in Bankruptcy, acknowledged to Dr. Marshall, the County Clerk, and myself, in the Clerk's Office, that the deed was executed in April, '42, and not in October, '41, as aforesaid, but that he was not privy to the fraud) — for (230) two hundred and thirty lots, or thereabouts, mostly in the ' White Purchase,' for the consideration of the sum of ONE DOLLAR to them in hand paid, on a just and lawful settlement between themselves in person, and the Church of Jesus Christ of Latter Day Saints, — Property worth from *one hundred and fifty to two hundred and thirty thousand dollars,* at the rate that Joe is selling it — *from five to fifteen hundred dollars a lot.*

"Another in book I, page 329, from Ebenezer F. Wiggins to Emma Smith, executed May 15, 1841, and recorded June 30, 1841, for west half of north-west quarter 30, 7 north, 8 west, and the west half of north-east 30, 7 north, 8 west, for the consideration of ($2,700) two thousand seven hundred dollars, — paid for by Joe, and worth about three thousand dollars.

"Another in the same book, (I,) page 243, from Daniel H. Wells and wife to Joseph Smith, Jr., (Joe's son,) executed May 5, 1841, and recorded May 6, 1841, for lots 1 and 4, block 22, in Wells's addition to Nauvoo, for the consideration of one hundred dollars.

"Another in the same book, page 354, from Robert B. Thompson and wife to Emma Smith, (Joe's wife,) executed July 24, 1841, and recorded July 27, 1841, for south-east fractional quarter of section 2, 6 north, 9 west, containing 123 43-100 acres, for the consideration of ($4,000) four thousand dollars.

9

" Another in same book, page 355, from same to Frederick G. W. Smith, (Joe's son,) executed July 24, 1841, and recorded July 27, 1841, for part of block 156, in Nauvoo, for the consideration of ($500) five hundred dollars."

If an official certificate is required, call upon Chauncey Robinson, Esq., the Recorder of Hancock, and he will certify that these are correct extracts from the county records. There are various other matters of record that could be made to operate against this king of swindlers and impostors, Joe Smith; but I presume that the foregoing will be sufficient to give him a comfortable home in the State Penitentiary, at Alton, for some years to come, if Missouri does not get him first.

If oral testimony is required, call upon General George W. Robinson, Colonel Francis M. Higbee, and others, who are acquainted with the transactions. Call out these witnesses in relation to the SHAM sales of valuable property made to Apostle Willard Richards, and Bishop N. K. Whitney, and others, by Joe, in order to prepare for the bankruptcy. The Hotchkiss Purchase, CALLED Church property, — but which is not paid for, — was given in by Joe in his schedule as his *own* individual property, which it undoubtedly was; but the White Purchase (south-east fractional quarter of section 2, 6 north, 9 west,) WHICH IS PAID FOR, was deeded to Thompson, Joe's clerk, who had no property, and from Thompson to Emma Smith, (Joe's wife,) and from Joseph Smith and wife to Joseph Smith, SOLE TRUSTEE IN TRUST, &c.

Remember that the White Purchase was CALLED Church property, but it was and is Joe's own individual estate. He said in a public congregation in Nauvoo, a few weeks ago, "I own a million of dollars in property, in this city and around it." Can this swindler take the benefit of the bankrupt law! Never! No, never!! Let a prosecution be at once instituted against his Holiness, and let the law have its just operations ONCE.

I shall now give the testimony of the Messrs. Kilbourns, of Iowa, in relation to Joe's swindling operations in Iowa lands.

From the Hawk-Eye and Patriot, October 7, 1841.

" It is generally known, that a tract of land, containing 119,000 acres, lying in the extreme southern part of our Territory, which from its form, — bounded as it is on the east by the Mississippi, and on the south and west by the Des Moines River, — may not inaptly be termed the Delta of Iowa, was in 1824 reserved by treaty for the use of the ' Half Breeds of the Sac and Fox Nation of Indians ; they holding it by the same title that other Indian lands are held,' — i. e. possession, — the United States retaining a reversionary interest, or the right to purchase it. In June, 1834, Congress relinquished to the ' Half-Breeds of the Sac and Fox Nation of Indians ' this reversionary interest, and authorized them to transfer their portions thereof by sale, devise, or descent.

" By an unaccountable oversight, the names of the individuals intended to be benefited by this reservation of land, were neither introduced into the treaty nor in the act of Congress alluded to, and the term ' Half Breeds ' of the Sac and Fox Nation was so indefinite, that a wide door was at once opened for the introduction of spurious and doubtful claims, and from forty or fifty in number, they soon increased to one hundred and sixty.

" In the summer and fall of 1836, a company of gentlemen from New York made extensive purchases of Half Breed shares. On account of the intimate knowledge that Doctor Galland was supposed to have of the ' Half Breeds,' he was admitted as a member of this company, and was constituted one of their five trustees. Their confidence, however, in his integrity was of short duration, and as a majority of the trustees controlled the affairs of the company, his power to injure *them* was of short continuance.

" In the winter of 1837–8, a law was passed for the partition of the Half Breed tract; commissioners were appointed to receive testimony, &c.; the succeeding legislature, however, repealed the law, and left the matter, if possible, worse than before. Every attempt that had been made to adjust the title, had not only signally failed, but seemed to increase the difficulties that clustered around it, and the public mind had settled down into the conviction that any further effort of the kind would be entirely fruitless.

" The ingenuity of Doctor Galland, however, found, in this state of things, a fine field for the exercise of his peculiar talents ; and in the year 1839, he matured the plan of a *stupendous fraud.* He wrote to Joe Smith, — who was then most righteously imprisoned in Missouri, on charges of *High Treason, Burglary, Arson,* &c. &c., — inviting him to purchase his land at Nauvoo, — 47 acres. — Smith, after making his escape, complied, and brought on his half-starved followers, a large number of whom settled on the ' Half Breed Reserve ' in Iowa. Doctor G. then commenced selling Half Breed lands, giving therefor *warrantee* deeds, which of course could convey no title while the lands remained undivided. He at first asserted that he was the owner of seven tenths of the tract, and finally claimed to be the *sole proprietor.*

" That he might the more successfully carry out the scheme of swindling thus commenced, he attached himself to the Mormon

Church! became a confederate of Joe Smith, and in order to dupe persons daily arriving among them, he deeded to Mormon *Bishops* and *Prophets*, thousands and *tens of thousands* of acres of the reservation alluded to, and they are daily deeding by warrantee deeds the lands thus acquired, and receiving therefor a valuable consideration.

" By a recent judicial decision it is ascertained that the interest to which this man Galland is entitled, is but a small, undefined, undivided portion of the Half Breed reservation.

" Our object is not so much to draw the portrait of Galland, — for his character is too well known to require an extended notice here, — as to show the connection between him and the swindling leaders of the Mormon society. With a full knowledge of all the facts here stated, he is sent out with a ' Proclamation to the Saints abroad — Greeting;' signed by Joseph Smith, Sidney Rigdon, and Hyrum Smith, — the two *latter* of whom, the Times and Seasons informs us, ' have been appointed, by revelation, Prophets, Seers, and Revelators,' — in which it is said that ' he (Galland) is the honored instrument the Lord used to prepare a home for us when we were driven from our inheritance, *having given him control of vast bodies of land, and prepared his heart to make the use of it the Lord intended he should.*'

" Many instances might be mentioned of individuals at the east, who have exchanged with the ' Agents of the Church ' their valuable possessions for these worthless land titles, and there are cases of suffering, of families reduced to beggary, by these villains, which would cause them, were they other than the heartless wretches they are, to relent, and desist from their cruel purpose.

" Do these Prophets share in the plunder ? If the reader has thrown the mantle of charity over them thus far, it will require enlarging to cover a pretended ' revelation ' upon matters and things in general, published in their paper of June 1, in which — speaking of the Nauvoo Boarding House — the following passage occurs : ' Let my servant, Isaac Galland, put stock in that house, for I the Lord *loveth* him for the works he has done, and will forgive *all* his sins, therefore let him be remembered for an interest in that house from generation to generation.'

" When it is known that one of these Prophets acts in the absence of Galland as his Agent for the sale of these lands, what further evidence, we ask, is wanted of the baseness and rascality of himself and his confederates ?   " D. W. Kilbourn,
                                          " Edward Kilbourn.

" Montrose, Iowa, *October* 6, 1841."

From the Hawk-Eye and Patriot of October 14, 1841.

" It is perhaps unnecessary to say that in these numbers it is not our purpose to enter into any controversy with the ' Mormons ' relevant to their religious belief. It is sufficiently humiliating to be compelled, by a strong sense of duty, to expose their *nefarious conduct.* Confining ourselves strictly to *facts*, we shall leave them for others to draw their own inferences. That there may be no misapprehension as to the individuals meant, we shall freely make use of their names, and should injustice be done them, they can resort to their legal remedy, assuring them that if a single statement of ours is denied, we stand prepared to establish its truth by a host of witnesses.

" In a previous number we gave a brief history of the ' Half Breed Reservation,' and stated that ' a company of New York gentlemen made extensive purchases of Half Breed claims.' The same gentlemen, by their agents, were placed in possession of the barracks at Camp Des Moines, on their abandonment by the United States dragoons in June, 1837, and soon after caused a town to be surveyed, to which the name of ' Montrose ' was given, and the name of the post-office was changed, at the request of the citizens, from ' Fort Des Moines ' to ' Montrose.'

" In addition to the numerous difficulties surrounding the ' Half Breed title,' an old ' Spanish claim ' was raked up from the oblivion of a former age, and a patent issued in 1839 to the claimants under it for a tract of land one mile square, including the town site of Montrose.

" The gentlemen in possession, however, having ' nine points of the law ' in their favor, could, of course, hold the premises against the world, till a final adjudication of the whole matter. This the ' Spanish claimants ' well knew, and recognized them as being in peaceable possession by instituting suit in our courts, which is still pending.

" The parties interested flattered themselves that when *their* conflicting claims should be settled, all obstacles to the improvement of the place, and its becoming — what, from the beauty of its situation, it was intended for by nature — a large and flourishing town, would be removed; but, alas! how vain and delusive are all human hopes and expectations. A *third* claimant appears in the person of Joe Smith, with a title purporting to be *Heaven derived.* Early one morning in March last, the quiet citizens of Montrose were surprised by a visit from some of Joe Smith's scullions from Nauvoo,— who to all appearance had but recently made their escape from a steel trap,— headed by Alanson Ripley, a Mormon *Bishop,* who says that ' *as to the technical niceties of the law of the land, he does not intend to regard them ; that the kingdom spoken of by the prophet Daniel has been set up, and that it is necessary every kingdom should be governed by its own laws.*' With compass and chain they strided through gates and over fences to the very doors of the ' Gentiles,' and drove the stakes for the lots of a city which, in extent at least,— four miles square,— should vie with some of the largest cities of the world. They heeded not enclosures; why should they? is not the earth the Lord's, and the fulness thereof? and shall not his ' Saints ' — of the Latter Day — inherit and possess it forever?

" ' The kingdom spoken of by the prophet Daniel ' having been set up, its ' laws ' authorized this Mormon Bishop to threaten personal violence to one of the undersigned, for removing a stake which had been driven within the bounds of his enclosure, without

9 *

his consent and contrary to his wishes, and to hold a club over the head of Mr. A. M. Bissell, while one of his 'steel trap' comrades drove a stake within the enclosure of Mr. Bissell, directly before his door, after having been forbidden by him to do so.

"A few days subsequently to these occurrences, it was ascertained that the exterior line of this 'four mile' town had been run by order of Joe Smith, and a plot of it made and recorded, to which he gave the name of Zarahemla.

"And who figures as proprietor of this renowned city? Joe Smith, to be sure, ' the Agent of Doctor Galland,' — a worthy agent for a worthy principal!

"Having sold to his dupes a large portion of the Half Breed tract, a happy thought strikes him that they can yet be 'bled;' he orders them by 'revelation' to leave their fine farms and move into the 'city,' sells them lots and conveys them by deeds. There would be some excuse for these proceedings had they taken place under any color of title, but he had not the shadow of a shade to found a right upon. In this view of the case, was there ever a more barefaced attempt at swindling than this?

"On the 6th of April, at a conference held at Nauvoo, a Mormon leader publicly read a pretended 'revelation' that the city of Zarahemla should be laid out and built up by the 'Latter Day Saints!' Joe Smith then stated that, 'in accordance with this revelation,' a city had been surveyed, and the Saints desirous of purchasing lots could now do so. 'The people over there,' said he, 'are very much opposed to it, but they must know — if they know any thing — that it would be for their interest to have 5000 inhabitants come in with back loads of money; why, I sometimes think they don't know beans when the bag is open; they needn't be scared; we don't want their improvements without paying them for them; we expect to pay them a good price for their possessions, and if that don't satisfy them, we'll have them any how.'

"Are the people of Iowa prepared to submit to such treatment from an Impostor as vile as ever disgraced humanity? Are we to be told that 'if you choose to sell, we will buy your possessions, if not, we will have them any how'? Is the title to land hereafter to be settled by revelation through Joe Smith? Has the time indeed arrived when 'the kingdom is to be set up by forcible means if necessary,' and when the riches of the Gentiles are to be consecrated to the true Israel? Such were the teachings of the leaders of this society in Missouri, and the facts here stated show conclusively that such are their teachings and practices now.

"Have we not some reason to believe that their Missouri troubles were not solely for righteousness' sake, but that they there, as here, disregarded all law, human and divine, and by their conduct brought down upon their own heads the vengeance of an outraged and insulted people? Robbery and theft with them are called 'consecrating the property of the Gentiles.' Since the publication of the second number of these articles, we were called from home by business, and during our absence our store was broken open in the early part of the evening of Wednesday, the 6th inst., before the young man who slept in the store retired for the night, and robbed of goods to the amount of between three and four hundred dollars, to wit:

42 pieces dark prints, (entire,)
5 or 6   "   "   satinets,
1   "   black circassian,

and a considerable quantity of cambric book muslins, jaconet, sarsenet, &c. &c. This stands on our list as robbery No. 14.

" The undersigned, however, are not the *only* sufferers; this our ' Gentile ' neighbors know by sad experience. The four wheels of a new farm wagon were stolen from the yard of Harman Booth, Esq., a few nights since; and the week previous, all the tools of the blacksmith shop of Mr. S. H. Burtis, with a fine two-horse wagon, were taken. Is it not a singular fact that the enclosures of the ' Gentiles,' and their buildings even, are entered, and property stolen, while the wagons and farming utensils of these ' *Latter Day* Saints ' stand exposed in the open street, far from any dwelling, and yet are perfectly secure ?

" Why is it that those who oppose this swindle are the principal, if not the only, sufferers ?

" D. W. Kilbourn,
" Edward Kilbourn

" Montrose, Iowa, *October* 13, 1841."

THE BOOK OF MORMON — ITS ORIGIN, AND THE EVIDENCE OF ITS TRUTH.

In this article, likewise, I shall extract from the works of Harris and Howe, and that of Professor J. B. Turner, of Illinois College, Jacksonville.

" Our first point respects the character and credibility of Joseph Smith, Jr., who announces himself, on the title-page of the first edition of the Book of Mormon, as ' *the* AUTHOR *and* PROPRIETOR ' of that work.

" We cannot conceive how any man of common sense could ever have imagined that God, or any other being, except Joe Smith, was either the author or proprietor of such a book. The only difficulty is, to see how God can be responsible for a work of which Joseph Smith is ' *Author and Proprietor;* ' and one ground on which such a claim must be sustained, is the admitted excellence and trustworthiness of Joseph Smith's moral character.

" We admit that a man may have great faults, and still be not only worthy of credit, but an.*accredited* and appropriate agent of the, Most High.

" All the ancient worthies, who spake as they were moved by the Holy Ghost, were frail and sinful men, like ourselves; still they became the approved and *accredited* messengers of God.

" We admit, also, that God often chooses ' the weak things of the world to confound the wise;' and that want of mere worldly talent, acquirement, or genius, is therefore no insuperable objection to the credibility of a prophet of the Lord.

" Still, we contend that God never has, and never will, choose a character notoriously weak, silly, profane, and rotten in all its parts, to deliver a new dispensation of his will to man.

" *What, then, was the* NOTORIOUS CHARACTER *of Joseph Smith* BEFORE, AND AT THE TIME *of the writing of the Book of Mormon?*" — *Mormonism in all Ages, by J. B. Turner,* pp. 150, 151.

" THE TESTIMONY OF THREE WITNESSES.

" ' Be it known unto all nations, kindreds, tongues, and peoples, unto whom this work shall come, that we, through the grace of God the Father, and our Lord Jesus Christ, have seen the plates which contain this record, which is a record of the people of Nephi, and also of the Lamanites, his brethren, and also of the people of Jared, which came from the tower of which hath been spoken; and we also know that they have been translated by the *gift and power of God, for his voice hath declared it unto us.* Wherefore we know of a surety that the work is true.

" ' And we also testify that we have seen the engravings, which are upon the plates, and they have been shown unto us by the *power of God,* and not of man. And we declare, with words of soberness, that an angel of God came from heaven, and he brought and laid before our eyes, that we beheld and saw the plates and the engravings thereon. And we know that it is by the grace of God the Father, and our Lord Jesus Christ, that we beheld, and bear record that these things are true : and it is marvellous in our eyes. Nevertheless, the *voice of the Lord commanded us* that we should bear record of it. Wherefore, to be obedient unto the commandments of God, we bear testimony to these things; and we know that if we are faithful in Christ we shall rid our garments of the blood of all men, and be found spotless before the judgment-seat of Christ, and shall dwell with him eternally in the heavens. And the honor be to the Father, and to the Son, and to the Holy Ghost, which is one God. Amen,

" ' OLIVER COWDERY,
" ' DAVID WHITMER,
" ' MARTIN HARRIS.'

" The reader is requested to notice particularly the words in Italics. One would indeed think, that if honest men had heard and seen such marvels, they ought, at least, themselves to have believed it through life, and lived accordingly, as the apostles did." — *Mormonism in all Ages, by J. B. Turner*, pp. 164, 165.

"As regards *the capacity* of the witnesses, the reader is referred to a revelation given, June, 1829, through Joseph Smith, to these three identical witnesses the year before they appended their names to the Book of Mormon, which we will transcribe.

"'Revelation to Oliver Cowdery, David Whitmer, and Martin Harris, given through Joseph Smith, June, 1829, *previous* to their viewing the plates containing the Book of Mormon.'

"1. 'Behold, I say unto you, that *you must rely upon my word;* which if you do *with full purpose of heart*, you shall have a view of the plates, and also of the breastplate, the sword of Laban, the Urim and Thummim, which were given to the brother of Jared, upon the mount, when he talked with the Lord face to face, and the miraculous directors, which were given to Lehi in the wilderness, on the borders of the Red Sea; and it is *by your faith* you shall *obtain a view* of them, even by that faith which was had by the prophets of old.'

"2. 'And after you *have obtained faith*, and have seen them with your eyes, *you shall testify of them by the power of God;* and this you shall do, that *my servant, Joseph Smith, Jr., may not be destroyed*, that I may bring about my righteous purposes unto the children of men in this work. *And ye shall testify that you have seen them, even as* my servant Joseph Smith, Jr., *has seen them;* for it is *by my power* he hath seen them, and it is because *he had faith.* And HE HAS TRANSLATED THE BOOK, even that part which I have commanded him, and AS YOUR LORD AND YOUR GOD LIVETH, IT IS TRUE.'

"3. 'Wherefore you HAVE received the *same power*, and the *same faith*, and the *same gift, like unto him.* And if you do *these last commandments* of mine, which I have given you, the gates of hell shall not prevail against you; for my grace is sufficient for you; and you shall be lifted up in the last day. And I, Jesus Christ, your Lord and your God, have spoken it unto you, that I might bring about my righteous purposes unto the children of men. *Amen.*'

"A revelation given to Martin Harris, by Smith, March, 1829, also contains the identical words paraded forth to the world in the testimony of the three witnesses.

"Verse 5. 'And then shall he (Harris) say unto the people of this generation : Behold, I have seen the things which the Lord hath shown to Joseph Smith, Jr., and *I know of a surety that they are true, for they have been shown unto me by the power of God, and not of man*, and these are the words he shall say,' &c.

"*The voice of the Lord*, then, it seems, which informed the witnesses that Smith had translated the plates, and caused them *to know of a surety that they are true*, and commanded them to bear record of it, in 1830, in the Book of Mormon — this same voice came to them through the mouth of the Lord's Prophet, Smith, in March and June preceding, that is, in 1829.

" They are told in this revelation that they should obtain a view of the plates, or see them, not with their natural eyes, but with those spiritual eyes of faith with which the Mormons see so many marvels, viz., by the ' eye of faith, even by that faith which was had by the prophets of old.' This accords with the admissions of Martin Harris, who expressly stated that he did not see the plates with his natural eyes, but with ' the eye of faith.'

" Here, then, is the ' mighty power of God, the angel, and voice of the Lord,' which revealed such marvels in 1830, all concentrated in the person, and pouring from the mouth, of the Lord's Prophet in 1829.

" Was there ever impudence and stupidity like this? Why did the dunce publish that revelation to the world, especially since he has retained in his own hands, to this day, hundreds of others equally inspired? Was it for the express purpose of disclosing his own impudence and knavery? Or was it (as he himself once remarked to Peter Ingersoll) to see what the ' d——d fools would believe' ?

" But after all, these witnesses of inspiration did not testify to one half that Smith's divinity commanded them to declare. They were so absorbed in their visions and golden dreams about the plates, that they forgot to testify, as commanded, of the 'breastplate,' the ' sword of Laban,' the ' Urim and Thummim,' the miraculous ' directors,' &c. &c. Perhaps this negligence was the reason that the said divinity gave them all over to subsequent unbelief and hardness of heart, to work all kind of abominations, and be ' guilty of all manner of debaucheries,' as the Prophet assures us is the fact.

" Their CAPACITY as witnesses, then, to say nothing of their honesty, amounts simply to this — Joe Smith puts the words of the Lord into their mouths, in 1829, and they repeat a part of the same to the world in 1830. Surely, if the Prophet, in his pious rebuke of his witnesses, had only thought to have referred to this transaction, he might not only have called them ' knaves and asses,' but proved them such. Doubtless he thought the world would take his inspired testimony to the fact, without logical proof; we only supply the proof, without questioning the fact." — Mormonism in all Ages, by J. B. Turner, pp. 172—175.

" The sublime testimony of the second phalanx of eight witnesses is as follows : —

" ' Be it known unto all nations, kindreds, tongues, and people, unto whom this work shall come, that Joseph Smith, Jr., AUTHOR and PROPRIETOR (! !) of this work, has shown unto us the plates, of which hath been spoken, which have the appearance of gold ; and as many leaves as the said Smith has translated, we did handle with our hands, and we saw the engravings thereon, all of which has the appearance of ancient work and of curious workmanship. And this we bear record, with words of soberness, that the said Smith has shown unto us, for we have seen, and hefted, and know of a surety, that the said Smith has got the plates of which we have spoken.

And we give our names unto the world, to witness unto the world that which we have seen, and we lie not, God bearing witness of it.

"'Christian Whitmer,
"'Jacob Whitmer,
"'Peter Whitmer, Jr.,
"'John Whitmer,
"'Hiram Page, brother-in-law of the Whitmers,
"'Joseph Smith, Sen.,
"'Hyrum Smith,
"'Samuel H. Smith.'

"By turning to the same revelation, quoted above, the reader will again see how this second platoon of witnesses 'hefted,' and 'knew of a surety,' that the said Smith had the plates 'of which hath been spoken.' It is Joe Smith, thought, style, and all, from a to izzard. And what does it all prove? First, that Joe Smith is author and proprietor of the Book of Mormon, as all the world knows. Second, that they saw and 'hefted' some plates shown them by Smith. What if they did? How did they know what or how many plates Smith had translated, when, by their own confession, they could not read a word on any of them? Joe Smith told them so. And this is all their testimony amounts to, on the face of it, by their own showing. We are not only willing, but anxious to admit that Smith did show some plates, of some sort; and that they actually testify to the truth, so far as they were capable of knowing it, we are not only willing, but anxious to admit, in order to keep up a just and charitable equilibrium between the knaves and fools, in Mormonism and the world at large. Three to eight is at once a happy and reasonable proportion. We will not disturb it. It is gratifying to human philanthropy to be able to account for all the facts in the case by this charitable solution.

"Three of these witnesses, we are boastingly told, died in the faith; and we should naturally have expected that any man who could have been induced to set his name to such a silly paper as that is, would have died in almost any faith. The only thing that looks strange about it is, that all the rest, except the brothers of the Prophet, have had sense enough to apostatize and leave the Church, (with proper discipline, of course.) Perhaps it is well for the world, and well for these three, that they did not live to go the same way with all the rest, and fall with Harris into 'all manner of abominations.'

"The whole, then, of this mighty array of bombast, nonsense, and blasphemy, resolves itself into this : —

"Joe Smith is not only author and proprietor of the Book of Mormon, as both he and his witnesses declare, but he is also 'power of God,' 'angel,' 'voice,' 'faith,' 'eyes,' ears and hands for the witnesses themselves; that is, all the evidence the world has for the Book of Mormon, after all this bluster, is 'Joe Smith's say so.' He says that God instructs him, he instructs the witnesses,

and the witnesses instruct the world. *Quod erat demonstrandum.*
David Whitmer reported that the angel, which appeared unto him,
' was like a man in gray clothes, having his throat cut.' This was
probably a prophetic vision, indicating the true desert of the real
author.

" In further elucidation of what Mormons mean by the ' power of
God,' the reader is referred to the Book of Mormon, pp. 420, 421;
the Book of Covenants, p. 102, v. 12—173, v. 5. It will there be
seen that this voice and power of God is a small affair, which every
enthusiast can have, and see at any time he pleases, especially if
Smith is at hand.

" Since, then, we are obliged, after all, to take Joe's word, simply,
for his new Bible, it may be interesting to the world to know how
he was enabled to translate it, out of the Reformed Egyptian, into
' *patent* English.' He has told us that he looked into his stone
spectacles, and saw the words pass before his mind. But he informs
us more explicitly still, in the famous book of Revelations and
Covenants, in which, after all, it must be candidly admitted, that
the Lord has clearly revealed some things — at least one, and that
is the KNAVERY OF JOE SMITH.

" If the reader will turn to the revelation given by Smith to O.
Cowdery, in Harmony, Pennsylvania, April, 1829, while translating
the Gold Bible, (see Book of Covenants, 110,) he will perceive
that Oliver's faith had begun to fail. He had got tired of writing
the gibberish of Smith, and needed a word of exhortation and encouragement. Smith's divinity gives him both, of course, and also,
to pacify him, grants him the gift to translate, ' even as my servant
Joseph,' (verse 11.) At this, it appears that Oliver took courage,
put on the spectacles, planted himself in due order, before the mystic plates, and looked with all his might, but saw nothing. Oliver,
of course, becomes more uneasy and intractable than ever. He
complains more than before, and with more reason too. And now,
for a new revelation, of the same date, *pat* upon the other, which
contained the grant of the gift to Oliver to translate.

" We will quote a verse or two of this revelation from Smith's
' unchanging Deity.' Verse 2, page 162: ' Be patient, my son Oliver, for it is wisdom in me, and it is not expedient that you should
translate *at this present time.* Behold, the work you are called to do
is *to write for my servant Joseph.* And behold, it is because you did
not continue, as you commenced, when you began to translate, that
I have taken away this privilege from you. Do not murmur, my
son, for it is wisdom in me that I have dealt with you after this
manner.' (Undoubtedly!!)

" Verse 3: ' Behold, you have not understood. You have supposed that I would *give it unto you,* when *you took no thought save
it was to ask me.* But behold, I say unto you, YOU MUST STUDY IT
OUT IN YOUR OWN MIND. (!) Then you must ask me if it be right;
and *if it is right,* I will cause that YOUR BOSOM SHALL BURN *within
you.* THEREFORE (!!) you shall FEEL that it is RIGHT. But
if it is *not* right, you shall have no such feelings; but you shall
have a STUPOR of *thought,* that shall cause you to *forget* the thing

which is *wrong*. THEREFORE (! !) you cannot write that which is *sacred*, save it be given you from me.' 2d ed.

" Here, in the first place, we see that Smith's Divinity found it expedient ' *to deviate a little*,' and retract the divinity-given gift conferred the same day.

" In the second, we have his patent divine prescription for writing *things sacred*, in detail ; and, of course, the method which Smith has followed in translating his Bible, and giving his other revelations to the world. He ' STUDIED IT OUT IN HIS OWN MIND,' and when he got it right, ' *his bosom burned*,' of course. With this patent recipe before him, we see not why any man might not translate, or give revelations, as well as Smith, unless he was afflicted with that unaccountable *stupor of thought*, which seems to unfit all other Mormons for the work, except Smith. Perhaps, if brother Cowdery should try his hand at it now, since he has had wit enough to leave the Mormons, he would succeed in raising the needful heat better than before.

" Those in other churches, who are in the habit of practising upon the same principle, would do well to commit Smith's rule to memory, since it accurately describes the process of securing miraculous confirmations of any known or imagined truth."

Mormonism in all Ages, by J. B. Turner, pp. 177—181.

From Mormonism Portrayed, by Rev. Wm. Harris.

" The Book of Mormon, which may be said to be at the foundation of Mormonism, was first published in the year 1830. Since that period, its believers and advocates have propagated its doctrines and absurdities, with a zeal worthy of a better cause. Through every State of the Union, and in Canada, the Apostles of this wild delusion have disseminated its principles, and duped hundreds to believe it true — they have crossed the ocean, and, in England, if their own accounts may be credited, have made thousands of converts ; and recently some of their missionaries have even been sent to Palestine. Such strenuous exertions having been, and still being made, to propagate the doctrines of this book, and such fruits having already appeared from the labors of its friends, it becomes a matter of some interest, to investigate its origin and claims.

" The Book of Mormon purports to be the record, or history, of a certain people, who inhabited America, previous to its discovery by Columbus. This people, according to it, were the descendants of one Lehi, who crossed the ocean, from the eastern continent, to this. Their history and records, containing prophecies and revelations, were engraven, by the command of God, on small plates, and deposited in the hill Comora, which appears to be situated in Western New York. Thus was preserved an account of this race, (together with their religious creed,) up to the period when the descendants of Laman, Lemuel, and Sam, who were the three eldest sons of Lehi, arose and destroyed the descendants of Nephi, who was the youngest son. From this period, the descendants of the eldest sons ' dwindled in unbelief,' and ' became a dark, loathsome, and filthy people.' The last-mentioned are our present Indians.

10

"The plates above mentioned remained in their depository until about the year 1825, when, as the Mormons say, they were found by Joseph Smith, Jr., who was directed in the discovery by the Angel of the Lord. On these plates were certain hieroglyphics, said to be of the Egyptian character, which Smith, by the direction of God, being instructed by inspiration, as to their meaning, proceeded to translate. This translation is the work which I propose now to examine.

"It will be here proper to remark, that a narrative so extraordinary as that contained in the Book of Mormon, translated from hieroglyphics, of which even the most learned have but a limited knowledge, and that, too, by an ignorant youth, who pretended to no other knowledge of the characters, than what he derived from inspiration, requires more than ordinary evidence to substantiate it. It will be my purpose therefore, in the remainder of this chapter, to inquire into the nature and degree of testimony which has been given to the world, to substantiate the claims of this extraordinary book.

"In the first place, the existence of the plates themselves has, ever since their alleged discovery, been in dispute. To this point it would be extremely easy to give some proof, by making an exhibition of them to the world. If they are so ancient as they are claimed to be, and designed for the purpose of transmitting the history of a people, and if they have laid for ages, deposited in the earth, their appearance would certainly indicate the fact. What evidence, then, have we of the existence of these plates? Why, none other than the mere dictum of Smith himself, and the certificates of eleven other individuals, who say that they have seen them; and upon this testimony we are required to believe this most extraordinary narrative, and are threatened with eternal punishment for not believing it.

"Now, even admitting, for the sake of argument, that these witnesses are all honest and credible men, yet what would be easier than for Smith to deceive them? Could he not easily procure plates to be made, and inscribe thereon a set of characters, no matter what, and then exhibit them to his intended witnesses as genuine? What would be easier than thus to impose on their credulity and weakness? And if it were necessary to give them the appearance of antiquity, a chemical process could easily effect the matter. But I do not admit that these witnesses were honest; for six of them, after having made the attestation to the world that they had seen the plates, left the Church; thus contradicting that to which they had certified. And one of these witnesses, Martin Harris, who is frequently mentioned in the Book of Covenants — who was a High Priest of the Church — who was one of the most infatuated of Smith's followers — who even gave his property in order to procure the publication of the Book of Mormon, having afterwards left the Church, Smith, in speaking of him in connection with others, said that they were so far beneath contempt, that a notice of them would be too great a sacrifice for a gentleman to make.

"But what reason does Smith give for not exhibiting the plates to the world? The only reason that I have ever heard, is, that God has forbidden him; but at the same time directed that he should show them to the eleven witnesses above spoken of. Now, the foreknowledge of God has never been denied; and is it to be presumed that the Almighty would direct Smith to exhibit the plates to men whom he knew would prove traitors? and more especially to so contemptible a man as Harris is described to be? If these plates are of divine origin, the witnesses to them must be considered as the witnesses of God; but what idea could be more ridiculous, than to suppose that six, out of eleven witnesses, chosen by the Almighty, for his own purpose, should prove recreant? Yet this is not more absurd, than to suppose God would require mankind to believe a matter so out of the ordinary course of nature, as are many things recorded in the Book of Mormon, from the simple attestation of eleven men. How different, in this respect, is Mormonism from Christianity! Did Christ exhibit the evidence of his Divinity before his twelve apostles only? No! nearly every miracle that is recorded was performed in the presence of great multitudes. Did he ask mankind to believe that his mission was from above, merely because his twelve apostles said that they had evidence of it? No! but he exhibited the proof wherever he went, and gave such clear and incontestable evidence of its nature, even in the presence of his enemies, that they were every where confounded. Now, is it probable that God, in one age of the world, should give such convincing proof of the truth of his word, and in another age, require us to believe on the mere *ipse dixit* of but eleven men, and the moral characters of these equivocal, to say the best of them, and according to the general evidence, very bad?

"But admitting the plates to exist, and that they have certain hieroglyphics inscribed upon them, yet how are we to know that the Book of Mormon is a correct translation? Smith, at the time of the alleged translation, was a young man, totally ignorant of any language, except his mother tongue. There is no way, therefore, in which he could have arrived at a correct translation of the plates, unless by the aid of divine inspiration: indeed, the first certificate attached to the Book of Mormon, avers that it was translated 'by the gift and power of God.' Now, the first evidence to show that they really were translated by the 'gift and power of God,' would be to show that the book is a correct translation of the plates. This could easily be done, by submitting the plates to the inspection of learned men, and procuring their attestation to the fact. Has this ever been done? Not one of the men to whom the plates were alleged to have been shown, possessed any knowledge of the language in which they were said to have been written. How, then, could they tell whether the book was a correct translation? Why, only by the same means that Smith professed to translate it, — namely, by inspiration. Indeed, Oliver Cowdery, David Whitmer, and Martin Harris, in the first certificate attached to the Book of Mormon, claim to be inspired. Speaking of the translation, they say, 'It is marvellous in our eyes; nevertheless, the *voice of the Lord commanded us that we should bear record of it.*' Here it will be observed, that there are a number of men, all professing to be inspired, and they are the only evidence of each other's inspiration.

Does this not look like collusion? Smith says, ' I am inspired,' and these men say, ' We believe it, for we have the evidence of its truth, by inspiration.' This is something like thieves proving each other honest men.

" A further remark here. There are two certificates attached to the Book of Mormon; the second of which is signed by eight witnesses. Now, this certificate does not say one word about the book being translated through the aid of inspiration; it simply avers that Smith is the translator. The only evidence, therefore, which we have that Smith translated the book by the aid of inspiration, is the first certificate, signed by Martin Harris, Oliver Cowdery, and David Whitmer. Now, as to Harris, by Smith's own showing, he is too contemptible to be noticed by a gentleman; therefore we will lay him on the shelf. The other two, Cowdery and Whitmer, left the Church, renounced Mormonism, and contradicted what they had certified. Here, then, are but three witnesses on all the Mormon records, to prove Smith's inspiration, one of which is too contemptible to notice, and the others have discredited themselves.

" Some of the Mormons have said (I know not whether it comes from the heads of the Church) that a copy of the plates was presented to Professor Anthon, a gentleman standing in the first rank as a classical scholar, and he attested to the faithfulness of the translation of the Book of Mormon. Now, let us hear what the Professor himself has to say of this matter. In a letter recently written by him to the Rev. T. W. Coit, of New Rochelle, N. Y., he professes to make a plain statement of all he knows of the Mormons. In this letter he says, —

" ' Many years ago, — the precise date I do not now recollect, — a plain-looking countryman called upon me with a letter from Dr. Samuel L. Mitchell, requesting me to examine, and give my opinion upon a certain paper, marked with various characters, which the Doctor confessed he could not decipher, and which the bearer of the note was very anxious to have explained. A very brief examination of the paper, convinced me that it was a mere *hoax*, and a very clumsy one too. The characters were arranged in columns, like the Chinese mode of writing, and presented the most singular medley that I had ever beheld. Greek, Hebrew, and all sorts of letters, more or less distorted, either through unskilfulness or from actual design, were intermingled with sundry delineations of half moons, stars, and other natural objects, and the whole ended in a rude representation of the Mexican zodiac. The conclusion was irresistible, that some cunning fellow had prepared the paper in question for the purpose of imposing upon the countryman who brought it, and I told the man so without any hesitation. He then proceeded to give me the history of the whole affair, which convinced me that he had fallen into the hands of some sharper, while it left me in great astonishment at his own simplicity.'

" He also states that he gave his opinion in writing to this man, that ' the marks on the paper appeared to be merely an imitation of various alphabetic characters and had no meaning at all connected with them.'

The plain-looking countryman referred to, the Professor states, he believes to have been no other than the Prophet Smith himself; but the probability is, that it was Martin Harris. Here, then, is a beautiful illustration of what Mormonism really is — a mere *hoax*, designed to take advantage of the gullibility of mankind, and thus to aggrandize its author and his coadjutors.

  " The only evidence that has ever been received to prove the inspiration of an individual, is this, — that he possessed the power to work miracles; in other words, to do some act impossible, according to the established laws of nature.   Now, has Smith ever performed an act of this description ? True, if he establishes the fact incontrovertibly, that he discovered plates on which were engraved certain characters in the Egyptian, or any other ancient language, and that he, being unlettered, made a correct translation of them, — this indeed would be a miracle.   But neither of these facts is established; not even by the slightest testimony.   For the certificates of the witnesses do not state where, or how, Smith obtained the plates, but simply that an Angel came from heaven, and brought, and laid the plates before their (the witnesses') eyes, that they ' beheld and saw the *plates*, and the engravings thereon.'   There is, then, no evidence of where Smith obtained the plates, except his own dicta; neither is there any evidence of the nature of the characters alleged to have been written thereon.

  " As for any other miracles, although I have heard of Smith's having performed such, yet, until he appears before a multitude, every opportunity being given for detecting fraud, and performs an act that could not be done without suspending the ordinary laws of nature, no credence can be given to the statements of bigoted and interested persons.   His miracles must be performed as were those of Christ, — in the presence of thousands, and before the eyes of his enemies.   Can he heal the sick ? if so, why, when he is himself sick, does he take ordinary medicines for relief? Can he prevent death ?   Why, then, are his nearest relations and most useful friends suffered to die in the vigor of manhood ?

  " I have now examined the sum total of the external evidence which has ever been given to prove the truth of the Book of Mormon.   True, numerous passages of Scripture are quoted, and, by forced constructions, are made to have reference to this book; but a fair interpretation will always show the fallacy of all arguments that can be drawn from this source.   With the same propriety that quotations are made to prove the truth of Mormonism, they can be made to prove it a horn of the great beast referred to by John.   Equally futile with the last, is the attempt of some to corroborate the narrative of the book, by producing facts to prove that this continent was once inhabited by a civilized race.   This only shows that the author of the book had a knowledge of that fact, and wrote it in reference thereto.

  " I cannot better close this chapter, than by giving an extract from a revelation to Smith, which will show what idea he has of inspiration.   It appears that Oliver Cowdery, who was appointed to assist Smith in translating the plates, finding that he was but

10 *

little aided by inspiration, complained of the fact; and Smith, for his encouragement, received the following revelation, which will be found in the Book of Covenants, page 162, and reads thus: — ' Be patient, my son, for it is wisdom in me, and it is not expedient that you should translate at this present time. Behold, the work which you are called to do, is to write for my servant Joseph, and behold, it is because that you did not continue as you commenced, when you began to translate, that I have taken away this privilege from you; do not murmur, my son, for it is wisdom in me, that I have dealt with you after this manner. Behold, you have not understood; you have supposed that I would give it unto you, when you took no thought, save it was to ask me; but, behold, I say unto you, *that you must study it out in your own mind; then you must ask me if it be right;* and if it be right, I will cause that your bosom shall burn within you; therefore you shall feel that it is right; but if it be not right, you shall have no such feelings; but you shall have a stupor of thought that shall cause you to forget the thing which is wrong.' Here is inspiration, with a vengeance! ' Study it out in your own mind!' no matter what it is! make the most plausible story that you can, and then, ah! then, you must come and ' ask me if it be right.' Is this any thing like to the inspiration spoken of in the Bible? Does it bear any analogy to the voice of God speaking to Abraham, when the burning coals, &c., passed between the parts of the sacrifice, at eventide; or to the burning bush of Moses; or the terrific grandeur of Sinai, when, in the presence of millions, the mountain shook, and burned with fire, and the trumpet waxed louder and louder, until Moses said, ' I exceedingly fear and quake'?

"Now, it will here be observed, that the translators of the Book of Mormon, by their own showing, were not under inspiration at the time of writing the translations. How, then, in the name of common sense, would a set of unlettered men, who could scarcely write their own language, and who were totally innocent of a knowledge of any other, proceed to make a translation of Egyptian hieroglyphics? We are told that they must ' study it out in their own minds,' without assistance from God; and after they had *imagined* what the characters meant, *then* the inspiration should come. Here, then, is direct evidence from Smith himself of what the Book of Mormon really is — namely, a mere fiction, conjured up from the brains of Smith, or his coadjutors, and designed for nothing else than to gull mankind, and to aggrandize themselves.

"One remark further. We are asked, if Smith was an unlettered youth, is not the fact of his producing a work such as the Book of Mormon, a proof of inspiration. I answer, that the style and matter of the book is nothing superior; but admitting that it was more than a youth like Smith could produce, is it not well known that he had coadjutors of acknowledged talents — fully ample to produce such a work? more especially as, in style and matter, it is written in imitation of the Scriptures? Some have intimated, however, that the book was obtained by Smith surreptitiously, from the executors of a man who had written it as a religious romance, and altered it to suit his own purposes."

Mormonism Portrayed, by William Harris, pp. 4—10.

From Mormonism Unveiled, by E. D. Howe, pp. 278—290.

" We think that facts and data have been elicited, sufficient, at least, to raise a strong presumption that the leading features of the ' Gold Bible ' were first conceived and concocted by one SOLOMON SPALDING, while a resident of Conneaut, Ashtabula county, Ohio. It is admitted by our soundest jurists, that a train of circumstances may often lead the mind to a more satisfactory and unerring conclusion, than positive testimony, unsupported by circumstantial evidence — for the plain reason, that the one species of testimony is more prone to falsehood than the other. But we proceed with our testimony.

" The first witness is Mr. *John Spalding,* a brother of Solomon, now a resident of Crawford county, Pa., who says, —

" Solomon Spalding was born in Ashford, Conn., in 1761, and in early life contracted a taste for literary pursuits. After he left school, he entered Plainfield Academy, where he made great proficiency in study, and excelled most of his classmates. He next commenced the study of law, in Windham county, in which he made little progress, having in the mean time turned his attention to religious subjects. He soon after entered Dartmouth College, with the intention of qualifying himself for the ministry, where he obtained the degree of A. M., and was afterwards regularly ordained. After preaching three or four years, he gave it up, removed to Cherry Valley, N. Y., and commenced the mercantile business, in company with his brother Josiah. In a few years he failed in business, and in the year 1809 removed to Conneaut, in Ohio. The year following, I removed to Ohio, and found him engaged in building a forge. I made him a visit in about three years after, and found that he had failed, and was considerably involved in debt. He then told me he had been writing a book, which he intended to have printed, the avails of which he thought would enable him to pay all his debts. The book was entitled the ' Manuscript Found,' of which he read to me many passages. It was an historical romance of the first settlers of America, endeavoring to show that the American Indians are the descendants of the Jews, or the lost tribes. It gave a detailed account of their journey from Jerusalem, by land and sea, till they arrived in America, under the command of NEPHI and LEHI. They afterwards had quarrels and contentions, and separated into two distinct nations, one of which he denominated Nephites, and the other Lamanites. Cruel and bloody wars ensued, in which great multitudes were slain. They buried their dead in large heaps, which caused the mounds so common in this country. Their arts, sciences, and civilization, were brought into view, in order to account for all the curious antiquities, found in various parts of North and South America. I have recently read the Book of Mormon, and to my great surprise I find nearly the same historical matter, names, &c., as they were in my brother's writings. I well remember that he wrote in the old style, and commenced about every sentence with ' And it came to pass,' or ' Now it came to pass,' the same as in the Book of Mormon, and according to the best of my recollection and belief, it is the same as my brother Solomon wrote, with the exception of

the religious matter. By what means it has fallen into the hands of
Joseph Smith, Jr., I am unable to determine.   JOHN SPALDING.

———

" Martha Spalding, the wife of John Spalding, says, —

" I was personally acquainted with Solomon Spalding, about
twenty years ago. I was at his house a short time before he left
Conneaut ; he was then writing an historical novel founded upon the
first settlers of America. He represented them as an enlightened
and warlike people. He had for many years contended that the ab-
origines of America were the descendants of some of the lost tribes
of Israel, and this idea he carried out in the book in question. The
lapse of time which has intervened, prevents my recollecting but few
of the leading incidents of his writings ; but the names of Nephi and
Lehi are yet fresh in my memory, as being the principal heroes of
his tale. They were officers of the company which first came off
from Jerusalem. He gave a particular account of their journey by
land and sea, till they arrived in America, after which, disputes arose
between the chiefs, which caused them to separate into different
bands, one of which was called Lamanites, and the other Nephites.
Between these were recounted tremendous battles, which frequently
covered the ground with the slain ; and their being buried in large
heaps was the cause of the numerous mounds in the country. Some
of these people he represented as being very large. I have read the
Book of Mormon, which has brought fresh to my recollection the
writings of Solomon Spalding ; and I have no manner of doubt that
the historical part of it is the same that I read and heard read more
than twenty years ago. The old, obsolete style, and the phrases of
' and it came to pass,' &c., are the same.   MARTHA SPALDING.

———

" We would here remark, by the way, that it would appear that
Sol. Spalding, like many other authors, was somewhat vain of his
writings, and was constantly showing and reading them to his neighbors. In this way most of his intimate acquaintances became con-
versant at that time with his writings and designs. We might therefore introduce a great number of witnesses, all testifying to the same
general facts ; but we have not taken the trouble to procure the
statements of but few, all of whom are the most respectable men, and
highly esteemed for their moral worth, and their characters for truth
and veracity are unimpeachable. In fact, the word of any one of
them would have more weight in any respectable community, than
the whole family of Smiths and Whitmers, who have told about
hearing the voice of an angel.

———

" CONNEAUT, Ashtabula Co., Ohio, *September*, 1833.

" I left the State of New York, late in the year 1810, and arrived
at this place, about the first of January following. Soon after my
arrival, I formed a copartnership with Solomon Spalding, for the
purpose of rebuilding a forge which he had commenced a year or two
before. He very frequently read to me from a manuscript which he
was writing, which he entitled the ' Manuscript Found,' and which

he represented as being found in this town. I spent many hours in hearing him read said writings, and became well acquainted with its contents. He wished me to assist him in getting his production printed, alleging that a book of that kind would meet with a rapid sale. I designed doing so, but the forge not meeting our anticipations, we failed in business, when I declined having any thing to do with the publication of the book. This book represented the American Indians as the descendants of the lost tribes, gave an account of their leaving Jerusalem, their contentions and wars, which were many and great. One time, when he was reading to me the tragic account of Laban, I pointed out to him what I considered an inconsistency, which he promised to correct; but by referring to the Book of Mormon, I find, to my surprise, that it stands there just as he read it to me then. Some months ago, I borrowed the Golden Bible, put it into my pocket, carried it home, and thought no more of it. About a week after, my wife found the book in my coat pocket, as it hung up, and commenced reading it aloud as I lay upon the bed. She had not read twenty minutes, till I was astonished to find the same passages in it that Spalding had read to me more than twenty years before, from his 'Manuscript Found.' Since that, I have more fully examined the said Golden Bible, and have no hesitation in saying that the historical part of it is principally, if not wholly, taken from the 'Manuscript Found.' I well recollect telling Mr. Spalding that the so frequent use of the words 'And it came to pass,' 'Now it came to pass,' rendered it ridiculous. Spalding left here in 1812, and I furnished him the means to carry him to Pittsburgh, where he said he would get the book printed, and pay me. But I never heard any more from him or his writings, till I saw them in the Book of Mormon. HENRY LAKE.

"SPRINGFIELD, Pa., *September*, 1833.

" In the year 1811, I was in the employ of Henry Lake and Solomon Spalding, at Conneaut, engaged in rebuilding a forge. While there, I boarded and lodged in the family of said Spalding, for several months. I was soon introduced to the manuscripts of Spalding, and perused them as often as I had leisure. He had written two or three books or pamphlets on different subjects; but that which more particularly drew my attention, was one which he called the 'Manuscript Found.' From this he would frequently read some humorous passages to the company present. It purported to be the history of the first settlement of America, before discovered by Columbus. He brought them off from Jerusalem, under their leaders; detailing their travels by land and water, their manners, customs, laws, wars, &c. He said that he designed it as an historical novel, and that in after years it would be believed by many people as much as the history of England. He soon after failed in business, and told me he should retire from the din of his creditors, finish his book and have it published, which would enable him to pay his debts and support his family. He soon after removed to Pittsburgh, as I understood.

" I have recently examined the Book of Mormon, and find in it the writings of Solomon Spalding, from beginning to end, but mixed up with Scripture and other religious matter, which I did not meet with in the 'Manuscript Found.' Many of the passages in the Mormon book are verbatim from Spalding, and others in part. The names of Nephi, Lehi, Moroni, and in fact all the principal names, are brought fresh to my recollection, by the Gold Bible. When Spalding divested his history of its fabulous names, by a verbal explanation, he landed his people near the Straits of Darien, which I am very confident he called *Zarahemla;* they were marched about that country for a length of time, in which wars and great bloodshed ensued; he brought them across North America in a north-east direction.   JOHN N. MILLER.

"CONNEAUT, *August,* 1833.

" I first became acquainted with Solomon Spalding in 1808 or '9, when he commenced building a forge on Conneaut Creek. When at his house, one day, he showed and read to me a history he was writing, of the lost tribes of Israel, purporting that they were the first settlers of America, and that the Indians were their descendants. Upon this subject we had frequent conversations. He traced their journey from Jerusalem to America, as it is given in the Book of Mormon, excepting the religious matter. The historical part of the Book of Mormon I know to be the same as I read and heard read from the writings of Spalding, more than twenty years ago; the names, more especially, are the same, without any alteration. He told me his object was to account for all the fortifications, &c., to be found in this country, and said that in time it would be fully believed by all, except learned men and historians. I once anticipated reading his writings in print, but little expected to see them in a new Bible. Spalding had many other manuscripts, which I expect to see when Smith translates his other plate. In conclusion, I will observe, that the names of, and most of the historical part of the Book of Mormon, were as familiar to me before I read it, as most modern history. If it is not Spalding's writing, it is the same as he wrote; and if Smith was inspired, I think it was by the same spirit that Spalding was, which he confessed to be the love of money.

                                   " AARON WRIGHT.

"CONNEAUT, *August,* 1833.

" When Solomon Spalding first came to this place, he purchased a tract of land, surveyed it out, and commenced selling it. While engaged in this business, he boarded at my house, in all nearly six months. All his leisure hours were occupied in writing an historical novel, founded upon the first settlers of this country. He said he intended to trace their journey from Jerusalem, by land and sea, till their arrival in America; give an account of their arts, sciences, civilization, wars, and contentions. In this way, he would give a satisfactory account of all of the old mounds, so common to this country. During the time he was at my house, I read and heard read one hundred pages or more. Nephi and Lehi were by him represented as leading characters, when they first started for America. Their main object was to escape the judgments which they supposed were coming upon the old world. But no religious matter was introduced, as I now recollect. Just before he left this place, Spalding sent for me to call on him, which I did. He then said, that although he was in my debt, he intended to leave the country, and hoped I would not prevent him. For, says he, you know I have been writing the history of the first settlement of America, and I intend to go to Pittsburgh, and there live a retired life, till I have completed the work, and when it is printed, it will bring me a fine sum of money, which will enable me to return and pay off all my debts. The book, you know, will sell, as every one is anxious to learn something upon that subject. This was the last I heard of Spalding or his book, until the Book of Mormon came into the neighborhood. When I heard the historical part of it related, I at once said it was the writings of old Solomon Spalding. Soon after, I obtained the book, and on reading it, found much of it the same as Spalding had written, more than twenty years before. OLIVER SMITH.

_____

" CONNEAUT, *August*, 1833.

" I first became acquainted with Solomon Spalding, in Dec, 1810. After that time, I frequently saw him at his house, and also at my house. I once, in conversation with him, expressed a surprise at not having any account of the inhabitants once in this country, who erected the old forts, mounds, &c. He then told me that he was writing a history of that race of people; and afterwards frequently showed me his writings, which I read. I have lately read the Book of Mormon, and believe it to be the same as Spalding wrote, except the religious part. He told me that he intended to get his writings published in Pittsburgh, and he thought that in one century from that time, it would be believed as much as any other history.

" NAHUM HOWARD.

_____

" Artemas Cunningham, of Perry, Geauga county, states as follows :

" In the month of October, 1811, I went from the township of Madison to Conneaut, for the purpose of securing a debt due me from Solomon Spalding. I tarried with him nearly two days, for the purpose of accomplishing my object, which I was finally unable to do. I found him destitute of the means of paying his debts. His only hope of ever paying his debts, appeared to be upon the sale of a book, which he had been writing. He endeavored to convince me, from the nature and character of the work, that it would meet with a ready sale. Before showing me his manuscripts, he went into a verbal relation of its outlines, saying that it was a fabulous or romantic history of the first settlement of this country, and as it purported to have been a record found buried in the earth, or in a cave, he had adopted the ancient or Scripture style of writing. He then presented his manuscripts, when we sat down, and spent a good share of the night in reading them, and conversing upon them. I well remember the name of Nephi, which appeared to be the principal hero of the story. The frequent repetition of the phrase, ' I Nephi,' I recollect as distinctly as though it was but yesterday, although the general features of the story have passed from my memory, through the lapse of twenty-two years. He attempted to account for the numerous antiquities which are found upon this continent, and remarked that, after this generation had passed away, his account of the first inhabitants of America would be considered as authentic as any other history. The Mormon Bible I have partially examined, and am fully of the opinion that Solomon Spalding had written its outlines before he left Conneaut.

———

"Statements of the same import might be multiplied to an indefinite length; but we deem it unnecessary. We are here willing to rest the question in the hands of any intelligent jury, with a certainty that their verdict would be, that Solomon Spalding first wrote the leading incidents of the Book of Mormon, instead of its being found by the Smith family, while digging for gold, and its contents afterwards made known by the Supreme Being.

"But our inquiries did not terminate here. Our next object was to ascertain, if possible, the disposition Spalding made of his manuscripts. For this purpose, a messenger was despatched to look up the widow of Spalding, who was found residing in Massachusetts. From her we learned that Spalding resided in Pittsburgh about two years, when he removed to the township of Amity, Washington county, Pennsylvania, where he lived about two years, and died in 1816. His widow then removed to Onondaga county, New York, married again, and lived in Otsego county, and subsequently removed to Massachusetts. She states that Spalding had a great variety of manuscripts, and recollects that one was entitled the 'Manuscript Found;' but of its contents she has now no distinct knowledge. While they lived in Pittsburgh, she thinks it was once taken to the printing-office of *Patterson and Lambdin;* but whether it was ever brought back to the house again, she is quite uncertain: if it was, however, it was then, with his other writings, in a trunk which she had left in Otsego county, New York. This is all the information that could be obtained from her, except that Mr. Spalding, while living, entertained a strong antipathy to the Masonic Institution, which may account for its being so frequently mentioned in the Book of Mormon. The fact, also, that Spalding, in the latter part of his life, inclined to infidelity, is established by a letter in his hand-writing, now in our possession.

"The trunk referred to by the widow, was subsequently examined, and found to contain only a single MS. book, in Spalding's handwriting, containing about one quire of paper. This is a romance, purporting to have been translated from the Latin, found on twenty-four rolls of parchment, in a cave, on the banks of Conneaut Creek, but written in modern style, and giving a fabulous account of a ship's being driven upon the American coast, while proceeding from Rome to Britain, a short time previous to the Christian era, this country then being inhabited by the Indians. This old MS. has been shown to several of the foregoing witnesses, who recognize it as Spalding's, he having told them that he had altered his first plan of writing, by going farther back with dates, and writing in the old Scripture style, in order that it might appear more ancient. They say that it bears no resemblance to the '*Manuscript Found.*'

"Here, then, our inquiries after facts partially cease, on this subject. We have fully shown that the Book of Mormon is the joint production of Solomon Spalding and some other designing knave, or, if it is what it purports to be, the Lord God has graciously condescended, in revealing to Smith his will, through spectacles, to place before him, and appropriate to his own use, the writings and names of men which had been invented by a person long before in the grave. Having established the fact, therefore, that most of the names and leading incidents contained in the Mormon Bible, originated with Solomon Spalding, it is not very material, as we conceive, to show the way and manner by which they fell into the hands of the Smith family. To do this, however, we have made some inquiries.

"It was inferred at once that some light might be shed upon this subject, and the mystery revealed, by applying to Patterson and Lambdin, in Pittsburgh. But here again death had interposed a barrier. That establishment was dissolved and broken up many years since, and Lambdin died about eight years ago. Mr. Patterson says he has no recollection of any such manuscript being brought there for publication, neither would he have been likely to have seen it, as the business of printing was conducted wholly by Lambdin at that time. He says, however, that many MS. books and pamphlets were brought to the office about that time, which remained upon their shelves for years, without being printed or even examined. Now, as Spalding's book can nowhere be found, or any thing heard of it after being carried to this establishment, there is the strongest presumption that it remained there in seclusion till about the year 1823 or '24, at which time *Sidney Rigdon* located himself in that city. We have been credibly informed that he was on terms of intimacy with Lambdin, being seen frequently in his shop. Rigdon resided in Pittsburgh about three years, and during the whole of that time, as he has since frequently asserted, abandoned preaching and all other employment, for the purpose of *studying the Bible.* He left there, and came into the county where he now resides, about the time Lambdin died, and commenced preaching some new points of doctrine, which were afterwards found to be inculcated in the Mormon Bible. He resided in this vicinity about four years previous to the appearance of the book, during which time he made several long visits to Pittsburgh, and perhaps to the Susquehannah, where Smith was then digging for money, or pretending to be translating plates. It may be observed also, that about the time Rigdon left Pittsburgh, the Smith family began to tell about finding a book that would contain a history of the first inhabitants of America, and that two years elapsed before they finally got possession of it.

"We are, then, irresistibly led to this conclusion — that Lambdin, after having failed in business, had recourse to the old manuscripts then in his possession, in order to *raise the wind*, by a book speculation, and placed the 'Manuscript Found,' of Spalding, in the hands of Rigdon, to be embellished, altered, and added to, as he might think expedient; and three years' study of the Bible, we should deem little time enough to garble it, as it is transferred to the Mormon book. The former, dying, left the latter the sole proprietor, who was obliged to resort to his wits, and in a miraculous way, to bring it before the world; for in no other manner could such a book be published without great sacrifice. And where could a more suitable character be found than Joe Smith, whose necromantic fame and arts of deception had already extended to a considerable distance? That Lambdin was a person every way qualified and fitted for such an enterprise, we have the testimony of his partner in business, and others of his acquaintance. Add to all these circumstances the facts that Rigdon had prepared the minds, in a great measure, of nearly a hundred of those who had attended his ministration, to be in readiness to embrace the first mysterious *ism* that should be presented; the appearance of Cowdery at his residence as soon as the book was printed; his sudden conversion, after many pretensions to disbelieve it; his immediately repairing to the residence of Smith, three hundred miles distant, where he was forthwith appointed an elder, high-priest, and a scribe to the Prophet; the pretended vision that his residence in Ohio was the ' promised land; ' the immediate removal of the whole Smith family thither, where they were soon raised from a state of poverty to comparative affluence. We, therefore, must hold out Sidney Rigdon to the world as being the original 'author and proprietor' of the whole Mormon conspiracy, until further light is elicited upon the lost writings of Solomon Spalding."

Mormonism Unveiled, by E. D. Howe, pp. 278—290.

Rev. J. N. T. Tucker's Statement.

MORMONISM.—SOME CURIOUS FACTS.

" MESSRS. EDITORS :

" Having noticed in a late number of the Signs of the Times, a notice of a work, entitled Mormon Delusions and Monstrosities, it occurred to me that it might, perhaps, be of service to the cause of truth, to state one circumstance in relation to the authenticity of the Book of Mormon, which occurred during its publication, at which time I was a practical printer, and engaged in the office where it was printed. and became familiar with the men and their principles, through whose agency it was 'got up.'

" The circumstance alluded to was as follows : — We had heard much said by Martin Harris, the man who paid for the printing, and the only one in the concern worth any property, about the wonderful wisdom of the translators of the mysterious plates, and resolved to test their wisdom. Accordingly, after putting one sheet in type, we laid it aside, and told Harris it was lost, and there would be a serious defection in the book in consequence, unless another sheet like the original could be produced. The announcement threw the old gentleman into quite an excitement. But after a few moments' reflection, he said he would try to obtain another. After two or three weeks, another sheet was produced, but no more like the original than any other sheet of paper would have been, written over by a common schoolboy, after having read, as they did, the manuscripts preceding and succeeding the lost sheet.

" As might be expected, the disclosure of the plan greatly annoyed the authors, and caused no little merriment among those who were acquainted with the circumstance. As we were none of us Christians, and only labored for the ' gold that perisheth,' we did not care for the delusion, only so far as to be careful to avoid it ourselves, and enjoy the hoax *Not one* of the hands in the office where the wonderful book was printed, ever became a convert to the system, although the writer of this was often assured by Harris, if he did not, he would be destroyed in 1832.

" I am well acquainted with the two gentlemen whose names appear on pages 50, 51, in the work referred to at the head of this article, and know the certificate above their names to be true. I have known several instances of the grossest impostures by them in their pretensions of working miracles, &c. &c., and am greatly surprised that such a man as Nickerson, of your city, can induce any rational person to follow in his pernicious ways.

" Mrs. Harris, the wife of Martin Harris, was so familiar with the monstrous wickedness and folly of her husband, and the trio who were engaged with him, that she would not follow him, nor live with him. His conduct was not such as a man of God would have been. After he had been absent about two years, and frequent reports of his having power to heal the sick, &c., had reached his neighborhood, he returned, and assured his wife that he could cure her of deafness, with which she was afflicted. But as a condition of so doing, he required her to put into his hands about $1500 of money which she had managed to secure out of the avails of his property, which he sold on joining the ' Latter Day Saints ' colony. She assured him he should have every dollar as soon as her hearing was restored. But he very wisely replied, he could ' have no evidence of her faith until she put the cash down; ' so, of course, she remained deaf, and Martin went back to the ' promised land ' with pockets as light as when he came.

" This is, no doubt, one of the great deceptions which should come upon the people on the eve of the second coming of the Son of Man. Let the saints of God beware of them. Let no persecution or violence be opposed to them, but simply an avoidance, and we shall soon find them without faith.

" Yours in the gospel of Christ,
" J. N. T. Tucker.

" Groton, *May* 23, 1842."

Signs of the Times, June 8, 1842.

I will remark here, in confirmation of the above, that the Book of Mormon was originally written by the Rev. Solomon Spalding, A. M., as a romance, and entitled the " Manuscript Found," and placed by him in the printing-office of Patterson and Lambdin, in the city of Pittsburg, from whence it was taken by a *conspicuous Mormon divine*, and re-modelled, *by adding the religious portion, placed by*

*him in Smith's possession, and then published to the world,
as the testimony exemplifies.* This I have from the CON-
FEDERATION, and of its perfect correctness there is not the
shadow of a doubt. There never were any *plates* of the
Book of Mormon, excepting what were seen by the SPIRIT-
UAL, and not the *natural*, eyes of the witnesses. The story
of the plates is all CHIMERICAL.

THE CLAIMS AND ABSURDITIES OF THE BOOK OF MORMON.

I quote from Harris's work : —

" Probably, in the history of the world, there is not to be found
an instance of more cool impudence, and deliberate blasphemy, than
is contained in the Book of Mormon. Coming forth, as has been
shown, without one shadow of evidence in its favor, either circumstantial or direct, except what has evidently been manufactured for
the occasion, it claims for itself, or the Mormons claim for it, a rank
and importance excelled by nothing that has gone before.

" In the first place, it is claimed to be a new and everlasting covenant, doing away with all former covenants. This is expressed in a
revelation given to Joseph Smith, Jr., Book of Covenants, pages 91
and 178: ' And this condemnation resteth on the children of Zion,
even all ; and they shall remain under this condemnation until they
repent and remember the new covenant, even the Book of Mormon.'
' Behold, I say unto you, that all old covenants have been done
away in this thing, and this is a new and an everlasting covenant.'

" Secondly, it is claimed to be the fulness of the everlasting gospel. Book of Covenants, page 180 : ' Behold, this is wisdom in me ;
therefore marvel not, for the hour cometh, that I will drink of the
fruit of the vine with you, on the earth, and with Moroni, whom I
have sent unto you, to reveal the Book of Mormon, containing the
fulness of my everlasting gospel.'

" Thirdly, it claims a preëminence over the Bible. Book of Mormon,* page 30, where the Roman church is referred to, as ' having
taken away from the gospel many parts which are plain and most
precious ; and also many covenants of the Lord have they taken
away,' &c. ; and on page 32 you find that the preference is taken to
itself, in that it professes to make known the ' plain and precious
things which have been taken away.'

" Here, then, are some of the claims of this truly wonderful book.
The world is informed that all old covenants are done away ; the
promises of the Bible, therefore, are void ; and hereafter we must
look alone for comfort to the Book of Mormon. Not only this, it is

---

* The first edition is referred to.

the complete gospel; of course the New Testament must be imper
fect. And above all, it corrects the errors in the present translation
of the Bible. Wonderful, indeed !!

"Having given the exhibition of the claims of the Book of Mormon, let us examine some of the absurdities and contradictions to
Scripture apparent on the face of it. These are very numerous, and
to point out the tithe of them would swell this pamphlet far beyond
my design.

"On page 65, we have the following : ' And now behold, if Adam
had not transgressed; he would not have fallen ; but he would have
remained in the garden of Eden. And all things which were created, must have remained in the same state which they were after
they were created; and they must have remained forever, and had
no end. And they would have had no children, wherefore, they
would have remained in a state of innocence, having no joy, for
they knew no misery; doing no good, for they knew no sin. But
behold, all things have been done in the wisdom of him who knoweth
all things. Adam fell, that men might be ; and men are, that they
might have joy.'

"Here we have Adam placed in a very sorry dilemma; for in
Genesis, i. 28, he is commanded to 'be fruitful, and multiply, and
replenish the earth;' and in chapter ii. 17, he is commanded not to
'eat of the tree of knowledge of good and evil.' But, according to
the Book of Mormon, had Adam not transgressed, he would have
had no children. If this be correct, Adam was obliged to transgress
the second command, above mentioned, that is, eat the fruit forbidden, in order that he might obey the first commandment, to multiply and replenish the earth. Was ever a contradiction made more
glaring? The truth of the Bible must be denied, or else the Book
of Mormon is untrue.

"But further: the passage says that our first parents ' had no joy,
for they knew no misery;' in other words, they were in a state of perfect neutrality, and incapable of enjoyment. If this be true, why did
God plant the garden of Eden, and cause in it to grow every tree
that is pleasant to the sight, and good for food? And why did he
place Adam in the garden to dress it and to keep it? Why, I ask, did
God place man in such a perfect Paradise, surrounded by every
thing to produce enjoyment, and nothing to disturb it, and yet not
confer on him the power of enjoyment? Such nonsense is too
trivial for argument.

"But further: the passage says, ' Adam did no good, for he knew
no sin.' According to this, there can be no good done without sin.
The angels, therefore, who sin not, do no good. But was Adam
doing no good when in a state of purity, obeying the commands of
God? Is not the rendition of such obedience the very height of
goodness? But if Adam, in a state of innocence, did no good, for
what did God create him? The conclusion is inevitable, that he
created him for no purpose at all, or else he created him to sin.
To suppose the former, would make God create man from a mere
whim; and to suppose the latter, would make *Him*, and not the Devil,
the author of sin. In either case, an absurdity necessarily follows.

11 *

" Here, then, is a short passage from this veritable book, containing nothing but contradiction, nonsense, and absurdity.

" Again, on the same page, (65,) we find the following: ' Wherefore men are free, according to the *flesh*, and all things are given them which is expedient unto man. And they are free to choose liberty, and eternal life, through the great mediation of all men.' Now, what are we to understand from this? Why, certainly, nothing more nor less, than that all men are mediators; and if we obtain liberty and eternal life, at all, it must be through the mediation of *all men*. What, then, becomes of the words of the apostle, in Tim. ii. 5, where he says, there is ' one Mediator between God and man.' Certainly the Book of Mormon, or else St. Paul, must be wrong.

" Again, on page 424, the following passage occurs : ' Behold they (speaking of oaths and covenants) were put into the heart of Gadianton, by that same being who did entice our first parents to partake of the forbidden fruit; yea, that same being, who did plot with Cain, that if he would murder his brother Abel, it should not be known unto the world.' ' And he did plot with Cain, and his followers, from that time forth And, also, it was that same being, who put it into the heads of the people, to build a Tower, sufficiently high, that they might get to heaven. And it was that same being which led on the people, which came from that tower, into this land.' Now, here it is positively stated, that the being who tempted Eve, &c., that is, the Devil, was the leader of the Jaredites, or the people who came from the Tower of Babel, in Babylon, to the American continent. But, by reference to pages 539 and 540, we will find the following : ' And it came to pass, the Lord did hear the brother of Jared, and he had compassion upon him, and said unto him, go to, and gather together thy flocks, both male and female, of every kind; and also, of the seed of the earth, of every kind, and thy families; and also, Jared, thy brother, and his family; and also thy friends, and their families. And when thou hast done this, thou shalt go at the head of them down into the valley which is northward, and there will I meet thee, and I will go before thee, into a land which is choice above all the land of the earth.' Here there is a positive contradiction. These two statements both refer to the same people, and to the same journey; in one of which, the Devil is represented as the leader, and in the other, the Lord. In reading these passages, one is reminded of the adage — ' Liars, to be consistent, should have good memories.'

" But now for the climax. On page 542, we have a description of the barges in which all the people, before referred to, crossed the ocean. It is in these words : ' And the Lord said, go to work, and build after the manner of barges, which ye have hitherto built. And it came to pass, that the brother of Jared did go to work, and also his brethren, and built barges after the manner which they had built, according to the instructions of the Lord. And they were small and they were light upon the water, even unto the lightness of a fowl, upon the water; and they were built after the manner that they were exceedingly tight, even that they would hold water like unto a dish; and the sides thereof were tight like unto a dish; and the ends were peaked : and the top thereof was tight like unto a dish; and the length thereof was the length of a tree; and the door thereof, when it was shut, was tight like unto a dish. And it came to pass, that the brother of Jared cried unto the Lord, saying : O Lord, I have performed the work which thou hast commanded me, and I have made the barges according as thou hast directed me. And, behold, in them there is no light, whither shall we steer? and also, we shall perish, for in them we cannot breathe, save it is the air that is in them; therefore are we to perish.

" ' And the Lord said unto the brother of Jared, behold thou shalt make a hole in the top thereof, and also in the bottom thereof, and when thou shalt suffer for air thou shalt unstop the hole thereof, and receive air.

" ' And if it be so that the water come in upon thee, behold ye shall stop the hole thereof, that ye may not perish in the floods.

" ' And it came to pass, that the brother of Jared did so, according as the Lord had commanded. And he cried again unto the Lord, saying, O Lord, behold I have done even as thou hast commanded me, and I have prepared the vessels for my people, and behold there is no light in them. Behold, O Lord! wilt thou suffer that we shall cross this great water in darkness? and the Lord said unto the brother of Jared, what will ye that I shall do, that ye may have light in your vessels? For behold ye cannot have windows,* for they will be dashed in pieces; neither shall ye take fire with you, for ye shall not go by the light of the fire : for, behold, ye shall be as a whale in the midst of the sea; for the mountain waves shall dash upon you. Nevertheless, I will bring you up again, out of the depths of the sea; for the winds have gone forth out of my mouth, and also the rains and the floods have I sent forth.'

" From this description, we learn that the boats were made perfectly tight, bottom, top, door, and sides; and were of the length of a tree. (Very definite! almost equal to the witness who described a stone that one man threw at another as being about the size of a piece of chalk.) But these boats, although made according to the direction of God himself, appear to have been very deficient; for they could not exist in them for want of air. (A strange oversight for God to make.) But the remedy is the funniest of all, viz., to make holes in both the top and bottom. Yet after they were made, it appears that they could be of but little use, for the boats were to be as a whale, sometimes under the water and sometimes on top. Of course, when they were under the water, they were in as bad a fix as ever; for they had to keep the holes stopped, in order to keep out the floods. But what did they want with that hole in the bottom? I was told by a Mormon expounder, that the holes in the top and bottom were so made on account of the roughness of the passage — the mountain waves dashing the boats over and over, so that sometimes the top would be uppermost, and sometimes the bottom.

---

* *Query.* What kind of windows are here referred to? If of glass, it will be recollected that such were not in use until modern times; and what other kind would have been dashed in pieces?

Hence the holes were made to suit either case. What an idea! men, women, children, flocks, bees, &c. &c., all confined in a t ght vessel, tumbling and rolling; one moment heads up and the next down; and this delightful commingling to last during the whole passage from India to America. What squealing there must have been! Truly, this was a perfect shaking together of the elements, by which the new continent was to be populated.

"But another idea. The brother of Jared, after he had finished the barges, which admitted neither light nor air, asks the Lord whither he shall steer. It will be remembered that the vessels were perfectly tight; there were no holes for either oars or rudder, and no sails, nor could they see any place without the boat, when once shut up in it; and yet he asks the Lord to what point he should steer! Truly, Smith's nautical genius must have been extremely limited, or he would have told a better yarn than this. But it does seem that he, in this description, used his utmost endeavors to see how far he could impose on the gullibility of mankind.

"It will be useless to make any further comments to prove the absurdities of this extraordinary book. Enough has been said, already, to show it to be a perfect humbug. A great number of other passages might be quoted, all tending to prove its absurdities; but the limits prescribed for this book compel me to forbear."

Mormonism Portrayed, pp. 10—14.

THE BOOK OF COVENANTS—ITS ABSURDITIES AND CONTRADICTIONS.

I again quote from Harris's work : —

"The Book of Covenants appears to be regarded by the Mormons as equal, in point of authority and inspiration, to the Bible. It contains, firstly, an exposition of the doctrines of the Church; and secondly, a number of revelations, given to Joseph Smith, Jr., and others, either explanatory of the Scriptures, or directory of the manner of governing the Church, both in things temporal and spiritual. Like the Book of Mormon, there appear on its face many absurdities and contradictions to Scripture, which it may be important, for the object of this work, for one moment to examine.

"On page 7, Heb. chapter xi. verse 3, is quoted thus : 'Through faith, we understand, that the worlds were formed by the word of God; so that things which are seen, were not made of things which do appear.' On this passage, the following wise commentary is made : 'By this we understand that the principle of power, which existed in the bosom of God, by which the worlds were framed, was faith, and that it is by reason of this principle of power, existing in the Deity, that all created things exist; so that all things in heaven, on earth, and under the earth, exist by reason of faith, as it exists in him.' 'Had it not been for the principle of faith, the worlds would never have been framed, neither would man have been formed of the dust; it is the principle by which Jehovah works, and through which he exercises power over all temporal as well as eternal things; take this principle or attribute (for it is an attribute) from the Deity, and he would cease to exist.' Here is a bright idea, and a bright perception of the meaning of language. 'The apostle, in the above quotation, says, ' Through faith *we* understand.' Who understand? ' We,' says the apostle. Understand what? ' That the worlds were framed by the word of God,' not by faith. The evident meaning to any man, even of the most ordinary perception, is, that the followers of Christ, through the aid of faith, understand or know that the worlds were made by the power of God. Faith must always have a subject; but in what could God have faith? What was there to have faith in, before the worlds were framed? But admitting that there were other beings, God was greater than they, and what aid could he derive from having faith in inferiors? To suppose that God, by having faith in others, could be aided, would be taking away his omnipotence; for that which is all powerful cannot be made stronger. Further, if I perform a miracle through faith in God, the miracle is not my work, but the work of God, done as a reward of my faith; to say, then, that God could not have made the worlds without faith in others, is to say he did not make them at all, but that they were made by those in whom he had faith. But perhaps we are to understand that God made the worlds through faith in himself. Now, faith in himself means nothing more than *confidence* in himself; to say, therefore, that God made the worlds by faith in himself, is to say that he made them by confidence in himself. What nonsense!

" On page 85, it is said that 'Enoch was twenty-five years old when he was ordained, under the hand of Adam; and he was sixty-five, and Adam blessed him, and he saw the Lord; and he walked with him, and was before his face continually, and he walked with God three hundred and sixty-five years, making him four hundred and thirty years old when he was translated.' *Per Contra.* Gen. iv. 23, reads thus : ' And all the days of Enoch were three hundred sixty and five years.' Here, then, is a difference of only sixty-five years between the Mosaic account of the age of Enoch, and that given by Joe Smith. Which is correct?

" On page 175, we have the following: ' For behold I, God, have suffered these things for all, that they might not suffer even as I ; which suffering caused myself, even God, the greatest of all, to tremble because of pain.' The idea of the Godhead, or Divinity, suffering involuntary pain, will excite a sneer by the mere mentioning.

" On page 102, it is said, ' The day shall come when you shall comprehend even God.' In these days it takes a shrewd man to comprehend a fool, but the Mormons are to comprehend even God; of course their comprehension must be at least commensurate with his power, which is infinite.

" The prophet Ezekiel said by the Lord, ' This proverb shall be no more heard in Israel, " The fathers have eaten sour grapes, and the children's teeth are set on edge." ' But the Mormons have revived this proverb, (page 219,) thus: after stating that if a person trespass against you, you shall forgive him three times, it says, ' But if he trespass against thee the fourth time, thou shalt not forgive him, but thou shalt bring these testimonies before the Lord, and they shall not be blotted out until he repent and reward thee fourfold in all things wherewith he has trespassed against thee, and if he do this thou shalt forgive him with all thine heart; and if he do not this, I, the Lord, will avenge thee of thine enemies an hundred fold; and upon his children, and his children's children, of all them that hate me, until the third and fourth generations.' Here is the old proverb revived with a vengeance! For it will be perceived, by reading the next few lines, that there is no forgiveness to the children unless they restore the trespass of their fathers, and that, too, fourfold. It reads thus: ' But if the children shall repent, or the children's children, and turn unto the Lord their God, with all their hearts, and with all their might, mind, and strength, and restore fourfold, for all their trespasses wherewith they have trespassed, and wherewith their fathers have trespassed, or their fathers' fathers, then thine indignation shall be turned away, and vengeance shall no more come upon them.' If this be true, hard fate for the Mormons.

"On page 106, in speaking of Christ, it is said, that ' The saints shall be filled with his glory, and receive their inheritance, and be made equal with him.' On this passage, Parley P. Pratt, in the Voice of Warning, (a standard work of the Mormons,) makes the following argument, which I give in this place as an illustration of the wild doctrines of Mormonism: ' See the prayer of Christ recorded by John, concerning his saints becoming one with him and the father, as they are one, and certainly they are equal: and again, the saints are joint heirs with him; and again, he that overcometh shall sit down with Christ on his throne, as he has overcome and set down with the father on his throne; and again, the spirit shall guide his saints unto all truth, God is in possession of all truth, and no more, consequently his saints will know what he knows; and it is an acknowledged principle that knowledge is power; consequently if they had the same knowledge that God has, they will have the same power. And this will fulfil the Scriptures which say, unto him that believeth all things are possible, and I am sure God can do no more than all things; consequently, there must be equality. Hence the propriety of calling them God's, even the sons of God.' Such is the reasoning of the Apostle Parley P. Pratt, and such is the doctrine of the Church, for they believe that they will have power to create worlds, and that those worlds will transgress the law given; consequently they will become saviors to those worlds, and redeem them; never, until all this is accomplished, will their glory be complete; and then there will be ' Lords many and Gods many.' "

Mormonism Portrayed, pp. 20—23.

MORMON PARADISE.

Harris says, —

"The Mormon idea of a Paradise is a singular feature in their creed. They, however, regard it as one which shows the superiority of their system over all others, and ridicule, as absurd, the notion generally entertained of the location and nature of heaven. As a matter of curiosity, then, as well as to make a further display of the absurdities of Mormonism, I will here insert a description of the Mormon Paradise, taken from the Voice of Warning, pages 179, 80 Alluding to a prophecy in the Book of Mormon, the author says, 'From this prophecy we learn, First, That America is a chosen land. Secondly, That it is the place of the new Jerusalem, which shall come down from God out of heaven upon the earth, when it is renewed. Thirdly, That a new Jerusalem is to be built in America, to the remnant of Joseph, (the Indians,) like unto or after a similar pattern to the old Jerusalem in the land of Canaan; and that the old Jerusalem shall be rebuilt at the same time; and this being done, both cities will continue in prosperity on the earth, until the great and last change, when the heavens and the earth are to be renewed. Fourth, We learn that when this change takes place, the two cities are caught up into heaven, together with the inhabitants thereof, and being changed, and made new, the one comes down on the American land, and the other to its own place as formerly. Fifth, We learn that the inhabitants are the same that gathered together and first builded them. The remnant of Joseph and those gathered with them, inherit the new Jerusalem; and the tribes of Israel, gathered from the north countries, and from the four quarters of the earth, inhabit the other, and thus all things being made new, we find those who were once strangers and pilgrims on the earth, in possession of that better country, and that city for which they sought.'

"Here, then, is a picture of the Mormon Paradise. Let us now, for a moment, compare it to the Paradise of God, or the city of inheritance, spoken of, and sought for, by the prophets and apostles.

"Christ said, when on earth, 'In my Father's house are many mansions; if it were not so, I would have told you. I go to prepare a place for you.' Now, where did Christ speak of going? To the earth? He was already there, and on the very spot where one of the new Jerusalems, according to the Mormons, is to be. He meant, evidently, to his Father's house, the place where is the throne of God. Paul, in his allusion to this passage, says, 'For we know, that if this earthly house of our tabernacle were dissolved, we have a building of God, a house not made with hands, eternal in the heavens.' And speaking of Abraham, 'For he looked for a city which hath foundations, whose maker and builder is God.' Here is Paul's idea of heaven, 'a house not made with hands, eternal (that is, existing from, and to, all eternity) in the heavens.' The Mormon Paradise, on the other hand, is to be built by men, (not by God, as was Abraham's,) and does not yet exist. Again, Peter says, 'Blessed be the

God and Father of our Lord Jesus Christ, which, according to his abundant mercy, hath begotten us again unto a lively hope, by the resurrection of Jesus Christ from the dead, to an inheritance incorruptible, undefiled, and that fadeth not away; reserved in the heavens for you, who are kept by the power of God, through faith, unto salvation, ready to be revealed in the last time.' Here Peter's inheritance is 'reserved in the heavens;' not to be built hereafter, but now being, and reserved 'ready to be revealed at the last time.'

"Again, Peter, in his 2d Epistle, 3d chapter, and 10—13th verses, says, 'The day of the Lord will come as a thief in the night, in the which the heavens shall pass away with a great noise, and the elements shall melt with fervent heat; the earth, also, and the works that are therein, shall be burned up. Seeing, then, that all these things shall be dissolved, what manner of persons ought ye to be in all holy conversation and godliness, looking for and hasting unto the coming of the day of God, wherein the heavens, being on fire, shall be dissolved, and the elements shall melt with fervent heat? nevertheless we, according to his promise, look for new heavens and a new earth, wherein dwelleth righteousness.' Now, here Peter says that the old earth shall pass away, and that, according to the promise of God, we look for a 'new heaven, and a new earth;' not the present heavens and the present earth renewed, as the Mormons have it. To renew merely implies to change; but Peter says that the earth shall pass away. Again, John, referring to the same, Rev. 21st chapter, 1st verse, says, 'And I saw a new heaven and a new earth, for the first heaven and the first earth had passed away, and there was no more sea.' Now, if there is to be no sea, how can the new earth be divided into continents? But the Mormons say there are to be two Jerusalems, one on the eastern and the other on the western continent. John goes on to say, 'And I saw the holy city, new Jerusalem, coming down from God out of heaven, prepared as a bride adorned for her husband.' He does not say that the city was caught up into heaven, brick houses and all made by men, and then let down again, as the Mormons have it, but, 'I saw the city (not two cities) coming down from God,' on the new earth. Further, in the same chapter, 22d verse, he says, 'And I saw no temple therein, for the Lord God Almighty and the Lamb are the temple of it.' Now, in the revelation giving directions for building the Mormon new Jerusalem, they are to build a Temple, &c., and, according to Pratt's account, the cities are to be caught up into heaven, and are to be let down after the earth is renewed; of course, there are to be temples literally speaking. A great number of other passages might be quoted, to show the dissimilarity between the Mormon Paradise and that which is described in the Scriptures; but enough has been said to prove theirs a mere invention of the imagination."

Mormonism Portrayed, by William Harris, pp. 23—25.

HISTORY OF THE MORMONS.

Mr. Harris observes, —

" An account of the origin of Smith, the discovery of the plates, and their translation, will be found in another portion of this work ; I shall therefore confine myself more particularly, in this chapter, to the history of the Mormon Church, with a view thereby more fully to illustrate its character. Its first organization, with only six members, was shortly after the publication of the Book of Mormon, in 1830. These first members, consisting mostly of persons who were engaged with Smith in the translation of the plates, forthwith set themselves with great zeal to building up the Church. Their first efforts were confined to Western New York and Pennsylvania, where they met with considerable success. After a number of converts had been made, Smith received a revelation, that he and all his followers should go to Kirtland, Ohio, and there take up their abode. Many obeyed this command, selling their possessions, and helping each other to settle in the spot designated. This place was the head-quarters of the Church, and the residence of the Prophet, until 1838 ; but it does not appear that they ever regarded it as a place of permanent settlement ; for in Book of Covenants, page 150, it is said, in speaking of Kirtland, ' I consecrate this land unto them for a little season, until I the Lord provide for them to go hence.'

" In the spring of 1831, Smith, Rigdon, and others, were directed, by revelation, (see Book of Covenants, page 193,) to go on a journey to Missouri, and there the Lord was to show them the place of the new Jerusalem. This journey was accordingly taken, and when they arrived, a revelation was received, (see B. C., p. 154,) pointing out the town of Independence, Jackson county, as the central place for the Land of Promise, where they were directed to build a temple, &c. Shortly after their return to Kirtland, a number of revelations were received, commanding the Saints, throughout the country, to purchase and settle in this Land of Promise. Accordingly many went and began there to build up Zion, as they called it.

" In the mean time, Smith, Rigdon, &c., devoted their labors in Kirtland to building up themselves and the Church.

" In 1831, a consecration law was established in the church, by revelation. It was first published in the Book of Commandments, page 93, and in the Evening and Morning Star, 1st ed., No. 3, Vol. I. It reads thus : ' If thou lovest me thou shalt keep my commandments, and thou shalt consecrate *all* of thy properties unto me, with a covenant and deed which cannot be broken.' This law, however, has been republished, in the Book of Covenants, page 122, and in the republication, has been altered. As modified, it reads thus : ' If thou lovest me thou shalt serve me and keep all of my commandments, and behold thou shalt remember the poor, and consecrate of thy properties for their support that which thou hast to impart unto them with a covenant and deed, which cannot be broken.' Let me digress for one moment, and ask why this alteration. It does ap-

12

pear to have been done by command of God, but purports to be
the same revelation as was first published. This is demonstration
that Smith makes and alters revelations, to suit his own purposes.

" The details of this consecration law will be found in Book of
Covenants, page 150, and reads thus : ' Hearken unto me, saith the
Lord your God, and I will speak unto my servant Edward Patridge,
and give unto him directions ; for it must needs be that he have
directions how to organize the people ; for it must needs be that
they are organized according to my laws. If otherwise, they will
be cut off ; wherefore let my servant Edward Patridge, and those
whom he has chosen in whom I am well pleased, appoint unto this
people their portion, every man equal according to their families,
according to circumstances, and their wants and needs ; and let my
servant Edward Patridge, when he shall appoint a man his portion,
give unto him a writing, that shall secure unto him his portion, that
he shall hold it, even this right and this inheritance in the Church,
until he transgresses and is not accounted worthy by the voice of
the Church, to belong to the Church, according to the laws and
covenants of the Church ; and if he shall transgress and is not accounted worthy to belong to the Church, he shall not have power to
claim that portion which he has consecrated unto the Bishop, for
the poor and the needy of my Church, therefore he shall not retain
the gift, but shall only have claim to that portion which is deeded
unto him. — And thus all things shall be made sure according to the
laws of the land.

" ' And let that which belongs to this people, be appointed unto
this people, and the money which is left unto this people, let there
be an agent appointed unto this people, to take the money to provide food and raiment according to the wants of this people. And
let every man deal honestly and be alike amongst this people, and
receive alike, that he may be even as I have commanded you.

" ' And let that which belongeth to this people not be taken and
given unto that of another church : wherefore if another church
would receive money of this Church, let them pay unto this Church
according as they shall agree, and this shall be done through the
Bishop or the agent, which shall be appointed by the voice of the
Church.'

" And again, ' Let the Bishop appoint a storehouse unto this
Church, and let all things both in money and in meat, which is more
than is needful for the wants of this people, be kept in the hands of
the Bishop. And let him also reserve unto himself for the wants of
his family, as he shall be employed in doing this business.' Again,
speaking of this law, ' Behold, this shall be an example unto my
servant Edward Patridge in other places, in all churches, and whoso
is found a faithful, a just, and wise steward, shall enter into the joy
of his Lord, and shall inherit eternal life. Verily I say unto you, I
am Jesus Christ, who cometh quickly, in an hour you think not ;
even so, Amen.'

" The penalty attached to a breach of this law will be found in
the Book of Covenants, page 241, thus : ' Therefore, if any man
shall take of the abundance which I have made, and impart not his

portion, according to the law of the gospel, unto the poor and the needy, he snall with the wicked lift up his eyes in hell, being in torment.'

" These were the provisions of the consecration laws, which, so far as I am informed, are yet unrepealed. They have never, however, been put in full operation ; because the people would not suffer it. The whole scheme was evidently designed for the benefit of Smith & Co., as will more fully appear by what follows.

" In April, 1832, a firm was established by revelation, ostensibly for the benefit of the Church, consisting of the principal members in Kirtland and in Independence. (See B. C., pages 219 and 220.) The members of th s firm were bound together by an oath and covenant, to ' manage the affairs of the poor, and all things pertaining to the bishopric, both in Zion (Missouri) and in Shinahar (Kirtland.) According to the consecration law, above quoted, the Bishop was to h ve charge of all consecrated property, also to have charge of the storehouse of the Church ; consequently, as this firm superseded the B shop, it had charge of all the consecrated property. In June, 1833, a revelation was received to lay off Kirtland in lots, and the proceeds of the sale were to go to this firm, (B. C., p. 234.) In 1834 or '5, the firm was divided by revelation, (B. C., 240,) so that those in Kirtland continued as one firm, and those in Missouri as another. In the same revelation, they are commanded to divide the consecrated property between the individuals of the firm, which each separately were to manage as stewards Previous to this, in 1833, a revelation was received to build a temple, (B. C., p. 213,) which was to be done by the consecrated funds in the management of the firm. In putting up this structure, the firm involved itself in debt to a large amount ; wherefore, in the revelation last mentioned above, the following appears: 'Inasmuch as ye are humble and faithful, and call on my name, behold I will give you the victory, I give unto you a promise that you shall be delivered this once out of your bondage, inasmuch as you obtain a chance to loan money by hundreds and thousands, even till you have obtained enough to deliver yourselves out of bondage.' This was a command to borrow money, in order to free themselves from the debt that oppressed them. They made the attempt, but failed to get sufficient to satisfy their purposes. This led to another expedient.

" In 1835, Smith, Rigdon, and others, formed a mercantile house, and purchased goods in Cleveland and in Buffalo, to a very large amount, on a credit of six months. In the fall, other houses were formed, and goods purchased in the eastern cities to a still greater amount. A great part of the goods of these houses went to pay the workmen on the Temple, and many were sold on credit, so that when the notes became due, the houses were not able to meet them. Smith, Rigdon, & Co., then attempted to borrow money, by issuing their notes payable at different periods after date. This expedient not being effectual, the idea of a Bank suggested itself. Accordingly, in 1837, the far-famed Kirtland Bank was put into operation, without charter. This institution, by which so many have been swindled, was formed after the following manner : Subscribers for stock were allowed to pay the amount of their subscriptions in town lots, at five or six times their real value ; others paid in personal property, at a high valuation; and some paid the cash. When the notes were first issued, they were current in the vicinity, and Smith took advantage of their credit to pay off, with them, the debts he and the brethren had contracted in the neighborhood, for land, &c. The eastern creditors, however, refused to take them. This led to the expedient of exchanging them for the notes of other banks. Accordingly, the elders were sent off the country to barter off Kirtland money, which they did with great zeal, and continued the operation, until the notes were not worth twelve and a half cents to the dollar. As might have been expected, this institution, after a few months, exploded, involving Smith and his brethren in inextricable difficulties. The consequence was, that he and most of the members of the Church set off, in the spring of 1838, for Far West, Mo., being pursued by their creditors, but to no effect.

" I will now go back for a short period. In 1836, an endowment meeting, or solemn assembly, was called, to be held in the Temple at Kirtland. It was given out that those who were in attendance at the meeting should receive an endowment, or blessing, similar to that experienced by the disciples of Christ on the day of Pentecost. When the day arrived, great numbers convened from the different Churches in the country. They spent the day in fasting and prayer, and in washing and perfuming their bodies ; they also washed their feet, and anointed their heads with what they called holy oil, and pronounced blessings. In the evening, they met for the endowment. The fast was then broken by eating light wheat bread, and drinking as much wine as they saw proper. Smith knew well how to infuse the spirit which they expected to receive ; so he encouraged the brethren to drink freely, telling them that the wine was consecrated, and would not make them drunk. As may be supposed, they drank to the purpose. After this, they began to prophesy, pronouncing blessings upon their friends, and curses upon their enemies. If I should be so unhappy as to go to the regions of the damned, I never expect to hear language more awful, or more becoming the infernal pit, than was uttered that night. The curses were pronounced principally upon the clergy of the present day, and upon the Jackson county mob in Missouri. After spending the night in alternate blessings and cursings, the meeting adjourned.

" I now return to Missouri. The Mormons who had settled in and about Independence, having become very arrogant, claiming the land as their own, — saying the Lord had given it to them, — and making the most haughty assumptions, so exasperated the old citizens, that a mob was raised, in 1833, and expelled the whole Mormon body from the county. They fled to Clay county, where the citizens permitted them to live in quiet, until 1836, when a mob spirit began to manifest itself, and the Mormons retired to a very thinly settled district of the country, where they began to make improvements. This district was, at the session of 1836–7 of the Missouri Legislature, erected into a county, by the name of Caldwell, with Far West for its county seat. Here the Mormons remained in

quiet, until after the Bank explosion in Kirtland, in 1838, when
Smith, Rigdon, &c. arrived.   Shortly after this, the Danite Society
was organized, — the object of which, at first, was to drive the dissenters out of the county.   The members of this society were bound
together by an oath and covenant, with the penalty of death attached
to a breach, to defend the Presidency, and each other, unto death, —
right or wrong.   They had their secret signs, by which they knew
each other, either by day or night; and were divided into bands of
tens and fifties, with a captain over each band, and a general over
the whole.   After this body was formed, notice was given to several
of the dissenters to leave the county, and they were threatened
severely, in case of disobedience.   The effect of this was, that many
of the dissenters left; amongst these were David Whitmer, John
Whitmer, Hiram Page, and Oliver Cowdery, all witnesses to the
Book of Mormon, also Lyman Johnson, one of the Twelve Apostles.
The day after John Whitmer left his house in Far West, it was
taken possession of by Sidney Rigdon.   About this time, Rigdon
preached his famous 'salt sermon.'   The text was — 'Ye are the
salt of the earth, but if the salt have lost its savor, wherewith shall
it be salted; it is thenceforth good for nothing, but to be cast out,
and to be trodden under foot of men.'   He informed the Mormons
that the Church was the salt, that dissenters were the salt that had lost
its savor, and that they were literally to be trodden under the feet
of the Church, until their bowels should be gushed out.   In order to
give weight to this interpretation, he attempted to sustain his position from the Bible !   He referred to the case of Judas, informing the
people that he did not fall headlong and his bowels gush out, without assistance, but that the apostles threw him, and with their feet
trampled them out !   He also said that Ananias and Sapphira, his
wife, did not fall down dead, as translated ; but that Peter and John
slew them, and the young men, or deacons, carried them out and
buried them.

    " In one of the meetings of the Danite Band, one of the leaders
informed them that the time was not far distant, when the elders of
the Church should go forth to the world with swords at their sides,
and that they would soon have to go through the State of Missouri,
and slay every man, woman, and child !   They had it in contemplation, at one time, to prophesy a dreadful pestilence in Missouri, and
then to poison the waters of the State, to bring it about, and thus to
destroy the inhabitants.

    " In the early part of the fall of the year 1838, the last disturb-
ance between the Mormons and the Missourians commenced.   It
had its origin at an election in Daviess county, where some of the
Mormons had located.   A citizen of Daviess, in conversation with a
Mormon, remarked that the Mormons all voted one way : this was
with warmth denied.   A violent contest ensued ; when at last the
Mormon called the Missourian a liar.   Upon this the Missourian
struck him.   A row between the Mormons and Missourians followed.

    " A day or two after this, Smith, with a company of men from
Far West, went into Daviess county, for the purpose, as they said,

to quell the mob; but when they arrived, there was no mob there. This excited the citizens of Daviess, and they gathered in turn. But the Mormons soon collected a force to the amount of three or four hundred, and compelled the citizens to retire. They fled, leaving the country deserted for a number of miles around. At this time they killed between one and two hundred hogs, a number of cattle, took at least forty or fifty stands of honey, and at the same time destroyed several fields of corn. The word was out, that the Lord had consecrated, through the Bishop, the spoils unto his host. All this was done when they had plenty of their own, and previous to the citizens in that section of the country taking aught of theirs. They continued these depredations for near a week, when the Clay county militia were ordered out. The history of what followed will be found in another chapter. Suffice it to say, here, that Smith, Rigdon, and many others, were finally taken, and at a court of inquiry were remanded over for trial. Rigdon was afterwards discharged on *habeas corpus*, and Smith and his comrades, after being in prison several months, escaped from their guards, and reached Quincy, Illinois. The Mormons had been before ordered to leave the State, by direction of the Governor; and many had retired to Illinois previous to Smith's arrival.

" Of this Missouri war, as it has been called, a great deal has been said, and public opinion, at the time, generally censured the conduct of Missouri. That the Missourians carried the matter too far, and treated the Mormons with an unnecessary degree of cruelty, in many instances, there can be no doubt; but that there was great cause of aggravation, there can be just as little. The truth is, that while the Mormon body, as a church, interfere with the pecuniary and political acts of its members, assuming the sole direction of both, it will be impossible for them to live in peace in any community. The necessary consequence of their regarding the words of Smith as the words of the Lord, is, that he can unite them whenever it may be necessary to effect his purposes. This, probably, would produce no jealousy, if his acts were confined to ecclesiastical government; but when they extend to controlling the political and pecuniary interests of his followers, it must inevitably produce distrust and enmity. Such a community, thus united, hold the rights of the neighboring citizens in their own hands; and in every contest they must come off victors. They have a capacity for secrecy, which enables them to commit any act of depredation, without the fear of detection; and when a crime has been committed by one of them, they are so united to each other's interests, as to render it almost impossible, through a legal formula, to obtain a conviction. Is it any wonder, then, that a body thus controlled — their interest confined within themselves, and inimical in its nature to that of the other citizens — should excite jealousy? And when we consider the materials of which the Church is made, the amount of ignorance, bigotry, and arrogance, that is displayed by its members, is it at all surprising that an explosion should take place between them and those by whom they are surrounded? Now, even admitting that the Mormons were honest, yet, taking all things into consideration, the Missourians acted, in the commencement of the difficulties, as would almost any community in the country. I do not justify their mobs; on the contrary, 1 say that a mob in ho case is justifiable; but I do say that, as society is now constituted, mobs will arise, under certain circumstances, in any community. Let, then, those who have regarded the Missourians as a set of unprincipled desperadoes, because of their conduct towards the Mormons, bethink them, that the same scenes, under the same circumstances, would, in all probability, have been enacted in their own neighborhoods. It was not the mere religion of the Mormons, that exasperated the Missourians; it was their arrogance, — their united purpose to protect each other, and to infringe on the rights of other citizens, — their thefts, and their concealments of each other's crimes. These were all, under the circumstances, injuries without legal remedies; and, although this does not justify a mob, yet there are few communities in this country, that would not, if placed in the same situation, have been exasperated to violence.

" The Mormons, as a body, arrived in Illinois in the early part of the year 1839. At this time they presented a spectacle of destitution and wretchedness almost unexampled. This, together with their tales of persecution and privation, wrought powerfully upon the sympathies of the citizens, and caused them to be received with the greatest hospitality and kindness. After the arrival of Smith, the greater part of them settled at Commerce, situated on the Mississippi River, at the head of the Des Moines, or Lower Rapids, — a site equal in beauty to any on the river. Here they began to build their habitations, and in the short space of two years have raised quite a city. At first, as was before said, on account of their former sufferings, and also of the great political power which they possessed, they were treated by the citizens of Illinois with great respect; but subsequent events have served to turn the tide of feeling against them. In the winter of 1840, they applied to the Legislature of the State for several charters — one for the city of Nauvoo, the name Smith had given to the town of Commerce, — one for the Nauvoo Legion, a military body, — one for manufacturing purposes, — and one for a University. The privileges which they asked for were very extensive; and such was the desire to secure their political favor, that they were granted for the mere asking. Indeed the great ones of our Legislature seemed to vie with each other in sycophancy to this set of fanatical strangers, — so anxious was each party to do some act that would secure their gratitude. This, together with the sycophancy of office-seekers, tended to produce jealousy in the minds of the neighboring citizens, and fears were expressed, lest a body, so united, both religiously and politically, would become dangerous to our free institutions. The Mormons had nearly all voted at every election with their leaders, and evidently under their direction; this alone made them formidable. The Legion had got under its direction a great portion of the arms of the State, and the whole body was placed under the strictest military discipline. These things, together with complaints similar to those which were made in Missouri, tended to arouse a strong feeling against them; when at last, in the early part of the summer of

1841, a political move was made by them, and the citizens organized a party in opposition. The Mormons were beaten in the contest. The disposition now manifested by the citizens appears to be, to act on the defensive ; but to maintain their rights at all hazards. If the Mormons consent to act as other citizens, they will not be molested on account of their religion ; but freemen will not submit to be trampled on by an organized body of men, no matter by what name they are called, or whose standard they follow.

" As regards the pecuniary transactions of the Mormons, since they have been in Illinois, — Smith still uses his power for his own benefit. His present operations are to purchase land at a low rate, lay it off into town lots, and sell them at a high price to his followers. Thus, lots that scarcely cost him a dollar, are frequently sold for a thousand. He has made several towns in this manner, both in Iowa and in Illinois.

" During the last year, he has made two proclamations to his followers abroad, to settle in the county of Hancock. These proclamations have been to a great extent obeyed, and hundreds are now flocking in, from the Eastern States, and from England. What is to be the result of all this, I am not able to tell; but one thing is certain, — that, in a political point of view, the Mormons are already dangerous; and as a consequence, they will be watched with jealousy by their neighbors."

Mormonism Portrayed, by William Harris, pp. 28—36

———◆———

THE DESIGNS OF MORMONISM.

Mr. Harris remarks, —

" The designs of Smith and his coadjutors, at the time of the first publication of the Book of Mormon, was, doubtlessly, nothing more than pecuniary aggrandizement. I do not believe, at that time, they expected that so many could ever be duped to admit it true. When, however, the delusion began to spread, the publishers saw the door opened not only for wealth, but also for extensive power ; and their history throughout shows that they have not been remiss in their efforts to acquire both. The extent of their desires is now by no means limited, for their writings and actions show a design to pursue the same path, and attain the same end by the same means, as did Mahomet. The idea of a second Mahomet arising in the nineteenth century, may excite a smile; but when we consider the steps now taking by the Mormons to concentrate their numbers, and their ultimate design to unite themselves with the Indians, it will not be at all surprising, if scenes unheard of since the days of feudalism should soon be reënacted.

" In the first place, Smith, by proclamations and by revelations, has called all his followers to settle immediately around him. The last revelation on this subject is published in the Times and Seasons dated June 1, 1841, from which I extract the following: 'Awake! O! Kings of the Earth! Come ye, O! Come ye, with your gold and your silver, to the help of my people, to the house of the Daughter of Zion, * * *. And again, verily I say unto you, let all my Saints come from afar; and send ye swift messengers, yea, chosen messengers, and say unto them, come ye with all your gold, and your silver, and your precious stones, and with your antiquities,' &c. They are further informed, in the course of this revelation, that after sufficient time has been allowed to build a baptismal font at Nauvoo, their baptisms for the dead shall not be acceptable in other places. The object of Smith, in all this, is evidently to collect all his followers into one place, and thus to concentrate all his power, and enable him the better to secure wealth.

"These quotations and statements are introduced to show that they are concentrating all their energies at one point, and that they teach their proselytes that it is the will of God that they should thus concentrate themselves. In accordance with this, I wish to make a few remarks: First, it is a notorious fact that they (the Mormons) *are gathering from every part of the world*, and all their teachers are instructed, by revelation, to gather them together at Nauvoo. Secondly, they have obtained an act of the Legislature, organizing the 'Nauvoo Legion,' (which may be increased to an indefinite number,) have obtained arms of the government, and are at this time more than one thousand strong, and increasing continually. Now, I ask, why all this gathering, so different from every other denomination, unless they have designs against the rights and liberties of others? Why are they using their best exertions for, and actually raising up, a large, well-drilled, well-armed, standing army? There can be no religion in this, every one knows; and hence it follows that they are not only contemplating, but actually preparing for, the execution of some murderous design. But as an illustration of what they intend to do, I make the following extracts from Rigdon's oration, delivered at Far West, July 4, 1838, and from their standard writings.

"In his oration, Mr. Rigdon said, 'We take God and all the holy angels to witness this day, that we warn all men in the name of Jesus Christ, to come on us no more forever. The man, or the set of men, who attempts it, does it at the expense of their lives. And that mob that comes on us to disturb us, it shall be between us and them a war of *extermination*, for we will follow them till the *last drop of their blood is spilled*, or else they will have to exterminate us. For we will carry the seat of *war* to their own *houses*, and their own *families*, and one party or the other shall be utterly destroyed. Remember it, then, all men. * * * No man shall be at liberty to come into our streets, to threaten us with mobs; for if he does, he shall atone for it before he leaves the place; neither shall he be at liberty to vilify and slander any of us, for suffer it we will not in this place. We, therefore, take all men to record this day, as did our fathers. And we pledge this day to one another our fortunes, our lives, and our sacred honors, to be delivered from the persecutions which we have had to endure, for the last

nine years, or nearly that. Neither will we indulge any man, or
set of men, in instituting vexatious lawsuits against us, to cheat us
out of our just rights ; if they attempt it, we say woe be unto them.
We this day, then, proclaim ourselves free, with a purpose and a
determination, that can never be broken, — *No, Never! No, Never* !!
NO, NEVER ! ! ! '

"What gives this testimony the more importance is this — it was
uttered some time previous to the disturbance in Missouri, in which
they were driven away, and hence shows, conclusively, that Rigdon
& Co. expected a disturbance, which could only have arisen
from an intention to act in such a, manner, that the Missourians
would not bear with them. But, further : —

"Book of Covenants, page 191. 'Wherefore, I say unto you,
that I have sent unto you mine everlasting *Covenants*, (namely, the
Book of Mormon,) even that which was from the beginning, and
that which I have promised I have so fulfilled, and the nations of the
earth *shall bow to it ;* and if not of themselves, *they shall come down ;
for that which is now exalted of itself shall be laid low of power.*'
Also, on page 76, 'Wherefore the voice of the Lord is unto the
ends of the earth, that all that will hear may ; prepare ye, prepare
ye, for that which is to come, for the Lord is nigh ; and the anger
of the Lord is kindled, and his sword is sheathed in heaven, and it
shall fall upon the inhabitants of the earth ; and the arm of the Lord
shall be revealed ; and the day cometh, that they who will not hear
the voice of his servants, neither give heed to the words of the
prophets and apostles, shall be cut off from among the people.'
Also, on page 95, (perhaps it ought to be remarked here, that in all
their revelations, and by all their declaimers, they represent themselves and Indians as the instruments by which these desolations are
to be brought about,) 'Go ye forth, as your circumstances shall permit, in your several callings, unto the great and notable cities
and villages, reproving the world in righteousness of all their
unrighteous and ungodly deeds, setting forth clearly and understand-
ingly, the desolation of abomination in the last days; *for with you,
saith the Lord Almighty, I will rend their kingdoms.*' Also, page
117, 'Wherefore, I have called upon the weak things of the world,
those who are unlearned and despised, to thrash the nations by the
power of my spirit; and their arm shall be my arm, and I will be
their shield and their buckler, and I will gird up their loins, and
they shall fight manfully for me ; and their *enemies shall be under
their feet ;* and I will let fall the *sword* in their behalf ; and by the
fire of mine indignation will I preserve them.'

"Voice of Warning, by Parley P. Pratt, one of the Twelve Apostles, page 186: 'The government of the United States has been
engaged, for upwards of seven years, in gathering the remnant of
Joseph (the Indians) to the very place where they will finally build
a new Jerusalem ; a city of Zion ; with the acquisition of the believing Gentiles, who will gather with them from all the nations of
the earth; and this gathering is clearly predicted in the Book of
Mormon, and other revelations; and the place before appointed, and
the time set for its fulfilment; and except the Gentiles repent of all
their abominations and embrace the same Covenant, (namely, the

Book of Mormon,) and come into the same place of gathering, *they will soon be destroyed from off the face of the land;*' as it is written by Isaiah, 'The nation and kingdom that will not serve thee shall perish. Yea, those nations shall be utterly wasted.' It is further stated, in the same work, that the Indians shall be gathered, and that they, in connection with the Mormons, shall be among the Gentiles as ' a young lion among the flock of sheep, *and none can deliver,*' and that the Gentiles (all Anti-Mormons) shall be ' as a thing long since passed away, and the remembrance of it almost gone from the earth.'

" But, to cap the climax, read the following : ' All who will not hearken to the Book of Mormon, shall be cut off from among the people ; and that too, in the day it comes forth to the Gentiles and is rejected by them.' And not only does this page set the time for the *overthrow of our government,* and *all other Gentile governments* on the AMERICAN CONTINENT, but the way and means of this *utter destruction* are clearly foretold ; namely, the remnant of Jacob (or Indians) will go through among the Gentiles and *tear them in pieces* like a lion among the flocks of sheep. Their hand shall be lifted up upon their adversaries, and all their enemies shall *be cut off.* This destruction includes an utter overthrow, and desolation of all our cities, forts and strong-holds, — an *entire annihilation of our race,* except such as embrace the Covenant, and are numbered with Israel ! ! ! ' And I will state, as a prophecy, that *there will not be an unbelieving Gentile on the face of this continent fifty years hence ;* and if they are not greatly scourged and in a great measure overthrown within five or ten years from this date, (1838,) then the Book of Mormon will have proved itself false.' This last quotation comes from Pratt's ' Mormonism Unveiled, or Truth Vindicated, ' — a work, by the way, so popular among them that it has already passed through several editions. Comment is unnecessary here; the fact stands proved, clearly and incontrovertibly proved, that they contemplate nothing less than the butchery ! murder !! and entire annihilation ! ! ! of all who will not subscribe to their ridiculous teachings. And what adds insult to injury is this — that they raise a long and loud cry of ' PERSECUTION,' when people are only defending themselves against their unlawful aggressions. In conclusion, permit me to ask my countrymen whether they are prepared to allow these ' wolves in sheep's clothing ' to impose upon them by the false cry of peace, when it is evident that they have only ' religion on their tongues,' at the same time ' holding a dagger in their hands, and murder in their hearts.' "

Mormonism Portrayed, by William Harris, pp. 44—47.

The Rev. L. Sunderland, in his *Mormonism Exposed,* in speaking on this subject, remarks, —

"MORMONS SAY THAT GOD HAS SENT DOWN FROM HEAVEN A CITY, CALLED THE ' NEW JERUSALEM,' AND LOCATED IT [IN INDEPENDENCE] IN THE WESTERN BOUNDARIES OF MISSOURI, WHERE HE REQUIRES ALL HIS TRUE FOLLOWERS TO GO, UNDER THE PAIN OF HIS WRATH.

" And it is a fundamental principle with them, that if they cannot buy the land, they are to *obtain it by the sword.*

" ' America is a chosen land of the Lord, above every other land ; it is the place of the new Jerusalem, which has *come down from God out of heaven,* upon the earth.' — *Voice of Warning,* p. 179.

" ' This is the will of God concerning his saints, that they shall assemble themselves together unto the land of Zion. Behold the land of Zion, I the Lord *holdeth* it in my own hands ; notwithstanding, I, the Lord, *rendereth* unto Cæsar the things which are Cæsar's. Wherefore, I, the Lord, *willeth* that you shall purchase the lands, that you may have advantage of the world, that you may have claim of the world, that they may not be stirred up unto anger; for Satan putteth it into their hearts to anger against you, and to the shedding of blood. Wherefore the land of Zion shall not be obtained but, by purchase, *or by blood;* otherwise there is none inheritance for you.' — *Doc. and Cov.,* p. 143.

" ' A revelation of Jesus Christ unto his servant Joseph Smith, Jr., and six elders, as they united their hearts and lifted up their voices on high, * * * for the gathering of his Saints to stand on Mount Zion, which shall be the city of New Jerusalem ; which shall be built, beginning at the Temple Lot, [in INDEPENDENCE,] appointed by the finger of the Lord, in the western boundaries of Missouri.' — *Ib.,* p. 88.

" ' And that it was the place of the new Jerusalem which should come down out of heaven, and the Holy Sanctuary of the Lord.' — *Book of Mormon,* p. 566.

" THE MORMON LEADERS HOLD THAT THEY, OR THEIR SECT, ARE JUSTLY ENTITLED TO THE TEMPORAL AND SPIRITUAL DOMINION OF THESE UNITED STATES, AND THAT IF THEY CANNOT OTHERWISE OBTAIN THIS DOMINION, THEY ARE TO GAIN IT BY THE SWORD.

" ' Wherefore the land of Zion shall not be obtained, but by purchase or *by blood.'* — *Doc. and Cov.,* p. 143.

" It is added in connection with the above, ' as ye are *forbidden* to shed blood.' But how the Mormons are forbidden to shed blood we shall see in the sequel.

" ' For behold, verily I say unto you, the Lord willeth that the disciples and the *children of men* should open their hearts even to purchase this *whole region of country,* as soon as time will permit. Behold, here is wisdom, let them do this, lest they receive none inheritance, save it be the *shedding of blood.'* — *Ib.,* p. 139.

" The following is designed to signify the UTTER DESTRUCTION of this nation, except it submits to Mormonism. By the Gentiles, he means the people of these United States.

" ' A remnant of the house of Jacob [as he calls our American Indians] shall be among the Gentiles ; yea, in the midst of them, as a lion among the beasts of the forest, as a young lion among the flocks of sheep, who, if he go through, both treadeth down and teareth in pieces, and none can deliver. Their hand shall be lifted up upon their adversaries, and all their enemies shall be cut off. Yea, *woe* be unto the Gentiles, except they repent : for it shall come to pass in that day, saith the Father, that I will cut off thy horses out of the midst of thee, and I will destroy thy chariots, and I will *cut off the cities of thy land,* and throw down thy strong-holds,' &c. — *Voice of Warning,* p. 188.

"'And the day cometh that they who will not hear the voice of the Lord, neither the voice of his servants, [the Mormons,] neither give heed to the words of the Prophets and Apostles, [Mormons,] shall be CUT OFF from among the people — for they have broken mine everlasting covenant.' — *Doc. and Cov.,* p. 76.

"'*Everlasting* covenant' broken!

"'Therefore, having so great witnesses, [Joe Smith and Oliver Cowdery,] by *them shall the world be judged,* even as many as shall hereafter come to a knowledge of this work — but those who harden their hearts in unbelief, and reject it, shall turn to their own con-demnation,' &c. — *Ib.,* p. 78.

"'Woe, I say again, unto that house, or that village, or city that rejecteth you, [Mormons,] or your words, or your testimony of me.' — *Ib.,* p. 93.

"'Let the Bishop go unto the city of New York, and also to the city of Albany, and also to the city of Boston, and warn the people of those cities with the sound of the gospel, with a loud voice, of the DESOLATION and UTTER ABOLISHMENT which awaits them if they do reject these things,' [Mormonism.] — *Ib.,* p. 95.

"'Verily I say unto you, [Mormons,] that in time, ye shall have *no king nor ruler,* for I will be your king and watch over you ; and you shall be a free people, and ye shall have no laws but my laws when I come.' — *Ib.,* p. 119.

"'Assemble yourselves together to rejoice upon the land of Mis-souri, which is the land of *your inheritance,* which is now in the hand of your enemies.'— *Ib.,* p. 194.

"'Therefore, get ye straightway unto my land; *break down* the walls of mine enemies, *throw down* their tower, and scatter their watchmen, avenge me of mine enemies, that by and by I may come and possess the land.'— *Ib.,* p. 238.

"MORMONISM DEMANDS MONEY AS THE CONDITION OF DISCIPLE-SHIP, UNDER THE PENALTY OF ETERNAL DAMNATION.

"'Whoso receiveth you, receiveth me, and the same will feed you, and clothe you, *and give you* MONEY —and he who doeth not these things is not my disciple.'— *Doc. and Cov.,* p. 93.

"Here it will be seen, that giving *money* to the Mormon leaders, is a condition of discipleship, and all who are not Mormon disciples are *doomed to hell !*

"ONE GRAND DESIGN OF MORMONISM IS, TO FILL THE POCK-ETS OF ITS ADVOCATES WITH MONEY.

"'It must needs be that ye save all the money that ye can, and that ye gain all ye can in righteousness.' *Doc. and Cov ,* p. 191.

"'It is wisdom in me, that my servant Martin Harris should be an example unto the Church, *in laying his moneys before the Bishop of the Church.* And also, this is a law unto *every man* that cometh unto this land, to receive an inheritance ; and he shall do with his moneys according as the law directs.' *Ib.,* p. 138.

13

" From the next extract, which is addressed to one Titus Billings, the grand object of Mormonism appears in full view.

" ' And let all the *moneys* which can be spared, *it mattereth not unto me whether it be little or much*, be sent up unto the land of Zion, unto those I have appointed to receive it.'— *Ib.* p. 143.

" Here it is again.   Money, money, money !

" ' And let all those (preachers) who have no families, who receive moneys, send it up unto the Bishop of Zion, or unto the Bishop in Ohio, th it it may be consecrated for the *bringing forth of the revelations*, and the printing thereof, and *establishing Zion*.'

" No ' revelations ' can be brought forth without money. The ' new Jerusalem ' cannot come down from heaven without money. Here it is again.

" ' Behold, this is my will, obtaining *moneys* even as I have directed.'— *Ib*., p. 143, 4.

" ' He that sendeth up *treasures* unto the land of Zion. shall receive an inheritance in this world.   And his work shall follow him. And also a reward in the world to come.'— *Ib*., p. 144.

" And we must believe that the foregoing language is from the mouth of the infinite God, under the penalty of eternal damnation !

" Look, also, to the following, said to be the words of the Most High : —

" ' I command that thou shalt not *covet thine own property*, but impart it freely to the printing of the Book of Mormon; which contains the truths of the word of God.'— *Ib*., p. 175.

" ' Impart a portion of thy property ; yea, even part of thy lands, and *all* save the support of thy family.'— *Ib* , p 176.

" The next extract is not only important, as it plainly shows the true Mormon solicitude about *money*, but it reveals an important fact with regard to Oliver Cowdery, one of the eleven witnesses upon whose *ipse dixit* we are commanded to believe the Book of Mormon.

" ' Hearken unto me, saith the Lord your God, for my servant Oliver Cowdery's sake.   It is not wisdom in me that he should be *intrusted* with the commandments and the *moneys*, which he shall carry up unto the land of Zion, *except one go with him who is true and faithful*   Wherefore, I, the Lord, willeth that my servant, John Whitmar, shall go with my servant, Oliver Cowdery.'— *Ib*., p. 138.

" Does the reader still doubt as to the grand design of Smith and his associates ?   Read the following : —

" ' It is meet that my servant. Joseph Smith, Jr., should have a *house built* in which to live and translate.   And, again, it is meet that my servant, Sidney Rigdon, should live *as seemeth him good*, inasmuch as he keepeth my commandments.'— *Ib* , p. 189.

" And from the following it will be seen that Joe Smith excuses himself from work, and has provided himself with ' WHATSOEVER *he needeth*.'   And this regulation is not only to last while he lives, but he is to hold his office in the world to come !

" ' Provide for him *food* and *raiment*, and *whatsoever* he needeth.' — *Ib*., p. 126.

" ' And in temporal labor thou (Smith) shalt not have strength, for this is *not thy calling.*'— *Ib.*, p 112.

" ' Verily, I say unto you, (Joseph Smith, Jr.,) the keys of the kingdom shall never be taken from you, while thou art in this world, neither in the world to come.'— *Ib.*, p. 114.

" Nor is this all. A new ' revelation' has recently ' come forth ' from this Impostor, in which he not only makes provision for himself during life, but, also, for his family connections after him, *forever!!* This revelation is dated January 19, 1841, and has appeared in the papers of the day. It orders the building of a *boarding-house.*

" ' And now, I say unto you, as pertaining to my *boarding-house,* which I commanded you to build for the boarding of strangers ; let it be built unto my name, and let my name be named upon it, and let my servant *Joseph* and *his house* have places therein from *generation to generation.* For this anointing have I put upon his head, that his blessing shall also be put upon the heads of *his posterity after him,* and as 1 said unto Abraham, concerning the kindreds of the earth, even so I say unto my servant Joseph, in thee, and in thy seed, shall the kindreds of the earth be blessed.

" 'Therefore, let my servant *Joseph, and his seed after him,* have place in that house from generation to generation forever and ever, saith the Lord, and let the name of that house be called the Nauvoo House.'

" MORMONS PROFESS TO ACT UNDER THE INFALLIBLE INSPIRATION OF GOD, AND TO HAVE POWER TO WORK MIRACLES.

" ' Without these gifts [prophecy, miracles, healing, and all other gifts] the Saints cannot be perfected ; the work of the ministry cannot proceed ; the body of Christ cannot be edified.'— *Voice of Warning,* pp. 118, 119.

" ' And as I said unto mine apostles, even so I say unto you; for ye are mine apostles — therefore as I said unto mine apostles, I say unto you again, that *every soul* who believeth on your word, and is baptized with water for the remission of sins, shall receive the Holy Ghost, and these signs *sha'l follow* them that believe : In my name they shall cast out devils — heal the sick — open the eyes of the blind — unstop the ears of the deaf — and if any man shall administer poison unto them it shall not hurt them.'— *Doc. and Cov.*, p. 92.

" MORMONS ARE PLEDGED TO WORK MIRACLES WHEN REQUIRED TO DO SO.

" ' Require not miracles, *except* I shall command you, *except* casting out devils, healing the sick, and against poisonous serpents, and against deadly poisons : and these things ye shall not do *except* it be required of you, by them who desire it, that the Scriptures might be fulfilled.'—*Doc. and Cov.*, p. 112.

" MORMONS AFFIRM, THAT THEIR BOOKS WERE WRITTEN, AND THAT THE BOOK OF MORMON WAS TRANSLATED, BY THE INSPIRATION OF GOD ; AND THAT THEY ARE OF EQUAL AUTHORITY WITH THE HOLY SCRIPTURES.

" The book called ' Doctrines and Covenants,' it seems, received the approbation of the Mormon General Assembly, August 17, 1835. Twelve *Mormons* bear the following testimony to its divine authority.

" ' We, therefore, feel willing to bear testimony to all the world of mankind, * * * that the Lord hath borne record to our souls, through the Holy Ghost shed forth upon us, that these commandments were given by inspiration of God, and are profitable for all men, and are verily true.'— *Doc. and Cov.*, p. 256.

" ' They shall speak as they are moved upon by the Holy Ghost; and what they shall speak when moved upon by the Holy Ghost, *shall be* SCRIPTURE.'— *Ib.*, p. 148.

" MORMONS PRETEND TO HAVE POWER TO GIVE THE HOLY GHOST TO THOSE ON WHOM THEY LAY THEIR HANDS FOR THIS PURPOSE.

" ' Behold, verily, verily, I say unto my servant, Sidney Rigdon, * * * I give unto thee a commandment, that thou shalt baptize with water, and they shall *receive the Holy Ghost by the laying on of hands*, EVEN *as the apostles of old.'— Doc. and Cov.*, p. 116.

" MORMONISM AUTHORIZES THEFT.

" ' Behold it is said in my laws, or forbidden to get in debt to thine enemies; *but*, behold, *it is not said*, at any time, that the *Lord* should not *take* when he please, and *pay as seemeth him good :* wherefore, *as ye are agents*, and *ye are on the Lord's errand*, and whatsoever ye do according to the will of the Lord is the Lord's business, and he *hath sent you to provide for his Saints*,' &c.— *Doc. and Cov* , p. 147.

" A Mormon has only to imagine himself an agent of God, and, according to the above precept, he may steal or commit any other crime, and fancy himself doing the will of God all the while. And these very things the Mormons have done."

From the Louisville Journal of July 27, 1842.

" ☞ General John C. Bennett, the author of the expositions of Joe Smith's character and conduct, passed through this city on Saturday. In consequence of some conversation we had with him, he has since sent us the following letter. The astounding facts that it sets forth are certainly worthy of the earnest consideration of the civil authorities of Illinois.

" ' STEAMER IMPORTER, *July* 23, A. D. 1842.

" ' To the Editors of the Louisville Journal : —

" ' As I promised to lay before you some of the strong points of objection to " *the gathering of the Saints*," or the congregating of THE MORMONS at *one point*, or *general head-quarters*, I now proceed to redeem the pledge.

" ' 1st. Nine hundred and ninety-nine thousandths of all the *faithful* of the Mormon Church regard Joe Smith as God's vicegerent on earth, and obey him accordingly ; and all the Danites of that Church (and, by the bye, they compose no very inconsiderable proportion of their mighty hosts) are sworn to receive him as the supreme head of the Church, and to obey him as the supreme God. If, therefore, any State officer, in the administration of public justice, happens to give offence to His Holiness the Prophet, it becomes the will of God, *as spoken by the mouth of his Prophet*, that that functionary should DIE ; and his followers, *the faithful Saints*, immediately set about the work of assassination, in obedience, as they suppose, to their Divine Master; and for which NOBLE DEED, they expect to receive an excellent and superior glory in the celestial kingdom !!! It does not require Argus eyes to see the incalculable mischief growing out of such a state of society ; and an intelligent community must look on with awful forebodings and fearful anticipations, where such a state of things is *suffered*. Great God! only look at the horrible picture ! The lives of thousands of human beings depending upon the whim or caprice of the most corrupt, Heaven-daring, and black-hearted Impostor that ever disgraced the earth ! The whole community are in the most imminent danger, from the common citizen to the highest public functionary, unless they chain their fate to the car of Mormon despotism.

" '2d. Where a large community, like the Mormons, are under the absolute dictation of a vacillating and capricious tyrant, like Joe Smith, who acts not under the influence of reason, but is wholly governed by impulses and selfish motives, political demagogues will become fawning sycophants, and the best interests of the country will be sacrificed to the ambitious views of an ancient or modern Prophet — a Mahomet or a Smith ! This state of things is fraught with the most fearful consequences — the subversion of governments ; the fall of kingdoms and empires ; the destruction of nations, by the shedding of rivers of human blood ; and, where consequences of a less serious nature accrue, it destroys natural affection, hardens the heart against the better feelings of our nature, and produces a state of savage barbarity, which causes a civilized man to shudder, and from which he turns with loathing and disgust.

" '3d. The standard of morality and Christian excellence with them is quite unstable. Joe Smith has but to speak the *word*, and it becomes the LAW *which they delight to obey* — BECAUSE IT COMES FROM GOD !!! Acts, therefore, which but yesterday were considered the most immoral, wicked, and devilish, to-day are the most moral, righteous, and God-like, because God, who makes right, has so declared it *by the mouth of his anointed Prophet !*

" '4th. Joe Smith designs to abolish all human laws, and establish a *Theocracy*, in which the word of God, *as spoken by his (Joe's) mouth*, shall be the only law ; and he now orders that his followers shall only obey such human laws as they are *compelled* to do, and declares that the time is at hand when all human institutions shall be abrogated ! Joe's *will* is to become the *law of right*, and *his power is to execute it*.

" '5th. Under the new order of things, *all* the property of *the Saints*, with their WIVES and little ones, is to be *consecrated* to Joe,

13 *

to subserve his purposes and gratify his passions! These are only SOME of the reasons which I shall hereafter, when time permits, consider more in detail; and, in the mean time, I should like your opinion on a matter of so much importance to *all* of our fellow-citizens.

"'With high considerations of respect and esteem, suffer me to subscribe myself—   Yours, respectfully,

"'JOHN C. BENNETT.'"

From the New York Herald of August 30, 1842.

"LATE AND IMPORTANT FROM THE MORMON COUNTRY.

"We have just received a variety of curious, strange, and original information from this part of the world. Some of it is political, some financial, some belligerent, some religious, and some personal.

"Among other items we have the following news, which was written on the outside of a letter received on Saturday, at one of the public offices, from Chicago, Illinois. 'A battle has been fought between the Mormons and Anti-Mormons. The extra says, thirty or forty were killed or wounded. The Governor has gone down with 200 men.'

"In connection with this we have the following letter from the head-quarters of Joe Smith, the Prophet, and second Mahomet himself:—

"'HEAD-QUARTERS, NAUVOO LEGION, CITY OF NAUVOO, *August* 4, 1842.

"'GENERAL ORDER.

"'As General John C. Bennett has retired from the service, General James Arlington Bennet, the next ranking officer, is hereby ordered to repair forthwith to the Head-Quarters of the Legion, and assume the command, accompanied by his chief Aid-de-Camp, General James Gordon Bennett.

"'The requisition from the Executive of Missouri, on the Executive of Illinois, for the person of the Lieutenant-General, (at the instance of their accomplice, Dr. John C. Bennett,) for the attempted assassination of Ex-Governor Boggs, makes it necessary that the most able and experienced officers should be in the field, for if the demand is persisted in, blood must be shed.

"'By order of Lieut. Gen. JOSEPH SMITH.

"'HUGH McFALL,
"'*Adjutant-General.*

"'This will be conveyed to New York by John Slade, Esq., who is just leaving the city for the east, to watch Dr. Bennett's movements.'

"In connection with the above, we have also received the following letter from General John C. Bennett, now in this city, enclosing one from the brother of Governor Boggs, of Missouri; we give them both:—

" ' New York, *August* 27, 1842.

" ' General James Gordon Bennett, LL. D. :

" ' Dear Sir, —

" ' As you have recently been presented with the appointment of, and commissioned as, Aid-de-Camp to His Imperial Holiness, Joseph Smith, Emperor of the Mormon Empire, with the rank and title of Brigadier-General, I presume that the perusal of the enclosed letter from Dr. Joseph O. Boggs will not be uninteresting to you. I have replied to the communication, and stand in readiness to obey the mandate of Missouri, to testify in the premises. The Mormon Pontiff shall tremble at the sight of gathering hosts, in the days of his captivity, like an aspen leaf in the wilderness.

" ' *Sævitque animis ignobile vulgus ;*
Jamque faces et saga volant : furor arma ministrat.'

" ' The rude rabble are enraged ; now the firebrands and stones are seen to fly about; their fury supplies them with arms.'

" ' But the Mormon Autocrat should remember the old adage.—

" ' *Sæpe intereunt aliis meditantes necem.'*

" ' Those who plot the destruction of others, very often fall themselves the victims.'

" ' Though his touch be as deadly as that of the Bohon Upas, I will tear the ermine of sanctity from the shoulders of His Pontifical Holiness, and dim the glory of his mitred head. It may justly be said of him, as a shawn-bawn once said to a stranger in Ireland, in speaking of two persons of the names of Pierce and Damer, (comparing the Mormon Mahomet to Damer,) — " Damer," said he, " was *worser* than Pierce, and Pierce was *worser* than Damer, and Damer himself was *worser* than the Devil."

" ' In the face of High Heaven he has perpetrated the blackest deeds of felony, and in the curling flames of Tartarus shall he drink the dregs of the culprit's cup.

" ' Nothing short of an excision of the cancer of Mormonism will effect a cure of that absorbing delusion, and the strong arm of military power must perform the operation at the edge of the sword, point of the bayonet, and mouth of the cannon.

" ' Yours, respectfully,
" ' John C. Bennett.'

" ' Independence, *August* 4, 1842.

" ' General J. C. Bennett :

" ' Sir, —

" ' I write in behalf of my brother, L. W. Boggs, to say that Governor Reynolds has demanded Joe Smith and O. P. Rockwell from the Governor of Illinois. The old indictments against Smith and others, for murder, arson, burglary, &c., were dismissed by the prosecuting attorney about two years ago. Affidavits were made by my brother against both, Rockwell as principal, and Joe Smith as accessory before the fact. It is to be regretted that you left St. Louis before the messenger despatched to Illinois reached there ; you could doubtless have advised him of the best means of securing Smith and Rockwell.

" ' We look for the return of the messenger in the course of ten
days. If he succeeds in securing the men, it will be necessary for
you to come on here immediately. I shall write to you again, as
soon as it is ascertained that they are within the State. In the mean
time, do you endeavor to have all the evidence collected that you
think will be required.

" ' Yours, respectfully,
" ' JOSEPH O. BOGGS.'

" With regard to going out to Nauvoo immediately, we shall state
our views shortly. In the mean time, we shall see, and hear, and
report what reasons General John C. Bennett can advance to-night
in his discourse that may prevent us from standing by Joe Smith,
until, as he says, blood shall flow."

From the New York Herald.

" MILITARY MOVEMENTS.

" I have just received the following, by military express, from the
Major-General : —

"ARLINGTON HOUSE, *August* 31, 1842.

" ' Sir, —

" ' As the ranking Major-General of the Nauvoo Legion, I
have received a General Order to repair immediately to head-
quarters, and assume the command, accompanied by my principal
Aid-de-Camp, Brigadier-General James Gordon Bennett.

" ' Now, sir, I shall ever hold myself ready to defend the Mormon
people, or any other people with whom I might be associated,
against mob violence ; but at the same time feel that I am not
bound to act against the constituted authorities of the State of Illinois, nor of any other State in the Union, nor would I do it were it
for a brother.

" ' I have transmitted the Order to his Excellency Governor
Carlin for instructions, while, at the same time, I shall repair immediately to Nauvoo, and take command of the Legion, where I expect
you will accompany me, in conformity with its mandate.

" ' I should desire no better fun than to despatch you with orders,
on my horse Cicero, among the whizzing bullets, or blue pills of
Galena.

" ' Most respectfully yours, &c.,
" ' JAMES ARLINGTON BENNET,
" ' *Inspector and Major-General of the Nauvoo Legion.*'

" Blood and 'ouns, I'll go. It never shall be said that the blood
of the Bennetts did not rise to the top. Who knows but I may get
one of these glorious bullets in the ' calf ' ? What would Colonel
Webb say if I disobeyed a military mandate ? In the mean time, I
highly approve of my superior in command ascertaining first the
constitutionality of the measure, by direct application to Governor
Carlin, to see if there be any necessity of a veto. But still, I must

prepare. I have no uniform. Egad, I must advertise for proposals. So here goes : —

" Wanted to Purchase. — A full suit of uniform for an officer of the rank of Brigadier-General in the Nauvoo Legion ; also, a fine horse, thirteen hands high, a sword, &c., including a good old Bible and Prayer-book. Nothing like being well provided with all sorts of ammunition."

It does not require Argus eyes to see that General J. Gordon Bennett has no idea of joining the Mormon Auto-crat. " *The Napoleon of the American Press*" is too smart a man, and too wily and shrewd an officer, to think of risking his precious carcass in the *tented field* in the *present crisis ;* and, in fact, the severe attack of *Coup-de-Soleil,* (the legitimate effects of the *scorching rays* of the New York Sun,) under which he is now laboring, wholly disables him for camp duty. The *Scotch* Bennetts were never proverbial for their military prowess ; and General J. Arlington Bennet, who, by the bye, is one of the most talented and experienced officers in the Union, cannot be cajoled by a military order from His Imperial Holiness, through a Jack-Mormon Adjutant-General, into palpable usurpation and open rebellion against the legal authorities.

From the New York Herald of June 17, 1842.

" HIGHLY IMPORTANT FROM THE MORMON EMPIRE. — WONDER-" FUL PROGRESS OF JOE SMITH, THE MODERN MAHOMET. —" SPREAD OF THE MORMON FAITH, AND A NEW RELIGIOUS REV-" OLUTION AT HAND.

" By the mails last evening we received a variety of letters and papers from Nauvoo, the capital of the new religious revolutionary empire, established by Joe Smith, and also from other towns in Illinois, exhibiting the extraordinary progress of this most extraordinary people, who call themselves the ' Latter Day Saints.'

" These letters and papers are as follows : — First — A letter from a United States artillery officer, travelling through Nauvoo, who gives a most original glimpse of the Mormon movement there. Second — An extract from the ' Sangamo Journal ' of the 3d of June, a newspaper in favor of the whig party, and opposed to the Mormons on account of their locofoco tendency, requiring a view of their military organization. Third — A law of the Mormon city of Nauvoo, extending toleration towards all religions, even Mohammedan, and assuming power to legislate for all with imperial *nonchalance.* Fourth — A public meeting of the Mormons in Nauvoo, developing their sentiments and position in the elections in Illinois. Fifth — A

letter to Mrs. Emma Smith, the wife of the Prophet, from a lady in
Edwardsville, exhibiting the singular mixture of piety, politics, tact,
and shrewdness, in those who believe in Mormonism.

"All these letters and documents disclose a most extraordinary
movement in human affairs. What they mean, we can hardly tell;
but is it not time for some great religious revolution, as radical as
Luther's, to take place in the Christian world?

" In the early ages of antiquity, before the dates of the monuments
of Egypt, we have distinguished names handed down to us by tra-
dition. Brama, Vishnu, Confucius, Zoroaster, Isis, Osiris, including Adam, Seth, Noah, Abraham, were the master-spirits of a great
antiquity throughout the ancient world. In later times, we have
Moses and the Prophets, Peter and Paul, and the apostles of Christ
— and even Mahomet, who acknowledged the truth of Christianity.
Each of these movements was a religious revolution, but that which
followed the time of Adam, Seth, Noah, Abraham, Moses, Christ,
and the apostles, has developed the only true system of morals, of
belief, of revelation, of prophecy, of man, of God, of eternity.
When the Christian church was overwhelmed with the follies and
superstition of Rome, and the thousand quarrelling sects of monks
and idlers, a fresh spirit arose in the world — a spark came down
from Heaven — Luther lifted up his voice, and a religious revolution
started at his word, and renovated Christianity. But a new age has
come — a fresh infusion of faith is required — a strong impulse is
rendered necessary.

" May not this wonderful Mormon movement be the signal for a
new religious revolution? Is not Joe Smith its master-spirit, and
General Bennett its military spirit? The vast progress of the last
century, in art and science, through steam and type, has changed
the nature of man and society. Is it not necessary that a new religion and a new faith should come down from Heaven, to carry out
the destiny of the race, under its present condition?

" It is very evident that the Mormons exhibit a remarkable degree
of tact, skill, shrewdness, energy, and enthusiasm. The particular
features of their faith are nothing against their success. Do they
believe their new Bible — their virgin revelation — their singular
creed? If they do so with enthusiasm, and practise their shrewd
precepts, the other sects will fall before them. This is certain —
this is human nature. In Illinois, they have already shown how to
acquire power and influence, by holding the balance of power between both the great parties. *They can already dictate to the State
of Illinois*, and if they pursue the same policy in other States, *will
they not soon dictate to Congress, and decide the Presidency?* In
all matters of public concernment, they act as one man, with one
soul, one mind, and one purpose. Their religious and moral principles bind them together firmly. They may be, and have been, abused
and calumniated — partly true — partly false — but whether true or
false, these attacks only increase their popularity and influence.
Unlike all other Christian sects, they adopt, at once, all the modern
improvements of society, in art or literature, and from their singular
religious faith, give the highest enthusiasm to the movement at large.

There is nothing odd, or singular, or absurd about them, that they will not cast away, if it interferes with their progress to power.

" Verily, verily, we are truly in the 'latter days;' and we should not be surprised to see that the Mormon religion is the real millennium already commenced. One thing is certain. The Mormons are so constituted, that, in these temperance times, they will swallow up all the other lukewarm Protestant sects; and the moral and religious world will be divided between the Pope and the Catholics on one side, and Joe Smith and the Mormons on the other. The oyster is opening, and will soon be equally divided.'

———

[" *Correspondence of the Herald.*]

" ' City of Nauvoo, Illinois, *May* 8, 1842.
" ' THE MORMONS, A VERY SINGULAR PEOPLE. — MILITARY, CIV-
" ' IL, AND LITERARY ORGANIZATION. — AMBITIOUS VIEWS AND
" ' PURPOSES.

" ' J. G. Bennett, LL. D.:

" ' I address you as Doctor, because I am assured that the University of this city has conferred on you the degree of LL. D.; and this is no small feather in your cap, when we consider the talent and learning possessed by the faculty of this chartered institution, which will, before long, be equal, if not superior, to any college in this country.

" ' Yesterday was a great day among the Mormons. Their Legion, to the number of two thousand men, was paraded by Generals Smith, Bennett, and others, and certainly made a very noble and imposing appearance. The evolutions of the troops directed by Major-General Bennett would do honor to any body of armed militia in any of the States, and approximates very closely to our regular forces. What does all this mean? Why this exact discipline of the Mormon corps? Do they intend to conquer Missouri, Illinois, Mexico? It is true they are part of the militia of the State of Illinois, by the charter of their Legion; but then there are no troops in the States like them in point of enthusiasm and warlike aspect, yea, warlike character. Before many years, this Legion will be twenty, and perhaps fifty thousand strong, and still augmenting. A fearful host, filled with religious enthusiasm, and led on by ambitious and talented officers, what may not be effected by them? Perhaps the subversion of the Constitution of the United States; and if this should be considered too great a task, foreign conquest will most certainly follow. Mexico will fall into their hands, even if Texas should first take it.

" ' These Mormons are accumulating, like a snow-ball rolling down an inclined plane, which, in the end, becomes an avalanche. They are also enrolling among their officers some of the first talent in the country, by titles or bribes, it don't matter which. They have appointed your namesake, Captain Bennet, late of the army of the United States, Inspector-General of their Legion, and he is commissioned as such by Governor Carlin. This gentleman is known to be well skilled in fortification, gunnery, ordnance, castrametation,

and military engineering generally, and I am assured that he is now
under pay, derived from the tithings of this warlike people. I have
seen his plans for fortifying Nauvoo, which are equal to any of
Vauban's.

"' General John C. Bennett, a New England man, is the Prophet's
great gun. They call him (though a man about the stature of Napoleon) the "forty-two pounder." He might have applied his talents
in a more honorable cause, but I am assured that he is well paid for
the important services he is rendering this people, or, I should rather
say, rendering the Prophet. This gentleman exhibits the highest
degree of field military talent, (field tactics,) united with extensive
learning. He may yet become dangerous to the States. He was
Quarter-Master-General of the State of Illinois, and at another time
a Professor in the Erie University. It will, therefore, be seen, that
nothing but a high price could have secured him to these fanatics.
Only a part of their officers, regents, and professors, however, are
Mormons; but then they are all united by a common interest, and will
act together on main points to a man   Those who are not Mormons
when they come here, very soon become so, either from interest or
conviction.

"' The Smiths are not without talent, and are said to be as brave as
lions. Joseph, the chief, is a noble-looking fellow, a Mahomet every
inch of him. The Postmaster, Sidney Rigdon, is a lawyer, philoso-
pher, and Saint. Their other Generals are also men of talents, and
some of them men of learning. I have no doubt that they are all
brave, as they are most unquestionably ambitious, and the tendency
of their religious creed is to annihilate all other sects; you may,
therefore, see that the time will come, when this gathering host of
religious fanatics will make this country shake to its centre. A
western empire is certain. Ecclesiastical history presents no parallel
to this people, inasmuch as they are establishing their religion on a
learned footing. All the sciences are taught, and to be taught, in
their colleges, with Latin, Greek, Hebrew, French, Italian, Spanish,
&c. &c. The mathematical sciences, pure and mixed, are now in
successful operation, under an extremely able Professor, of the name
of Pratt; and a graduate of Trinity College, Dublin, is President of
their University.

"' Now, sir, what do you think of Joseph, the modern Mahomet?
"' I arrived here, incog., on the first inst., and from the great preparation for the military parade, was induced to stay to see the turn-
out, which I confess has astonished and filled me with fears for
future consequences. The Mormons, it is true, are now peaceable,
but the lion is asleep. Take care, and don't rouse him.

"' The city of Nauvoo contains about ten thousand souls, and is
rapidly increasing. It is well laid out, and the municipal affairs
appear to be well conducted. The adjoining country is a beautiful
prairie. Who will say that the Mormon Prophet is not among the
great spirits of the age?

"' The Mormons number, in Europe and America, about one hundred and fifty thousand, and are constantly pouring into Nauvoo and
the neighboring country. There are, probably, in and about this

city, and adjacent territories, not far from 30,000 of these warlike
fanatics, this place having been settled by them only three years ago.
"'An Officer of the U. S. Artillery.

[" ' *From the Sangamo* (Illinois) *Journal*.]

" ' Since the attempt upon the life of Governor Boggs, it has been
feared that some emissaries might visit Nauvoo, for the purpose of
retaliating upon the Mormon Prophet; and for that reason, it is
rumored, a guard is now provided for the city. The official notices
of the establishment of this guard, are given in the " Wasp," which
are here copied : —

" ' Major-General's Office, Nauvoo Legion,)
City of Nauvoo, (Ill.,) *May* 20, 1842.)

" ' To the Citizens of the City of Nauvoo : —

" ' I have this day received an order from General
Joseph Smith, Mayor of said city, to detail a regular night watch for
the city, which I have executed, by selecting and placing on duty
the following named persons, to wit : — D. B. Huntington, W. D.
Huntington, L. N. Scovil, C. Allen, A. P. Rockwood, N. Rogers,
S. Roundy, and J. Arnold; who will hereafter be obeyed and respected as such, until further orders.

" ' John C. Bennett, *Major-General.*"

" ' Mayor's Office, City of Nauvoo, *May* 20, A. D. 1842.

" To the City Watch : —

" ' You are hereby directed to appear at my office daily,
at 6 o'clock, P. M., to receive orders, and at 6 o'clock, A. M., to
make reports, until regularly disbanded by the Major-General of
the Legion, by my order. Joseph Smith, *Mayor.*" '

" ' From these official notices, it would appear that the Mormons
have a government entirely of their own, an army of their own,
portions of which are detached on the requisition of the Mayor of
Nauvoo, when he pleases to make a requisition upon the commanding officer for their services. This is, indeed, a curious state of
things. A Christian sect in Illinois, keeping up a military organization for their own particular purposes ! What would be thought,
if the Baptists, Methodists, Presbyterians, or Episcopalians of this
State, had separate military organizations, and that their respective
legions of troops were in constant practice of military discipline?
These Mormon troops are said now to amount to 2000 men, and
that they are as well drilled as regular soldiers.

" ' The laws of incorporation under which the Mormons are now
enjoying exclusive privileges, have given rise, latterly, to some public
discussions. We have now before us a communication from Mount
Vernon, Jefferson county, in this State, which possesses much interest. It appears from this communication, that the laws in question were passed by our locofoco legislature, (a legislature, by the
bye, which professed an utter aversion to monopolies in the shape

14

of incorporations,) for political purposes ; that they were passed to
secure the Mormon vote. There can now be no doubt of the fact,
that the proclamation issued by Lieutenant-General Smith, to his
people, requiring them to vote for Messrs. Snyder and Moore, was
the result of the passage of these laws by the locofoco legislature.

" ' AN ORDINANCE IN RELATION TO RELIGIOUS SOCIETIES.

" ' Sec. 1. Be it ordained by the City Council of the City of Nauvoo, that the Catholics, Presbyterians, Methodists, Baptists, Latter
Day Saints, Quakers, Episcopalians, Universalists, Unitarians, Mohammedans, and all other religious sects and denominations whatever,
shall have toleration and equal privileges in this city ; and should
any person be guilty of ridiculing, abusing, or otherwise depreciat-
ing another, in consequence of his religion, or of disturbing or in-
terrupting any religious meeting within the limits of this city, he
shall, on conviction thereof before the Mayor, or Municipal Court,
be considered a disturber of the public peace, and fined in any
sum not exceeding five hundred dollars, or imprisoned not exceeding six months, or both, at the discretion of said Mayor, or Court.

" ' Sec. 3. This ordinance to take effect and be in force from and
after its passage. Passed, March 1, A. D. 1841.

" ' JOHN C. BENNETT, Mayor.
" ' JAMES SLOAN, Recorder.

" ' PUBLIC MEETING.

" ' According to previous notice, a very large and respectable
meeting of the citizens of the city of Nauvoo convened at the Temple ground, on Thursday, the 26th day of May, at one o'clock, P. M.

" ' The meeting was called to order by General Bennett, on
whose motion the assembly was duly organized by the appointment
of General Joseph Smith, Chairman, and Colonel James Sloan,
Secretary.

" ' The object of the meeting was then stated, in a speech of considerable length, by General Smith, distinctly avowing his intention
not to coöperate or vote with either the whig or democratic parties,
as such.

" ' The meeting then unanimously disapproved of the remarks of
the Quincy Whig, in relation to the participation of General Smith
in the violent death of Governor Boggs, of Missouri, and unanimously concurred in the opinion that General Smith had never made
such a prediction.

" ' General Bennett, at the solicitation of the Chairman, then
spoke at length on State and general politics, and nominated Sidney
Rigdon and Orson Pratt, for representatives for the county of Hancock, at the approaching August election, which nominations were
unanimously concurred in by the assembly.

" ' George Miller then made a speech, recommending the selection
of a full ticket, which was concurred in ; and George Miller put in
nomination for the State Senate, from Hancock ; Hiram Kimball,
for County Commissioner ; and William Backenstos, for Sheriff.

A committee was then appointed to take the names of the legal voters in the Nauvoo precinct, and report to the next general meeting of the people, on two weeks from this day, at the same time and place.

" ' The meeting then adjourned for two weeks.

" ' JOSEPH SMITH, *Chairman.*

" ' JAMES SLOAN, *Secretary.*' "

The *Sangamo Journal* of July 8, 1842, in commenting upon the above article, says, —

"The people of this State are well aware of the fact, that the Mormon College at Nauvoo have conferred on J. Gordon Bennett, the editor of the New York Herald, the degree of *Doctor of Laws.* The same paper has been selected by Joe Smith as his organ in New York city; and the City Council of Nauvoo, by resolutions, have recommended the Herald to the patronage of the Mormon Church throughout the country. These facts, with the additional one that Joe Smith, by some of his followers, carries on a CONFIDENTIAL CORRESPONDENCE WITH THE EDITOR OF THE HERALD, stamp with authority the statements of that paper in relation to the policy and designs of Joe Smith."

Yes, the *New York Herald* is the *Mormon official organ* in the eastern metropolis, and its ALIEN *editor* the *premonstration* of the *Prophet himself.* This, together with his failing to obtain the printing of this *Exposé,* as contemplated, will account for the gratuitous vituperative editorial attacks of that "*Napoleon*" Editor on the author of this work. He is likely to be the CHANCELLOR OF THE EXCHEQUER *in the Cabinet of the Mormon Autocratic Emperor of the* "WESTERN EMPIRE," and perhaps the DAUPHIN *to the regal crown!* Else why so opposed to every thing American? The Herald Editor is a MORMO-CATHOLIC, and sustains those two creeds against the Protestant Christian world. That able man could employ his fine editorial talents to much better advantage in the advocacy of unsophisticated truth.

From the New York Herald, August 13, 1842.

"RISING IN THE WORLD.

" ' Since you will buckle Fortune on my back,
To bear her burden whe'er I will or no,
I must have patience to endure the load.'

"We are rising very rapidly in this sinful world. A short time ago, the Corporation of Nauvoo, Illinois, conferred upon us the freedom of the city. How far this freedom extends we know not, but we suppose it embraces a vast number of DELICIOUS PRIVILEGES, *according to the Mormon creed.* The next step was to raise us to the dignity of LL. D., a regular Doctor of Laws, by the University of Nauvoo, *an honor which we highly prize,* and which is as good, and perhaps better, than that conferred on General Jackson by the University of Harvard, or that on His Excellency, Edward Everett, by the University of Cambridge, in England. But this is not all. Yesterday, — blessed be the day! — we received by a special messenger from Illinois, the intelligence that that State had gone entirely for the Mormons and locofocos, in the elections ; and also an enclosure which contained the parchment, *conferring a high military rank upon us,* of which document the following is a true copy — the original being in our salamander safe, with the titles of the Herald building : —

"'THOMAS CARLIN, Governor of the State of Illinois, to all to whom these presents shall come, greeting :

"'Know ye, That James Gordon Bennett having been duly elected to the office of Aid-de-Camp (with the rank and title of Brigadier-General) to the Major-General of the Nauvoo Legion of the Militia of the State of Illinois, I, Thomas Carlin, Governor of said State, for and on behalf of the People of said State, do commission him Aid-de-Camp to said Major-General, with rank and title as aforesaid, to take rank from the twenty-eighth day of May, 1842. He is, therefore, carefully and diligently to discharge the duties of said office, by doing and performing all manner of things thereunto belonging; and I do strictly require all officers and soldiers under his command to be obedient to his orders; and he is to obey such orders and directions as he shall receive from time to time from his Commander-in-Chief, or his superior officer.

" ' In testimony whereof, I have hereunto set my hand, and caused the Great Seal of State to be hereunto affixed. Done at Springfield, this second day of June, in the year of our Lord one thousand eight hundred and forty-two, and of the Independence of the United States the sixty-sixth.

"' By the Governor,   "'THO. CARLIN.
        "'LYMAN TRUMBULL, *Secretary of State.*'

" There's honor — there's distinction — there's salt and greens for a modest, simple, calm, patient, industrious editor. We now take legitimate rank, far above Colonel Webb, Major Noah, Colonel Stone, General George P. Morris, or all the military editors around and about the country. We are only inferior in rank — and that but half a step — to good old General Jackson — he being Major-General and LL. D. — we being Brigadier and LL. D. also.

" In an hour after the arrival of this precious document, but before I received it, I found myself two inches taller, three inches more in circumference, and so wolfish about the head and shoulders that I could have fought a duel with Marshall, provided he had given me the 'same terms on the ' bandanna handkerchief plan ' that he generously gave to Colonel Webb. It was no doubt caused by the military title approximating to its owner. ' God tempers the wind to the shorn lamb ' — the devil heats the fire to suit the sinner, and I must bear the honors that are thickening around me.

"It will be seen, therefore, that I am *Aid-de-Camp,* with the rank of Brigadier-General, to the Major-General of the famous Nauvoo Legion. *This Major-General is no less a man than the* PROPHET JOE SMITH, *who is very busy establishing an* ORIGINAL RELIGIOUS EMPIRE *in the west, that may swallow up all the other different sects and* CLIQUES, as the rod of Moses, turned into a serpent, swallowed up, without salt, the rods of Jannes and Jambres, and the other magicians of Egypt. Heavens! how we apples swim, as the sprat said to the whale, Mount Etna bawling out at the same time, ' Let's have another segar.' Wonders will never cease. Hereafter, I am James Gordon Bennett, Freeman of the Holy City of Nauvoo, LL. D. of the University of Nauvoo, and Aid-de-Camp to the Major-General, and Brigadier-General to the Nauvoo Legion, with a fair prospect of being a prophet soon, and a saint in heaven hereafter."

It will be seen by the foregoing from the *New York Herald* of August 13, 1842, (the very day on which "The (Nauvoo) Wasp" published the *famous Algerine Habeas Corpus Ordinance,* (a very remarkable coincidence,) that the *Editor of the Herald* (JOE's OFFICIAL ORGAN IN THE EAST) has been constituted one of the *general officers* of the NAUVOO LEGION *of near three thousand regular troops,* and, as one of the *Cabinet Ministers (the Keeper of the Privy Seal)* of the MORMON EMPEROR, fully intrusted with the *secrets of the Administration :* consequently *all who do not savor strongly of* MORMONISM *may expect to have the vials of the Herald's fierce wrath and fiery indignation poured out upon their devoted heads, without mixture and in great fury.* UPAS'S RICHEST SAP WILL NOT BE HALF SO DEADLY. *I am prophet enough to foretell that.* So, —

" Lay on, Macduff,
And damned be he who first cries, Hold! enough!' "

"The time was when we supposed Mormonism too great an *absurdity* to be received by any person of common sense, who believed the Bible. But we know no system of error was ever broached too monstrous to be believed, by any one. All the impostures ever concocted, have, in their time, had their advocates. And no system of fanaticism, in any previous age, has combined so many *fatal* errors

14 *

as this Mormonism, which has been delineated in these extracts. Here you have it, as plain as language can make it, that Mormonism *authorizes* and approves the most horrid crimes which it is possible for any one to perpetrate. *Deception, lying, fraud, theft, plunder, arson, treason, and murder,* are among the crimes which have characterized this miserable delusion.

" And will it be said that these deluded creatures committed these dreadful crimes in *self-defence?* Treason, theft, and murder, in self-defence? What kind of religion is that which leads its votary to perpetrate such crimes under the pretence that he is doing it in self-defence? The truth is, Mormons believe that the whole of this country belongs, of right, to them ; and they are training their followers, and preparing them, to obtain possession of the country, either by ' purchase or by *blood.*' We may laugh at these as idle pretensions, and persuade ourselves that they cannot amount to any thing. So the good people of the west thought ; but we now see that Mormonism has actually involved one portion of our land in all the horrors of a civil war. And what it has done in Missouri it will do in other places, just as soon as it can find a sufficient number silly enough to yield their hearts and property to its unreasonable, unscriptural, and wicked claims." — *Mormonism Exposed,* pp. 63, 64.

ORGANIZATION AND DOCTRINE OF THE MORMONS.

Professor Turner, in his " Mormonism in all Ages," published by Platt and Peters, (from which I quote more liberally than I otherwise should, in order to give my readers a fair sample of the great ability and superior excellence of that work, the purchase of which I strongly recommend to all the patrons of my Exposé, as being one of the most correct expositions of the Mormon delusion now extant,) says, —

" The ' Latter Day Saints ' have two distinct classes of arguments, which they advance in their own behalf. One class is to prove the divine authority of Smith's book, the other to show the necessity and superiority of the peculiar organization, doctrines, and discipline, of their Church.

" The apostolic and democratic simplicity of their Church government will first claim our attention.

" They have two distinct orders of church dignitaries : 1. The MELCHIZEDEC, or High Priesthood, consisting of High Priests and Elders ; 2. The AARONIC, or Lesser Priesthood, consisting of Bishops,

Priests, Teachers, and Deacons. The former preside over the spiritual interests of the Church; the latter administer its ordinances, and manage its temporal concerns.

" Three of the Melchizedec or High Priests are appointed Presidents, to preside over all the churches in all the world. They are called the *First Presidency.*

" The church in Jackson county, Mo., is called ' Zion,' and is *still to become* the great centre, both of gathering and of ruling; at least so says Smith's divinity. Governor Boggs seems to be of a different opinion. Which knows best, it is hard to say.

" Other churches, established by revelations given to Smith, are called ' Stakes of Zion,' or simply ' Stakes.' Hence the *Stakes* at Kirtland, Nauvoo, &c.

" Each of these Stakes, also, is ruled by a subordinate Presidency, of three High Priests, whose jurisdiction is confined to the limits of the Stake.

" The divine appointment of these Stakes, in new regions, gives a fine opportunity of speculating in town lots.

" They have also a High Council, consisting of twelve High Priests, and constituting the court of ultimate appeal, at each Stake. The Bishop and his two Counsellors, from the Lesser Priesthood, constitute the court of immediate jurisdiction, for the first trial of transgressors, and for administering things temporal at each Stake.

" A travelling High Council, consisting also of twelve High Priests, and called the ' *Twelve Apostles,*' are sent forth with power to preach the gospel to all the world, and to discipline and govern all un organized churches. One of these is called ' President of the Twelve.'

" The first, second, and third ' Seventies,' consisted of seventy Elders each, whose duty it was to preach the Mormon gospel abroad, under the direction of the Twelve Apostles.

" In addition to these dignitaries, there is an innumerable host of Bishops, Elders, Priests, Deacons, &c., employed by the Church, either to edify the ' Saints ' at home, or to gain proselytes abroad. Each of these furnishes himself with the Book of Covenants and Pratt's Voice of Warning, from which they are soon able to acquire at once their proof-texts, their logic, and their faith.

" The First Presidency, the High Council, and each of the Seventies, have the right to discipline their own members, within their respective limits, and a decision of either body is final, and reversible only at the General Council of all the bodies conjointly.

" The High Priests, Elders, and Priests, travel and preach; but Teachers and Deacons are the stationary officers of the Church.

" All these functionaries are created, and, according to the doctrine and teaching of Smith, can be removed, at any time, by the voice of their constituents, the people.

" All this is so purely and beautifully democratic, that the Saints seem to forget that their democratic monarch, Smith, has reserved exclusively to himself the sole right of receiving and promulgating revelations from the Lord, touching even the most minute of all the interests of the Church, to which, of course, they are ever to yield the most implicit obedience, on penalty of eternal damnation. Hence — though, as Smith tells them, all these functionaries are merely their servants — Joe Smith himself is virtually the God both of them and their servants, for his voice is the voice of God in all things, great and small, whenever he chooses to call it so; and that, too, in spite of the command of God, given March, 1829, and found in the Book of Covenants, 158. By turning to that same revelation, as it stands on the tenth page of the first edition of the Book of Commandments, published in 1833, before the Prophet saw fully what powers it would be convenient for him to assume in the Church, the reader will see that, at the end of the second verse, God commands Smith to pretend to '*no other gift*' except to translate, and expressly declares that he will '*grant him no other gift*.' Doubtless the Prophet thought this sufficient at the time. But, in publishing the second edition, two years after, it was found expedient to add a saving clause or two, so as effectually to annihilate at once the command and the promise, and leave Smith still free to usurp whatever power he pleased. The second edition is made to read thus: '*I have commanded that you should pretend to no other gift*' (save to translate) '*until my purpose is fulfilled in this*,' '*for I will grant you no other gift until it is finished*.' The words in Italics are interpolated in the second edition, but not found in the first. Doubtless this was a mere correction of the type, like the taking away of a whole page of the preface from the second edition of the Book of Mormon. Smith did not see the necessity of correcting the type in '33, but in '35 it became apparent. The power of a simple translator was too narrow for the exigency of the times. It would have been well for the world if Smith's divinity, instead of giving him a pair of stone spectacles, had given him a divine printer, and a divine press, and such types that he might have been enabled to fix the meaning of his inspired revelations, so that it would be possible to let them stand, at *least two years*, without abstracting, interpolating, altering, or garbling, to suit the times. But the ways of Smith's providence are indeed mysterious. We will not pretend to judge. The Prophet needed other gifts, and he took them; not by piecemeal, but by wholesale; or rather, he had already taken them before.

" In a revelation given to Smith, April 6, 1830, the very day the first Mormon church of six was organized at Fayette, New York,* Smith is appointed ' *Seer, Translator, Prophet, Apostle* of Jesus Christ, and *Elder* of the Church, through the will of God, the Father, and the grace of our Lord Jesus Christ.' He is also declared to be 'inspired of the Holy Ghost, to lay the foundation of the Church, and build it up in the most holy faith ; ' and the Church is commanded to keep a *perpetual record* of these titles.

" ' Wherefore, the Church shall give heed to *all his words and commandments*, which he shall give unto you : for his word shall ye receive, as if from mine own mouth, in all patience and faith.' Again, on page 88, the First President is to preside over the whole Church,

* B. C., 177.

and be like unto Moses, to be a *Seer, Revelator, Translator, Prophet,* having *all the gifts* which God bestows upon the *head of the Church.*

" These are the moderate qualifications, indispensable, in order to be even a candidate for the office of First President of the Mormon Church. But, in a revelation given February, 1831, page 126, Smith's divinity confers on him not only the *exclusive* right to receive and give forth commandments from the Lord, but also power to appoint his successor ; and the Church are commanded to ' uphold him, to appoint him, to provide him food and raiment, and *whatsoever things* he needeth to accomplish his work,' with threats for disobedience, as usual. Hence, none but Smith, or his appointed successor, can ever be elected to stand at the head of the Church, without direct disobedience and rebellion against the Mormon God, that is, Joe Smith.

" In a revelation of September, 1831, page 145, all Smith's dignities and titles are conferred on him for life. True, he may be removed for misconduct; but who is to judge ? The Lord, surely ; but by whose mouth ? By the mouth of his servant, Joseph Smith ! This is first-rate democracy, to say nothing of apostolic humility and simplicity.

" In a revelation, page 111, the world is informed of what they very well knew before, that Joe Smith '*had no strength to work*,' though he is one of the best wrestlers in the county. Therefore the churches are commanded to support him, with the usual benedictions and cursings. See also Book of Commandments, 181, where the Church are commanded to obey him, even as Aaron. By comparing also the revelation on page 214 with the ' Times and Seasons,' Vol. II , No. 7, pages 305 and 307, the reader will see that Smith has the power of holding the keys of the kingdom of God forever, and that this is only the modest power of eternal salvation or damnation over the flock, the same as is arrogated by the spiritual descendant of St. Peter at Rome, and is to be perpetuated to the spiritual descendants of brother Jose, the democratic General at Nauvoo.

" So much for the beautiful symmetry, simplicity, and freedom of Mormon democracy, and the admirable consistency, humility, patience, and self-denial of their servant, the Prophet Joseph Smith, Jr., General of Nauvoo Militia, and head of the Church throughout the earth.

" According to reports from England, it appears that they there have about one church dignitary, of some sort, to every ten private members. In the early history of the Church in this country, the proportion was much greater. Here lies the secret of their success ; every thing in the shape of a man, that can walk and carry his catechisms, is forthwith dubbed High Priest, Elder, or Apostle, (or something large,) and sent forth to trudge and beg, with a single comrade, in quest of adventure and proselytes. This arrangement operates at once as a motive and a means of conquest. Every ejected or discontented dunce, in other denominations, feels sure that, if he joins the Mormons, he shall be dubbed a knight of the altar, and may in turn trudge forth in quest of new apostles, until perchance he tires in his new labors, or fails of his full share of blushing honors, doffs the badges of the apostle for the sackcloth of the apostate, and yields up his faith in Joe Smith, for faith in nothing save his own folly and delusion.

" We will next consider some of the fundamental doctrines of the Church.

" 1. *The nature of faith.* Their doctrines, on this fundamental item of all religion, may be seen at large in the first part of the Book of Covenants.   There can be no doubt that faith, or rational belief, in things not seen, is the foundation of all power, all energy, all efficiency, and all good, temporal and eternal, so far as man is concerned.   But when we are referred to Heb. xi. 3, to prove that faith enabled God to create the world, it shocks all reason, and all common sense. The apostle tells us that *we understand it* through faith, not that God *created the world* through faith.

" Most will admit also, that it is probable that the first idea of a Supreme Being has travelled down from Adam, to whom it was given by direct revelation.   But does it follow from this, that our belief in a Supreme Being rests, either in whole or in part, on mere human testimony?   Doubtless our parents first suggested to our minds the idea of a supreme Divinity.   But with the heavens over our heads, and the earth under our feet, all declaring and demonstrating his being, and glory, and power, do we still believe it on the bare ground of human testimony?   If so, we must be dolts indeed.   This is as though one should maintain that his belief in the existence of the sun rested on human testimony, because, forsooth, his father happened first to point it out to him.

" The writer next proceeds to show that we also come to the knowledge of the moral attributes of God by revelations made to men, which we receive on the mere ground of human testimony. This is like believing that the sun is warm, because our grandfathers sat under his beams and have told us so. Suppose that we found, from our own actual individual experience, that God was, in all possible ways, constantly endeavoring to deceive and torment us, instead of endeavoring to do us good, hour by hour, and day by day; should we, forsooth, in that case, believe that he was wise, and good, and holy, because he had condescended to tell our grandfathers so? No; — we believe that God is good, not on human testimony, nor yet on his own testimony, for we must first *know* that he is good, before we can rationally believe a word he says. But we believe that he is good, because we observe and experience the results of his goodness in our own persons every hour of our lives.

" We have been more explicit in our remarks on the first four lectures on faith, because we perceive here a sort of entering wedge to the whole system of Mormonism. The absurd and contemptible sophisms, in these four chapters on faith, are intended to lie as an immovable foundation to the whole system.   Hence, by a sort of logical agony, the profound effort was made, by beginning away back at the creation, with the fundamental idea of a first cause, and gradually and carefully creeping along up, with their new doctrine of faith, through all the divine attributes, to the sublime conclusion, that all religious faith does and must, from the very nature of things, rest on the contemptible foundation of *mere human testimony.* But the final end, the inevitable conclusion, from all this Jesuitical sophistry, is cautiously and prudently suppressed, until a more suitable opportunity for its development. We think it a good time now to drag this detestable inference forth from its hiding-place, and to present the whole syllogism in broad daylight, where all men may at once both see and detest, not only the sophism, but the meanness of its authors. It is this: All faith, even in a Supreme Being, rests of necessity on mere human testimony for its foundation. Ergo, (now comes the real inference, meanly suppressed,) therefore you MUST BELIEVE IN JOE SMITH, Martin Harris, Oliver Cowdery, and David Whitmer, or whatever other 'knaves, dupes, or debauchees,' choose to draw on a long face and come to you in the name of the Lord.

"This is the sublime logic of the first four chapters on faith!! And the knavery and hypocrisy of omitting the necessary, inevitable, and *intended* inference from the whole, are surely not the least detestable parts of the effort.

" We believe neither in God, nor in his attributes, nor in any part or portion of divine revelation, on the ground of mere human testimony, and we never shall, so long as we retain our common sense; but we believe in all these on much higher ground than the mere conjoint testimony of even the whole human race, as has been shown.

" Much less shall we believe in the testimony of those whom this professed Prophet of the Lord himself has pronounced 'liars, debauchees, and asses.' Nor shall we believe in the lying, money-digging, drunken deceiver, who duped them to give their testimony to such contemptible gibberish as the Book of Mormon.

" The reader will pardon our extended notice of this puerile doctrine of faith. It is not worth discussing, I am well aware; but I had the edification of the Saints in view. Besides, it is fundamental in Mormonism, as well as in some other fanaticisms.

" The fourth lecture on faith treats of the Trinity, or rather of the Duality, as they explain it. We commend it to the careful perusal of those who think they can understand and explain the precise mode in which the Supreme Intelligence of the universe exists, as readily as they can the properties of an ellipse or a triangle, and who are enabled to expound and adjust all the powers and relations of the Trinity, with the same facility that they can the various compartments of an hour-glass.

" We presume a criticism on this paragraph of Mormon faith, from such exalted geniuses, who, by the mystic aid of ' substances ' and ' essences,' are enabled to solve what angels cannot comprehend, would be amusing, if not important to the public. We leave it to them.

" In the sixth lecture on faith, the proposition is announced and maintained, that men know their acceptance with God ' only through the medium of the sacrifice of all earthly things.' Verse 7.

" In the first place, we would inquire, What is meant by ' the sacrifice of all earthly things,' if our eternal reward is to consist in similar things — eternal cities, eternal gold, and eternal farms, instead of temporal cities, gold, and farms? Again : Are these sacrifices of all worldly things to be made at the bidding of Joe Smith and his counsellors? Are we to yield them up to God through their hands, or are we not?

" The language of these exhortations would be well enough, were they not in known connection with the ends and aims of Smith and his comrades. But as it is, the plain meaning is this : You must give up all worldly things to God, as an indispensable condition of salvation. Very well — agreed. But who is to inform us of what things God has need? Why, the Lord's Prophet at Nauvoo, to be sure. And to whom are we to pay it over? To the Lord's servants at Nauvoo. *All* our wealth, according to the first edition of the Book of Covenants, and *part* of it only, according to the second edition. Very well. All this is nice. We think we will take our chance of salvation on some other ground.

" This lecture on the sacrifice of all things, we are informed, is so plain, that the customary catechism upon it at the end is deemed unnecessary. We have supplied one, with appropriate answers, which we would respectfully commend to the ' Saints,' to be appended to the next edition of this plausible lecture. It would constitute a better typographical correction than the Prophet is wont to make in his revelations, even where he adds whole pages to the original text. The student is also advised, by the Mormons, to commit the whole lecture to memory, it is so important. We advise him to do the same, and to take our catechism with it, since the Prophet has supplied none. The concluding, seventh lecture on faith we would also commend to theological mystics and systemmongers of all creeds. Faith here is made to mount up into regions where they delight to soar. We fear we should fall from the giddy height. We choose, then, to stand on terra firma, and stretch up our necks, to see how other geese rise and fly through these aerial heights.

" We have already noticed the fundamental dogma and final exhortation of Mormonism, and of all other spurious creeds, viz., You must believe on mere human testimony, and then give all you have to God's appointed *witnesses of the faith;* we have dragged them forth from their lurking-places by the incipient catechism on faith, and that is all we can do at present.

" The next move of the Mormons, after having thus got a firm foothold upon the credulity of their followers, is to remove one insuperable objection to their scheme, viz., utter want of all accredited or rational evidence that it is from God. This they do, by denying that the miracles of the Bible were wrought of old by God, in attestation of the veracity of his servants, before the world; but they affirm that they were wrought simply for the benefit of those who believe, or the Saints.

" To prove this, instead of taking the Bible literally, where Moses is said to have wrought signs to show that he was commissioned of God, and also in John x. 37, xv. 24, Acts ii. 3, and numberless other passages, on almost every page of the Bible, where even Christ himself is represented as commanding the Jews not to take nim at his word, but to look at his works, or miracles, because ' he that beareth witness of himself is not true; ' all these they virtually deny, or contradict, and then tell us that they take them literally. Still, they contend that there can be no true church on earth, without prophets, apostles, power of miracles, gifts of tongues, of healing, etc. etc., and that their Church alone possesses these.

" These extravagant dogmas and absurd claims, common to all impostors, in all ages, they base on the following passages of Scripture. It is said in Mark xvi. 17, 'These signs shall follow them that believe,' (enumerating the signs.) They fall into a mistake here, which is common to them and all other fanatics, viz., that of understanding all that was said by Christ and his apostles *to their hearers*, as of course said to them. Hence they infer that these signs were to follow, not only those who believed on the twelve apostles, as the text literally asserts, and as was the case at the day of Pentecost, and on various other occasions, but, forsooth, they maintain that these signs were to follow *all those* who should afterwards believe the *gospel*, in *all ages of the world*, which the text does not assert. This they call a *literal* interpretation. But when we grant them this position, and say, Very well; bravo! now show us the signs, and we will believe; their ready reply is, ' A wicked and adulterous generation seeketh for a sign, and verily there shall no sign be given them; ' and here they stop, forgetting to refer us to any past or future sign, as the Savior referred those whom he rebuked in this passage, because they had before refused to look at the multitude of signs he had already given them.

" And now, for a long time, the teeth of the Mormons have been chattering with the ague, induced by the trials of poverty and want, which have been brought upon them by their frequent removals from place to place, and the stone temple, bank stock, mercantile, prairie land, and tavern-house speculations of the Lord's Prophet and his compeers; and their teeth still chatter, and their bones still burn and ache, though they alone, of all others, possess the miraculous gifts of healing, given, as we are assured, for the express purpose of comforting the Saints on earth, and for no other purpose.

" But all this, we are told, is because, forsooth, after ten years' trial, they cannot bring their faith up to the sticking-point necessary to cure this ague. And yet we are told that sometimes they achieve wonders with the hysterics and the 'blues,' which we believe are the only kind of devils they have ever succeeded in casting out.

" We are assured, also, that there can be no church, without prophets and apostles. We ask them to prophesy; and the Prophet, in 1831, points us to the destruction which awaits the Mormons in the eastern country, and withdraws them from impending ruin to Mount Zion, Jackson county, Missouri, the *everlasting possession*

15

of the Saints, the fairie land of Mormon faith, Mormon peace, and Mormon bliss.*

"We ask them, Whom did the apostles appoint as their successors in their apostleship, and whether it was not their fault that the office ended with them? The Mormons make no reply.

"Again, we ask, Who is empowered to revive the long-lost succession? All caps are thrown up, and all voices at once shout, 'Joe Smith! Joe Smith!! He is the Prophet of the Lord!' He holds both the keys and the cash of the Church, though, as we have seen, he once, in time of danger, committed the sword to his favorite mastiff.

"To cap the climax of these absurdities, Parley Pratt contends that the general commission referred to in Mark, to preach the gospel, was limited to those who heard it, while the many signs that were to follow are granted to all coming generations!! So that, while we must all wait for a new revelation to preach, we all have liberty to cast out devils as soon as we believe!!† I hope he will not complain that I have omitted the former, and am trying my hand at the latter.

"They next refer to 1 Cor. xii., which they expound with marvellous ability.

"From the rear of this invaluable breastwork of logic, Parley opens an inspired cannonade of commingled metaphysics, eloquence, and pathos, and concludes with the prayer 'that the vision should be shut up;' in which prayer, all men of common sense, I presume, will heartily unite. So here we drop it.

'I would just suggest that he and all other Mormons have forgotten to read and interpret, literally, the apostle's argument through, to the end of the 13th chapter of 1 Corinthians. They are particularly silent upon that verse in which the apostle says, literally, that prophecies shall fail, and tongues shall cease, and all else but faith, (not Mormon faith, we presume,) hope, and charity.

"The outlines of their despotic hierarchy have already been presented. The names indeed of their several orders and offices are found in the Scriptures. But that the name is nothing, and the powers of an office every thing, some other apostolic sects would do well to learn, as well as the Mormons. We look in vain for the origin of the definite powers of such hierarchies, baptized with Scripture names, except in the crania of their respective godfathers. In this case, Joseph Smith, Jr., General of Nauvoo Militia, happens to be the man.

"The system also establishes a somewhat more perfect despotism than has been reached by any other hierarchy. It concentrates all power in the person of the valorous translator. This is the principal difference between the Joe Smith of Illinois, and other Joe Smiths who have trodden the path of hierarchal fame before him. They, one and all, from Pope Linus downward, demonstrate the divine

* See B. C., p. 151, 12; p. 190, 2; p. 192, 1; p. 194, 9; p. 139, 11, 12, 13; p. 154, 1, 2.
† See Voice of Warning, p. 112.

origin of their religious oligarchies from Scripture, because, forsooth, the names with which they have chosen to christen their several functionaries are found in that sacred volume. The progress which Joseph has made in the divine favor, since the typographical correction of that unlucky revelation, 'Thou shalt aspire to no other gift, save to translate,' may be seen from an enumeration of his accumulating titles in the Book of Covenants, 177 and 88, also at the close of the former.

"The next chapter on the fundamental doctrines of Mormonism, which we shall notice, is 'the witness of the Spirit,' as they term it. This is always the last resort. After running the whole round of argument, discussing the merits of Joseph's bough, and its literal leap across the wall of the Atlantic Ocean; glancing at the upspringing truth and downlooking righteousness of David; brandishing, with triumphant flourishes, the two sticks of Ezekiel; gazing at the angel flying away with the Book of Mormon; and having appealed to Mark's limited charter for preaching the gospel, and general permission to cast out devils, there is a solemn pause. You ask for a sign; but verily no sign shall be given you. You demand proof; the ready reply is, 'I know that Mormonism is true, for God has revealed it to me, in my soul.' Very good; but how shall I know it? 'Ask in faith, as I have done, and it shall be given you.' That is, first believe it, then ask, and then you shall know it is true. To require this process is much the same as to require one to eat his dinner raw, and to cook it afterwards.

"By this patent mode of procedure, both Pratt and Rigdon assure us that they discovered ultimately that what they had at first pronounced a base fabrication, was indeed a new and wonderful revelation from God. It should be noticed, here, that asking in faith, according to the Book of Covenants, is actual believing; for' where doubt and uncertainty is,' say they, 'there faith is not, nor can be.'* Doubtless any one might discover the truth of any thing in the same way.

"The fanatical doctrine of the Spirit is more fully discussed upon another page.† We only repeat, here, that the man who neglects the employment of the written word, natural reason, and conscience, which God has given him for his guidance, and yields himself up to his own internal impulses and fantasies, from that moment throws himself out from under the guidance of God, and yields himself up to the guidance of darkness and delusion. And the spirit of darkness will not be slow to instruct and guide him in whatever way he sees fit. He will soon know, with dogmatical assurance, every thing in the universe, save one, viz., that he himself has become a religious lunatic, bereft of all common sense.

"I have reserved one choice specimen of 'Mormon logic and literal interpretation of the Scriptures,' with which to grace the climax of this Mormon Babel. I have done this, partly because it holds and deserves the highest place in the system, and partly because I wish so to hold it up, that all men may look at this hideous

* B. C., 62, 12.   † See Mormonism in all Ages, pp. 115, 116.

and ,blasphemous abortion of all Scripture, all reason,. all decency, and all sense.

" Christ prayed, say they, that all the saints might be one with him and the Father. He has declared, also, that they are joint heirs with him, and shall sit down with him on his throne, as he has overcome and sat down with the Father on his throne; that to those that believe, all things are possible, &c. Now, what logical, literal, and inspired inference, are we to make from this? Why, truly, nothing else than that the saints are all to become equal with God himself!! in knowledge, and power, and glory, equal to the Father!! But this is not all; Christ assured his disciples, that they should do even greater things than these. Therefore, say they, we shall create, uphold, redeem, save, and reign forever, over still greater worlds than this which Christ governs!!*

" This is almost as literal as the bough and the wall, the two sticks, and the flying angel. What part the ' liars, knaves, swindlers, debauchees, and asses,' (who bore witness to, and constitute the foundation of the Book of Mormon, and on whose shoulders the whole superstructure rests,) are to have in these displays of Mormon glory, we are not definitely told. But since, according to Mormon doctrine, they have been the principal means of turning many to righteousness, doubtless they will shine as stars somewhere in this new firmament of gods, higher than the Highest.

" Surely, when this notable day shall come, all things will be created new, with a vengeance!! We see here what it is that inspires the ardor and inflates the zeal of the idiot multitude of that professed Church. They are to possess the fulness and wealth of the earth here, and reign with Christ in Mount Zion, Missouri, a thousand years, and hereafter they are to become, not demigods, but literal deities, one and all of them. Why, then, talk about sacrifices? They can afford to empty their pockets into the coffers of Smith and Company, and to traverse the world, barefoot, in quest of new Zions and new proselytes, with such a splendid reversion in prospect.

" But every Mormon is not only to be a God hereafter; he has, in his own belief, been a demigod from all eternity, or at least an angel heretofore.

" Their sublime faith teaches them that their action and destiny here are the result, and can be explained only upon the admission, of their existence and action before they inhabited their present bodies. This notion, however, does not distinctly appear in their published revelations. It was at one time promulgated, but from its unpopularity, their leaders suppressed the full development of their peculiar scheme of preëxistence until faith on the earth should increase.†

" These general theories of humanity enable them, as they think, to give a full and literal interpretation to the language of Scripture, which, without these enlarged views, as they call them, of the origin and destiny of man, are utterly inexplicable. Reader, remember that

* See Pratt's Truth Vindicated, p. 27.
† B. C., 211, 115.

when you meet a full-blooded Mormon, you meet an angel that *was,* a Mormon that *is,* and a God that IS TO BE. As in the case of the man who fell down stairs, and ran up again, you will find the lowest point in the climax in the middle of his career.

" Probably, however, not one Mormon in fifty knows what is really taught in their own sacred books. In preaching and writing creeds in new places, they do not generally even allude to the peculiarities of Mormonism as such. They take their texts, and preach a some-what peculiar form of Christianity, which, in truth, is as much like the Mormonism at ·Nauvoo, as it is like paganism, and no more so. This, at first, they call *Mormonism.* But the doctrines of their sacred books and teachers are quite another thing. Every believer, either in Smith or the Book of Mormon, must believe that that book and the Book of Covenants, or revelations to Smith, are on a level with the Bible, and that all who thus receive them will be saved, and that all others will be damned.*

" 2. They believe the Bible only as Smith interprets and explains, or new translates and supplies the lost parts.†

" 3. They believe in four different future states ; the celestial, te-lestial, terrestrial, and the lake of fire.‡

" If the reader has doubts on any of these points, he is requested to compare the pages and passages cited in proof with care.

" 4. Their 'literal interpretation of Scripture not only involves giving to the Deity a human form, and implements of human enter-prise, but also the literal future levelling of mountains, annihilating seas, and, bringing the whole earth into one vast plain, without weeds, thorns, briers, or any useless or hurtful thing — all as neat and as smooth as the head of a pair of brass andirons ; and it is to be smelted and polished into shape much in the same way.

" 5. The Book of Covenants and Revelations, as it is called, which is the real basis of the practical faith of the Mormons, con-tains only a small part of the revelations that have actually been given to Smith, as he pretends. There is still a large folio of un-published revelations of many hundreds, which it would be indis-creet to expose to the rude gaze of unbelievers, but which a Mormon is really bound to believe and obey wherever he meets them, or else believe that Smith, to whom they are given, is an impostor : for he has declared them all to be from God, and printed only so many of them as he deemed prudent. Some of those not published occa-sionally meet us, through either the indiscretion of the brethren or the kindness of seceders.

" The revelations in the Book of Covenants cannot be understood without carefully comparing them with the history and position of the Mormon Church at the time they were given. The transfers of town-lots, tanyards, &c. &c., to Smith and Company, by ex-press revelation, are also artfully concealed by the use of antiquated, fictitious names, both for the persons and the property. It should

---

* In proof of this, see B. C., pp. 77, 74, 180, 159, 78, 75, 93, 95, 104, 113, 23, 250, 174, 175, 176, 189, in order.
† B. C., 7, 16, 111 ; B. M., 30, 31, first edition ; B. C., 76, 117, 166.
‡ B. C., 225.

15 *

also be remembered that revelations, said to be given to others, are always given through Smith, who is sole translator, and who, according to one revelation, aspires to no other gift,* but, according to another, claims all gifts and all authority.

" In 1833, an edition of these revelations was published, in the order of their dates, and called the ' Book of Commandments,' with explanatory captions at the head of each revelation. That edition has been wisely suppressed. It was quite too luminous for Mormonism. In 1835, the present book came forth, with the type, &c., corrected. The captions are left out, and the revelations are scattered here and there, without any order of time or date. It now takes a *Mormon* to hunt them out, and compare them with facts in their history. Nor is this all; whole clauses, sections, and, in some cases, almost entire pages, are either added or suppressed, as new exigencies require, in these said divine revelations. Let not the ' pious Saint ' complain of this. It is the duty of his Prophet to see that the revelations are corrected, from time to time. The disciple has nothing to do but to believe.

" When old Mr. Smith, the father of Joe, was alive, he, among the rest, needed something to do. He was consequently dubbed Patriarch, and it was his duty to pronounce a patriarchal blessing, in the name of Jesus Christ, on the head of all the fatherless children in the Mormon Church. He had a wonderful gift of *prophecy*, which, like a cider-barrel tapped at both ends, spun out both towards the past and the future. He *predicted* to these sons of the Church both their pedigree and their destiny ; told them what particular tribe of Israel they were from, and what their future career would be, in this world and the next."

----◆----

REMARKABLE EVENTS.

" The reader will already have observed, that a great variety of contradictory stories were related by the Smith family, before they had any fixed plan of operation, respecting the finding of the plates, from which their book was translated. One is, that after the plates were taken from their hiding-place by Joe, he again laid them down, looked into the hole, where he saw a *toad*, which immediately transformed itself into a spirit, and gave him a tremendous blow. Another is, that, after he had got the plates, a spirit assaulted him with the intention of getting them from his possession, and actually jerked them out of his hands; Joe, nothing daunted, in return seized them again, and started to run, when his Satanic Majesty (or the spirit) applied his foot to the Prophet's seat of honor, which raised him three or four feet from the ground. That the Prophet has related a story of this kind, to some of his ' weak Saints,' we have no manner of doubt.

* B. C., 126.

" Here, then, is the finding of the plates, containing a new revelation from Heaven ; and the *modus operandi* may seem to the
Mormon truly wonderful, and in character with that Being who
upholds and sustains the Universe ; but to the rational mind it can
excite no other emotion than contempt for his species.

" Mr. Copley testified that, after the Mormon brethren arrived
here from the Susquehannah, one of them, by the name of Joseph
Knight, related to him a story, as having been related to him by
Joseph Smith, Jr., which exciting some curiosity in his mind, he
determined to ask Joseph more particularly about it, on the first
opportunity. Not long after, it was confirmed to him by Joseph
himself, who again related it in the following manner : ' After he
had finished translating the Book of Mormon, he again buried up
the plates in the side of a mountain, by command of the Lord. Some
time after this, he was going through a piece of woods, on a by-path,
when he discovered an old man dressed in ordinary gray apparel,
sitting upon a log, having in his hand, or near by, a small box. On
approaching him, he asked him what he had in his box. To which
the old man replied, that he had a MONKEY, and for five coppers he
might see it. Joseph answered, that he would not give a cent to
see a monkey, for he had seen a hundred of them. He then asked
the old man where he was going, who said he was going to *Charzee.*
Joseph then passed on, and, not recollecting any such place in that
part of the country, began to ponder over the strange interview, and
finally asked the Lord the meaning of it. The Lord told him that
the man he saw was MORONI, with the plates, and if he had given
him the five coppers, he might have got his plates again.'

" Here we have a story related by our modern Prophet, to his
followers, for no other purpose, as we conceive, but to make his
pretensions more ' marvellous in their eyes.' A celebrated Mormon
prophet, of ancient times, and one of modern date, have an interview in the woods, and hold a conversation about a MONKEY ; one
prophet of the Lord relating a falsehood to another ! ! ! "

Howe's excellent and able book, pp. 275—277.

Shortly after I located in Nauvoo, Joe proposed to me
to go to New York, and get some plates engraved, and
bring them to him, so that he could exhibit them as the
genuine plates of the Book of Mormon, which he pretended
had been taken from him, and " *hid up* " by an angel, and
which he would profess to have recovered. He calculated
upon making considerable money by this trick, as there
would of course be a great anxiety to see the plates, which
he intended to exhibit at twenty-five cents a sight. I mentioned this proposition to Mrs. Sarah M. Pratt, on the day
the Prophet made it, and requested her to keep it in
memory, as it might be of much importance.

As an illustration of the hypocrisy of Joe Smith, I will

mention a short conversation that passed between him and myself, as we were one day riding together up the banks of the Mississippi. After a short interval of silence, Smith suddenly said to me, in a peculiarly inquiring manner, —

"General, Harris (meaning George W. Harris, Esq., the present husband of the widow of the late William Morgan, a very pretty and intelligent woman, who has a very beautiful daughter married to Colonel David B. Smith) says that you have no faith, and that you do not believe we shall ever obtain our inheritances in Jackson county, Missouri." Though somewhat perplexed by the Prophet's remark, and still more by his manner, I coldly replied, "What does Harris know about my belief, or the real state of my mind? I like to tease him now and then about it, as he is so firm in the faith, and takes it all in such good part." "Well," said Joe, laughing heartily, "I guess you have got about as much faith as I have. Ha! ha! ha!" "I should judge about as much," was my reply.

My friend, General George W. Robinson, once related to me a curious circumstance, which occurred in Missouri, when he was clerk of the Church. One day, Joe, the Prophet, was gravely dictating to him a revelation which he had just received from the Lord. Robinson, according to custom, wrote down the very words the Lord spoke to Joe, and in the exact order in which the latter heard them. He had written for some considerable time, when Smith's inspiration began to flag, and, to gain breath, he requested Robinson to read over what he had written. He did so until he came to a particular passage, when Smith interrupted him, and desired to have that read again. Robinson complied, and Smith, shaking his head, knitting his brows, and looking very much perplexed, said, "That will never do. You must alter that, George."

Robinson, though not a little surprised at the "*Lord's blunder*," did as he was directed, and changed the offensive passage into one more fit for the inspection of the Gentiles.

One of the most remarkable of the Mormon miracles is related by Rev. Mr. Tucker to have occurred in the following manner:—

Towards the close of a fine summer's day, a farmer, in

one of the States, found a respectable-looking man at his gate, who requested permission to pass the night under his roof. The hospitable farmer readily complied : the stranger was invited into the house, and a warm and substantial supper set before him.

After he had eaten, the farmer, who appeared to be a jovial, warm-hearted, humorous, and withal shrewd old man, passed several hours in pleasant conversation with his guest, who seemed to be very ill at ease, both in body and mind, yet, as if desirous of pleasing his entertainer, replied courteously and agreeably to whatever was said to him. Finally, he pleaded fatigue and illness as an excuse for retiring to rest, and was conducted by the farmer to an upper chamber, where he went to bed.

About the middle of the night, the farmer and his family were awakened by the most dreadful groans, which they soon ascertained proceeded from the chamber of the traveller. On going to investigate the matter, they found that the stranger was dreadfully ill, suffering the most acute pains and uttering the most doleful cries, apparently without any consciousness of what was passing around him. Every thing that kindness and experience could suggest, was done to relieve the sick man ; but all efforts were in vain, and to the consternation of the farmer and his family, their guest expired in the course of a few hours.

In the midst of their trouble and anxiety, at an early hour in the morning, two travellers came to the gate, and requested entertainment. The farmer told them that he would willingly offer them hospitality, but that just now his household was in the greatest confusion on account of the death of the stranger, the particulars of which he proceeded to relate to them. They appeared to be much surprised and grieved at the poor man's calamity, and politely requested permission to see the corpse. This of course the farmer readily granted, and conducted them to the chamber in which lay the dead body. They looked at it for a few minutes in silence, and then the oldest of the pair gravely told the farmer, that they were Elders of the Church of Jesus Christ of Latter Day Saints, and were empowered by God to perform miracles, even to the extent of raising the dead ; and that they felt quite assured they could bring to life the dead man before them!

The farmer was of course pretty considerably astonished by the quality and powers of the persons who addressed him, and rather incredulously asked if they were quite sure that they could perform all they professed to.

" O certainly! Not a doubt of it. The Lord has commissioned us expressly to work miracles, in order to prove the truth of the Prophet Joseph Smith, and the inspiration of the books and doctrines revealed to him. Send for all your neighbors, that, in the presence of a multitude, we may bring the dead man to life, and that the Lord and his Church may be glorified to all men."

The farmer, after a little consideration, agreed to let the miracle-workers proceed, and, as they desired, sent his children to his neighbors, who, attracted by the expectation of a miracle, flocked to the house in considerable numbers.

The Mormon Elders commenced their task by kneeling and praying before the body with uplifted hands and eyes, and with most stentorian lungs. Before they had proceeded far with their prayer, a sudden idea struck the farmer, who quietly quitted the house for a few minutes, and then returned, and waited patiently by the bedside until the prayer was finished, and the Elders ready to perform their miracle. Before they began, he respectfully said to them, that, with their permission, he wished to ask them a few questions upon the subject of this miracle. They replied that they had no objection. The farmer then asked, " You are quite certain that you can bring this man to life again?" "We are." " How do you know that you can?" "We have just received a revelation from the Lord, informing us that we can." " Are you quite sure that the revelation was from the Lord?" " Yes; we cannot be mistaken about it." " Does your power to raise this man to life again depend upon the particular nature of his disease? or could you now bring any dead man to life?" " It makes no difference to us: we could bring any corpse to life." " Well, if this man had been killed, and one of his arms cut off, could you bring him to life, and also restore to him his arm?" " Certainly, — there is no limit to the power given us by the Lord. It would make no difference, even if both his arms and his legs were cut off." "Could you restore him if his head had been cut off?" "Certainly we could." " Well,". said the farmer, with a quiet smile upon his features, " I do not doubt the truth of what such holy men assert, but I am desirous that my neighbors here should be fully converted by having the miracle performed in the completest manner possible. So, by your leave, if it makes no difference whatever, I will proceed to cut off the head of this corpse." Accordingly he produced a huge and well-sharpened broad axe from beneath his coat, which he swung above his head, and was apparently about to bring it down upon the neck of the corpse, when, lo and behold! to the amazement of all present, the dead man started up in great agitation, and swore he would not have his head cut off for any consideration whatever!

The company immediately seized the Mormons, and soon made them confess that the pretended dead man was also a Mormon Elder, and that they had sent him to the farmer's house, with directions to die there at a particular hour, when they would drop in, as if by accident, and perform a miracle that would astonish every body. The farmer, after giving the impostors a severe chastisement, let them depart to practise their humbuggery in some other quarter.

I give the following from the Times and Seasons, Vol. III., No. 8, page 701, *verbatim, et literatim, et punctatim,* as a sample of the Prophet's editorial taste in doing up hymeneal notices, and as an evidence of his purity and chastity of thought on subjects of that kind. Any Gentile editor would be hooted out of society for penning and publishing such contemptible stuff.

" MARRIED—In this city on the 6th inst. by the Rev. Erastus H. Derby, Mr. Gilbert H. Rolfe, to Miss Eliza Jane Bates, all of this city.
" On receipt of the above notice, we were favored with a rich and delightful loaf of cake—by no means *below* the *medium* size ; which makes us anxious that all their acts through life may be *justified ;* and when life wanes and they find a peaceful abode in the ' narrow house,' may the *many outs* and *ins* they have made, leave to the world an abundant posterity to celebrate their glorious example.'

PHRENOLOGICAL CHARTS.

I here insert two phrenological charts, about which much has been said and written, simply as a matter of curiosity. That of the Prophet was taken in Nauvoo, Illinois, by Doctor Crane, in June last; mine was taken in Fairfield, Illinois, by Doctor Parnell, between two and three years since.

"SMITH'S CHART, BY CRANE.

In this chart the figures range from 1 to 12; 1 is the minimum, 7 the medium, and 12 the maximum.

From the Nauvoo Wasp, of July 2, 1842.
" Mr. Editor:

" Sir, — I take the liberty to inform you that a large number of persons in different places have manifested a desire to know the phrenological development of Joseph Smith's head. I have examined the Prophet's head, and he is perfectly willing to have the chart published. You will please publish in your paper such portions of it as I have marked, showing the development of his much-talked-of brain, and let the public judge for themselves whether phrenology proves the reports against him true or false Time will prove all things, and a ' word to the wise is sufficient.'

" Yours, respectfully,
" A. Crane.''

"A PHRENOLOGICAL CHART.
" By A. Crane, M. D., *Professor of Phrenology.*
" PROPENSITIES

" 11; L. *Amativeness.* — Extreme susceptibility; passionately fond of the company of the other sex.

" 9; L. *Philoprogenitiveness.* — Strong parental affection, great solicitude for their happiness.

" 5; F. *Inhabitiveness.* — Attached to place of long residence; no desire to change residence.

" 8; F. *Adhesiveness.* — Solicitous for the happiness of friends, and ardent attachments to the other sex.

" 8; L. *Combativeness.* — Indomitable perseverance; great courage; force; ability to overpower.

" 6; M. *Destructiveness.* — Ability to control the passions; and is not disposed to extreme measures.

" 10; L. *Secretiveness.* — Great propensity and ability to conceal feelings, plans, &c.

" 9; L. *Acquisitiveness.* — Strong love of riches; desire to make and save money.

"9; L. *Alimentiveness.* — Strong relish for food; keen and severe appetite.

"4; M. or S. *Vitativeness.* — Indifference to life; views the approach of death without fear.

"FEELINGS.

"7; F. *Cautiousness.* — Provision against prospective dangers and ills, without hesitation or irresolution.

"10; L. *Approbativeness.* — Ambition for distinction; sense of character; sensibility to reproach; fear of scandal.

"10; L. *Self-esteem.* — High-mindedness; independence; self-confidence; dignity; aspiration for greatness.

"7; F. *Concentrativeness.* — Can dwell on a subject without fatigue, and control the imagination.

"SENTIMENTS.

"10; L. *Benevolence.* — Kindness; goodness; tenderness; sympathy.

"6; F. *Veneration.* — Religion without great awe or enthusiasm; reasonable deference to superiority.

"10; L. *Firmness.* — Stability and decision of character and purpose.

"8; L. *Conscientiousness.* — High regard for duty, integrity, moral principle, justice, obligation, truth, &c.

"10; L. *Hope.* — Cheerfulness; sanguine expectation of success and enjoyment.

"10; L. *Marvellousness.* — Wonder; credulity; belief in the supernatural.

"5; M. *Imitation.* — Inferior imitative powers; failure to copy, describe, relate stories, &c.

"8; L. or F. *Prepossession.* — Attached to certain notions; not disposed to change them, &c.

"9; L. *Ideality.* — Lively imagination; fancy; taste; love of poetry, elegance, eloquence, excellence, &c.

"PERCEPTIVES.

"8; F. or M. *Admonition.* — Desirous to know what others are doing; ready to counsel and give hints of a fault or duty, &c.

"7; F. *Constructiveness.* — Respectable ingenuity, without uncommon skill, tact, or facility in making, &c.

"5; F. or M. *Tune.* — Love of music, without quickness to catch or learn tunes by the ear.

"11; V. L. or L. *Time.* — Distinct impressions as to the time when, how long, &c.

"11; V. L or L. *Locality.* — Great memory of places and position.

"11; V. L. *Eventuality.* — Extraordinary recollection of minute circumstances.

"10; L. *Individuality.* — Great desire to see; power of observation.

"10; F. *Form.* — Cognizance, and distinct recollection of shapes, countenances, &c.

16

"11; V. L., L. or F. *Size.*—Ability to judge of proportionate size, &c.

"9; V. L., L. or F. *Weight.*—Knowledge of gravitation, momentum, &c.

"9; F. or M. *Color.*—Moderate skill in judging of colors, comparing and arranging them.

"6; F. *Language.*—Freedom of expression, without fluency or verbosity; no great loquacity.

"9; L. *Order.*—Love of arrangement; every thing in its particular place.

"7; *Number.*—Respectable aptness in arithmetical calculations, without extraordinary talent.

"REFLECTIVES.

"10; L. *Mirthfulness.*—Wit; fun; mirth; perception and love of the ludicrous.

"9; L. *Causality.*—Ability to think and reason clearly, and perceive the relations of cause and effect.

"11; V. L. *Comparison.*—Extraordinary critical acumen; great power of analysis.

"THERE ARE FOUR TEMPERAMENTS.

"The Lymphatic, or Phlegmatic, in which the *secreting glands* are the most active portion of the system, produces both corporeal and mental languor, dulness, and inactivity.

"The Sanguine, in which the *arterial* portion of the system is most active, gives strong feelings and passions, and more ardor, zeal, and activity, than of strength or power.

"The Bilious, in which the *muscular* portion predominates in activity, produces strength, power, and endurance of body, with great force and energy of mind and character.

"The Nervous, in which the *brain* and *nervous system* are most active, gives the highest degree of activity, with clearness of perception and of thought, but less endurance. Sharp and prominent organs denote activity; smooth and broad ones, intensity and strength.

"EXPLANATION OF THE CHART.

"The figures in the margin opposite the organs, and ranging in a scale from 1 to 12, indicate the various *degrees* in which the respective organs are developed in the head of the individual examined: thus, 1, 2, indicate that the organ is VERY SMALL, or almost wholly wanting; 3, 4, means SMALL, or feeble, and inactive; 5, 6, MODERATE, or active only in a subordinate degree; 7, 8, FULL or fair, and a little above par; 9, 10, LARGE, or quite energetic, and having a marked influence upon the character; 11, 12, VERY LARGE, or giving a controlling influence, and extreme liability to perversion. The SIZE OF THE BRAIN, COMBINATIONS OF THE FACULTIES, and TEMPERAMENT, of the individual may be indicated in the same manner as the degrees of the faculties or organs.

The initials V. L. denote very large; L. large; F. full; M. moderate; S. small; V. S. very small.

COMBINATION OF THE FACULTIES.

" The fore part of the head is called the *frontal* portion ; and the back, the *occipital ;* the base, or lower part, is denominated the *basilar* region ; and the upper portion, the *coronal.*

" Phrenology has ascertained what *portion* of the brain the mind employs in the exercise of each mental function ; and hence, by determining how much *larger* one part of the brain is than another, it can tell how much an individual exercises certain classes of mental functions more than he does others. The combinations of the organs have, also, great influence upon the mental manifestations. The rule is, that the *larger* organs control the *smaller.*

" When the occipital portion is larger than the frontal, there will be more of feeling than reason ; of passion than intellect ; of brutality than humanity ; of propelling than directing power; of action than judgment. But when the frontal region is much larger than the occipital, as in the heads of Melancthon, Franklin, Washington, and Clinton, the individual will combine pure morality with great depth and power of intellect ; a strong mind with virtuous feelings ; and sound practical sense, with nobleness of conduct.

" One having large or very large intellectual organs, combined with moderate or small organs of the propensities, will possess great mental power with a want of impetus ; high intellectual and moral qualities, with inefficiency ; but with the propensities well developed, and the intellectual faculties very large, will combine great strength of mind with great energy of character, and both directed by the human sentiments, and applied to moral and intellectual objects : Washington, Franklin, Clinton, and Lafayette.

" One having very large perceptive faculties, combined with only full reasoning organs, will possess a practical matter-of-fact talent, and an uncommon share of general information, yet lack depth of mind and strength of intellect, and a talent for adapting means to ends.

" One having the perceptive organs full or large, with very large reflective faculties, will have a universal talent, and ability both to *plan* and *execute ;* to attend to general principles and to details ; and, with full or large propensities, be capable of employing extraordinary talents to the best advantage, and of rising to eminence : Franklin, Washington, Clinton, Bonaparte.

" One having very large reasoning organs, with only moderate or full perceptive faculties, will possess great depth and originality of mind, and profound philosophical acumen ; but will *think* and *reason* more than *observe.*

" One in whom the basilar region greatly predominates over the coronal, will possess great force of character, and a ready talent for business, but strong passions applied to selfish purposes, with little morality and elevation of character and feeling.

" An evenness of the head indicates *uniformity* of character ; and unevenness *eccentricities* and strong *traits.*"

BENNETT'S CHART, BY PARNELL.

In this chart the figures range from 1 to 22; 1 is the minimum, 14 the medium, and 22 the maximum.

"*Phrenological Developments of General John C. Bennett.*

"REMARKS.— The brain may be more or less active, from temperament and texture, — the former to be determined by the comparative size of the head, thorax, and abdomen, the latter by observing the fibre of the skin. The size of the head is always compared with the size of the body of the same individual, and the size of the faculties with the faculties of the same head. If the size of the faculties are marked by figures, those used will be from 1 to 22; the medium, 14 : if by words, V. S. stands for very small; S. for small; R. S. for rather small; M. for moderate; F. for full; V. F. for very full; L. for large; V. L. for very large.

"FEELINGS, OR AFFECTIVE FACULTIES.

" GENUS ONE — PROPENSITIES.

" 17. *Vitativeness.* — Use; to preserve life. Abuse; too great a fear of death. Want; careless of health and life.

" 17. *Alimentiveness.* — Use; to prompt to take food. Abuse; drunkenness and gluttony. Want; careless of the kind of food.

" 18. *Destructiveness.* — Use; to destroy animals for food. Abuse; anger, revenge, murder. Want; inability to destroy.

" 18. *Amativeness.* — Use; propagation of the species — affection for the opposite sex. Abuse; jealousy, lust, lasciviousness, rapes, seduction. Want; incapacity to love the opposite sex.

" 14. *Philoprogenitiveness.* — Use; protection of offspring. Abuse; too great a fondness for children. Want; neglect of them, hatred of children.

" 16. *Adhesiveness.* — Use; attachment, friendship. Abuse; too great a fondness for society. Want; averse to friendship and social society.

" 14. *Concentrativeness.* — Use; to give continuity to feelings and intellect. Abuse; too great a love of home, place, country, and a disposition to dwell too long on one subject. Want; incapacity to locate and be content, and to keep the intellect on one subject.

" 19. *Combativeness.* — Use; courage, self-defence. Abuse; contention, quarrelling, war. Want; timidity.

" 14. *Secretiveness.* — Use; prudence, to conceal. Abuse; suspicion, deceit, lying. Want; inability to conceal.

" 13. *Acquisitiveness.* — Use; to provide for present and future wants. Abuse; avarice and theft. Want; prodigality, spendthrift.

" 13. *Constructiveness.* — Use; to construct, build, and invent. Abuse; picklocks, too great a desire to invent, and to build without judgment. Want; want of mechanical genius.

"GENUS TWO — SENTIMENTS.

"13. *Cautiousness.* — Use; circumspection, care — to keep from danger. Abuse; fear, melancholy, bashfulness, hesitation. Want; reckless, hasty in speech and action.

"16. *Approbativeness.* — Use; to gain the good-will and esteem of others, proper ambition. Abuse; vanity, and too great a love of glory, fame, and applause. Want; regardless of the opinion of others, want of proper ambition.

"14. *Self-Esteem.* — Use; proper self-respect. Abuse; pride, and too great a love of power. Want; want of confidence, distrust of one's abilities.

"14. Q. A love of the pathetic, sublime, and awful.

"16. *Benevolence.* — Use; mercy, charity, and forgiveness. Abuse; relieving the lazy, idle, and unworthy. Want; indifferent to the wants and woes of others, unforgiving.

"16. *Veneration.* — Use; to revere, respect, and reverence laws, parents, the Creator and his laws, and what is great and good. Abuse; servility and the worship of what is evil. Want; disrespect, neglect of parents, disregard for the Creator and the laws of the land.

"16. *Firmness.* — Use; perseverance, fortitude, and steadiness of purpose. Abuse; stubbornness, wilfulness, and desperation. Want; fickleness of purpose and opinion.

"18. *Conscientiousness.* — Use; perfect justice to all. Abuse; too great a sensitiveness. Want; disregard for the rights of others.

"10. *Hope.* — Use; to lead one to endeavor to obtain what the other faculties properly desire. Abuse; castle-building, too great expectation. Want; doubt and despondency.

"9. *Marvellousness.* — Use; faith, confidence, and proper belief. Abuse; credulity, fanaticism, — a belief in the supernatural, ghosts, and witches. Want; unbelief, want of confidence in others.

"11. *Ideality.* — Use; desire of perfection, poetry. Abuse; fastidiousness, too great a disposition to raise the mind above reality and sober reason Want; regardless of improvement.

"16. *Mirthfulness.* — Use; cheerfulness, mirth, wit, and gayety. Abuse; sarcasm, too great a love of the ridiculous, and of ridicule. Want; inability to enjoy mirth and conviviality.

"12. *Imitation.* — Use; natural language — to imitate in nature and the arts. Abuse; mimicry, forgery, and counterfeiting. Want inability to copy.

"INTELLECTUAL FACULTIES.

"GENUS ONE — PERCEPTIVE FACULTIES.

"18. *Individuality.* — The observing faculty. Memory of things.
"16. *Form.* — Memory of persons, drawing.
"17. *Size.* — Judge of size, distance, and perpendicularity.
"17. *Weight.* — Judge of weight and gravity.
"18. *Coloring.* — Painting, flowers, beauties of nature.
"19. *Locality.* — Love of travel, memory of places.
16 *

" 15. *Order.* — Love of arrangement.
" 16. *Number.* — Love of figures, memory of numbers.
" 14. *Eventuality.* — Love of history, memory of historical events.
" 14. *Time.* — Chronology, time in music.
" 13. *Tune.* — Tones in music, memory of sound.
" 16. *Language.* — Memory of words.

" GENUS TWO — REFLECTIVE FACULTIES.

" 16. *Comparison.* — Judgment, logical reason.
" 13. *Causality.* — Gives one the power to reason abstractly, a love
of metaphysics, and to trace effects to their causes.
" 12. *Inference.* — The power to draw conclusions from premises.

" TEMPERAMENT. — Sanguine and bilious.

" The animal passions and intellectual powers prevail in this head
in a great degree over the superior sentiments; consequently, he
has great energy and indomptable perseverance, and much more
force and power, than goodness and fine feeling; he was made for
war, rapine, plunder, and destruction; to fill some high station,
where he could have power, take the command, and he would gain
all his ends by force and storm.   He is very tenacious of life, but
still a man of great courage.   He is an epicure, and fond of good living; and quite amorous; strong in friendship, but still stronger in
his feelings of hatred and desire of revenge.   He is quite ambitious;
desires fame, glory, and renown; is hasty, rash, violent; wants
patience and prudence.   He would sacrifice money both for fame
and power.   He is very generous, and would relieve the distressed.
He wants faith and hope, and is not fond of the marvellous; must
have facts before his mind can be convinced.   He is not a wit, poet,
or musician; but is very severe, satirical, and has some of the poetry
of love, and is very fond of amorous and martial music.   He is good
to imitate from observation and recollection, but not from feeling.
His pride would prevent him from being guilty of small, mean acts.
He is governed very much by his feelings, and is too liable to jump
at conclusions.   He has very strong powers of observation, and
memory of things, facts, faces, places, and dates; good, of events,
language, and time; poor, of tones.   He is very fond of the physical
sciences, geography, travel; of order, discipline, and epistolary
writing.   He is a most accurate judge of size, distance, proportion,
location, and color; should be a first-rate surgeon, or a fair linguist;
reasons by comparison.

                                        " B. A. PARNELL."

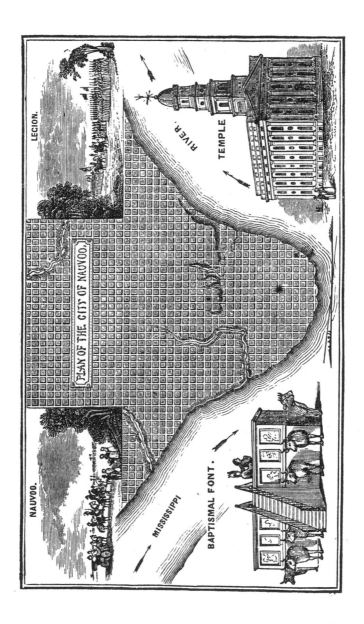

PLAN OF THE CITY OF NAUVOO.

LECION.

TEMPLE

RIVER.

NAUVOO.

MISSISSIPPI

BAPTISMAL FONT.

DESCRIPTION OF NAUVOO.

Nauvoo, the Holy City of the Mormons and present capital of their empire, is situated in the north-western part of Illinois, on the east bank of the Mississippi, in latitude N. 40° 35′, and longitude W. 14° 23′. It is bounded on the north, south, and west, by the river, which there forms a large curve, and is nearly two miles wide. Eastward of the city is a beautiful undulating prairie. It is distant ten miles from Fort Madison, in Iowa, is fifty-five miles above Quincy, Illinois, and more than two hundred above St. Louis.

Before the Mormons gathered there, the place was named *Commerce*, and was but a small and obscure village of some twenty houses. So rapidly, however, have they accumulated, that there are now, within three years of their first settlement, upwards of seven thousand inhabitants in the city, and three thousand more, of the Saints, in its immediate vicinity.

The surface of the ground upon which Nauvoo is built, is very uneven, though there are no great elevations. A few feet below the soil is a vast bed of limestone, from which excellent building material can be quarried, to almost any extent. A number of tumuli, or ancient mounds, are found within the limits of the city, proving it to have been a place of some importance with the extinct inhabitants of this continent.

The space comprised within the city limits is about four miles in its greatest length, and three in its greatest breadth, but is very irregular in its outline, and does not cover so much ground as the above measurement would seem to indicate.

The city is regularly laid out — the streets crossing each other at right angles, and being generally of considerable length, and of convenient width. The majority of the houses are as yet merely whitewashed log-cabins, but latterly quite a number of frame and brick houses have been erected.

The chief edifices of Nauvoo are the Temple, and a ho-

tel, called the Nauvoo House, neither of which is yet finished. The latter is of brick, upon a stone foundation, and
presents a front, on two streets, of one hundred and twenty
feet each, by forty feet deep, and is to be three stories high,
exclusive of the basement; and, though intended chiefly for
the reception and entertainment of strangers and travellers,
contains, or, rather, when completed is to contain, a splendid suite of apartments, for the especial accommodation of
the Prophet Joe Smith, and his heirs and descendants forever!

The privilege of this accommodation he pretends was
granted him by the Lord, in a special revelation, on account of his services to the Church. It is most extraordinary that Americans, imbued with democratic sentiments
and an utter aversion to hereditary privileges of any kind,
could for a moment be blinded to the selfishness of the
scoundrel, who thus coolly provided for himself and his
latest posterity a palace and a maintenance. We may,
however, safely predict that his Imperial Majesty will not
continue long in the enjoyment of his palace, and that, if
he escapes the fate of Haman, it will only be to wander,
like Cain, a vagabond on the face of the earth.

The Mormon Temple is a splendid structure of stone,
quarried within the bounds of the city. Its breadth is
eighty feet, and its length one hundred and twenty, besides
an outer court of thirty feet, making the length of the whole
structure one hundred and fifty feet.

In the basement of the Temple is the baptismal font,
constructed in imitation of the famous brazen sea of Solomon. It is upborne by twelve oxen, handsomely carved,
and overlaid with gold. Upon the surface of it, in panels,
are represented various scenes, handsomely painted. This
font is used for baptism of various kinds, viz., baptism for
admission into the Church — baptism for the healing of
the sick — baptism for the remission of sins — and lastly,
which is the most singular of all, baptism for the *dead*. By
this latter rite, living persons, selected as the representatives of persons deceased, are baptized for them, and thus
the dead are released from the penalty of their sins! This
baptism was performed, I recollect, for General Washington, among many others.

The upper story of the Temple will, when finished, be used as a lodge-room for Order Lodge, and other secret societies.

In the body of the Temple, where it is intended that the congregation shall assemble, are two sets of pulpits; one for the Melchisedec priesthood, and the other for the Aaronic and Levitical priesthood.

The cost of this noble edifice has been defrayed by tithing the whole Mormon Church. Those who reside at Nauvoo, and are able to labor, have been obliged to work every tenth day in quarrying stone, and also upon the Temple itself; and those who reside at a distance have been levied upon to the amount of one tenth of their property.

Besides the Temple, there are in Nauvoo two extensive steam saw mills, a large steam flouring mill, a tool factory, on a handsome scale, a foundry, and a company of considerable wealth, from Staffordshire, England, are establishing the manufacture of English china-ware.

It has often been asserted, in the Eastern States, that the Mormon settlement in Illinois had a community of goods; but this is not the case. Individual property is held, and society organized, as in other American cities. Not far from the city, however, is a community farm, which is cultivated in common by the poorer classes; but in the city itself each family has an acre allotted to it.

The neighborhood of Nauvoo is pretty thickly populated, and chiefly, though not exclusively, by Mormons.

The population of the Holy City itself is rather of a motley kind. The general gathering of the Saints has, of course, brought together men of all classes and characters. The great majority of them are uneducated and unpolished persons, who are undoubtedly sincere believers in the Prophet and his doctrines. A great proportion of them consists of the ignorant, brutalized converts from the English manufacturing districts, who were easily persuaded by Smith's missionaries to exchange their wretchedness at home for ease and plenty in the Promised Land. These men are devotedly attached to the Prophet's will, and obey his dictates as they would those of God himself.

These aliens can, by the law of Illinois, vote, after six months' residence in the State; and they consequently go

blindly to the polls, and cast their ballots for whoever is in
favor with Joe Smith, and has the expressed approbation
of that holy personage. To such an extent does his will
influence them, that at the last election in Nauvoo there
were but six votes against the candidates he supported!
The former inhabitants of Hancock county, those who re-
deemed it from the wilderness, are almost disfranchised by
these new-comers, whose numbers and unanimity give them
the political control of the county, and enable them to monopolize all civil and military offices.

I need say but little more of Nauvoo and its inhabitants,
except to remark that the great mass of the population is
composed of Mormons, and what are vulgarly styled *Jack
Mormons*, who are those attached to the Church from interest, but who do not possess overmuch faith in its doctrines, and, indeed, are not considered Mormons.

Of the Mormons, I believe the majority to be ignorant,
deluded men, really and earnestly devoted to their religion.
But their leaders are men of intellect, who are infidels, and
profess Mormonism because of the wealth, titles, rank, and
power, it procures them. The missionaries who are sent
out to convert the Gentiles, are chiefly sincere men, whom
Joe cannot trust with a knowledge of his iniquity, and who,
from their intelligence, would soon find him out, if they
lived at Nauvoo. Their wives, also, are sometimes wanted
for the cloister, and consequently the husbands are kept at
a distance.

As a military position, Nauvoo, garrisoned by twenty or
thirty thousand fanatics, armed to the teeth, and well supplied with provisions, would be one of the most formidable
in the world. It is unapproachable upon any side but the
east, and there the nature of the ground offers great obstacles to besieging operations. It is Smith's intention to
congregate his followers there, until they accumulate a
force that can defy any thing that can be brought against
him.

Nauvoo is a *Hebrew* word, and signifies *a beautiful
habitation for man*, carrying with it the idea of REST; it
is not, however, considered by the Mormons their FINAL
HOME, but a *resting-place only* — for they only intend to
remain there until they have gathered force sufficient to

enable them to conquer INDEPENDENCE, IN JACKSON COUN-
TY, MISSOURI, *which is one of the most fertile, pleasant,
and desirable countries on the face of the earth, possessing
a soil unsurpassed in any region.*   *Independence* they consider their ZION, and they there intend to rear their GREAT
TEMPLE, the corner-stone of which is already laid.   There
is to be the *great gathering-place* for all the Saints, and in
that delightful and healthy country they expect to find their
EDEN, and build the NEW JERUSALEM.   The Missourians
are proverbial for their hospitality, but they will never yield
a country of such surpassing beauty, superior excellence,
and unbounded fertility, to the *Latter Day* Saints, or any
other saints, without a valuable consideration.   The Mormons will never obtain it " BY BLOOD," as they contemplate,
and as their books teach.

" LOOK WELL TO THE WEST !! "   Why, only think of
WESTERN MISSOURI, the EDEN OF AMERICA, and the great
ST. LOUIS, the METROPOLIS OF THE WESTERN WORLD,
with her stupendous, stately edifices, of surpassing beauty
and gorgeous, princely structure, whose future glory *civic
prophets* can readily see without the assistance of the
Urim and Thummim, falling into the hands of a set of
MORMON DESPERADOES!!   Joe had better take another
look through his PEEP-STONE, for he was certainly mistaken
when he made the prediction.   The Lord intends that
WHITE FOLKS, and not *Mormons,* shall possess that goodly
land, a land truly " flowing with milk and honey," — the
desire of nations — the glory of the whole earth.

----◆----

CHARTERS, ORDINANCES, ETC. ETC.

When connected with the Mormons, I wrote and procured the passage of the following charters and ordinances, with the exception of the *Algerine Ordinance.*   My
limits will allow me to publish only a few of the ordinances : the Rules of Order, and other matters connected
with the City and University, will be found in another part
of this Exposé.

17

Extracts from Conference Minutes.

" On motion. *Resolved*, That a committee be appointed to draft a bill for the incorporating of the town of Nauvoo, and other purposes.

" *Resolved*, That Joseph Smith, Jr., Dr. J. C. Bennett, and R. B. Thompson, compose said committee.

" *Resolved*, That Dr. J. C. Bennett be appointed delegate to Springfield, to urge the passage of said bill through the legislature.

" Dr. Bennett, from the committee to draft a charter for the city, and for other purposes, reported the outlines of the same.

" On motion. *Resolved*, That the same be adopted."

Times and Seasons, Vol. I., No. 12, p. 186.

" By the politeness of Doctor Bennett, we have been favored with the following legislative act, incorporating our City, Legion, and University, for publication, which will, no doubt, be read with great satisfaction by all who have an interest in the future greatness and prosperity of our people ; to wit : —

" Charters of the ' City of Nauvoo,' the ' Nauvoo Legion,' and the ' University of the City of Nauvoo.'

" ' AN ACT TO INCORPORATE THE CITY OF NAUVOO.

" ' Sec. 1. *Be it enacted*, by the people of the State of Illinois, represented in the General Assembly, That all that district of country embraced within the following boundaries, to wit : beginning at the north-east corner of section thirty-one, in township seven, north of range eight, west of the fourth principal meridian, in the county of Hancock, and running thence west to the north-west corner of said section, thence north to the Mississippi River, thence west to the middle of the main channel of the said river, thence down the middle of said channel to a point due west of the south-east corner of fractional section number twelve, in township six, north of range nine, west of the fourth principal meridian, thence east to the south-east corner of said section twelve, thence north on the range line between township six north and range eight and nine west, to the south-west corner of section six, in township six, north of range eight west, thence east to the south-east corner of said section, thence north to the place of beginning, including the town plats of Commerce and Nauvoo, shall hereafter be called, and known, by the name of the ' City of Nauvoo,' and the inhabitants thereof are hereby constituted a body corporate and politic by the name aforesaid, and shall have perpetual succession, and may have, and use, a common seal, which they may change, and alter, at pleasure.

" ' Sec. 2. Whenever any tract of land adjoining the ' City of Nauvoo ' shall have been laid out into town lots, and duly recorded according to law, the same shall form a part of the ' City of Nauvoo.'

" ' Sec. 3. The inhabitants of said city, by the name and style aforesaid, shall have power to sue and be sued, to plead and be impleaded, defend and be defended, in all courts of law and equity, and in all actions whatsoever ; to purchase, receive, and hold property, real and personal, in said city ; to purchase, receive, and hold real property beyond the city for burying grounds, or for other public purposes, for the use of the inhabitants of said city; to sell, lease, convey, or dispose of property, real and personal, for the benefit of the city; to improve and protect such property, and to do all other things in relation thereto as natural persons.

"'Sec. 4. There shall be a City Council, to consist of a Mayor, four Aldermen, and nine Councillors, who shall have the qualifications of electors of said city, and shall be chosen by the qualified voters thereof, and shall hold their offices for two years, and until their successors shall be elected and qualified. The City Council shall judge of the qualifications, elections, and returns, of their own members, and a majority of them shall form a quorum to do business, but a smaller number may adjourn from day to day, and compel the attendance of absent members under such penalties as may be prescribed by ordinance.

"'Sec. 5. The Mayor, Aldermen, and Councillors, before entering upon the duties of their offices, shall take and subscribe an oath or affirmation that they will support the Constitution of the United States, and of this State, and that they will well and truly perform the duties of their offices to the best of their skill and abilities.

"'Sec. 6. On the first Monday of February next, and every two years thereafter, an election shall be held for the election of one Mayor, four Aldermen, and nine Councillors; and at the first election under this act, three judges shall be chosen, *viva voce*, by the electors present; the said judges shall choose two clerks, and the judges and clerks, before entering upon their duties, shall take and subscribe an oath or affirmation such as is now required by law to be taken by judges and clerks of other elections; and at all subsequent elections, the necessary number of judges and clerks shall be appointed by the City Council. At the first election so held the polls shall be opened at 9 o'clock, A. M, and closed at 6 o'clock, P. M.; at the close of the polls the votes shall be counted and a statement thereof proclaimed at the front door of the house at which said election shall be held; and the clerks shall leave with each person elected, or at his usual place of residence, within five days after the election, a written notice of his election, and each person so notified shall within ten days after the election take the oath or affirmation herein before mentioned, a certificate of which oath shall be deposited with the Recorder whose appointment is hereafter provided for, and be by him preserved; and all subsequent elections shall be held, conducted, and returns thereof made, as may be provided for by ordinance of the City Council.

"'Sec. 7. All free white male inhabitants who are of the age of twenty-one years, who are entitled to vote for State officers, and who shall have been actual residents of said city sixty days next preceding said election, shall be entitled to vote for city officers.

"'Sec. 8. The City Council shall have authority to levy and collect taxes for city purposes upon all property, real and personal, within the limits of the city, not exceeding one half per cent. per annum, upon the assessed value thereof, and may enforce the payment of the same in any manner to be provided by ordinance, not repugnant to the Constitution of the United States, or of this State.

"'Sec. 9. The City Council shall have power to appoint a Recorder, Treasurer, Assessor, Marshal, Supervisor of Streets, and all such other officers as may be necessary, and to prescribe their duties, and remove them from office at pleasure.

"'Sec. 10. The City Council shall have power to require of all officers appointed in pursuance of this act, bonds, with penalty and security, for the faithful performance of their respective duties, such as may be deemed expedient; and, also, to require all officers appointed as aforesaid to take an oath for the faithful performance of the duties of their respective offices.

"'Sec. 11. The City Council shall have power and authority to make, ordain, establish, and execute, all such ordinances, not repugnant to the Constitution of the United States, or of this State, as they may deem necessary for the peace, benefit, good order, regulation, convenience, and cleanliness, of said city; for the protection of property therein from destruction by fire, or otherwise, and for the health, and happiness, thereof; they shall have power to fill all vacancies that may happen by death, resignation, or removal, in any of the offices herein made elective; to fix and establish all the fees of the officers of said corporation not herein established; to impose such fines, not exceeding one hundred dollars, for each offence, as they may deem just, for refusing to accept any office in or under the corporation, or for misconduct therein; to divide the city into wards, to add to the number of Aldermen and Councillors, and apportion them among the several wards, as may be most just and conducive to the interest of the city.

"'Sec. 12. To license, tax, and regulate, auctions, merchants, retailers, grocers, hawkers, pedlers, brokers, pawn-brokers, and money-changers.

"'Sec. 13. The City Council shall have exclusive power within the city, by ordinance, to license, regulate, and restrain, the keeping of ferries; to regulate the police of the city; to impose fines, forfeitures and penalties, for the breach of any ordinance, and provide for the recovery of such fines and forfeitures, and the enforcement of such penalties, and to pass such ordinances as may be necessary and proper for carrying into execution the powers specified in this act; *Provided*, such ordinances are not repugnant to the Constitution of the United States, or of this State : and, in fine, to exercise such other legislative powers as are conferred on the City Council of the City of Springfield, by an act entitled 'An Act to incorporate the City of Springfield,' approved, February third, one thousand eight hundred and forty.

"'Sec. 14. All ordinances passed by the City Council shall, within one month after they shall have been passed, be published in some newspaper printed in the city, or certified copies thereof be posted up in three of the most public places in the city.

"'Sec. 15. All ordinances of the city may be proven by the seal of the corporation, and when printed or published in book or pamphlet form, purporting to be printed or published by authority of the corporation, the same shall be received in evidence in all courts or places without further proof.

"'Sec. 16. The Mayor and Aldermen shall be conservators of the peace within the limits of said city, and shall have all the powers of Justices of the Peace therein, both in civil and criminal cases arising under the laws of the State : they shall, as Justices of the Peace, within the limits of said city, perform the same duties, be governed by the same laws, give the same bonds and security, as other Justices of the Peace, and be commissioned as Justices of the Peace in and for said city by the Governor.

" ' Sec. 17. The Mayor shall have exclusive jurisdiction in all cases arising under the ordinances of the corporation, and shall issue such process as may be necessary to carry said ordinances into execution and effect; appeals may be had from any decision or judgment of said Mayor or Aldermen, arising under the city ordinances, to the Municipal Court, under such regulations as may be presented by ordinance; which court shall be composed of the Mayor as Chief Justice, and the Aldermen as Associate Justices, and from the final judgment of the Municipal Court, to the Circuit Court of Hancock county, in the same manner as appeals are taken from judgments of Justices of the Peace; Provided, that the parties litigant shall have a right to a trial by a jury of twelve men, in all cases before the Municipal Court. The Municipal Court shall have power to grant writs of habeas corpus in all cases arising under the ordinances of the City Council.

" ' Sec. 18. The Municipal Court shall sit on the first Monday of every month, and the City Council at such times and place as may be prescribed by city ordinance; special meetings of which may at any time be called by the Mayor or any two Aldermen.

" ' Sec. 19. All process issued by the Mayor, Aldermen, or Municipal Court, shall be directed to the Marshal, and in the execution thereof he shall be governed by the same laws as are, or may be, prescribed for the direction and compensation of Constables in similar cases. The Marshal shall also perform such other duties as may be required of him under the ordinances of said city, and shall be the principal ministerial officer.

" ' Sec. 20. It shall be the duty of the Recorder to make and keep accurate records of all ordinances made by the City Council, and of all their proceedings in their corporate capacity, which record shall at all times be open to the inspection of the electors of said city, and shall perform such other duties as may be required of him by the ordinances of the City Council, and shall serve as Clerk of the Municipal Court.

" ' Sec. 21. When it shall be necessary to take private property for opening, widening, or altering, any public street, lane, avenue, or alley, the corporation shall make a just compensation therefor to the person whose property is so taken, and if the amount of such compensation cannot be agreed upon, the Mayor shall cause the same to be ascertained by a jury of six disinterested freeholders of the city.

" ' Sec. 22. All jurors empanneled to inquire into the amount of benefits or damages that shall happen to the owners of property so proposed to be taken, shall first be sworn to that effect, and shall return to the Mayor their inquest in writing, signed by each juror.

" ' Sec. 23. In case the Mayor shall at any time be guilty of a palpable omission of duty, or shall wilfully and corruptly be guilty of oppression, mal-conduct, or partiality in the discharge of the duties of his office, he shall be liable to be indicted in the Circuit Court of Hancock county, and, on conviction, he shall be fined not more than two hundred dollars, and the court shall have power,

17 *

on the recommendation of the jury, to add to the judgment of the court that he be removed from office.

" ' Sec. 24. The City Council may establish and organize an institution of learning within the limits of the city, for the teaching of the arts, sciences, and learned professions, to be called the ' University of the City of Nauvoo,' which institution shall be under the control and management of a Board of Trustees, consisting of a Chancellor, Registrar, and twenty-three Regents, which board shall thereafter be a body corporate and politic, with perpetual succession, by the name of the ' Chancellor and Regents of the University of the City of Nauvoo,' and shall have full power to pass, ordain, establish and execute all such laws and ordinances as they may consider necessary for the welfare and prosperity of said University, its officers and students; Provided, that the said laws and ordinances shall not be repugnant to the Constitution of the United States, or of this State ; and Provided, also, that the Trustees shall at all times be appointed by the City Council, and shall have all the powers and privileges for the advancement of the cause of education which appertain to the Trustees of any other College or University of this State.

" ' Sec. 25. The City Council may organize the inhabitants of said city, subject to military duty, into a body of independent military men to be called the ' Nauvoo Legion,' the Court Martial of which shall be composed of the commissioned officers of said Legion, and constitute the law-making department, with full powers and authority to make, ordain, establish, and execute all such laws and ordinances as may be considered necessary for the benefit, government, and regulation of said Legion ; Provided, said Court Martial shall pass no law or act repugnant to, or inconsistent with, the Constitution of the United States or of this State ; and Provided, also, that the officers of the Legion shall be commissioned by the Governor of the State. The said Legion shall perform the same amount of military duty as is now or may be hereafter required of the regular militia of the State, and shall be at the disposal of the Mayor in executing the laws and ordinances of the city corporation and the laws of the State, and at the disposal of the Governor for the public defence, and the execution of the laws of the State or of the United States, and shall be entitled to their proportion of the public arms; and Provided, also, that said Legion shall be exempt from all other military duty.

" ' Sec. 26. The inhabitants of the ' City of Nauvoo' are hereby exempted from working on any road beyond the limits of the city, and for the purpose of keeping the streets, lanes, avenues, and alleys, in repair, to require of the male inhabitants of said city, over the age of twenty-one, and under fifty years, to labor on said streets, lanes, avenues, and alleys, not exceeding three days in each year ; any person failing to perform such labor when duly notified by the Supervisor, shall forfeit and pay the sum of one dollar per day for each day so neglected or refused.

" ' Sec. 27. The City Council shall have power to provide for the punishment of offenders, by imprisonment in the county or city jail, in all cases when such offenders shall fail or refuse to pay the fines and forfeitures which may be recovered against them.

" ' Sec. 28. This act is hereby declared to be a public act, and shall take effect on the first Monday of February next.

" ' Wm. L. D. Ewing,
" ' *Speaker of the House of Representatives.*
" ' S. H. Anderson,
" ' *Speaker of the Senate.*

" ' Approved, December 16, 1840.

" ' Tho. Carlin.' "

———

" State of Illinois, }
Office of Secretary of State. }

" I, Stephen A. Douglass, Secretary of State, do hereby certify that the foregoing is a true and perfect copy of the enrolled law now on file in my office.

[L. S.]   " Witness my hand, and Seal of State, at Springfield, this 18th day of December, A. D. 1840.

" S. A. Douglass,
" *Secretary of State.*"

———

" The following are the legislative powers alluded to in the 13th section of the foregoing act, as pertaining to the City Council of the city of Springfield, and which, consequently, become a part of the charter of the city of Nauvoo; to wit: —

" ' OF THE LEGISLATIVE POWERS OF THE CITY COUNCIL.

" ' Sec. 1. The City Council shall have powers and authority to levy and collect taxes upon all property, real and personal, within the city, not exceeding one half per cent. per annum upon the assessed value thereof, and may enforce the payment of the same in any manner prescribed by ordinance not repugnant to the Constitution of the United States and of this State.

" ' Sec. 2. The City Council shall have power to require of all officers appointed in pursuance of this charter, bonds, with penalty and security for the faithful performance of their respective duties, as may be deemed expedient, and also to require all officers appointed as aforesaid to take an oath for the faithful performance of the duties of their respective offices upon entering upon the discharge of the same.

" ' Sec. 3. To establish, support, and regulate common schools, to borrow money on the credit of the city; Provided, That no sum or sums of money shall be borrowed at a greater interest than six per cent. per annum, nor shall the interest on the aggregate of all the sums borrowed and outstanding ever exceed one half of the city revenue arising for taxes assessed on real property within the corporation.

" ' Sec. 4. To make regulations to prevent the introduction of contagious diseases into the city, to make quarantine laws for that purpose, and enforce the same.

" ' Sec. 5. To appropriate and provide for the payment of the debt [and] expenses of the city.

"'Sec. 6. To establish hospitals, and make regulations for the government of the same.

"'Sec. 7. To make regulations to secure the general health of the inhabitants, to declare what shall be a nuisance, and to prevent and remove the same.

"'Sec. 8. To provide the city with water, to dig wells and erect pumps in the streets for the extinguishment of fires, and convenience of the inhabitants.

"'Sec. 9. To open, alter, widen, extend, establish, grade, pave, or otherwise improve and keep in repair streets, avenues, lanes, and alleys.

"'Sec. 10. To establish, erect, and keep in repair, bridges.

"'Sec. 11. To divide the city into wards, and specify the boundaries thereof, and create additional wards, as the occasion may require.

"'Seç. 12. To provide for lighting the streets and erecting lamp-posts.

"'Sec. 13. To establish, support, and regulate night watches.

"'Sec. 14. To erect market-houses, establish markets and market-places, and provide for the government and regulation thereof.

"'Sec. 15. To provide for erecting all needful buildings for the use of the city.

"'Sec. 16. To provide for enclosing, improving, [and] regulating all public grounds belonging to the city.

"'Sec. 17. To license, tax, [and] regulate auctioneers, merchants, and retailers, grocers, taverns, ordinaries, hawkers, pedlers, brokers, pawn-brokers, and money-changers.

"'Sec. 18. To license, tax, and regulate hacking, carriages, wagons, carts, and drays, and fix the rates to be charged for the carriage of persons, and for the wagonage, cartage, and drayage of property.

"'Sec. 19. To license and regulate porters, and fix the rates of porterage.

"'Sec. 20. To license and regulate theatrical and other exhibitions, shows, and amusements.

"'Sec. 21. To tax, restrain, prohibit, and suppress tippling-houses, dram-shops, gaming-houses, bawdy and other disorderly houses.

"'Sec. 22. To provide for the prevention and extinguishment of fires, and to organize and establish fire companies.

"'Sec. 23. To regulate the fixing of chimneys and the flues thereof, and stove-pipes.

"'Sec. 24. To regulate the storage of gunpowder, tar, pitch, rosin, and other combustible materials.

"'Sec. 25. To regulate and order parapet walls and partition fences.

"'Sec. 26. To establish standard weights and measures, and regulate the weights and measures to be used in the city, in all other cases not provided for by law.

"'Sec. 27. To provide for the inspection and measuring of lumber and other building materials; and for the measurement of all kinds of mechanical work.

"'Sec. 28. To provide for the inspection and weighing of hay, lime, and stone coal, the measuring of charcoal, firewood, and other fuel, to be sold or used within the city.

" ' Sec. 29. To provide for and regulate the inspection of tobacco, and of beef, pork, flour, meal, and whisky in barrels.

" ' Sec. 30. To regulate the weight, quality, and price of bread sold and used in the city.

" ' Sec. 31. To provide for taking the enumeration of the inhabitants of the city.

" ' Sec. 32. To regulate the election of city officers, and provide for removing from office any person holding an office created by ordinance.

" ' Sec. 33. To fix the compensation of all city officers, and regulate the fees of jurors, witnesses, and others, for services rendered under this act or any ordinance.

" ' Sec. 34. To regulate the police of the city, to impose fines, and forfeitures, and penalties, for the breach of any ordinance, and provide for the recovery and appropriation of such fines and forfeitures, and the enforcement of such penalties.

" ' Sec. 35. The City Council shall have exclusive power within the city, by ordinance, to license, regulate, and suppress and restrain billiard tables, and from one to twenty pin alleys, and every other description of gaming or gambling.

" ' Sec. 36. The City Council shall have power to make all ordinances which shall be necessary and proper for carrying into execution the powers specified in this act, so that such ordinance be not repugnant to, nor inconsistent with, the Constitution of the United States or of this State.

" ' Sec. 37. The style of the ordinances of the city shall be : " Be it ordained by the City Council of the city of Springfield."

" ' Sec. 38. All ordinances passed by the City Council shall, within one month after they shall have been passed, be published in some newspaper published in the city, and shall not be in force until they shall have been published as aforesaid.

" ' Sec. 39. All ordinances of the city may be proven by the seal of the corporation, and when printed and published by authority of the corporation, the same shall be received in evidence in all courts and places without further proof? ' "

Times and Seasons, Vol. II., No. 6, p. 231—236.

"NAUVOO LEGION.

" By a letter from the Hon. S. H. Little, of the State Senate, to General Bennett, it appears that the following additional section in relation to our Legion, recently forwarded to Esquire Little by General Bennett, has become a law, to wit: —

" ' *Any citizen of Hancock county, may, by voluntary enrolment, attach himself to the Nauvoo Legion, with all the privileges which appertain to that independent military body.*'

" This is quite a privilege; and we say to our friends — Come on and enroll yourselves, so that there may be a perfect organization by the *4th of July next* — which day we wish to celebrate with appropriate military honors. The Legion will be called out, likewise, on the *6th of April.*" — *Times and Seasons*, Vol. II., No. 8, p. 320.

"AN ACT

TO INCORPORATE THE NAUVOO AGRICULTURAL AND MANU-
FACTURING ASSOCIATION IN THE COUNTY OF HANCOCK.

"Sec. 1. Be it enacted by the people of the State of Illinois represented in the General Assembly, That Sidney Rigdon, George W. Robinson, Samuel James, Wilson Law, Daniel H. Wells, Hyrum Smith, George Miller, William Marks, Peter Haws, Vinson Knight, John Scott, D. C. Smith, William Huntington. Sen., Ebenezer Robinson, R. B Thompson, William Law, James Allred, John T. Barnett, Theodore Turley, John C. Bennett, Elias Higbee, Isaac Higbee, Joseph Smith, A. Cutler, Israel Barlow, R. D. Foster, John F. Olney, John Snider, Leonard Soby, Orson Pratt, James Kelly, Sidney Knowlton, John P. Greene, John F. Weld, and their associates and successors, are hereby constituted a body corporate and politic, by the name of the Nauvoo Agricultural and Manufacturing Association, and by that name shall be capable of suing and being sued, pleading and being impleaded, answering and being answered, in all courts and places, and may have a common seal, and may alter the same at pleasure.

"Sec. 2. The sole object and purpose of said association shall be for the promotion of agriculture and husbandry in all its branches, and for the manufacture of flour, lumber, and such other useful articles as are necessary for the ordinary purposes of life.

"Sec. 3. The capital stock of said association shall be one hundred thousand dollars, with the privilege of increasing it to the sum of three hundred thousand dollars, to be divided into shares of fifty dollars, which shall be considered personal property, and be assignable in such manner as the said corporation may by its by-laws provide; which capital stock shall be exclusively devoted to the object and purposes set forth in the second section of this act, and to no other object and purposes, and to the same end the said corporation shall have power to purchase, hold, and convey real estate and other property to the amount of its capital.

"Sec. 4. Said corporation shall have power by its Trustees, or a majority of them present at any regularly-called meeting, to make by-laws for its own government, for the purpose of carrying out the objects of this association, *Provided*, the same are not repugnant to the laws and Constitution of this State, or of the United States.

"Sec. 5. Joseph Smith, Sidney Rigdon, and William Law, shall be commissioners to receive subscriptions for, and distribute said capital stock for said corporation; said commissioners, or a majority of them, shall within six months after the passage of this act, either by themselves or their duly-appointed agents, open a subscription book for said stock, at such times and places as they shall appoint, and at the time of subscription for such stock, at least ten per cent. upon each share subscribed for shall be paid to said commissioners, or their duly-appointed agents, and the remainder of said stock so subscribed for, shall be paid in such sums, and at such times, as shall be provided for by the by-laws of said corporation.

" Sec. 6. In case the stock of said corporation shall not all be taken up within one year from the passage of this act, the duties of said commissioners shall cease, and the Trustees of said corporation, or a quorum thereof, may thereafter receive subscriptions to said stock from time to time until the whole shall be subscribed.

" Sec. 7. The stock, property and concerns of said corporation shall be managed by twenty Trustees, who shall be stockholders of said corporation, any five of whom, to be designated by a majority of the Trustees, shall form a quorum for the transaction of all ordinary business of said corporation, the election of which Trustees shall be annual. The first-mentioned twenty persons, whose names are recited in the first section of this act, shall be the first Trustees of said corporation, and shall hold their offices until the first Monday in September, A. D. 1841, and until others shall be elected in their places.

" Sec. 8. The Trustees of said corporation for every subsequent year, shall be elected on the first Monday of September in each and every year, at such place as the Trustees for the time being shall appoint, and of which election they shall give at least fifteen days' previous notice, by advertisement in some newspaper in or near the city of Nauvoo. At every election of Trustees, each stockholder shall be entitled to one vote on each share of stock owned by him, *Provided*, that no stockholder shall be entitled to more than twenty votes, and said stockholders may vote either in person or by proxy. The election for Trustees shall be conducted in such manner as shall be pointed out by the by-laws of said corporation, and whenever a vacancy shall happen by death, resignation, or otherwise, among the Trustees, the remaining Trustees shall have power to fill such vacancy until the next general election for Trustees.

" Sec. 9. The Trustees of said corporation, as soon as may be after their appointment or election under this act, shall proceed to elect out of their number a President, Treasurer, and Secretary, who shall respectively hold their offices during one year, and until others shall be elected to fill their places, and whose duties shall be defined and prescribed by the by-laws of the corporation, and said Trustees shall also appoint such agents and other persons as may be necessary to conduct the proper business, and accomplish the declared objects of said corporation, and shall likewise have power to fill any vacancy occasioned by the death, resignation or removal of any officer of said corporation.

" Sec. 10. This act shall be construed as a public act, and continue in force for the period of twenty years. And the Trustees appointed under the provisions of this act, shall hold their first meeting at the city of Nauvoo, on the first Monday of April, A. D. 1841.   " Wm. L. D. Ewing,
                    " *Speaker of the House of Representatives.*
                        " S. H. Anderson,
                            " *Speaker of the Senate.*
" Approved, February 27, 1841.
                        " Tho. Carlin."

"STATE OF ILLINOIS, }
OFFICE OF SECRETARY OF STATE. }

" I, Lyman Trumbull, Secretary of State, do hereby certify the foregoing to be a true and perfect copy of the enrolled law on file in my office.

" Given under my hand, and Seal of State, Springfield, March 10, 1841.

" LYMAN TRUMBULL,
" *Secretary of State.*"

Times and Seasons, Vol. II., No. 10, pp. 355, 356.

———◆———

"AN ACT

" TO INCORPORATE THE NAUVOO HOUSE ASSOCIATION.

" Sec. 1.   Be it enacted by the people of the State of Illinois represented in the General Assembly, That George Miller, Lyman Wight, John Snider, and Peter Haws and their associates are hereby declared a body corporate, under the name and style of the ' *Nauvoo House Association,*' and they are hereby authorized to erect and furnish a public house of entertainment to be called the ' Nauvoo House.'

" Sec. 2.   The above-named George Miller, Lyman Wight, John Snider, and Peter Haws, are hereby declared to be the Trustees of said association, with full power and authority to hold in joint tenancy by themselves and their successors in office, a certain lot in the city of Nauvoo, in the county of Hancock, and state of Illinois, known and designated on the plot of said city, as the south half of lot numbered fifty-six, for the purpose of erecting thereon the house contemplated in the first section of this act.

" Sec. 3.   The said Trustees are further authorized and empowered to obtain by stock subscription, by themselves or their duly authorized agents, the sum of one hundred and fifty thousand dollars, which shall be divided into shares of fifty dollars each.

" Sec. 4.   No individual shall be permitted to hold more than three hundred nor less than one shares of stock, and certificates of stock shall be delivered to subscribers, so soon as their subscriptions are paid in, and not before.

" Sec. 5.   As soon as the above contemplated house shall have been completed and furnished, the stockholders shall appoint such agents, as the Trustees may deem necessary in the management of the affairs of said association.

" Sec. 6.   The Trustees shall have power to sue and be sued, plead and be impleaded in any court of this State, in the name and style of the ' Trustees of the Nauvoo House Association.'

" Sec. 7.   They shall also take the general care and supervision in procuring materials for said house and constructing and erecting the same, and further to superintend its general management, and to do and perform all matters and things which may be necessary to be done, in order to secure the interests and promote the objects of this association.

" Sec. 8.   This association shall continue twenty years from the passage of this act, and the house herein provided for, shall be kept for the accommodation of strangers, travellers, and all otner persons who may resort thereto, for rest and refreshment.

"Sec. 9. It is moreover established as a perpetual rule of said house, to be observed by all persons who may keep or occupy the same, that spirituous liquors of every description are prohibited, and that such liquors shall never be vended as a beverage, or introduced into common use, in said house.

"Sec. 10. And whereas Joseph Smith has furnished the said association with the ground whereon to erect said house, it is further declared, that the said Smith and his heirs shall hold by perpetual succession a suite of rooms in the said house, to be set apart and conveyed in due form of law to him and his heirs by said Trustees as soon as the same are completed.

"Sec. 11. The Board of Trustees shall appoint one of their number as president thereof.

"WM. L. D. EWING,
"Speaker of the House of Representatives.

"S. H. ANDERSON,
"Speaker of the Senate.

"Approved, February 23, 1841.

"THO. CARLIN."

—

"STATE OF ILLINOIS,   }
OFFICE OF SECRETARY OF STATE. }

"I, Lyman Trumbull, Secretary of State, do hereby certify the foregoing to be a true and perfect copy of the enrolled law on file in my office.

"Given under my hand, and Seal of State, Springfield, March 10, 1841.   LYMAN TRUMBULL,
                         Secretary of State."

Times and Seasons, Vol. II., No. 11, pp. 370, 371.

"OFFICERS OF THE CITY OF NAUVOO.

"Mayor: John C. Bennett. — Recorder: James Sloan. — Attorney: Sidney Rigdon. — Notary Public: E. Robinson. — Marshal: H. G. Sherwood. — Marshal ad interim: D. B. Huntington. — Treasurer: John S. Fulmer. — Surveyor: A. Ripley. — Assessor and Collector: Lewis Robison. — Supervisor of Streets: James Allred. — Weigher and Sealer: Theodore Turley. — Market Master: Stephen Markham. — Sexton: W. D. Huntington.

"FIRST WARD.

"Aldermen: Samuel H. Smith, Hiram Kimball. — Councillors. John P. Green, Vinson Knight, Orson Pratt, Willard Richards. — High Constable: D. B. Huntington.

"SECOND WARD.

"Aldermen: N. K. Whitney, Orson Spencer. — Councillors: Hy·

18

rum Smith, Lyman Wight, Wilford Woodruff, John Taylor. —
High Constable: George Morey.

"THIRD WARD.

"*Aldermen:* Daniel H. Wells, Gustavus Hills. — *Councillors:*
John T. Barnett, C. C. Rich, Hugh McFall, H. C. Kimball. —
High Constable: Lewis Robison.

"FOURTH WARD.

"*Aldermen:* William Marks, George W. Harris. — *Councillors:*
Joseph Smith, Wilson Law, Brigham Young, William Law. —
High Constable: W. D. Huntington.

"THE CITY COUNCIL consists of the Mayor, Aldermen, and Councillors, and sits on the first and third Saturday of every month,
commencing at 6 o'clock, P. M.

"MUNICIPAL COURT.

"*Chief Justice:* John C. Bennett. — *Associate Justices:* Samuel
H. Smith, Hiram Kimball, N. K. Whitney, Orson Spencer, Daniel
H. Wells, Gustavus Hills, William Marks, George W. Harris. —
Clerk: James Sloan.

"The Municipal Court sits on the first Monday in every month,
commencing at 10 o'clock, A. M.

"MAYOR'S COURT.

"This is the Criminal Court of the city, and sits at such times
as the business of the city requires — the Mayor presiding."

Times and Seasons, Vol. III., No. 4, p. 638.

"AN ORDINANCE
IN RELATION TO THE CITY COUNCIL.

"Sec. 1. Be it ordained by the City Council of the city of
Nauvoo, That should any member of the City Council absent himself from, or neglect or refuse to attend, any regular or special meeting of said Council, for more than thirty minutes after the time
appointed, or should the Marshal or Recorder be guilty of a like
offence, he shall be fined in the sum of two dollars for each offence.

"Sec. 2. Should any member of said Council neglect, or refuse,
to attend said meetings, forthwith, on a summons from the Mayor,
served by the Marshal, or special messenger of said Council, he shall
be fined in the sum of twenty-five dollars, for each offence ; Provided, That the City Council may, on good cause shown, remit any
fine herein, or by this ordinance, assessed.

"Sec. 3. The above fines to be collected as other debts before
the Mayor, at the suit of the city corporation. This ordinance to
take effect, and be in force, from and after its passage.

"Passed, February 8, A. D. 1841.

"JOHN C. BENNETT, *Mayor.*

"JAMES SLOAN, *Recorder.*"

Times and Seasons, Vol. II., No. 8, p. 322.

"AN ORDINANCE

FIXING THE COMPENSATION OF THE CITY COUNCIL, AND FOR OTHER PURPOSES.

" Sec. 1. Be it ordained by the City Council of the city of Nauvoo, That from and after the passage of this ordinance, the City Council shall meet on the second Saturday of every month, at 10 o'clock, A. M., and shall continue in session during the day, and evening, if the business of the city requires it — allowing one hour for dinner, and one for supper; and the said monthly meetings shall be called ' The Regular Meetings of the City Council.'

" Sec. 2. Each member of the City Council and the Recorder, and Marshal, shall be allowed two dollars per day for attendance, coöperation, and services, at said regular meetings; and each person aforesaid, shall be fined in the sum of two dollars for neglecting to attend at any such regular meeting, without an excuse satisfactory to the City Council; and for each part of a day so attended, or neglected, a proportionate allowance, or fine, shall be granted, or assessed, as the case may be.

" Sec. 3. It is hereby made the duty of the Recorder to keep a just and accurate record of the members present, including the Recorder and Marshal, at every such regular meeting, together with a full list of absentees, which list shall be returned to the Mayor for collection of fines quarterly.

" Sec. 4. Special meetings of the City Council, called by order of the Mayor, by summons or otherwise, shall be governed by the aforesaid regulations.

" Sec. 5. All ordinances, or parts of ordinances, contrary to the provisions of this ordinance, are hereby repealed. This ordinance to take effect, and be in force, from and after its passage.

" Passed January 22, A. D. 1842.

" JOHN C. BENNETT, *Mayor.*

" JAMES SLOAN, *Recorder.*"

Times and Seasons, Vol. III., No. 8, p. 701.

———◆———

By what stupid knave the following nondescript *Algerine Ordinance* was penned I am unable to say. Suffice it to observe, it is in open contravention of the constitutional and statute laws, and a palpable violation of vested chartered rights. I give it as it is, as a civic curiosity.

From " The (Nauvoo) Wasp" of August 13, 1842.

"AN ORDINANCE

REGULATING THE MODE OF PROCEEDING IN CASES OF HABEAS CORPUS, BEFORE THE MUNICIPAL COURT.

" Sec. 1. Be it ordained by the City Council of the city of Nauvoo, That in all cases where any person or persons, shall at any time hereafter, be arrested, or under arrest, in this city, under any writ or process, and shall be brought before the Municipal Court of this city, by virtue of a writ of Habeas Corpus, the court shall in every such case have power and authority and are hereby required to examine into the origin, validity, and legality of the writ or process, under which such arrest was made, and if it shall appear to the court upon sufficient testimony, that said writ or process was illegally or not legally issued, or did not proceed from proper authority, then the court shall discharge the prisoner from under said arrest, but if it shall appear to the court, that said writ or process had issued from proper authority, and was a legal process, the court shall then proceed and fully hear the merits of the case, upon which such arrest was made, upon such evidence as may be produced and sworn before said court, and shall have power to adjourn the hearing, and also issue process from time to time in their discretion, in order to procure the attendance of witnesses, so that a fair and impartial trial and decision may be obtained in every such case.

"Sec. 2. And be it further ordained, That if upon investigation it shall be proven before the Municipal Court, that the writ or process has been issued, either through private pique, malicious intent, religious or other persecution, falsehood or misrepresentation, contrary to the Constitution of this State, or of the United States, the said writ or process shall be quashed and considered of no force or effect, and the prisoner or prisoners shall be released and discharged therefrom.

"Sec. 3. And be it also further ordained, That in the absence, sickness, debility, or other circumstances disqualifying or preventing the Mayor from officiating in his office, as Chief Justice of the Municipal Court, the aldermen present shall appoint one from amongst them, to act as Chief Justice *pro tempore.*

"Sec. 4. This ordinance to take effect, and be in force, from and after its passage.   HYRUM SMITH,
                    " *Vice-Mayor and President pro tempore.*

"Passed August 8, 1842.   "JAMES SLOAN, *Recorder.*"

The *Sangamo Journal* of September 2, 1842, in commenting upon this ordinance for the protection of Mormon culprits and outlaws, concocted, probably, and passed by the influence of the Mormon *Collegium de Propaganda Fide,* for the especial protection of Joe Smith and other murderers and criminals, very justly remarks,—

"We copy the above ordinance in order to show our readers the barefaced effrontery with which the holy brotherhood at Nauvoo set at defiance the civil authorities of the State. No man having claims to even an ordinary share of common sense, can ever believe that there is the least shadow of authority in the City Council of Nauvoo to pass such an ordinance as the above; indeed the legislature of this State has not power to do it. The City Charter gives to the Municipal Court power to issue writs of *Habeas Corpus.* Evidently this power is only granted in reference to cases of arrest under the municipal laws, and, by the most latitudinarian construction, cannot be made to extend to cases of an arrest under the laws of the State ; but this Mormon ordinance not only extends to *all* cases of arrest, but sets the laws of the United States at defiance, by giving authority to the Municipal Court to inquire into the *causes* of the arrest — a power which even the legislature of this State cannot confer.

" By the Constitution and laws of the United States, the Governor of this State is bound to deliver up fugitives from justice on the requisition of the Governor of any other State ; and the judiciary of this State have no right to inquire, under any circumstances, into any thing further than the sufficiency of the writ on which the arrest is made. If this is in due form, and properly served, there is no power for any tribunal in this State to make any further inquiry. The guilt or innocence of the accused must be determined by the courts of the State from whence the requisition issued ; and any court of law, which institutes any inquiry of this nature, oversteps the boundaries of its jurisdiction, and openly sets at defiance the laws of the land.

" Now, we ask our citizens, what think you of this barefaced defiance of our laws by the City Council of Nauvoo ? and, if persisted in, what must be the final result ? If these things are suffered to pass unheeded by the authorities of this State, who is safe, whether in his person or property ? A Mormon cut-throat may take the life of one of our citizens, and returning to the City of the Saints, set at defiance the laws of the land.

" Independent of the ordinance above quoted, which was evidently designed to give some semblance of legality to the protection of criminals, we believe that the Mormon Church is just such a body as can be shelter to every blackleg, cut-throat, or horse-thief, who chooses to take refuge amongst them. While under the protection of Joe, who can harm them ? What means has an officer of either discovering or arresting a man sheltered by a band who regard the laws of the land as secondary to the commands of their Prophet ? "

This is an act of " *outlawry* " with a vengeance ! The Mormon Prophet places himself above the operation of the laws, and puts at defiance every principle of criminal jurisprudence, and the legitimately-constituted authorities of his country !!! *Sic transit gloria mundi !* But must these things be tolerated ? *Never !* No, NEVER !! NO, NEVER !!! Retributive justice must put forth the arm of power, and pass from the FORUM to the FIELD, if that be necessary, to capture refugees and fugitives from justice, and make them bow to the supremacy of the laws. Good officers cannot, will not, long be foiled in the execution of a high public trust, and one, too, in which every citizen of the commonwealth is so deeply interested.

18*

UNIVERSITY OF THE CITY OF NAUVOO.

BOARD OF REGENTS.

Chancellor: Gen. John C. Bennett, M. D. — *Registrar:* Gen. William Law. — *Regents:* Gen. Joseph Smith, Sidney Rigdon, Esq., Attorney at Law, Gen. Hyrum Smith, Rev. William Marks, Rev. Samuel H. Smith, Daniel H. Wells, Esq., Bishop N. K. Whitney, Gen. Charles C. Rich, Capt. John T. Barnett, Gen. Wilson Law, Rev. John P. Greene, Bishop Vinson Knight, Isaac Galland, M. D., Judge Elias Higbee, Rev. Robert D. Foster, M. D., Judge James Adams, Rev. Samuel Bennett, M. D., Ebenezer Robinson, Esq., Rev. John Snider, Rt. Rev. George Miller, Lenos M. Knight, M. D., Rev. John Taylor, and Rev. Heber C. Kimball.

FACULTY.

James Kelly, A. M., *President.*
Orson Pratt, A. M., *Professor of Mathematics and English Literature.*
Orson Spencer, A. M., *Professor of Languages.*
Sidney Rigdon, D. D., *Professor of Church History.*

SCHOOL WARDENS FOR COMMON SCHOOLS.

Wardens of First Ward: John P. Greene, N. K. Whitney, and A. Morrison.
Wardens of Second Ward: Charles C. Rich, Wilson Law, and Elias Higbee.
Wardens of Third Ward: Daniel H. Wells, R. D. Foster, and S. Winchester.
Wardens of Fourth Ward: Vinson Knight, William Law, and E. Robinson.

President Kelly is a graduate of Trinity College, Dublin, and is a ripe scholar.

Professor Pratt is a self-made man, and has had to encounter great difficulties in the acquisition of an education; but he has surmounted them all. As a teacher of mathematics and English literature he is equalled by few, and surpassed by none, this side of the great waters, as the proficiency of the matriculates of the university under his care and tuition abundantly testifies. He is a gentleman of the first order of talents — than whom there is, probably, no better man on earth.

Professor Spencer is a graduate of Union College, N. Y., in the arts, and of the Baptist Literary and Theological Seminary, N. Y., in divinity.

Professor Rigdon has long been regarded, by both enemies and friends, as an accomplished belles-lettres scholar and eloquent orator, possessing both the *suaviter in modo* and the *fortiter in re*,—deeply learned in that department of collegiate education which has been assigned him in the university. His Character, and that of his entire family, is considered above reproach. Nothing can be brought against him, I am persuaded, but his connection with the Book of Mormon and Mormonism.

"University of the City of Nauvoo, Illinois, *August* 10, A. D. 1841.

"The Regents of the University of the City of Nauvoo will convene at the office of General Joseph Smith, on Saturday, the 4th day of September, proximo, at half past 10 o'clock, A. M., for the transaction of important business. Punctual attendance is requested.

"The Department of English Literature is now in successful operation under the supervision of Professor Orson Pratt—a gentleman of varied knowledge and extensive acquirements, who is admirably qualified for the full execution of the high trust reposed in him, as an able and accomplished teacher

"In this department, a general Course of Mathematics, including Arithmetic, Algebra, Geometry, Conic Sections, Plane Trigonometry, Mensuration, Surveying, Navigation, Analytical, Plane and Spherical Trigonometry, Analytical Geometry, and the Differential and Integral Calculus;—Philosophy;—Astronomy;—Chemistry;—etc. etc., will be extensively taught.

"Tuition.—Five Dollars per quarter, payable semi-quarterly, in advance.

"John C. Bennett, *Chancellor.*

"William Law, *Registrar.*"

Times and Seasons, Vol. II., No. 20, p. 517.

NAUVOO LEGION.

This military organization comprises between two and three thousand well-disciplined troops, and constitutes a portion of the militia of the State of Illinois; and might, under proper management, be made very useful to the country. It is a division divided into two cohorts, or brigades, and these cohorts subdivided into regiments, battalions, and companies. The organization is intended to represent a Roman legion. I have not space in this Exposé for the full rank-roll, and must, therefore, content myself with giving the names of a few of the most accomplished, brave, and efficient of the corps; and amongst them I would enumerate,—

Gen. George W. Robinson, Capt. C. M. Kreymyer, Gen. Charles C. Rich, Col. John F. Weld, M. D., Col. Orson Pratt, A. M., Capt. Darwin Chase, Col. Francis M. Higbee, Col. Carlos Gove, Col. Chauncey L. Higbee, Capt. John F. Olney, Capt. Justus Morse, Gen. Davison Hibard, Gen. Hiram Kimball, Capt. William M. Allred, Gen. W. P. Lyon, Capt. L. N. Scovil, Capt. Charles Allen, Col. James Sloan, Lieut. Stephen H. Goddard, Capt. Marcellus Bates, Col. George Schindle, Col. Amasa Lyman, Col. D. B. Smith, Col. George Coulson, M. D., Col. Alexander McRea, Gen. A. P. Rockwood, Capt. Amos Davis, Col. Jacob B. Backenstos, Capt. Samuel Hicks, Col. L. Woodworth, and some others of the staff and line.

Joseph Smith, the Lieutenant-General, is a military novice of the first water and magnitude, scarcely knowing the difference between a general and a corporal — if it only has the *ral* as the suffix, Joe is therewith content. By the bye, however, the office of Lieutenant-General is unknown to the Constitution of the State, and is, therefore, a nullity. There are, likewise, various other officers who would disgrace the forces of His Tartarean Majesty, amongst whom I would enumerate Gen. Robert D. Foster, M. D., Maj. Willard Richards, Maj. Hosea Stout, Capt. D. B. Huntington, and others of the staff and line.

The troops are very tractable, and obedient to the word of command, and conduct themselves on parade in a highly creditable and the most orderly manner — *à la militaire.*

"COURT MARTIAL OF THE NAUVOO LEGION.

"ORDINANCE No. 1.

" Sec. 1. Be it ordained by the Court Martial of the Nauvoo Legion in general court assembled, That the discipline, drill, rules, regulations, and uniforms of the United States' Army, so far as applicable, be and they hereby are adopted for the Legion ; Provided, That each company may adopt its own uniform for the non-commissioned officers and privates belonging to it.

" Sec. 2. That from and after the 15th day of April next, it shall be the duty of every white male inhabitant of the city of Nauvoo, between eighteen and forty-five years of age, to enroll himself in some company of the Legion, by reporting himself to the Captain thereof, within fifteen days ; and every person neglecting or refusing to do so shall, on conviction thereof before a regular court martial, forfeit and pay the sum of one dollar, and the further sum of one dollar for every subsequent fifteen days' neglect.

" Sec. 3. The Legion shall hold a general parade on the 1st Saturday of May and September, and the 4th day of July, (the 3d when the 4th comes on Sunday,) in, or near the city of Nauvoo; a battalion parade on the 3d Saturday of June and October, in their respective precincts; a company parade on the 4th Saturday of April, June, and August, in their respective precincts; and an officer drill on the Thursday and Friday preceding each general parade, in the city of Nauvoo; and such other musters or parades as the Lieutenant-General, and the Major-General, may jointly direct, in each year: and any non-commissioned officer, musician, or private, who shall neglect or refuse to appear on said days, shall be fined in the sum of one dollar for each company, or battalion parade, and two dollars for each general parade — and the commissioned officers neglecting or refusing to appear in their appropriate places on parade shall be fined in the following sums, to wit: the Lieutenant-General and the Major-General — thirty dollars; Brevet Major-Generals and Brigadier-Generals — twenty-five dollars; Colonels — fifteen dollars; Lieutenant-Colonels and Majors — ten dollars; Captains — six dollars; Lieutenants — four dollars; and every commissioned officer, non-commissioned officer, musician, or private, who shall neglect or refuse to uniform himself in full, after the lapse of eight months from the passage of this act, shall be fined in the same sums, in addition, for each day of parade — every commissioned officer, non commissioned officer, or musician, who shall neglect or refuse to attend officer drills, shall be fined in half the sums aforesaid — and any commissioned officer who shall neglect or refuse to attend their appropriate courts martial shall be fined in one half the sums aforesaid — and any commissioned officer neglecting, or refusing, to discharge any duty devolving upon him shall, in addition, be cashiered and disgraced, by a general court martial, detailed by the Major-General by order of the Lieutenant-General: Provided, always, That all members of this corporation, who are unable to attend parades on account of sickness in their families, or any other reasonable excuse, satisfactory to the court martial, shall, for the time being, be exempt from all such fines.

" Sec. 4. That no person whatever, residing within the limits of the city of Nauvoo, of fifteen days' residence, between the ages of 18 and 45 years, excepting such as are exempted by the laws of the United States, shall be exempt from military duty, unless exempted by a special act of the court martial of the Legion; or a certificate of inability, under oath, signed by the Lieutenant-General, countersigned by the Surgeon-General, and recorded by the Major-General's War Secretary.

" Sec. 5. Each regimental court of assessment of fines shall be composed of the Major as President — the Adjutant as Secretary — and the Captains of companies as members; and the court of appeals shall be composed of the Colonel as President — the Adjutant as Secretary — and the Lieutenant-Colonel and Major as members, — the court of assessment shall sit on the Saturday succeeding each general parade, and the court of appeals on the second Saturday thereafter, at such places as the Colonel may direct.

" Sec. 6. The regular court and law days of the court martial of the Legion, constituting the law-making department of the corporation, shall be the 1st Friday of March, June, September, and December, and such other days as may be appointed by the joint general orders of the Lieutenant-General and the Major-General, within the city of Nauvoo, on a notice of ten days.

" Sec. 7. The staff of the Lieutenant-General shall consist of an Inspector-General with the rank of Major-General, a Drill officer, a Judge-Advocate, and four Aids-de-Camp, with the rank of Colonels; and a guard of twelve Aids-de-Camp, and a Herald and Armor-Bearer, with the rank of Captain.

" Sec. 8. The staff of the Major-General shall consist of an Adjutant-General, a Surgeon-General, a Cornet, a Quarter-Master-General, a Commissary-General, a Pay-Master-General, a Chaplain, two Assistant Inspectors-General, four Aids-de-Camp, and a War Secretary, with the rank of Colonel; a Quarter-Master, Sergeant, Sergeant-Major, and Chief Musician, with the rank of Major; and four Musicians, and a Herald and Armor-Bearer, with the rank of Captain.

" Sec. 9. The staff of each Brigadier-General shall consist of two Aids-de-Camp, an Assistant Quarter-Master-General, an Assistant Commissary-General, and a Surgeon, with the rank of Lieutenant-Colonel; six Assistant Chaplains, with the rank of Major; and a Herald and Armor-Bearer, with the rank of Captain.

" Sec. 10. The staff of each Colonel shall consist of an Adjutant, a Quarter-Master-Sergeant, and a Sergeant-Major, with the rank of Captain.

" Sec. 11. Each Regiment shall be officered with a Colonel, a Lieutenant-Colonel, a Major, and company officers.

" Sec. 12. Each Company shall be officered with a Captain, three Lieutenants, five Sergeants, one Pioneer, and four Corporals.

" Sec. 13. The Lieutenant-General, and the Major-General, may by their joint act grant brevet commissions to such persons as may merit appointment and promotion at their hands.

" Sec. 14. That all laws, and parts of laws, inconsistent with this ordinance, be and they hereby are repealed.

" Passed March 12th, 1842.

" JOSEPH SMITH,
" *Lieutenant-General, and President of the Court Martial.*
" JOHN C. BENNETT,
" *Major-General, and Secretary of the Court Martial.*"
Times and Seasons, Vol. III., No. 10, pp. 733, 734.

THE CALL.

The *Sangamo Journal,* of July 1, 1842, says that the recent acts of the Prophet and the position of the Mormons have attracted

" ——— public attention to the movements of Joe Smith, —

to the tyranny exercised by him over his followers, — to the moral principles by which he is governed; and it is now not likely that he will much longer deceive the mass of the people, however much he may deceive those who have surrendered all their interests — spiritual and temporal — into his hands.

" There are individuals in his flock, possessed of talents and disposition to use them for the benefit of their sect and the country. Among these individuals we reckon General Bennett, Sidney Rigdon, Esq., Mr. George Robinson, and others. But the Prophet will scarcely permit them to think or act, except in entire subservience to his wishes. It is now understood that, within a few days past, Smith has made a desperate, blackguard, and abusive public attack on General Bennett, Mr. Rigdon, and Mr. Robinson; and reports — and we place great reliance upon them — go so far as to say that the life of the former has been threatened, and that orders have been issued to the *Danite* Band to murder him in a clandestine manner on the first opportunity. Indeed, the report goes further, and states that two of the *Danites* have been in hot pursuit of General Bennett for several days, in order to accomplish the nefarious purpose, and thus prevent a public exposition of the corruptions of the great Impostor.

" We call upon the people of our State to have an eye upon this matter, and, if either of the individuals mentioned should be missing, that there shall be no hesitation in placing the responsibility of the act upon its proper authors, and in making them feel in their own persons that murder shall be avenged.

" We take no pleasure in placing these remarks upon paper. If a secret band of assassins shall prowl about among this community, who is safe? The fate of Governor Boggs is an event not to be unheeded. But we should be unworthy of our position, should we fail to meet this matter as it deserves. And we now call upon General Bennett, if the rumors we have stated have just foundation, ' to take his life into his hands,' if that be required, and, with the true spirit of a soldier and a patriot, expose the crimes, if such exist, of the Heaven-daring Impostor. We call upon General Bennett to come out NOW. We appeal to him to do this in behalf of his fellow-citizens, who claim this of him, by all the considerations which can be presented to him as a lover of his species and as the servant of his God. Such an exposure may save life — may expose corruption — may avert consequences which no man can contemplate without fearful apprehensions. We call upon General Bennett to produce documentary evidence, that the public may form opinions that cannot be gainsaid — that they may understand the entire character, as it stands naked before his God, of a long successful religious Impostor.

" Among the subjects which we call upon General Bennett, Messrs. S. Rigdon, G. W. Robinson, and others, to notice, are the rumors that Joe Smith, some short time before he applied for the benefits of the bankrupt law, was in possession of most valuable property — a part of which he made over to *himself* as *sole* trustee for the use of the Mormon Church, and another part for the use of his wife and children. The records of Hancock county will show if these things are so. And if these rumors are true, we call upon Mr. Robinson to come here with his proof, and let it be placed before the U. S. Circuit Court at its first session. We trust that there will be no hesitation in doing this—that there will be no compromise—no efforts to injure the innocent, and no pains spared to expose the guilty.

" Such is the opinion we hold of General Bennett, that we shall expect he will respond to the calls made in this article. It appears to us, under all the circumstances of the case, he will not refuse to do so. While he will be upon his guard against midnight assassination—while he will regard with contempt the ' bulls of excommunication ' issued against him—he will proceed to make developments that will astonish the world."

To this *Call* I have responded, and this Exposé contains the evidence that I have been enabled to procure. The public can now judge for themselves. I will simply say that my motives have been impugned, and my conduct animadverted upon, by those persons and presses only who are either in the pay of the Prophet, or profoundly ignorant of the nature of the Mormon difficulties. The leading public journals of the country have sustained me, and the cause of truth, morality, and true religion, against knavery, corruption, and religious fraud and imposture. The truth of the disclosures in this Exposé does not at all depend upon my testimony, but upon a concatenation of circumstances and events, substantiated by depositions, affidavits, and statements, of so irresistible a character, as to carry conviction to the mind of every intelligent, honest individual. The truth is as clear as the sun in the firmament at noonday — whatever may be said to the contrary, by the Prophet and his myrmidons in the Holy City, or their powerful, but mistaken, ally — the able " Napoleon" Editor of the Herald, in the eastern metropolis. The public press has always been, and will always be, divided into two grand parties — the one contends for GOLDEN LORE, and sustains the cause of *truth* and *virtue*, — the other contends for GOLDEN ORE, and pleads the cause of *falsehood, corruption*, and *fraud:* the *former* embraces the grand mass of leading journals; the latter, the scurrilous, egotistical, puff-ball sheets, which so often infest the community, and prove a serious annoyance to the moral commonwealth. " Truth is mighty, and will prevail," and the God of all truth will sustain it at the winding-up scene. Though the earth be dissolved, and the heavens fall, the truth of the disclosures in this Exposé will appear brighter and brighter, until the great day of final retribution.

THE MORMON SERAGLIO.

From the Louisville Journal.

" General Bennett has written us another letter. How long are the God-defying leaders of the Mormons to be allowed to perpetrate their horrible outrages with impunity ?

" *To the Editors of the Louisville Journal :*

"CLEVELAND, Ohio, *July* 30, 1842.

" I wrote you from Cincinnati, according to promise, and I presume you are in receipt of that hurried production, which, however, may not be wholly uninteresting. This letter will, of necessity, be short and hurried as the former, as all communications *written upon the wing*, must necessarily be.

" In the New York Herald, of the 26th inst., the editor says, ' This presents a strange and curious state of things for the centre of the nineteenth century; and the developments are the most remarkable we ever heard of. The initiatory proceedings at Joe's "Order Lodge" resemble those practised by Matthias at Pearson's house, only his members were females, and they danced round a stone, whilst Matthias anointed them. But, perhaps, after all, Joe Smith has a secret lodge of women ! We shall see.' Yes, Joe *has* a secret lodge of women! and the editor *will* see. Joe's female lodge (the Mormon inquisition, and seraglio) is the most singular thing of the age. The *anointing*, A LA JOE, is a caution to David Crocket. The *investment*, the *oath*, the *ceremonies*, the *lectures*, and the GRAND FINALE, are all done up in such a manner, as to place Matthias in the *shade*, and to cover Mahomet, the Oriental prophet, in the rubbish of things that were. The ' History of the Saints ' will give a full account of this nondescript lodge of the Mormon ladies of pleasure and the fine arts, including all their *Cloistered,* *Chambered*, and *Cyprian maids and maidens ! !*

" The elections will terminate next Monday, and I hope that Missouri will then demand Joe, and secure him. I will be ready to make good the charges; and politicians will then see whether the Mormon disclosures were made for *political effect*. Time will develop facts, and show the *truth*, the *undeniable truth*, of *all* the charges against Smith, as clear as the sun in the firmament at noonday. The Roman pontiff never exercised the domination over the minds and property of the Catholic church, as Joe, the chief of the Mormon hierarchy, does over his subjects — *the faithful;* and the pontifical bull is harmless in comparison with the Mormon bull, (Joe's letter of marque and reprisal,) as the latter terminates not in spiritual excommunication and damnation from all Mormon gospel privileges from off the face of God's earth, but in murder, cold-blooded, Danite murder ! Joe is now making a desperate struggle to save himself from merited disgrace and condign punishment, by the forgeries and perjuries of his Cyprian girls, cloistered and chambered

19

mistresses, and the Danites. If you will take the trouble to examine all the evidence, you will find that forgery, perjury, theft, robbery, burglary, arson, treason, and murder, are *very little things* in the eyes of the Mormons, so long as the Holy Joe can, by a ' *Thus saith the Lord*,' pardon iniquity, transgression, and sin !! Joe's father, the devil, was a liar from the beginning, and the world believed him not; neither will they believe Joe, the son, the *delectable* modern Prophet of the Latter Day Sinners; nor the sworn Danites, the grand-children, though covered with all the habiliments of latter day glory.

"Joe's *words* are *lies*, and the *affidavits* of his followers and friends, PATENT LIES. They swear as they are moved upon by Joe's holy ghost, and say the things that gold, or interest, or the Prophet's mandate, dictates !!

"In haste, yours, respectfully,
"JOHN C. BENNETT."

The most extraordinary and infamous feature of the social and religious system established by the Mormon Prophet, and one in which he closely resembles his master and model, Mahomet, is the secret regulations he has formed for directing the relations of the sexes.

The scenes and practices I am about to reveal, will, I am aware, be considered almost incredible, when related as occurring in a civilized and Christian country, and in the enlightened nineteenth century. Their enormity would appear marvellous, if they had been transacted in the most luxurious and corrupt empires of pagan antiquity, or at any of those licentious Oriental courts, where debauchery has been, for ages, systematized and sanctioned by law and religion, on the most extensive scale. The profligacy of Sardanapalus, of Solomon, of Tiberius, of Heliogabalus, and of the modern Turkish and Moorish sultans, has been fully equalled by that of an American citizen in our own day, and one, too, who professes to be the Prophet of the Lord, and the founder of a new and more holy religion than any now existing.

Before proceeding to describe the Mormon seraglio, it may not be amiss to speak of similar institutions on the eastern continent, from which, undoubtedly, the Holy Joe first derived the idea of his more extensive and elaborate system. The earliest one on record, we believe, is that of King Solomon, formed by him after he had fallen from his religion, and become corrupted and enslaved by the fascinations of the women of Egypt. The Hebrew records give us no other details of his harem, than the mere number of its inmates.

It is in the histories, however, of the Oriental and African monarchs, both in ancient and modern times, that we find the most glaring examples of the practice of polygamy and concubinage. We read of Persian, Chinese, and Moorish sovereigns, who kept thousands of women confined in the interiors of their palaces, and to whom were born hundreds of sons, and uncounted numbers of daughters. But the most renowned and remarkable potentate, in this respect, is the African king of Dahomey, who is by law obliged to maintain no less than thirty-three thousand three hundred and thirty-three wives! It is supposed that the stability of the monarchy depends upon this magical number, which is vigilantly kept complete. In numbers, at least, this black patriarch must be acknowledged to exceed the Holy Joe.

Perhaps, however, the most striking parallel to the career of the Mormon, in this, and indeed in other particulars, is that of the Veiled Prophet of Khorassan, the famous Mokanna, whose defeat and downfall have been celebrated by Thomas Moore in his Lalla Rookh.

The poet gives the following brilliant description of this impostor's harem : —

" Between the porphyry pillars that uphold
The rich moresque work of the roof of gold,
Aloft the harem's curtained galleries rise,
Where, through the silken net-work, glancing eyes,
From time to time, like sudden gleams that glow
Through autumn clouds, shine o'er the pomp below.
What impious tongue, ye blushing saints, would dare
To hint that aught but Heaven hath placed you there?
Or that the loves of this light world could bind
In their gross chain your Prophet's soaring mind?
No — wrongful thought! commissioned from above
To people Eden's bowers with shapes of love,
(Creatures so bright, that the same lips and eyes
They wear on earth will serve in paradise,)
There to recline among heaven's native maids,
And crown th' elect with bliss that never fades ! —
Well hath the Prophet-Chief his bidding done ;
And every beauteous race beneath the sun,
From those who kneel at Bramah's burning founts
To the fresh nymphs bounding o'er Yemen's mounts ;
From Persia's eyes of full and fawn-like ray,
To the small, half-shut glances of Kathay ;

And Georgia's bloom and Azab's darker smiles,
And the gold ringlets of the western isles;
All, all are there; — each land its flower hath given
To form that fair young nursery for heaven!"

I will now proceed to describe the seraglio of the modern Mokanna, the Holy Joseph, who differs as much from
his Hebrew namesake, the younger son of Jacob, in
chastity as in other virtues.

The Mormon seraglio is very strictly and systematically
organized. It forms a grand lodge, as it were, and is
divided into three distinct orders, or degrees. The first
and lowest of these is styled the "*Cyprian Saints;*" the
second, the "*Chambered Sisters of Charity;*" and the
third and highest degree is called the "*Cloistered
Saints,*" or "*Consecratees of the Cloister.*"

To give a clear idea of the system. it will be necessary
to treat of these in regular order.

THE CYPRIAN SAINTS.

The members of the Female Relief Society, who are
ever upon the watch for victims, have the power, when
they know, or even suspect, that any Mormon female has,
however slightly, lapsed from the straight path of virtue,
without the sanction or knowledge of the Prophet, of bringing her at once before the Inquisition. This body is
solemnly organized in secret and select council, and by its
members, the poor, terrified female is questioned and threatened, until she confesses the crime she has committed, or
perhaps, in her confusion and terror, accuses herself of
what she was never guilty of. She is immediately, by the
council, pronounced a Cyprian, and is excluded from any
further connection with the Relief Society. She takes
the *White Veil*, and her name and failing are stealthily promulgated among the *trustworthy* members of the Church,
at whose command she is, for licentious purposes, forever
after. Many young and beautiful females have thus been
ruined eternally, who, even after a single fault, might have
lived to redeem, by repentance and future good conduct,
their names and characters from degradation, and their souls
from guilt and from remorse. But the secret council of

the Inquisition instantly condemns them, on the confession or proof of their transgression, to perpetual association with a class devoted to the most infamous purposes; a class set apart and appropriated to the gratification of the vilest appetites of the brutal Priests and Elders of the Mormon Church. Was there ever known, in the history of the world, a more diabolical system than this? Instead of interposing the sacred priestly and prophetical character and influence for the salvation and reformation of an erring sister, to go deliberately to work, to sink her irreclaimably into the pit of crime and misery! Do not the authors and abettors of this horrid, this monstrous system deserve most richly the execration and prompt vengeance of an outraged and indignant community? Should such miscreants be longer suffered to pollute, with their contaminating presence, a Christian and civilized land? Humanity and decency loudly demand their punishment, and the rescue of their victims, many of whom realize the beautiful description of the poet —

> " Rich and rare were the gems she wore,
> And a bright gold ring on her wand she bore;
> But, O ! her beauty was far beyond
> Her sparkling gems or snow-white wand."

But even the means used to increase the order of Cyprian Saints do not exhaust the depraved ingenuity of the *Holy Old White Hat Prophet*, and his confidential counsellors. Let us examine the second degree of his female lodge, which is entitled

THE CHAMBERED SISTERS OF CHARITY.

This order comprises that class of females who indulge their sensual propensities, without restraint, whether married or single, by the express permission of the Prophet.

Whenever one of the "Saints," (as the Mormons style themselves,) of the male sex, becomes enamored of a female, and she responds to the feeling by a reciprocal manifestation, the loving brother goes to Holy Joe, and states the case. It makes, by the bye, no difference whatever if one or both the parties are already provided with conjugal helpmates. The Prophet gravely buries his

19 *

face in his hat, in which lies his peep-stone, and inquires
of the Lord what are his will and pleasure in the matter.
Sometimes, when Joe wants the woman for his own purposes, an unfavorable answer is given; but, generally, the
reply permits the parties to follow the bent of their inclina-
tions, which they do without further ceremony, though
with a strict observance of secrecy, on account of the
Gentiles, who have no right to the blessings and privileges
so liberally granted to the Latter Day Saints.

Thus these poor, deluded females, while incited by their
very religion (if it deserves that name) to indulgence
in the most degrading passions, have their consciences
soothed, and their scruples appeased, by the sanction of
the pretended Apostle and Prophet of the Lord, in whom
they have the utmost confidence, and whose lightest word
is with them a law.

The result of this system is, that not unfrequently men
having wives of their own are living in licentious intercourse with other women, and not unfrequently with other
men's wives; thus multiplying their adulteries, and producing an incalculable amount of domestic discord and
misery.   Families are estranged and separated, children
neglected, and all the tender and important relations of
society outraged and perverted.

The *Chambered Sisters of Charity* are much more numerous than the *Cyprian Saints*.   This results naturally
from the greater respectability of their order.   They are
" *Saints of the Green Veil,*" and are by no means nig-
gardly of their favors to any of the faithful.   Provided the
Holy Joe does not desire to monopolize any of them, they
are at the service of each and all of the Apostles, High
Priests, and Elders of Israel.

It occurs to me, however, that, when the uninitiated
portion of the Mormon Church discover how their wives
and daughters are used by their rulers, and spiritual guides,
and teachers, there will be some slight disturbance of the
peace in the Holy City of Nauvoo.   I cannot think it
probable that Americans, however deluded by an artful
Impostor, will tamely permit those dearest to them to be
prostituted, even to gratify the immaculate Joe himself.

The third and highest order of the Mormon harem is
that which is styled

THE CONSECRATEES OF THE CLOISTER, OR CLOISTERED SAINTS.

This degree is composed of females, whether married or unmarried, who, by an express grant and gift of God, through his Prophet the Holy Joe, are set apart and consecrated to the use and benefit of particular individuals, as *secret, spiritual wives.* They are the *Saints of the Black Veil,* and are accounted the special favorites of Heaven, and the most honorable among the daughters of Jacob. Their spiritual husbands are altogether from the most eminent members of the Mormon Church, and participate in the holiness of their consecrated wives. In the words of the poet, they can say, not unaptly, —

> " From the *consecrate* girl of my soul shall I fly
> To seek somewhere else a more orthodox kiss?
> No! *perish the hearts and the laws* that would try
> Truth, valor, or love, by a standard like this!"

This is the highest degree in the Harem, and, in the order of the Prophet's licentious arrangements, is held as the very acme of perfection, and it is, indeed, the *ne plus ultra* of depravity. Its ranks are filled up in the following manner: When an Apostle, High Priest, Elder, or Scribe, conceives an affection for a female, and he has satisfactorily ascertained that she experiences a mutual flame, he communicates confidentially to the Prophet his *affaire du cœur,* and requests him to inquire of the Lord whether or not it would be right and proper for him to take unto himself the said woman for his spiritual wife. It is no obstacle whatever to this spiritual marriage if one or both of the parties should happen to have a husband or wife, already united to them according to the laws of the land.

The Prophet puts this queer question to the Lord, and, if he receives an answer in the affirmative, which is always the case where the parties are in favor with Joe, His Holiness, either in person or by a duly-authorized administrator, proceeds to consecrate the sacred sister in the following solemn manner : —

The parties assemble in the lodge room, and place themselves kneeling before the altar; the administrator commences the ceremony by saying, —

" You, separately and jointly, in the name of Jesus Christ, the Son of God, do solemnly covenant and agree that you will not disclose any matter relating to the sacred act now in progress of consummation, whereby any Gentile shall come to a knowledge of the secret purposes of this order, or whereby the Saints may suffer persecution ; your lives being the forfeit.''

After the bow of assent is given by each of the pair, the administrator then proceeds —

" In the name of Jesus Christ, and by the authority of the holy priesthood, I now consecrate you and set you apart by the imposition of my hands, as husband and wife, according to the laws of Zion, and the will of God our heavenly Father; for which especial favor you now agree to serve him with a perfect heart and a willing mind, and to obey his Prophet in all things according to his divine will.''

Again the nod of assent is given by the man and woman, and the administrator continues in a solemn and impressive manner —

" I now anoint you with holy, consecrated oil, in the name of Jesus Christ, and by the authority of the holy priesthood, that you may be fully and unreservedly consecrated to each other, and to the service of God, and that with affection and fidelity you may nourish and cherish each other, so long as you shall continue faithful and true in the fellowship of the Saints ; and I now pronounce upon you the blessings of Jacob, whom God honored and protected in the enjoyment of like special favors ; and may the peace of Heaven, which passeth all understanding, rest upon you in time and in eternity ! ''

The parties then rise and embrace each other, and the robe of investiture is placed upon and around them by the administrator, who says, —

" According to the prototype, I now pronounce you *one flesh*, in the name of the Father, and of the Son, and of the Holy Ghost. Amen.''

The robe is then removed, and the parties leave the cloister, with generally a firm belief, at least on the part of the female, in the sacredness and validity of the ceremonial, and thereafter consider themselves as united in spiritual marriage, the duties and privileges of which are in no particular different from those of any other marriage covenant.

> " Here we dwell in holiest bowers,
>   Where angels of light o'er our orisons bend,
> Where sighs of devotion and breathings of flowers
>   To heaven in mingled odors ascend !
>   Do not disturb our calm, O Love !
>   So like is thy form to the cherubs above,
> It well might deceive such hearts as ours.''

The above is a faithful and unexaggerated account of the most enormous and detestable system of depravity that was ever concocted by the corrupt heart of a human being. The extensive scale upon which it was carried on, and the lofty and sacred character pretended to by the arch villain who contrived and perpetrated it, are equally remarkable. Is it not astonishing that a man professing to be the Apostle and Prophet of the Most High and Pure God, and the founder of a new and holy religion, based, in some degree, upon the Christian Scriptures, — a man claiming daily and hourly familiar intercourse with the Creator of heaven and earth, should, despite these high pretensions, which, however false, ought to have made him endeavor to act in some degree of accordance with them, — is it not astonishing, I say, that this man should so deliberately and shamelessly have gone to work to gratify, in so monstrous a manner, his abominable lusts? Will it not hereafter be deemed incredible that hundreds and thousands, yea, tens of thousands, of Americans and Christians, were, in the year of our Lord one thousand eight hundred and forty-two, so miserably, so awfully deceived as to believe that this monster of iniquity, this brutally sensual wretch, was the Prophet and Vicegerent of God upon earth?

And will it not be deemed still more incredible, that chaste and pious women should also be so far deluded by his arts and impostures, as to sacrifice themselves, body and soul, to him and to his myrmidons, despite all restraints of their former religious education, and of that decency and modesty which seem inherent qualities of the female soul?

But there is no absurdity so great that it will not be believed, no enormity so monstrous that it will not be practised, by those who have once yielded up their minds to the sway of superstition. The imposture of Joseph Smith has never had its parallel, if we consider not only its magnitude and grossness, but the age and the people when and among whom it was devised and promulgated.

In quitting this subject, I can only say that I have not told the tenth part of the Prophet's licentiousness. Numerous scenes and incidents could not, of course, be related, because of their obscene and disgusting nature, and because they involve the names and future reputation of his victims.

AMOURS, ATTEMPTED SEDUCTIONS, AND CRIM. CON. CASES.

Under this head I shall arrange two descriptions of cases ; — the *amours and attempted seductions,* as in the cases of Mrs. Sarah M. Pratt, Mrs. Emeline White, Miss Martha H. Brotherton, and Miss Nancy Rigdon, where the Prince of the Seraglio was signally defeated ; and the *amours and crim. con. cases,* as in the instances of Mrs. Warren, (late widow Fuller,) Mrs. Miller, and the long retinue of Cyprians, Chambered, and Cloistered Saints, where the Lord of the Harem glutted his brutal lusts to the maximum of his sensual desires, in his halcyon days of prophetic glory.

AMOURS AND ATTEMPTED SEDUCTIONS.

MRS. SARAH M. PRATT.

This lady is the wife of Orson Pratt, A. M., Professor of Mathematics in the University of the City of Nauvoo, and is one of the most elegant, graceful, amiable, and accomplished women in the place. Mr. S. Francis, editor of the Sangamo Journal, in speaking of her, says, " It will be recollected that Mrs. Schindle, in her affidavit detailing the attempt of Smith upon her, said, ' He then told her that she must never tell of his propositions to her, for he had ALL influence in that place, and if she told, *he would ruin her character, and she would be under the necessity of leaving.'* This same scheme has been carried out in reference to Mrs. Pratt. She ' told ' on the Impostor, and was marked by him for destruction. In a public speech in Nauvoo, on the 14th July, Joe spoke of this lady — a woman whose reputation had been as fair as virtue could make it until she came in contact with him — in a manner only befitting the lowest and most degraded vagabond in existence." Yes, her reputation was unsullied, and her character as pure as the virgin snow ; nor was even the Mormon Don Juan able to blight this blooming flower. — This noble and lovely woman was marked out by Joe as a victim. Her husband was sent to Europe

to convert the heathen, under a solemn promise that his
family should be honorably provided for by the Church;
but, as Mrs. Pratt was a beautiful and charming woman,
Joe's real object was to CONVERT HER in another way —
from virtue, unsophisticated virtue, to vice, soul-damning
vice, — from the path of innocence and peace, to the polluted way of the libertine, — from the pure teachings of
heaven's high King, to the loathsome caresses of the *beast
and the false prophet;* but the fowler's snare was broken,
and the intended victim saved. Mrs. Pratt is a highly-
educated lady, and had always been used to living well;
but no sooner had her husband crossed the ocean, than
Joe ordered the Bishops to restrict her in her allowance,
and reduce her to a state of absolute want and suffering, in
order to make her a more easy prey. The mandate was
obeyed, and, in drear winter, without fuel or food, she
found herself in a miserable hovel, with her darling child,
exposed to storm and tempest, and dependent upon the
tender mercies of a cold and unfeeling fraternity to supply her actual wants! ! ! The sufferings and privations
through which she passed are indescribable; the blackest
fiends of hell would shudder at the thought of such inhu-
man treatment; but, alas! she drank the bitter cup, and
sipped the dregs. A public contribution was then taken
up for her, and *pocketed by the Bishop;* but the venerable
prelate, Vinson Knight, was willing to see her provided
for on one condition, and *that was, the sacrifice of virtue!*
But she spurned his proffered mercies, and doffed the
mitre from his reverend brow. Joe Smith and Vinson
Knight — *par fratrum nobile!* Emma, the *Electa Syria*
of the Church, and wife of the Holy Joe, the male Cassandra of the Mormon Hierarchy, (who was very envious
of Mrs. Pratt's superior intellectual endowments,) advised
her to hire out as a servant to some Mormon nabob; but
that base attempt at human degradation of one in every
way superior to herself, became abortive; and Mrs. Pratt
turned from the delectable Emma, the Lady Abbess of the
Seraglio, or " Mother of the Maids," as Lord Byron calls
it, with loathing and ineffable contempt. Mrs. Pratt,
however, by the assistance of a few humane individuals,
and her persevering industry, was enabled to support her-

self and little boy, until the return of her husband from a
two years' mission, which was greeted with acclamations
of joy.   The cup of sorrow was broken, and she rejoiced
once more in the society of a *protector*, a husband, and a
friend.   But she had a dreadful tale to tell.

Joe Smith told me, *confidentially*, during the absence
of her husband, that he intended to make Mrs. Pratt
one of his *spiritual wives*, one of the *Cloistered Saints*,
for the Lord had given her to him as a special favor
for his faithfulness and zeal ; and, as I had influence with
her, he desired me to assist him in the consummation of
his hellish purposes; but I refused compliance, and told
him that she had been much neglected and abused by the
Church, in order to *cloister* her, so far without success,
and that, if the Lord had given her to him, he must attend
to it himself, for I should never offer her an indignity.
"Well," said he, "I shall approach her, for there is no
harm in it if she submits to be cloistered, and if her husband should never find it out ; and if she should expose
me, as she did Bishop Knight, *I will blast her character;*
so there is no material risk for so desirable a person."   I
then called upon Mrs. Pratt, and apprized her of Joe's
contemplated attack on her virtue, *in the name of the
Lord*, and that she must prepare to repulse him, in so
infamous an assault, *by opposing revelation to revelation.*
She replied, "Joseph cannot be such a man; I cannot
believe it until I know it for myself, or have it from his
own lips ; he cannot be so corrupt."   I told her that she
would see, unless he changed his mind, for he was an unprincipled libertine, unequalled in the history of civilized
man.   Accordingly, in a few days, Joe proposed to me a
visit to Ramus, which I accepted, and we started from his
house, in an open carriage, about 4 o'clock, P. M., rode
into the prairie a few miles, and returned to the house of
Captain John T. Barnett, in Nauvoo, about dusk, where
we put up the horse, with Barnett's permission.   Joe pretended we were looking for thieves.   After perambulating
for an hour or two, we proceeded to the residence of Mrs.
Pratt, and found her at home, and alone, with the exception of her little boy, who was then asleep in bed.   We
were hospitably received, and our situation rendered as

comfortable and agreeable as the tenement would admit of. After considerable desultory conversation, Joe asked her if she would keep a secret for him; to which she assented. "Do you pledge me your honor," said he, "that you will never tell without my permission?" She replied in the affirmative. He then continued, "Sister Pratt, the Lord has given you to me as one of my *spiritual wives.* I have the blessings of Jacob granted me, as God granted holy men of old; and as I have long looked upon you with favor, and an earnest desire of connubial bliss, I hope you will not repulse or deny me." She replied, "And is that the great secret that I am not to utter? Am I called upon to break the marriage covenant, and prove recreant to my lawful husband? *I never will.* My sex shall not be disgraced, nor my honor sullied. I care not for the blessings of Jacob, and I believe in no such revelations, neither will I consent, under any circumstances whatever. I have one good husband, and that is enough for me." He then went off to see Miss Louisa Beeman, at the house of Mrs. Sherman, and remained with her about two hours, when we returned to Barnett's, harnessed our horse, started for Ramus, arrived at Carthage early in the morning, and took breakfast at Mr. Hamilton's. We then went to Ramus, transacted some business in relation to real estate, returned to Carthage that night, and put up at the house of Esquire Comer. Next day, we returned to Nauvoo. I then called upon Mrs. Pratt, and asked her if her opinion of Joseph, the Prophet, was the same as heretofore. She replied, "No; he is a bad man, beyond a doubt — 'wicked, sensual, devilish;' but it will not do for me to express myself openly, or my life might atone for it. It becomes me to move in this matter with much circumspection; I must be as 'wise as a serpent, and harmless as a dove;' for I see plainly that Joseph is determined to transgress the laws, change the ordinance, and break the everlasting covenant of our heavenly Father, and to set at open defiance every principle of true godliness and moral rectitude. I exceedingly fear and tremble for the weak and uneducated of my sex; for an unprincipled libertine, sensualist, and debauchee, of such unbounded prophetic influence, in a community like this, may utterly

20

ruin hundreds of pious, unsuspecting females, under the
potent dictum of a ' THUS SAITH THE LORD ; ' and all the
proof they would require would be his simple *ipse dixit.*
O, WHAT TOTAL DEPRAVITY ! ! What ignorance and impudence in a land of Bibles, where *Christians* ought to
dwell, and worship the Great Ruler of the Universe in the
beauty of holiness ! Surely God will not suffer it long !
I remember well when you told me of his desiring you to
procure the engraving of new plates of the Book of Mormon, for the further and more perfect blinding of the
people — of his gross wickedness and perfidy — of his
fraud and corruption — of his spiritual wickedness in high
places, and his secret abominations, — and so forth ; but I
could never *realize* it before. I had a better opinion of
human nature ; but, alas ! I was deceived. The scales,
however, have fallen from my eyes, and ' *whereas I
was once blind,* NOW I SEE.' I am in great trouble on
another account. My husband is a good and pious man,
and *a true believer in Mormonism,* DEVOTEDLY attached to
Joseph as the spiritual leader of the Church. He believes
him to be a pure man, and a Prophet of the Lord. Now,
if I should tell him the true story of my sufferings, privations, and insults, and Joseph should circumvent or meet
it with his *infallible rebuff* of a ' VERILY, THUS SAITH THE
LORD,' I fear that Orson would believe him in preference
to me, *unless his faith can be shaken.* How shall I extricate myself from this fearful dilemma ? As a confidential
friend, I look to you for advice and protection, until the
return of Mr. Pratt." " Be quiet," said I, " Sarah, under
these circumstances, until some event transpires by which
Orson can have ocular and auricular demonstration of the
palpable imposture of the whole scheme of Mormonism,
and of the infidelity and brutality of the *Mormon Mountebank,* that *Sui Generis Prophet,* who was constituted *per
se,* and *not by the appointment of* ALMIGHTY GOD ; and
such an event must soon be consummated, unless there
should be a manifest change in the Mormon Administration."

Joe afterwards tried to convince Mrs. Pratt of the propriety of his spiritual wife doctrine, and she at last told
him peremptorily, " Joseph, if you ever attempt any thing

of the kind with me again, I will make a full disclosure to Mr. Pratt on his return home. Depend upon it, *I will certainly do it.*" Joe replied, "Sister Pratt, I hope you will not expose me, for if I suffer, all must suffer; so do not expose me. Will you promise me that you will not do it?" "If," said she, "you will never insult me again, I will not expose you, unless strong circumstances should require it." "If you should tell," said he, "I will ruin your reputation; *remember that ;* and as you have repulsed me, it becomes sin, unless *sacrifice* is offered." He then desired that a lamb should be procured and slain, and the door-posts and the gate sprinkled with its blood, and the kidneys and entrails taken and offered upon an altar of twelve stones that had not been touched with a hammer, as a burnt sin-offering, for the purpose of saving him and his priesthood. His desire was complied with, and the lamb procured from Captain Barnett, and slain by Lieutenant Stephen H. Goddard ; and the kidneys and entrails were offered in sacrifice, as Joe desired ; and he observed, "All is now safe; the Destroying Angel will pass over without harming any of us." About this time, Mrs. Pratt, in a conversation with Mrs. Goddard, observed, "Sister Goddard, Joseph is a corrupt man ; I know it, for he made an attempt upon me, *in the name of the Lord.* I now detest *the man.*" Time passed on without further molestation, until one day, after Mr. Pratt's return from Europe, Joe called at her new house, and, looking at Mrs. Pratt, thought, —

> "And, O ! how often in these eyes,
> Which melting beamed like azure skies
> In dewy vernal weather —
> How often have I raptured read
> The burning glance, that silent said,
> Now, love, *we feel together,*" —

and grossly insulted her again, by stealthily approaching and kissing her. This highly offended her, and she told her husband, Colonel Orson Pratt, who was highly incensed, and gave Joe a SEVERE REBUKE. Joe observed, "I did not desire to kiss her ; *Bennett made me do it !*" Joe couldn't come the "*extreme unction*" over that intelligent lady ; she was far above his polluted breath, his ribaldry, low vituperation, calumny, and detraction. *He lied to her in the name of Israel's God.* Let the base blasphemer remember that, and weep! Let him look at his black catalogue of crimes — his seductions and attempted seductions, *in the name of the Lord* — his thefts — his robberies — and his murders! Why, Satan blushes to behold so corrupt and loathsome a mortal, — one whose daring deeds of crime so far surpass hell's darkest counsels, as to hide the sable Prince in impenetrable darkness forever! If Joe Smith is not destined for the *Devil*, all I can say is, that the *duties* of a devil have not been clearly understood.

> "I've had a dream that bodes no good
> Unto the Holy Brotherhood.
> I can't be wrong, and I confess —
> As far as it is right or lawful
> For one, *no conjurer*, to guess —
> It seems to me extremely awful."

Joe lied to Colonel Pratt afterwards, IN THE NAME OF THE LORD. This shook his faith, and he told the Prophet to his face that *he was a liar*, AN INFAMOUS LIAR; and his noble voice has since been heard thundering against that Uncircumcised Philistine, the fell Monster of Iniquity, and that at the very portals of the Temple. Deploy column, Colonel Pratt, and let your heavy ordnance and battering-rams ply upon the ramparts of General Joe's imperial fortifications! Demolish the bastions and curtains of his fortresses! Open your artillery upon his concealed recesses, and storm his strong-holds! Let loose the dogs of war upon his gathering hosts of Tartarean fugitives and refugees, and secure to yourself an imperishable reputation as a moral victor, and a servant of your God; and Mormonism will soon be numbered with the things that were, the glory of which is now in the sear and yellow leaf.

From Mrs. Emeline White.

"NAUVOO, *August* 3, 1842.

"GENERAL JOHN C. BENNETT:
  "Respected friend, —
            *   *   *   *   *   *   *
"Your friends are anxiously awaiting your return to the west. If it is possible, be here by the 1st of September. You can avert

a great calamity, and add greatly to the amount of human happiness by so doing. I dare not write you to what I allude, but
wou'd gladly tell you. I called on Mrs. Pratt this morning, in order
to learn where to address you; and she and Mr. Pratt dined at
father's to-day. We had a long talk with them about the troubled
waters, the present attitude in which they are placed, and the ultimate issue or final result of the *exposé*. I was much pleased to see
them so happy, and firm in the advocacy of truth. Mr. Pratt has
publicly defended her, from the stand, against the foul aspersions
attempted to be cast upon her irreproachable reputation by her interested persecutors. She is certainly one of the best of women,
above reproach, of noble bearing, and great moral excellence ; and
Mr. Pratt will ever sustain her in exposing corruption and fraud.
They request me to say to you that you must excuse them for not
writing, as their time has hitherto been so completely engrossed.
They are your unwavering friends, and cannot be driven from the
truth by your enemies. Some here have dealt very treacherously
with you, and they shall reap their reward hereafter; the curses of
Heaven will fall upon their heads, for God will protect you in a virtuous cause. May all your undertakings prosper, and may God bless,
and guardian angels watch over and hover around you, in this your
time of danger and peril ! Your friends here are firm as the adaman-
tine rocks, and will ever sustain you in defending virtue and exposing vice. Father and mother join me in their respects to you.
Please to write circumstantially at your earliest convenience
                              " Respectfully, yours,
                                        " EMELINE WHITE."

The following affidavit of Messrs. Carter, Whiting, and
Leland, though unexpected by me, is quite opportune : —

                              " BOSTON, *September* 17, 1842.
" TO THE PUBLIC :

      " Without solicitation or the previous knowledge of any one,
we would respectfully state that we have seen letters from four
individuals, residing in and near Nauvoo, addressed to and received
by different gentlemen in the States of New York and Massachusetts, through the post-office department, tending fully and unequivocally to confirm the truth of the disclosures of General Bennett, in
relation to Joseph Smith, the Mormon Prophet, and his followers,
especially so far as regards the Seraglio and Order Lodge, and the
cases of Mrs. Sarah M. Pratt, Miss Nancy Rigdon, and Mrs. Emeline White. The writers of these letters are persons of great respectability, holding high official stations. They request that their names
shall not be made public, for fear of secret murder by the Mormon
Destroying Angel, or the Daughter of Zion.
                              " ROBERT CARTER,
                              " WILLARD J. WHITING,
                              " EMERSON LELAND."

20 *

"Suffolk, ss. *September* 17, 1842.

"Then personally appeared the above-named Robert Carter, Willard J. Whiting, and Emerson Leland, and made oath that the above affidavit, by them subscribed, is true.

"Before me,   BRADFORD SUMNER,
                                        "*Justice of the Peace.*"

The *Sangamo Journal*, of July 22, 1842, in commenting on the Prophet's amours and secret abominations, says, —

"In this community, we verily believe that there is not a man, disconnected with the Mormons, who does not place implicit confidence in the disclosures of General Bennett. These disclosures show that the rulers of this Mormon confederacy are steeped in pollutions of the blackest dye — pollutions and crimes violatory of all laws, human and divine — and for which we can hardly find a parallel, without going back to the ingulfed ' cities of the plain.' "

It will be seen that the affidavit of Messrs. Carter, Whiting, and Leland, unequivocally sustains various other matters disclosed in this Exposé ; and the whole testimony places Mrs. Pratt high on the vantage-ground, and far above reproach. Thus, by the assistance of a most powerful intellect, and the great God, has this noble lady signally triumphed over her insidiously persecuting enemies, and placed her foot upon the neck of the Monster of Iniquity, the Beast and the False Prophet ; and her noble husband, too, has done himself immortal honor in battering down the bulwarks of prophetic security, behind which the Mormon Pontiff screened himself from merited infamy and disgrace. The course of the Prophet has been very singular in its inception, its prosecution, and its termination.

MRS. EMELINE WHITE.

Mrs. White is no Mormon. Her father, General Davison Hibard, resided at Nauvoo before the Mormons located themselves there. She is, however, what is much better, one of the most beautiful and accomplished women in the Holy City. Her form is noble, yet exquisitely proportioned ; her features regular, and glowing with a thousand charms, not the least attractive of which is the amiable gayety that beams from every line of her countenance. She possesses fine musical talent, and realizes, in every way, the description of the poet, —

" She sung of love — while o'er her lyre
        The rosy rays of evening fell,
    As if to feed with their soft fire
        The soul within that trembling shell.
    The same rich light hung o'er her cheek,
        And played around those lips that sung
    And spoke as flowers would sing and speak,
        If love could lend their leaves a tongue."

The fine intellect and superior intelligence of this lovely woman secured her effectually from falling into the Mormon delusion. She rejected, with decision and contempt, their base and absurd belief; and, so far as I am aware, rose triumphant above the libertine arts and temptations of the Prophet himself, though those arts and those temptations were put forth with all his strength.

The following letter was addressed to her by Joe, who was, when he wrote it, in Springfield, Illinois : —

"MY SWEET EMELINE :

"You know that my love for you, as David said to Jonathan, is ' wonderful, passing the love of women.' And how can that be ? You know it is only *figurative.* I mean you have my *most supreme affections.* O that I had yours as truly ! May I not hope that it will be so ? At all events, be my *friend,* my *best friend.* If you want any thing while I am gone, call upon either of the Bishops, — Vinson Knight or Alanson Ripley, — and show them the signature of ' Old White Hat,' and they will provide for you. Do not be afraid to receive any thing from me, and these men are *confidential.* You need not fear to write me ; and I do assure you that a few lines would be very consoling on a journey. Sign it ' Rosanna.'   " Your humble servant,
                                "OLD WHITE HAT."

This letter had no other effect upon this virtuous lady, than to excite her scorn and indignation. She saw through the Monster and his detestable doctrines, and could not be persuaded, by any offers, to participate in his vileness.

I am informed by General Robinson and Colonel Higbee, that the brother of Dr. John F. Weld has in his possession two other letters from this Old White Hat Prophet to Mrs. White, which are said to be exceedingly rich specimens of rigmarole, abounding in the warmest protestations of love; interlarded with quotations from Scripture.

The Mormon Don Juan failed again in the application of the "*extreme unction,*" and virtue once more triumphed over the insidious arts and machinations of a malevolent

caliph. The unbounded courage and inflexible moral purity
of purpose of this beautiful lady, combined with a vigorous
intellect, enabled her to hold the tyrant at bay, even in the
Holy City of the Saints, until she could effectually present
the *shield* and *rapier*. This she did, and vanquished. Noble woman! may the escutcheon of her honor ever remain
as spotless as the album of Diana, and the God of virtue
will be her Protector and her Friend.

MISS MARTHA H. BROTHERTON.

Miss Brotherton is a very good-looking, amiable, and
accomplished English lady, of highly respectable parent-
age, cultivated intellect, and spotless moral character.
She was selected as one of the victims for the *Cloister*, in
order to be consecrated to apostolic brutality. The Right
Reverend Brigham Young, the President of the Mormon
College of Apostles, (*Collegium de Propaganda Fide*,) it
is well known regarded her with an evil eye, and she was
also eagerly sought after by the Holy Prophet Joe, and by
Apostle Heber C. Kimball. Gods! what a triumvirate!
and united, too, for such a sanctified purpose! These
celestial gladiators, armed with the " sword of the Spirit,"
leaguing themselves in a Holy Alliance for the destruction
of a defenceless and innocent woman, and urging on their
work of sin and pollution with the most fiendish zeal and
malignity! " Tell it not in Gath, publish it not in the
streets of Askelon." These three Mormon demigods,
these Prophets and Apostles, were completely foiled in their
hopeful scheme, and utterly defeated by the determined
resistance of their intended victim, as will be seen by the
following graphic letter from her own pen : —

" St. Louis, Missouri, *July* 13, A. D. 1842.

" General John C. Bennett :

" Dear Sir, —
        " I left Warsaw a short time since for this city, and having
been called upon by you, through the ' Sangamo Journal,' to come
out and disclose to the world the facts of the case in relation to
certain propositions made to me at Nauvoo, by some of the Mormon
leaders, I now proceed to respond to the call, and discharge what I
consider to be a duty devolving upon me as an innocent, but insulted
and abused female. I had been at Nauvoo near three weeks, during

which time my father's family received frequent visits from Elders Brigham Young and Heber C. Kimball, two of the Mormon Apostles; when, early one morning, they both came to my brother-in-law's (John McIlwrick's) house, at which place I then was on a visit, and particularly requested me to go and spend a few days with them. I told them I could not at that time, as my brother-in-law was not at home; however, they urged me to go the next day, and spend one day with them. The day being fine, I accordingly went. When I arrived at the foot of the hill, Young and Kimball were standing conversing together. They both came to me, and, after several flattering compliments, Kimball wished me to go to his house first. I said it was immaterial to me, and accordingly went. We had not, however, gone many steps when Young suddenly stopped, and said he would go to that brother's, (pointing to a little log hut a few yards distant,) and tell him that you (speaking to Kimball) and brother Glover, or Grover, (I do not remember which,) will value his land. When he had gone, Kimball turned to me and said, 'Martha, I want you to say to my wife, when you go to my house, that you want to buy some things at Joseph's store, (Joseph Smith's,) and I will say I am going with you, to show you the way. You know you want to see the Prophet, and you will then have an opportunity.' I made no reply. Young again made his appearance, and the subject was dropped. We soon reached Kimball's house, where Young took his leave, saying, 'I shall see you again, Martha.' I remained at Kimball's near an hour, when Kimball, seeing that I would not tell the lies he wished me to, told them to his wife himself. He then went and whispered in her ear, and asked if that would please her. 'Yes,' said she, 'or I can go along with you and Martha.' 'No,' said he, 'I have some business to do, and I will call for you afterwards to go with me to the debate,' meaning the debate between yourself and Joseph. To this she consented. So Kimball and I went to the store together. As we were going along, he said, 'Sister Martha, are you willing to do all that the Prophet requires you to do?' I said I believed I was, thinking of course *he* would require nothing wrong. 'Then,' said he, 'are you ready to take counsel?' I answered in the affirmative, thinking of the great and glorious blessings that had been pronounced upon my head, if I adhered to the counsel of those placed over me in the Lord. 'Well,' said he, 'there are many things revealed in these last days that the world would laugh and scoff at; but unto us is given to know the mysteries of the kingdom.' He further observed, 'Martha, you must learn to hold your tongue, and it will be well with you. You will see Joseph, and very likely have some conversation with him, and he will tell you what you shall do.' When we reached the building, he led me up some stairs to a small room, the door of which was locked, and on it the following inscription: 'Positively no admittance.' He observed, 'Ah! brother Joseph must be sick, for, strange to say, he is not here. Come down into the tithing-office, Martha.' He then left me in the tithing-office, and went out, I know not where. In this office were two men writing, one of whom, William Clayton, I had seen in England; the other I did not know. Young came in, and seated himself before me, and asked where Kimball was. I said he had gone out. He said it was all right. Soon after, Joseph came in, and spoke to one of the clerks, and then went up stairs, followed by Young. Immediately after, Kimball came in. ' Now, Martha,' said he, ' the Prophet has come; come up stairs.' I went, and we found Young and the Prophet alone. I was introduced to the Prophet by Young. Joseph offered me his seat, and, to my astonishment, the moment I was seated, Joseph and Kimball walked out of the room, and left me with Young, who arose, locked the door, closed the window, and drew the curtain. He then came and sat before me, and said, ' This is our private room, Martha.' ' Indeed, sir,' said I, ' I must be highly honored to be permitted to enter it.' He smiled, and then proceeded — ' Sister Martha, I 'want to ask you a few questions; will you answer them ? ' ' Yes, sir,' said I. ' And will you promise not to mention them to any one ? ' ' If it is your desire, sir,' said I, ' I will not.' ' And you will not think any the worse of me for it, will you, Martha ? ' said he. ' No, sir,' I replied. ' Well,' said he, ' what are your feelings towards me ? ' I replied, ' My feelings are just the same towards you that they ever were, sir.' ' But, to come to the point more closely,' said he, ' have not you an affection for me, that, were it lawful and right, you could accept of me for your husband and companion ? ' My feelings at that moment were indescribable. God only knows them. What, thought I, are these men, that I thought almost perfection itself, *deceivers ?* and is all my fancied happiness but a dream ? 'Twas even so; but my next thought was, which is the best way for me to act at this time ? If I say *no*, they may do as they think proper ; and to say *yes*, I never would. So I considered it best to ask for time to think and pray about it. I therefore said, ' If it was lawful and right, perhaps I might ; but you know, sir, it is not.' ' Well, but,' said he, ' brother Joseph has had a revelation from God that it is lawful and right for a man to have two wives ; for, as it was in the days of Abraham, so it shall be in these last days, and whoever is the first that is willing to take up the cross will receive the greatest blessings ; and if you will accept of me, I will take you straight to the celestial kingdom ; and if you will have me in this world, I will have you in that which is to come, and brother Joseph will marry us here to-day, and you can go home this evening, and your parents will not know any thing about it.' ' Sir,' said I, ' I should not like to do any thing of the kind without the permission of my parents.' ' Well, but,' said he, ' you are of age, are you not ?' ' No, sir,' said I, ' I shall not be until the 24th of May.' ' Well,' said he, ' that does not make any difference. You will be of age before they know, and you need not fear. If you will take my counsel, it will be well with you, for I know it to be right before God, and if there is any sin in it, I will answer for it. But brother Joseph wishes to have some talk with you on the subject — he will explain things — will you hear him ? ' ' I do not mind,' said I. ' Well, but I want you to say something,' said he. ' I want time to think about it,' said I. ' Well,' said he, ' I will have a kiss, any how,' and then rose, and said he would bring Joseph. He then unlocked the door, and took the key, and locked me up alone. He was absent about ten minutes, and then returned with Joseph. ' Well,' said Young,

' sister Martha would be willing if she knew it was lawful and right before God.' ' Well, Martha,' said Joseph, ' it is lawful and right before God — I *know* it is. Look here, sis; don't you believe in me ? ' I did not answer. ' Well, Martha,' said Joseph, ' just go ahead, and do as Brigham wants you to — he is the best man in the world, except me.' ' O ! ' said Brigham, ' then you are as good.' ' Yes,' said Joseph. ' Well,' said Young, ' we believe Joseph to be a Prophet. I have known him near eight years, and always found him the same. ' Yes,' said Joseph, ' and I know that this is lawful and right before God, and if there is any sin in it, I will answer for it before God ; and I have the keys of the kingdom, and whatever I bind on earth is bound in heaven, and whatever I loose on earth is loosed in heaven , and if you will accept of Brigham, you shall be blessed — God shall bless you, and my blessing shall rest upon you ; and if you will be led by him, you will do well ; for I know Brigham will take care of you, and if he don't do his duty to you, come to me, and I will make him ; and if you do not like it in a month or two, come to me, and I will make you free again ; and if he turns you off, I will take you on.' ' Sir,' said I, rather warmly, ' it will be too late to think in a month or two after. I want time to think first.' ' Well, but,' said he, ' the old proverb is, " Nothing ventured, nothing gained ; " and it would be the greatest blessing that was ever bestowed upon you.' ' Yes,' said Young, ' and you will never have reason to repent it — that is, if I do not turn from righteousness, and that I trust I never shall ; for I believe God, who has kept me so long, will continue to keep me faithful. Did you ever see me act in any way wrong in England, Martha ? ' ' No, sir,' said I. ' No,' said he ; ' neither can any one else lay any thing to my charge.' ' Well, then,' said Joseph, ' what are you afraid of, sis ? Come, let me do the business for you.' ' Sir,' said I, ' do let me have a little time to think about it, and I will promise not to mention it to any one.' ' Well, but look here,' said he ; ' you know a fellow will never be damned for doing the best he knows how.' ' Well, then,' said I, ' the best way I know of, is to go home and think and pray about it.' ' Well,' said Young, ' I shall leave it with brother Joseph, whether it would be best for you to have time or not.' ' Well,' said Joseph, ' I see no harm in her having time to think, if she will not fall into temptation.' ' O, sir,' said I, ' there is no fear of my falling into temptation.' ' Well, but,' said Brigham, ' you must promise me you will never mention it to any one.' ' I do promise it,' said I. ' Well,' said Joseph, ' you must promise me the same.' I promised him the same. ' Upon your honor,' said he, ' you will not tell. ' No, sir, I will lose my life first,' said I. ' Well, that will do,' said he ; ' that is the principle we go upon. I think I can trust you, Martha,' said he. ' Yes,' said I, ' I think you ought.' Joseph said, ' She looks as if she could keep a secret.' I then rose to go, when Joseph commenced to beg of me again. He said it was the best opportunity they might have for months, for the room was often engaged. I, however, had determined what to do. ' Well,' said Young, ' I will see you to-morrow. I am going to preach at the school-house, opposite your house. I have never preached there yet ; you will be there, I suppose.' ' Yes,' said I. — The next day being Sunday, 1 sat down, instead of going to meeting, and wrote the conversation, and gave it to my sister, who was not a little surprised; but she said it would be best to go to meeting in the afternoon.   We went, and Young administered the sacrament.   After it was over, I was passing out, and Young stopped me, saying, ' Wait, Martha, I am coming.'   I said, ' I cannot; my sister is waiting for me.'   He then threw his coat over his shoulders, and followed me out, and whispered, ' Have you made up your mind, Martha?' ' Not exactly, sir,' said I; and we parted.   I shall proceed to a justice of the peace, and make oath to the truth of these statements, and you are at liberty to make what use of them you may think best.

" Yours, respectfully,
" MARTHA H. BROTHERTON.

" Sworn to and subscribed before me, this 13th day of July, A. D. 1842.   " DU BOUFFAY FREMON,
"Justice of the Peace for St. Louis County."

What a tale of infamy ! What a record of black-hearted villany and depravity !   Well does this young lady deserve the praise of her sex and the world, for her courage and virtue in resisting and repulsing with such signal success the foul miscreants who were tempting her to crime by the most insidious and powerful arts.

The *North-Western Gazette and Galena Advertiser* of July 23, 1842, a paper edited by H. H. Haughton, Esq., in speaking on this subject, says, —

" In our columns to-day will be found the affidavit of MARTHA H. BROTHERTON, who, it will be remembered, was called upon to make a public statement of her treatment while among the Mormons.   Her story is told in an artless manner, and goes strongly to corroborate Bennett's statement.   There is something peculiarly infamous in the practice of sending to England to induce simplehearted females to leave their homes, to be exposed to the arts of as shrewd a set of scamps as could well be congregated together."

The *Pittsburgh Morning Chronicle* of July 26, 1842, a paper edited by J. Heron Foster, Esq., and Wm. H. Whitney, Esq., in alluding to the same circumstance, remarks, —

" The last Nauvoo Wasp, a Mormon paper, contains Joe Smith's phrenological chart, in which the organ of ' Amativeness ' is set down as ' very large — giving a controlling influence, and very liable to perversion.'   We think the affidavit of Miss Brotherton, in another column, proves the truth of the science of phrenology conclusively."

I should think as much.   Joe's "Amativeness" is *large,* VERY LARGE, — and perfectly unrestrained.   There are eyes that see that he knows not of, and ears that hear that he understands not, and that *Uncircumcised Philistine* will

find that *Samson* will be upon him in a day when he looks
not for him, and in an hour when he thinks not.

MISS NANCY RIGDON.

Miss Rigdon is the eldest unmarried daughter of Sidney
Rigdon, Esq., and is a beautiful girl, of irreproachable
fame, great moral excellence, and superior intellectual endowments. She is a young lady of many charms and
varied attractions; but she, too, was marked out for the
Cloister. Joe could not suffer a pretty woman to escape
without a *trial.* The *inquisitorial seraglio* must swallow
up most cases, and secure the beautiful birds of gaudy
plumage or fascinating charms. If they fail to be in-
snared by the *Cyprian Saints,* they are liable to be taken
in the net of the *Chambered Sisters of Charity;* if they
pass that fiery ordeal, the poisoned arrows of the *Consecratees of the Cloister* await them : but this girl passed the
Rubicon with heroic firmness. Knowing that I had much
influence with Mr. Rigdon's family, Joe Smith said to me,
one day last summer, when riding together over the lawn,
in Nauvoo, " If you will assist me in procuring Nancy as
one of my spiritual wives, I will give you five hundred
dollars, or the best lot on Main Street." I replied, " I
cannot agree to it. Elder Rigdon is one of my best
friends, and his family are now pure and spotless, and it
would be a great pity to approach the truly virtuous."
" But," said Joe, " the Lord has given her to me to wife.
I have the blessings of Jacob, [meaning thereby a plurality
of wives,] and there is no wickedness in it. It would be
wicked to approach her, unless I had permission of the
Lord ; but, as it is, it is as correct as to have a *legal* wife,
in a *moral* point of view." I replied that it might be so,
but that he must see her himself, as I could not approach
her on a subject of that kind. There I supposed the
matter had ended ; but, at the funeral of Mr. Ephraim
R. Marks, Mrs. Hyde told Miss Rigdon that Joseph desired to see her at the printing-office, where Mrs. Hyde
and Dr. Richards resided, on special business. She said
she would go, and accordingly did ; but Joe was busily engaged at his store. Dr. Willard Richards, however, one
21

of the holy twelve Mormon Apostles, and Spiritual High
Priest, and Pander-General for Lust, whom I had long
suspected as being up to his eyes in the business with Joe,
came in, and said, " Miss Nancy, Joseph cannot be in to-
day; please call again on Thursday." This she agreed to
do; but she communicated the matter to Colonel Francis
M. Higbee, who was addressing her, and asked his advice
as to the second visit. I then came to a knowledge of the
facts, and went immediately to Joe, and said to him,
" Joseph, you are a Master Mason, and Nancy is a Master
Mason's daughter, [so is Mrs. Pratt, the daughter of Mr.
Bates;] so stay your hand, or you will get into trouble —
remember your obligation." Joe replied, " You are my
enemy, and wish to oppose me." I then went to Colonel
Higbee, and told him Joe's designs, and requested him to
go immediately and see Miss Rigdon, and tell her the infernal plot — that Joe would approach her in the name of
the Lord, by special revelation, &c., and to put her on
her guard, but advise her to go and see for herself what
Joe would do. He did so, and she went down. Joe
was there, took her into a private room, (his favorite as-
signation room,) and LOCKED' THE DOOR, undoubtedly
thinking somewhat in the strain of the poet, —

> " NANCY, my love, we ne'er were sages,
>   But, trust me, all that Tully's zeal
> Expressed for Plato's glowing pages,
>   All that, *and more*, for thee I feel '

> " Whate'er the heartless world decree,
>   Howe'er unfeeling prudes condemn,
> NANCY! *I'd rather sin with thee*,
>   Than live and die a *saint* with them.'

Joe then swore her to secrecy, and told her that she
had long been the idol of his affections, and that he had
asked the Lord for her, and that it was his holy will that
he should have her as one of the *Chambered Sisters of
Charity;* but that, if she had any *scruples* on the subject,
he would *consecrate her with the Cloistered Saints,* AND
MARRY HER IMMEDIATELY — *that it would not prevent her
from marrying any other person* — that he had the blessings of Jacob granted to him — and that all was lawful

and right before God. He then attempted to kiss her, and desired her to kiss him. — But we must again quote the bard to express the scene : —

> " I ne'er on that lip for a minute have gazed,
>   But a thousand temptations beset me ;
> And I've thought, as the dear little rubies you raised,
>   How delicious 'twould be — if you'd let me !

> " Then be not so angry for what I have done,
>   Nor say that you've sworn to forget me ;
> They were buds of temptation too pouting to shun,
>   And I thought that — you could not but let me !

> " When your lip with a whisper came close to my cheek,
>   O, think how bewitching it met me !
> And plain as the eye of a Venus could speak,
>   Your eye seemed to say — you *would* let me !

> " Then forgive the transgression, and bid me remain,
>   For, in truth, if I go you'll regret me ;
> Or, O ! — let me try the transgression again,
>   And I'll do all you wish — *will you let me ?* "

But Joe couldn't come it — he had to stand back a little, where he could see better — the Old Fox found sour grapes once more! She told him she would alarm the neighbors if he did not open the door and let her out *immediately.* He did so ; and, as she was much agitated, he requested Mrs. Hyde to explain matters to her ; and, after agreeing to write her a doctrinal letter, left the house. Mrs. Hyde told her that these things looked strange to her *at first,* but that she would become more reconciled on mature reflection. Miss Rigdon replied, " I never shall," left the house, and returned home. In a day or two, Dr. Richards, who is so notorious for *Hyde*-ing in these last days, handed her the following letter from the Prophet Joe, (written by Richards, by Joe's dictation,) and requested her to burn it after reading, to wit : —

" Happiness is the object and design of our existence, and will be the end thereof, if we pursue the path that leads to it ; and this path is virtue, uprightness, faithfulness, holiness, and keeping *all the commandments of God ;* but we cannot keep ALL the commandments without first *knowing* them, and we cannot expect to KNOW ALL, or more than we *now know,* unless we *comply with* or *keep* those we

have ALREADY RECEIVED! That which is *wrong* under one circumstance, may be, and often is, *right* under another. God said,
Thou shalt *not kill;* at another time he said, Thou shalt *utterly destroy.*
This is the principle on which the government of Heaven is conducted, by REVELATION adapted to the circumstances in which
the children of the kingdom are placed. *Whatever God requires is
right,* NO MATTER WHAT IT IS, although we may not see the reason
thereof till long after the events transpire. If we seek first the
kingdom of God, *all good things* will be added. So with *Solomon;*
first he asked *wisdom,* and God gave it him, and with it EVERY DE-
SIRE OF HIS HEART; even things which might be considered
ABOMINABLE to all who understand the order of Heaven ONLY IN
PART, but which, *in reality,* were *right,* because God *gave and sanctioned* by SPECIAL REVELATION. A parent may whip a child, and
justly too, because he stole an apple; whereas, if the child had
asked for the apple, and the parent had given it, the child would
have eaten it with a better appetite; there would have been no
stripes; all the *pleasures* of the apple would have been secured, all
the *misery* of stealing lost. This principle will justly apply to *all*
of God's dealings with his children. Every thing that God gives
us is *lawful and right,* and it is proper that we should ENJOY *his gifts
and blessings,* WHENEVER AND WHEREVER he is disposed to bestow;
but if we should seize upon those same blessings and enjoyments
without *law,* without REVELATION, without COMMANDMENT,
those *blessings and enjoyments* would prove cursings and vexations
in the end, and we should have to lie down in sorrow and wailings
of everlasting regret. But in *obedience* there is joy and peace un-
spotted, unalloyed; and as God has designed our happiness, the
happiness of all his creatures, he never has, he never will, institute
an ordinance or give a commandment to his people that is not calculated in its nature to promote that happiness which he has designed, and which will not end in the greatest amount of good and
glory to those who become the recipients of his law and ordinances.
Blessings offered, but rejected, are no longer *blessings,* but become
like *the talent hid in the earth* BY THE WICKED AND SLOTHFUL
SERVANT; the proffered good returns to the giver; the *blessing* is bestowed on *those who will receive, and occupy;* for unto him that hath
shall be given, and he shall have ABUNDANTLY, but unto him that
hath not, or *will not receive,* shall be taken away that which he hath,
or *might have had.*

"   ' *Be wise to-day; 'tis madness to defer!*
      Next day the fatal precedent may plead;
      Thus on till wisdom is pushed out of time,' into eternity.

"Our Heavenly Father is more *liberal* in his views, and *boundless*
in his mercies and blessings, than we are ready to believe or receive,
and, at the same time, is more terrible to the workers of iniquity,
more awful in the executions of his punishments, and more ready
to detect every *false way* than we are apt to suppose him to be; he
will be *inquired of* by his children; he says, *Ask* and ye SHALL RE-
CEIVE, *seek* and ye SHALL FIND; but, if ye will take that which is

not your own, or which I have not given you, you shall be rewarded according to your deeds; but *no good thing will I withhold from them who walk uprightly before me,* and do my will in *all* things; who will listen to my voice and *to the voice of* MY SERVANT WHOM I HAVE SENT ; for I delight in those who seek diligently to know my precepts, and *abide* by the *laws of my kingdom;* for ALL THINGS SHALL BE MADE KNOWN UNTO THEM IN MINE OWN DUE TIME, *and in the end* THEY SHALL HAVE JOY."

The original, of which the above is a literal copy, in the hand-writing of Dr. Richards, is now in my possession. It was handed me by Colonel F. M. Higbee, in the presence of General George W. Robinson.

Here you have the *doctrine,* in bold relief, as taught in the upper sanctuary of the great Mormon Seraglio. On Tuesday, the 28th day of June last, Joe went to Mr. Rigdon's, accompanied by his High Priest, George Miller, *of Sable Sister notoriety,* for a witness for him that he had successfully confronted Miss Rigdon, and, by boisterous words and violent gestures, tried to deny the attempted seduction and alarm the girl; but, with daring bravery, she met the *Monster of Iniquity,* and told him he was a *" cursed liar;"* that *all* that she had said of him was true to the letter, and dared him to face her to the contrary. Joe then made a full acknowledgment of the whole affair, in presence of the family, and several other persons who were present. The Demoniacal High Priest, George Miller, then groaned in the spirit, and cried aloud, *" You must not harm the Lord's Anointed; the Lord will not suffer his Anointed to fall ! ! ! "* If Joe did not offer another lamb in sacrifice, as a burnt sin-offering, on an altar of twelve stones, I fear the *Destroying Angel* will get him, for even the fiends of his father's kingdom have *demurred* to the spiritual doctrines of his seraglio.

Extract of a letter from General George W. Robinson to General James Arlington Bennet, LL. D., which I take the responsibility of publishing, as it is a material document, and pertinent to the case under consideration.

" NAUVOO, *July* 27, 1842.

" Dear Sir, —

*   *   *   *   *   *   *   *   *   *   *

" Smith and Bennett have always been on VERY friendly terms, and were together a great deal, and I have no doubt

21 *

but that Bennett was Smith's confidant in nearly all things. It appears from General Bennett's story, that Smith stated that the doctrine of a plurality of wives was correct, and that *he* intended to *practise* upon the principles, and that he enjoined secrecy on Bennett, as also on the females to whom he made known his desires and doctrine. Bennett says that he (Smith) succeeded admirably in many instances, and in others, he privately married the females who had any scruples of conscience about con———, &c. &c. General Bennett states that Smith offered him $500, or his choice in town lots on Main Street, if he would succeed in getting him Mr. Rigdon's eldest unmarried daughter for a spiritual wife. *Bennett utterly refused to have any thing to do with the matter, and cautioned Smith against such an attempt.* Smith says, 'You are my enemy,' &c. Bennett says to Smith, ' If you go there, you will get into trouble;' but Smith, it seems, persisted, and was determined to succeed in all his undertakings. Smith sent for Miss Rigdon to come to the house of Mrs. Hyde, who lived in the under rooms of the printing-office. Miss Rigdon inquired of the messenger who came for her what was wanting, and the only reply was, that Smith wanted to see her. General Bennett came to Miss Rigdon, and *cautioned her, and advised her not to place too much reliance on* REVELATION; but did not enlighten her on the object of Smith, but advised her to go down to Mrs. Hyde's, and see Smith. She accordingly went, and Smith took her into *another room*, and LOCKED THE DOOR, and then stated to her that he had had an affection for her for several years, and wished that she should be his; that the Lord was well pleased with this matter, for he had got a REVELATION on the subject, and God had given him all the *blessings of Jacob*, &c. &c., and that there was no sin in it whatever; but, if she had any scruples of conscience about the matter, *he would marry her* PRIVATELY, and enjoined her to secrecy, &c. &c. She repulsed him, and was about to raise the neighbors if he did not unlock the door and let her out; and she left him with disgust, and came home and told her father of the transaction; upon which Smith was sent for. He came. She told the tale in the presence of all the family, and to Smith's face. *I was present.* Smith attempted to deny it *at first*, and *face her down with the lie;* but she told the facts with so much earnestness, and THE FACT OF A LETTER BEING PRESENT, WHICH HE HAD CAUSED TO BE WRITTEN TO HER, ON THE SAME SUBJECT, the day after the attempt made on her virtue, *breathing the same spirit*, and *which he had fondly hoped was* DESTROYED, — all came with such force that he could not withstand the testimony ; and he then and there *acknowledged that every word of Miss Rigdon's testimony was true.* Now for his *excuse*, which he made for such a *base attempt*, and for using the *name of the Lord* in vain, on that occasion. HE WISHED TO ASCERTAIN WHETHER SHE WAS VIRTUOUS OR NOT, AND TOOK THAT COURSE TO LEARN THE FACTS!!! I would say, sir, that *I have reason to believe General Bennett's story in his disclosures of Smith's rascality; although I am not a witness to* ALL *of the facts, yet I am to* SOME. *I liked to have forgotten to state that the affair with Miss Rigdon was the* CAUSE *of Smith's coming out so on Bennett, he having suspicions that* BENNETT HAD CAUTIONED HER ON THE MATTER — *and he was further afraid that Bennett would make disclosures of* OTHER MATTERS.

*   *   *   *   *   *   *   *   *   *   *

"Very respectfully, yours, &c.,

"GEORGE W. ROBINSON."

———

From General Robinson to the Author.

"NAUVOO, *August* 8, 1842.

" GENERAL JOHN C. BENNETT:

" Dear Sir, —

*   *   *   *   *   *   *   *   *   *   *

"I have written General James Arlington Bennet, and given him to understand the difficulties between yourself and Smith. I have not yet responded to the call in the Sangamo Journal, but intend to do so soon. Orson Pratt will respond, in part, this week; and then, when 'The Wasp' shall attack him, he will respond more at length. There has been a d * * * * of a stir here. They have encompassed sea and land to get a counter-statement out of every person you have mentioned in your published letters, or those you call upon to come out and state to the public what they know. They have tried me to their satisfaction, and have given me up as a reprobate. Frank has stated in 'The Wasp' that he knew nothing about the *murder* of a prisoner in Missouri; but he did not say he knew nothing about a prisoner's being *shot*, as was *ordered* by *Smith*, and who *was* shot, but afterwards recovered. Frank will come out soon; he is doing a good work. Mrs. Pratt will come out, and so will Mr. Pratt. Mrs. White will come out. She was at Mr. Rigdon's yesterday. She said she would tell what she did know, but did not tell what it would be. Vinson Knight died last Sunday — sick only two or three days. Mrs. Pratt will criminate Knight: he heard that she was telling on him, and he roared through the streets like a mad bull, and went to Alderman Marks to get a warrant for her. Marks could not make it out then, and before Knight had time to get it, he went whence he will not return. Mr. Rigdon will say something as soon as he is able to write. He has letters from all quarters, making inquiries about your accusations against Smith; he invariably answers them with regard to the case of Nancy as it was, but says he knows nothing of the balance, as he has been sick for some time, and did not know what was going on; but so eager were the *worthies* to get something from him, that they have taken an extract from a letter which he wrote to H. Smith, some time ago, and they have put it in 'The Wasp,' as an answer to your call. Mr. Rigdon says, 'Drowning men catch at straws.' Nancy don't like to be called into the field, to say any thing about her case herself, but says I may mention it, *which I shall most assuredly do.* I have something new to communicate respecting ORDER LODGE, (though I do not expect it is new to *you*.) After they are initiated into the lodge, they have

oil poured on them, and then a mark or hole cut in the breast of
their shirts, which shirts must not be worn any more, but laid up
to keep the Destroying Angel from them and their families, and
they should never die; but Knight's shirt would not save him.   No
one must have charge of their shirts but their wives.

*   *   *   *   *   *   *   *   *   *   *

" Respectfully yours,
" GEORGE W. ROBINSON."

From General Robinson to the Author.

" NAUVOO, September 16, 1842.

" GENERAL BENNETT :
    " Dear Sir, —
        " Your letter of August 26, written from New York,
was received yesterday.   I was truly glad to hear from you once
more.   I am here on business, as you know I now reside at La Harpe.
Joe keeps hid yet; he dare not show himself publicly.   Hyrum
Smith and William Law have gone east PREACHING!! *as they say;*
that is all I know about it.   Some three or four hundred Mormons
have gone out, and are going, to put down the excitement which
you have raised, and to rebut your statements.   They have an extra
'Wasp' *filled* with affidavits to overflowing: SOME OF THE MOST
CURSED LIES IN IT THAT WERE EVER PRINTED OR THOUGHT OF.
They are kept secret from the people here, but are to be used when
away, FOR A LIE IS JUST AS GOOD FOR THEIR USE AS ANY THING ELSE,
SO THAT PEOPLE KNOW NOTHING ABOUT IT TO THE CONTRARY.
Stephen Markham swore that he saw improper conduct between you
and Nancy in the post-office.   The young men in the city came forward, and gave certificates against Markham, stating that they believed Markham wilfully and maliciously lied to injure the character
of Miss Rigdon, and to help Smith out of his dilemma, and that they
could not believe Markham under oath.   You will see that Joe
wants prodigiously to get around the affair with Nancy, and will
try to do it at the expense of her character.   Mr. Rigdon has employed a lawyer (Calvin A. Warren, Esq.) to prosecute Markham
on his affidavit.   Smith sent a letter to be read publicly in the congregation last Sunday, written to General James Arlington Bennet,
of Flatbush, stating to him that he was sorry to inform him that the
Nauvoo post-office was corrupt; and that he was sorry to inform
him that John C. Bennett robbed the post-office, while he was here,
of all the moneys and letters addressed to him; and that since you
went away, it has been robbed regularly by your confederates, (Mr.
Rigdon and myself, I suppose,) but called no names.   Frank Higbee
[Colonel Francis M. Higbee] has gone to Ohio.   He did not intend
to contradict your statements, but he knew of no prisoner *killed;*
yet he did not say that there were no prisoners *ordered to be shot,*
neither did he say that there was no prisoner or prisoners SHOT,
but not *killed.*   Frank is *true blue;* but, I fear, like some others here,
he lacks MORAL COURAGE !!   I am writing another article for the San-

gamo Journal, in obedience to the call, and I intend to give them
' JESSE. Captain John F. Olney has, likewise, written an excellent
article as a response to the call. Nancy stands firm in the cause of
virtue, and opposes Joe to the last. I am going to try to get Mrs.
White to come out with her ' *Budget*.' Can't she tell a tale on Joe,
if she is disposed? You know. *Orson Pratt has been* EXPELLED !!
and *Amasa Lyman* takes his place, as one of the Apostles, in the
Quorum of the Twelve!!! * * *

" In haste,

" Yours, as ever,

" GEORGE W. ROBINSON."

The brave Captain Olney has spoken. Hear him.

From the Sangamo Journal of September 14, 1842.

" MORE OF JOE SMITH'S VILLANIES!

" COMMUNICATION OF J. F. OLNEY, A SECEDING MORMON.

" LA HARPE, Hancock Co., *September* 10, 1842.

" *Editor of the Sangamo Journal :*

" Dear Sir, —

" I wish to make, through the medium of your paper, a public withdrawal from the Church of Latter Day Saints, as I cannot
longer consent to remain a member of said Church while polygamy,
lasciviousness, and adultery, are practised by some of its leaders.
That crimes of the deepest dye are tolerated and practised by them,
cannot be doubted.

" I have heard the circumstances of Smith's attack upon Miss
Rigdon, from the family as well as herself; and knowing her to be
a young lady who sustains a good moral character, and also of undoubted veracity, I must place implicit confidence in her statement,
the foul insinuations of that miserable little insect, '*The Wasp*,' to the
contrary notwithstanding.

" And having a *personal* knowledge of Smith's lying at different
times in the name of the Lord, I cannot for a moment doubt but he
did so in the case above alluded to. Smith is so fearful that his
character (which is poorest where best known) is about to take a
sudden flight to parts unknown, that he has lately, either by himself on the public stand, or by his organ ' The Wasp,' attacked the
character of every person, who, he thinks, will *demur*, and proclaim
against his conduct, or, which is still worse, REMAIN NEUTRAL, who
have been referred to by General Bennett, as witnesses of said
Smith's conduct, and been called upon by the public to state what
they know about the matter, and who have thus far refrained from
taking part with either side. *These are they* who feel the indignation and wrath of the Prophet Smith, and who suffer in the
MORMON community by the foul calumny of these debauchees.

" I know that Miss Rigdon has been greatly mortified by being
obtruded before the public; nevertheless, it was unavoidable on her
part, and if Smith succeeds in extricating himself from the awful
dilemma in which he *has placed himself*, by obtaining her certificate

to the contrary, then I am much mistaken in the character of Miss Rigdon. It is true that Mr. Rigdon has endeavored to allay the excitement upon this subject, and has evaded a direct answer to the public, as far as he could consistently with *truth ;* but that part which *is true* he has left untouched. The fact of Smith's wishing to marry Miss Rigdon as a spiritual wife, of his attack upon her virtue, his teachings about his having the blessings of Jacob, &c. &c., as stated in General Bennett's letters, ARE TRUE; and if I am called upon to prove it, I SHALL DO IT, to the satisfaction of the public, and to the *chagrin and mortification* of Smith and others. The letter published purporting to be from Smith to Miss Rigdon, was not in Smith's hand-writing, but in the hand-writing of Dr. Willard Richards, who officiated not only as *scribe*, but *post boy*, for the Prophet, and who DID say that he wrote the letter as *dictated by Joseph Smith*, and said Joseph Smith *did* say, on a certain occasion, that he did direct said Richards to write a letter to Miss Nancy Rigdon ; and I now say I stand ready to prove these allegations by as respectable WITNESSES as can be produced in Hancock county, and if Smith has no other means by which he can extricate himself from this *complexio argumenti bicornis*, than by endeavoring to blast the characters of the innocent and unoffending, to shield himself from infamy and disgrace, then let him fire his *Tormentum Murale — and be gathered unto his Fathers.*

"GENERAL GEORGE W. ROBINSON. I have been acquainted with this gentleman upwards of ten years. I have only to say, where he is known, and in the community and circle in which he moves, he is far above the reach of that foul 'Wasp,' and is altogether above reproach. I was present when the transaction took place between this gentleman and H. S. Eldridge, who then and there expressed himself perfectly satisfied, and I presume that *feeble effort* would never have been made to injure the reputation of General Robinson, if he had not made public his withdrawal from the Church. Said Robinson was formerly Joseph Smith's Secretary, and was General Church Clerk, and Recorder for the Church ; and I have heard Smith say that Robinson was the bravest man in the Mormon Band, and that he (Robinson) had not a drop of cowardly blood in his veins, and other eulogiums of the same nature. But alas, how fallen ! — how fallen !!

"STEPHEN MARKHAM, who has favored the public with his affidavit,* with the apparent design to help Smith out of his dilemma

---

* *Note by the Editor of the Journal.* — " As our readers are not acquainted with the facts in relation to Markham's affidavit, a few words of explanation seem to be necessary. It is well understood that when any of those ladies who are insulted by Joe, resent his insults, and make an exposure of his baseness, he at once, with his servile tools, attempts to destroy their character. Such was the case in the present instance. Unable to corrupt Miss Rigdon, the miserable man, Markham, was employed to make an affidavit against Miss Rigdon. But so well were the community of Nauvoo satisfied of the unsullied purity of Miss R., and the villany of Markham, that after the publication of Markham's affidavit, the editor of 'The Wasp,' by Joe Smith's directions, was made to say that he (Joe Smith) did not procure for publication the said affidavit of Markham! What a scene of villany is here disclosed! What putrid and corrupt wretches are acting in behalf of Joe Smith to further his infamous designs !

in the extraordinary affair with Miss Rigdon, is a man of little or no reputation, and I could not believe his statement, although made under oath; and Smith, it appears in 'The Wasp' of 3d inst., has already become disgusted with this worthy help-meet, and it certainly is a wonder that others of the same character should not share the same fate, for Smith must know they are an injury to his cause. The Mormon Elders are now scattering in every direction through our country, laden with lies to injure the innocent and oppressed.

" Very respectfully, &c.

" John F. Olney.

" P. S. Please publish the above, and you may hear from me again soon. My family sickness, as also my own, may be sufficient excuse for the long delay to respond to your call.

" J. F. O.

" N. B. Since writing the above, I have received several certificates, and *many others* proffered, to show to the public in what light they may look upon the certificate of Stephen Markham, against the character of Miss Rigdon. You will confer a favor by publishing them to the world, and requesting other periodicals to do the same; for Smith has just sent out about three hundred Elders from Nauvoo, and many others from other places, *heavily laden* with such certificates, to rebut the statements of General Bennett. I have not entertained the least doubt, but that the certificates of Miss Brotherton, Mrs. Schindle, and many others, are true to the very letter, concerning the conduct of Smith and others.

" J. F. O.

" Certificate of Colonel Carlos Gove.

"' Nauvoo, *September* 3, 1842.

"' Having been personally acquainted with Miss Nancy Rigdon, for some time, I take pleasure in saying to the public, that I verily believe Miss Rigdon a lady who sustains a virtuous, chaste, moral, and upright character, and that she has never given reason for any one whereon to rest a *suspicion* to the contrary, — and that the affidavit of Stephen Markham was procured for purposes well known to the public, — and I also believe said Markham to be a liar, disturber of the peace, and what may justly be termed a loafer.

"' Carlos Gove.'

" Certificate of Sidney Rigdon, Esq.

"' Nauvoo, *September* 3, 1842.

"' Personally appeared before me, E. Robinson, a Justice of the Peace, within and for the county of Hancock, and State of Illinois, Sidney Rigdon, who, being duly sworn, deposeth and saith, that he is personally acquainted with Stephen Markham, of this city, and that said Markham is not to be believed; that his word for truth and veracity is not good ; that he could not believe said Markham under oath, and that he did on a certain occasion testify under oath to that which deponent knows to be false, and he verily believes said Markham knew the same to be false while testifying ; and further this deponent saith not.   SIDNEY RIGDON.'

" 'Sworn to, this third day of September, A. D. 1842, before me,
                                " 'E. ROBINSON, *J. P.*'

" *Certificate of General George W. Robinson.*

" 'NAUVOO, *September* 3, 1842.

" 'Having been acquainted with Stephen Markham, of the city of Nauvoo, for many years, I can safely say that his character for truth and veracity is not good, and that I could not believe him under oath ; and that I am personally knowing to his lying, and that his character in general is that of a loafer, disturber of the peace, liar, &c. ; and that he did come into the house of Sidney Rigdon, as stated in his affidavit, and that Dr. Bennett and Miss Rigdon were present, as well as myself, and that Miss Rigdon was then sick, and Dr John C. Bennett was the attending physician ; and I do further state that no such *conversation* or *gestures* as said Markham states, took place or came under my observation ; and I do further believe that said Markham did invent, concoct, and put in circulation, said stories with a malicious design and intent to injure the character of Miss Rigdon, and more particularly for the use of the Elders, who are going out preaching to rebut Dr. Bennett's statements; and further this deponent saith not.   GEORGE W. ROBINSON.'

" 'Sworn to before me, L. R. Chaffin, a Justice of the Peace, within and for the county of Hancock, and State of Illinois, this ninth day of September, 1842.   LEWIS R. CHAFFIN, *J. P.*'

" *Certificate of Colonel Henry Marks.*

" 'Having been acquainted with Miss Nancy Rigdon for nearly six years, I can say that she is a lady of a virtuous, chaste, and upright moral character, and I do not believe she ever gave any occasion for the least suspicion to the contrary ; and I do further believe the certificate of Stephen Markham to be false, and given with a malicious design and intent to injure the character of Miss Rigdon unjustly.   HENRY MARKS.

" 'LA HARPE, Illinois, *September* 10, 1842.' "

AMOURS AND CRIMINAL CONVERSATION CASES.

WIDOW FULLER — NOW MRS. WARREN.

Mrs. Warren is a woman of ordinary intellect, and not particularly attractive in person, though far from being ugly. She is, however, very licentious. In the fall of 1841, *I saw her and Joe, the Prophet,* IN BED TOGETHER.

> " Angels and ministers of grace defend us —
> Be thou a spirit of health or goblin damned,
> Bring with thee airs from heaven, or blasts from hell,
> Be thy intents wicked or charitable,
> Thou comest in such a questionable shape
> That I will speak to thee.
> Save me and hover o'er me with your wings,
> You heavenly guards ! — What would your gracious figure ? "

This was at the time alluded to by Mrs. Schindle, wife of Colonel George Schindle, in her affidavit, procured by that indefatigable officer, Colonel Chauncey L. Higbee.

" STATE OF ILLINOIS, } ss.
    McDonough County, }

" Personally appeared before me, Abram Fulkerson, one of the Justices of the Peace in and for said county, Melissa Schindle, who, being duly sworn according to law, deposeth and saith that in the fall of 1841, she was staying one night with the widow Fuller, who has recently been married to a Mr. Warren, in the city of Nauvoo, and that Joseph Smith came into the room where she was sleeping about ten o'clock at night, and after making a few remarks, came to her bedside, and asked her if he could have the privilege of sleeping with her. She immediately replied, No. He, on the receipt of the above answer, told her that it was the will of the Lord that he should have illicit intercourse with her, and that he never proceeded to do any thing of that kind with any woman, without first having the will of the Lord on the subject; and further he told her that if she would consent to let him have such intercourse with her, she could make his house her home as long as she wished to do so, and that she should never want for any thing it was in his power to assist her to; but she would not consent to it. He then told her that if she would let him sleep with her that night, he would give her five dollars; but she refused all his propositions. He then told her that she must never tell of his propositions to her, for he had ALL influence in that place, and if she told he would ruin her character, and she would be under the necessity of leaving. He then went to an adjoining bed, where the widow Fuller was sleeping, got into bed

22

with her, and lay there until about one o'clock, when he got up, bade them good night, and left them; and further this deponent saith not.

her ˙

" MELISSA ✠ SCHINDLE,

mark.

" Subscribed and sworn to before me, this 2d day of July, 1842.

" A. FULKERSON, <i>J. P.</i>"

———

Joe, did you offer another sacrifice? If not, the Destroying Angel will come. But as you succeeded with Mrs. Fuller that night, as you told me, —

> " A little still she strove, and much repented,
>   And whispering, ' I will ne'er consent,' *consented*," —

that may take off the curse. Joe says, " There are wonderful things in the land of Ham, and terrible things by the Red Sea," but that he has no *desire* to do such things; he only does it to show that *he is a* MAN as well as a *Prophet*, and *to try the faith of the Saints!* He certainly takes a very delightful way to *show himself a man*, and *try the faith of the Saints*. This is certainly several degrees beyond the MILKING OF THE GENTILES! *O tempora! O mores!* When the Pontifical Head of the Mormon Harem fails in one case, he succeeds at least in a triplicate ratio. As the HARLOT'S PARAMOUR, he takes them *Coup-de-Main*. His manipulations and unsophisticated affections are wonderful, —

> " But always without malice; if he warred
>   Or loved, it was with what we call ' the best
>   Intentions,' which form all mankind's *trump card*,
>   To be produced when brought up to the test.
>   The statesman, hero, harlot, lawyer, ward
>   Off each attack, when people are in quest
>   Of their designs, by saying they *meant well;*
>   'Tis pity ' that such meaning should pave hell.' "

If the devil don't get Joe Smith, there is no use in having any devil.

> " Just Heaven! what must be thy look
>   When such a wretch before thee stands,
>   Unblushing, with thy sacred book,
>   Turning the leaves with blood-stained hands,
>   And wresting from its page sublime
>   His creed of lust, and hate, and crime! "

Mrs. Schindle is a woman of ordinary capacity, rather handsome, firm in her integrity, and inflexible in her purposes. The Prophet opened upon this lady the *vial of the wrath of his fornication,* in order to invalidate her testimony; but she held the *antidote,* and has signally triumphed over His Holiness, the *Prophet and Heir Apparent to the* THRONE OF HIS TARTAREAN MAJESTY. Col. Schindle should teach the Monster a lesson not soon to be forgotten, by exhibiting to him the IGNEOUS ———.

" Who would be free, *themselves* must strike the blow !
By their right arm the conquest must be wrought : "—

" A word to the wise is sufficient." The Mormon Mountebank will never cease his folly, brutality, and crime, until he is made to *feel, in propria persona,* the penalty of violated laws. He may *buy up* many whom he has grossly insulted, to perjure themselves for his safety and deliverance, but the public now know how to appreciate Mormon statements and Mormon testimony, — as the evidence of a murderous and prostituted race, the dregs and outcasts of society !

" God quit you in his mercy ! Hear your sentence :
You have conspired against my quiet person,
Joined with an enemy, and FROM HIS COFFERS
RECEIVED THE GOLDEN EARNEST OF MY DEATH ;
Wherein you have sold your chief to slaughter,
His friends and his compeers to servitude.
Touching my person, I seek no revenge ;
But I my nation's safety must so tender,
Whose ruin you have sought, that to her laws
I do deliver you. Go therefore hence,
Poor miserable wretches, to your death,
The taste whereof God of his mercy give
You patience to endure, and true repentance
Of all your dire offences."

WIDOW MILLER.

Mrs. Miller is one of Joe's most notorious Cyprian Saints. She became so by means of the Inquisition, before whom she confessed that she had been seduced by the Prophet, under an assurance that the proceeding was all

correct, and in accordance with the will and express permission of the Lord.   She is a voluptuous woman, of ordinary capacity, black hair and eyes, round features, and
free and lively disposition.

Joe looked upon her, and thought, —

" O Pleasure ! you're indeed a pleasant thing,
Although one must be damned for you, no doubt;
I make a resolution every spring
Of reformation, ere the year run out ;
But, somehow, this my vestal vow takes wing,
Yet still, I trust, it may be kept throughout :
I'm very sorry, very much ashamed,
And mean next winter to be quite reclaimed."

But,

" Alas ! the love of women ! it is known
To be a lovely and a fearful thing;
For all of theirs upon that die is thrown,
And if 'tis lost, life hath no more to bring
To them but mockeries of the past alone,
And their revenge is as the tiger's spring,
Deadly, and quick, and crushing ; yet as real
Torture is theirs ; what they inflict they feel."

I might mention a vast number of similar cases if I had
space in this Exposé, and was not restrained by a desire
to do no injury to Joe's unfortunate victims, who have
already suffered more than death, as aptly described by
the poet, —

" Poison be their drink,
Gall, worse than gall, the daintiest meat they taste;
Their sweetest shade a grove of cypress-trees,
Their sweetest prospects murdering basilisks,
Their softest touch as smart as lizard's stings,
Their music frightful as the serpent's hiss,
And boding screech-owls make the concert full ;
All the foul terrors of dark-seated hell."

But I desist.

In concluding this subject, however, I will semi-state
two or more cases, among the vast number, where Joe
Smith was privately married to his spiritual wives — in the
case of Mrs. A**** S****, by Apostle Brigham Young;
and in that of Miss L***** B*****, by Elder Joseph
Bates Noble.   Then there are the cases of Mrs. B****,
Mrs. D*****, Mrs. S********, Mrs. G*****, Miss B*****,
etc. etc.

" Ah, *Joseph !* with eyes of heavy mind,
I see thy glory, like a shooting star,
Fall to the base earth, from the firmament!
Thy sun sits weeping in the lowly west,
Witnessing storms to come, woe, and unrest;
Thy friends are fled, to wait upon thy foes,
And crossly to thy good all fortune goes."

This thing of sending off the Elders to preach, in order to cloister their wives, sisters, and daughters, is *Latter Day*-ism with a vengeance ! " *There are none so blind as they that* won't *see.*"

" Would curses kill, as doth the mandrake's groan,
I would invent as bitter searching terms,
As curst, as harsh, and horrible to hear,
Delivered strongly through my fixed teeth,
With full as many signs of deadly hate
As lean-faced Envy in her loathsome cave.
My tongue should stumble in mine earnest words,
Mine eyes should sparkle like the beaten flint,
Mine hair be fixed on end like one distract,
Ay, every joint should seem to curse and ban;
And, even now my burdened heart would break,
Should I not curse them

It appears from the mass of evidence in this Exposé, that the Mormon Hierarchy are guilty of infidelity, deism, atheism; lying, deception, blasphemy; debauchery, lasciviousness, bestiality; madness, fraud, plunder; larceny, burglary, robbery, perjury; fornication, adultery, rape, incest; arson, treason, and murder; and they have out-heroded Herod, and out-deviled the devil, slandered God Almighty, Jesus Christ, and the holy angels, and even the devil himself, when they supposed him inimical to their plans and operations; and it is not, therefore, to be wondered at, that they should pour forth, with great fury and without mixture, the vials of their fierce wrath and fiery indignation, through their eastern and western official organs, upon the head of the author of this work; but their liquid Tartarean lava and barbed arrows, dipped in the quintessence of Mormon ribaldry, shall be turned, by the helmet of truth, against themselves — the uncircumcised

22*

Philistines, foul fiends of iniquity, and devoted worshippers of Mammon. *" Cease, vipers ;* YOU BITE A FILE.*"* The GREAT GOD is with me, and will plead my righteous cause against FALSE WITNESSES and *persecuting fiends.*

" Plead my cause, O LORD, with them that strive with me: fight against them that fight against me. Take hold of shield and buckler, and stand up for my help. Draw out also the spear, and stop the way against them that persecute me: say unto my soul, I am thy salvation. Let them be confounded and put to shame that seek after my soul: let them be turned back and brought to confusion that devise my hurt. Let them be as chaff before the wind: and let the angel of the Lord chase them. Let their way be dark and slippery: and let the angel of the Lord persecute them. For without cause have they hid for me their net in a pit which without cause they have digged for my soul. Let destruction come upon him at unawares ; and let his net that he hath hid catch himself: into that very destruction let him fall. And my soul shall be joyful in the LORD : it shall rejoice in his salvation. All my bones shall say, LORD, who is like unto thee, which deliverest the poor from him that is too strong for him, yea, the poor and the needy from him that spoileth him ? FALSE WITNESSES DID RISE UP ; they laid to my charge things that I knew not. They rewarded me evil for good to the spoiling of my soul. But as for me, when they were sick, my clothing was sackcloth : I humbled my soul with fasting, and my prayer returned into mine own bosom. I behaved myself as though he had been my friend or brother : I bowed down heavily, as one that mourneth for his mother. But in mine adversity they rejoiced, and gathered themselves together: yea, the abjects gathered themselves together against me, and I knew it not; they did tear me, and ceased not : with hypocritical mockers in feasts, they gnashed upon me with their teeth. LORD, how long wilt thou look on ? rescue my soul from their destructions, my darling from the lions. I will give thee thanks in the great congregation : I will praise thee among much people. Let not them that are mine enemies wrongfully rejoice over me : neither let them wink with the eye that hate me without a cause. For they speak not peace : but they devise deceitful matters against them that are quiet in the land. Yea, they opened their mouth wide against me, and said, Aha, aha ! our eye hath seen it. This thou hast seen, O LORD : keep not silence. O LORD, be not far from me. Stir up thyself, and awake to my judgment, even unto my cause, my God, and my LORD. Judge me, O LORD my God, according to thy righteousness ; and let them not rejoice over me Let them not say in their hearts, Ah, so would we have it : let them not say, We have swallowed him up. Let them be ashamed and brought to confusion together that rejoice at my hurt: let them be clothed with shame and dishonor that magnify themselves against me. Let them shout for joy, and be glad, that favor my righteous cause : yea, let them say continually, Let the LORD be magnified, which hath pleasure in the prosperity of his servant. And my tongue shall speak of thy righteousness and of thy praise all the day long." — *Ps.* xxxv.

Though the Prophet *buys off*, WITH A HEAVY PRICE, the *Saints* and *Jacks* to swear against me, though he buys up *all* with promises of *gold and glory*, I'll stand alone with shield and rapier, and fight the fearful odds until I'm vanquished, or crowned a victor in the battle-field; but, looking through the vista of time, I see a mighty host, myriads, coming to the rescue; and still they come; the air darkens with the gathering throng; they come " to the help of the Lord, to the help of the Lord against the mighty." The noble and brave General George W. Robinson has issued his bull excommunicating the Mormon Church from his fellowship. His voice is heard in the west like the thunderings of Sinai! The proffered gold could not tempt him from the path of truth, and he now cries, "GOD AND LIBERTY!!" All who have the *moral courage* will follow in the train, until the MORMON BABEL shall become a *solitary*, and its BAAL a *wandering vagabond!* Those who cannot be bought with *gold and glory* will now abjure the *Dauphin Prince of hell*, (the Holy Joe,) and celebrate his HEGIRA as an epoch of returning sanity!

Hear the impious Prophet speak.

From the Boston Daily Mail of October 7, 1842.

"A VOICE FROM JOE SMITH'S HIDING-PLACE.

" The following letter from Joe Smith, published in the Times and Seasons, the Mormon paper at Nauvoo, shows that the whereabouts of the miserable Impostor is still unknown to the world. It is rather inglorious for a man who claims the power of working miracles, thus to crawl into his hole with fear. But his letter is a rich one, for all that. Joe's 'spiritual wives' must be in great tribulation.

" ' To all the Saints in Nauvoo:

"' *September* 1, 1842.

" ' Forasmuch as the Lord has revealed unto me that my enemies, both of Missouri and this State, were again on the pursuit of me; and inasmuch as they pursue me without cause, and have not the least shadow or coloring of justice or right on their side, in the getting up of their prosecutions against me; and inasmuch as their pretensions are all founded in falsehood, of the blackest dye, I have thought it expedient, and wisdom in me, to leave the place for a short season, for my own safety and the safety of this people. I would say to all those with whom I have business, that I have left my affairs with agents and clerks, who will transact all business in a prompt and proper manner; and will see that all my debts are cancelled in due time, by turning out property, or otherwise as the case may require, or as the circumstances may admit of. When I learn that the storm is fully blown over, then I will return to you again.

" ' And as for the perils which I am called to pass through, they seem but a small thing to me, as the envy and wrath of man have been my common lot all the days of my life ; and for what cause, it seems mysterious, unless I was ordained from before the foundation of the world, for some good end, or bad, as you may choose to call it.   Judge ye for yourselves.   God knoweth all these things, whether it be good or bad.   But nevertheless, deep water is what I am wont to swim in ; it all has become a second nature to me.   And I feel, like Paul, to glory in tribulation, for to this day has the God of my fathers delivered me out of them all, and will deliver me henceforth ; for behold, and lo, I shall triumph over all my enemies, for the Lord God hath spoken it.

" ' Let all the Saints rejoice, therefore, and be exceeding glad, for Israel's God is their God ; and he will mete out a just recompense of reward upon the heads of all your oppressors.

" ' And again, verily thus saith the Lord, Let the work of my Temple, and all the works which I have appointed unto you, be continued on, and not cease ; and let your diligence, and your perseverance, and patience, and your works be redoubled ; and you shall in no wise lose your reward, saith the Lord of Hosts.   And if they persecute, so persecuted they the Prophets, and righteous men that were before you.   For all this there is a reward in heaven.

" ' And again I give unto you a word in relation to the baptism for your dead.   Verily, thus saith the Lord unto you concerning your dead, When any of you are baptized for your dead, let there be a Recorder ; and let him be eye-witness of your baptisms ; let him hear with his ears, that he may testify of a truth, saith the Lord ; that in all your recordings, it may be recorded in heaven ; that whatsoever you bind on earth, may be bound in heaven ; whatsoever you loose on earth, may be loosed in heaven ; for I am about to restore many things to the earth, pertaining to the priesthood, saith the Lord of Hosts.

" ' And again, Let all the records be had in order, that they may be put in the archives of my Holy Temple, to be held in remembrance from generation to generation, saith the Lord of Hosts.

" ' I will say to all the Saints, that I desired, with exceeding great desire, to have addressed them from the stand, on the subject of baptism for the dead, on the following Sabbath.   But inasmuch as it is out of my power to do so, I will write the word of the Lord from time to time, on that subject, and send it you by mail, as well as many other things.

" ' I now close my letter for the present, for the want of more time , for the enemy is on the alert, and as the Savior said, The prince of this world cometh, but he hath nothing in me.

" ' Behold my prayer to God is, that you all may be saved.   And I subscribe myself your servant in the Lord, Prophet and Seer of the Church of Jesus Christ of Latter Day Saints.

" ' JOSEPH SMITH.' "

From Colonel F. M. Higbee to the Author.

"NAUVOO, *August* 16, 1842.

" GENERAL BENNETT :

" Sir, —

"The Mormon confusion is great; Joe Smith has run away, and the sheriffs are still here watching for him. Every one is struck with consternation and dismay; trouble has seized upon every breast. Joe's strength is delivered into captivity, and his glory into the hands of his enemies; and the days of his glory are as if they had never been. Some say Joe has gone to Texas, some to Canada, some to Santa Fe, and some say to heaven; others think he is really translated ; and, in fact, I am led to conclude that he is translated from earth to h***. His place is no more on the banks of the pleasant Mississippi ; he will have to seek safety in some crevice of the Hæmus Mountains, or enjoy the comfortable pursuits of a Merrill, a Rathbun, or an Edwards ; which, if Missouri should fail to furnish him, undoubtedly Illinois will not.

" You had better hasten your march here, for all are looking to you — as Israel did to Joshua the son of Nun — for a great and energetic movement.

" Robinson has come out, as strong as thunder, in the Sangamo Journal, and is continuing it. I have all sorts of times, once in a while, with the Saints, I assure you. Rigdon and Pratt are the same. Mrs. Pratt is going to give her certificate ; and *if Mrs. White can get away*, she will give a full history of the concern. Won't it be great? Statements have been FORCED from several ; you have seen *mine ;* but, *great God !* that's all from this child ! Go it strong, Doc., now or never. I have just been to see Mrs. White. Great Scotland! what a tale she can tell ! You know, Doc. O ! how the '*worthies* ' curse you ! They curse the day of your birth, and more than that.

" The Governor will order a force here to guard the *diggings* for a while. Joe and Porter were taken by the authority of the executive writ, and released on a Habeas Corpus. The inglorious ordinance, passed for the occasion, is published in ' The Wasp ' of the 13th of August. Joe is in the Islands, and Hyrum has to act as Mayor, as you will see.

" Miss Eliza Rigdon (God save her soul, for she is a good girl) [yes, one of the best that this world ever saw] is at the point of death ; yes, I think she is dying. [By more recent letters I learn she has since recovered ; and may that pious Christian still continue to be a bright ornament to her kind father's house.]

" You have friends here truer than death; just as they should be. * * *

" Your friend and well-wisher,
under all circumstances, and at all times,

" FRANCIS M. HIGBEE.'

From Colonel C. L. Higbee to the Author.

"NAUVOO, *August* 14, 1842.

" GENERAL BENNETT :

"Dear Sir, —

*   *   *   *   *   *   *   *   *   *

"Doctor Weld favored me with the perusal of your letter of July 19; and why you have not written me is entirely a mystery. I cannot believe, for a moment, that you have forgotten a person who has stood by you as I have done, both in prosperity and exile; for I assure you, Doctor, that 1 shall never forsake or forget *you*, nor the scenes through which we have passed together. There is quite a *rip up* in our city this week. A demand has been made by Governor Reynolds, of Missouri, on the affidavit of Ex-Governor Boggs, for O. P. Rockwell and Joseph Smith; on which demand Governor Carlin, last Saturday, issued his writ. On Monday, the officers (Thomas C. King and James M. Pitman) [two excellent ministerial officers] arrived in this city. Rockwell and Joe surrendered themselves, and immediately applied to the Municipal Court for a writ of Habeas Corpus. The writ was issued forthwith, and immediately served by the Marshal on King and Pitman, who refused to give up the prisoners, by disputing the legality of the writ, as any men who were determined to do their duty would do. They agreed to settle the matter, however, by Joe's making some masonic pledges to the officers to deliver himself and Rockwell up at any time when called for. The officers returned to Quincy to take advice as to the legality of the writ of Habeas Corpus; but before they had time to return, the prisoners *sloped*. Pitman is here watching, and King has returned to Warsaw to publish them. Hyrum Smith stated to-day, in the stand, that Rockwell and Joe had gone to Washington city, and were going from thence to England; but it is my opinion that they are here in the neighborhood. There is a great deal of confusion here amongst the Saints. Some are for going to the Oregon Territory, and some one place and some another. The Prophet prophesied on the stand, about four weeks since, that ' Bennett never would have influence enough to get a demand made for him;' but, alas! he has, at this late hour, realized his mistake. Eliza Rigdon is said to be dying. [She is one of the most devoutly pious girls in the world, and I am truly happy to learn, by more recent letters, that she is fast recovering.]

"Your friends here are firm, and desire to see you very much. Your presence is now required in the west, and I advise you to come immediately on. Your presence would give fresh courage to your friends, and a zest to the whole proceedings that could not be otherwise inspired. ' Napoleon should be in the field.'

"I have scrupulously attended to the business, which you confided to my care. All the friends desire to be respectfully remembered to you.   "Your friend,

"CHAUNCEY L. HIGBEE."

I shall be in INDEPENDENCE, Jackson county, Missouri, *as soon as possible,* to put the ball in motion; (to which

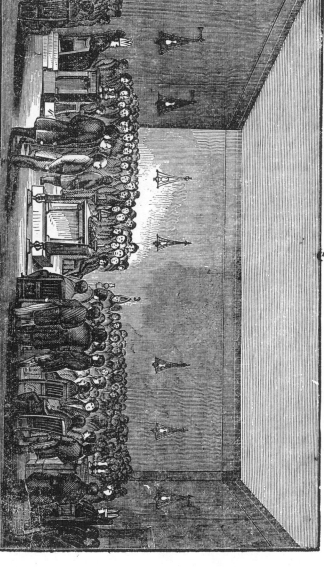

DAUGHTER OF ZION.

1. Joe Smith.   2. Hyrum Smith.   3. George Miller.   4. Willard Richards.   5. Robert D. Foster.

place my friends will hereafter direct their communications to me;) and if the war must be carried to the knife, and *the knife to the hilt*, the sons of thunder will drive it through. The eyes of a Boggs will never slumber nor sleep, *until the rod of Aaron divides the waters*, and the supremacy of the Constitution and the laws is acknowledged in the land, and violence and misrule hide their hydra head; and I shall hold the *rapier of justice* in my right hand, and my left arm shall bear the *shield of truth*, until I bruise the Serpent's head.

DAUGHTER OF ZION.

This is a secret society of many years' standing, and was first formed in Missouri : the great majority of the members are among the "*huge paws*" of the Mormons, and they compose as pretty a set of ruffians as can be found in Christendom or elsewhere. The society was instituted for the purpose of driving out from the Holy Land, *their earthly paradise*, in Missouri, all apostates or dissenters from the Mormon faith. It was, therefore, at first called the "*Big Fan*," inasmuch as it fanned out the chaff from the wheat. This name, however, did not seem sufficiently dignified for so holy a body, and was soon set aside for a scriptural appellation; they were called the "Brother of Gideon;" but the *rationale* of this title I have never been able to discover. They are usually styled *Danites*, and sometimes *Daughter of Zion*, for the origin of which names, see Micah iv. 13; read the whole chapter; also Judges xvii. and xviii.

The following is the constitution of this society : —

"Whereas, in all bodies laws are necessary for the permanency, safety, and well-being of society, we, the members of the society of the Daughter of Zion, do agree to regulate ourselves under such laws as, in righteousness, shall be deemed necessary for the preservation of our holy religion, and of our most sacred rights, and of the rights of our wives and children. But to be explicit on the subject, it is especially our object to support and defend the rights conferred on us by our venerable sires, who purchased them with the pledges

23

of their lives, their fortunes, and their sacred honors. And now, to prove ourselves worthy of the liberty conferred on us by them, in the providence of God, we do agree to be governed by such laws as shall perpetuate these high privileges, of which we know ourselves to be the rightful possessors, and of which privileges wicked and designing men have tried to deprive us, by all manner of evil, and that purely in consequence of the tenacity we have manifested in the discharge of our duty towards our God, who had given us those rights and privileges, and a right in common with others, to dwell on this land. But we, not having the privileges of others allowed unto us, have determined, like unto our fathers, to resist tyranny, whether it be in kings or in the people. It is all alike unto us. Our rights we must have, and our rights we shall have, in the name of Israel's God.

" Art. 1. All power belongs originally and legitimately to the people, and they have a right to dispose of it as they shall deem fit; but, as it is inconvenient and impossible to convene the people in all cases, the legislative powers have been given by them, from time to time, into the hands of a representation composed of delegates from the people themselves. This is and has been the law, both in civil and religious bodies, and is the true principle.

" Art. 2. The executive power shall be vested in the *President of the whole Church,* and *his Councillors.*

" Art. 3. The legislative powers shall reside in the *President* and *his Councillors* together, and with the *Generals* and *Colonels* of the society. By them all laws shall be made regulating the society.

" Art. 4. All offices shall be during life and good behavior, or to be regulated by the law of God.

" Art. 5. The society reserves the power of electing its own officers, with the exception of the Aids and Clerks which the officers may need in their various stations; the nomination to go from the Presidency to his second, and from the second to the third in rank, and so down through all the various grades. Each branch or department retains the power of electing its own particular officers.

" Art. 6. Punishment shall be administered to the guilty in accordance to the offence; and no member shall be punished without law, or by any others than those appointed by law for that purpose. The *legislature* shall have power to make laws *regulating punishments,* as, *in their judgments,* shall be wisdom and righteousness.

" Art. 7. There shall be a Secretary, whose business it shall be to keep all the legislative records of the society; also to keep a register of the names of every member of the society; also the rank of the officers. He shall also communicate the laws to the Generals, as directed by laws made for the regulation of such business by the legislature.

" Art. 8. All officers shall be subject to the commands of the Captain-General, given through the Secretary of War; and so all officers shall be subject to their superiors in rank, according to laws made for that purpose."

The oath by which the Danites were bound in Missouri, is as follows : —

"In the name of Jesus Christ, the Son of God, I do solemnly obligate myself ever to conceal, and never to reveal, the secret purposes of this society, called the Daughter of Zion. Should I ever do the same, I hold my life as the forfeiture."

This obligation was, however, subsequently altered, in a secret council of the Inquisition at Nauvoo, so as to read, —

"In the name of Jesus Christ, the Son of God, I do solemnly obligate myself ever to regard the Prophet, and First Presidency of the Church of Jesus Christ of Latter Day Saints, as the Supreme Head of the Church on Earth, and to obey them in all things the same as the Supreme God; that I will stand by my brethren in danger or difficulty, and will uphold the Presidency, right or wrong : and that I will ever conceal, and never reveal, the secret purposes of this society, called the Daughter of Zion. Should I ever do the same, I hold my life as the forfeiture, in a caldron of boiling oil."

Those who belonged to the society when under its old organization, but refused to take the new oath, were, together with those whose fidelity was doubtful, absolved from the Missouri obligation. But to the faithful of the band, and to about twelve hundred new members, the Nauvoo oath was administered by Joe Smith in person. While the candidate was yet kneeling before the altar, after having taken the oath, the Holy Prophet, assisted by Hyrum Smith, the Patriarch of the Church, and George Miller, the President of the High Priest's Quorum, approached, and said, —

"In the name of Jesus Christ, the Son of God, and by the authority of the Holy Priesthood, we, the First President, Patriarch, and High Priest, of the Church of Jesus Christ of Latter Day Saints, representing the First, Second, and Third Gods in Heaven, — the Father, the Son, and the Holy Ghost, — do now anoint you with holy, consecrated oil, and by the imposition of our hands, do ordain, consecrate, and set you apart, for the holy calling, whereunto you are called ; that you may consecrate the riches of the Gentiles to the House of Israel, bring swift destruction upon apostate sinners, and execute the decrees of Heaven, without fear of what man can do unto you. So mote it be. Amen."

It will be perceived from the above, that the Danites are solemnly bound, under penalty of forfeiting their lives in a horrid manner, to obey and execute the decrees of the Mormon leaders, whether the latter are right or wrong! No matter if they are commanded to commit treason, murder, arson, burglary, perjury, or any crime whatever; do it they must, or violate their oath, and forfeit, in consequence, their life. And, in fact, all these crimes *have* been committed by them, in many instances, no doubt, under the impression that they were doing God service! So grossly has the Prophet deluded his miserable followers!

That they make no scruple whatever to commit perjury, when deemed requisite for the welfare of their Church, or of its priests and chief men, is abundantly proved, not only by the atrocious falsehoods they have propagated about me, — falsehoods so gross as to be almost unworthy of notice or refutation, — but by the testimony given before Judge King, of Missouri, and published in 1841, by order of the General Assembly of that State; which testimony affords ample proof, that the Mormons of the Danite Order had no hesitation in committing the most barefaced perjuries, when they could thereby advance the interests of their rulers. This is particularly shown in the testimony of Colonel George M. Hinkle, T. C. Burch, Esq., Fanny Brewer, and others, which I have copied into this work.

Now, what material difference is there between this Joseph Smith and the leader of a band of highway robbers, or the captain of a crew of pirates? Does not the Mormon deserve more utter condemnation than either the bandit or the buccaneer, inasmuch as his wickedness is upon a more extensive scale, and is perpetrated in the name of religion and of the Most High God, thus blaspheming and desecrating the holiest names and objects to the vilest and most atrocious purposes?

The number of Danites is now about two thousand, or two thousand five hundred, and, as I before observed, they are drawn from the " *huge paws* " of the Mormon Church.

DESTROYING ANGEL.

From the *élite* of the Danites, or Daughter of Zion, twelve men are selected, who are called *Destructives*, or *Destroying Angel*, and sometimes *Flying Angel*. Their

DESTROYING ANGEL.

"Do as he hath said, and fall upon him, and bury him." — 1 Kings, ii. 31.

1. Joe Smith.   2. D. B. Huntington.   3. R. D. Foster.   4. Willard Richards.

duty is to act as spies, and watch the movements of all persons, both Saints and Gentiles, and to report all that they hear and observe to the First Presidency, as circumstances may require.

This band was at first called only "Destructives," or "Destructionists," and their leader or captain the "Destroying Angel;" but in time, the latter appellation was given to the whole body. They are bound by the following oath : —

" In the name of Jesus Christ, the Son of God, I do covenant and agree to support the First Presidency of the Church of Jesus Christ of Latter Day Saints, in all things, right or wrong ; I will faithfully guard them, and report to them the acts of all men, as far as in my power lies ; I will assist in executing all the decrees of the First President, Patriarch or President of the Twelve ; and that I will cause all who speak evil of the Presidency, or Heads of the Church, to die the death of dissenters and apostates, unless they speedily confess and repent ; for pestilence, persecution, and death, shall follow the enemies of Zion.   I will be a swift herald of salvation, and messenger of peace to the Saints, and I will never make known the secret purposes of this society, called the DESTROYING ANGEL, my life being the forfeiture in a fire of burning tar and brimstone.   So help me God, and keep me steadfast."

The members of this band, when engaged in the execution of any important decree, are clothed in female apparel, wearing a snow-white robe and a scarlet girdle.   This is the band alluded to by Judge King in his communication to the Executive of Missouri, and by Thomas B. Marsh and others.   They are bound to consecrate the riches of the Gentiles to the house of Israel, which, in plain English, means, to rob and plunder the people who are not Mormons, and appropriate the spoils to the use of the Church. They also pledge themselves to poison the wells and the food and drink of dissenters, apostates, and all enemies of Zion, and to murder those who refuse to tithe or contribute the tenth part of their property to the use of the Church, and, in short, to destroy by fire and sword all the enemies of Mormonism, and to assist in all things in building up the kingdom spoken of by the prophet Daniel.

These Destructives, in their capacities of spies and informers, are of great service to the Prophet, and assist materially in extending and confirming his influence over the Mormons.   They generally call upon him every morning, and make a detailed report of the sayings and doings of various persons in Nauvoo, or elsewhere, as the Prophet may direct them.   These reports are listened to with great attention by Holy Joe, and carefully treasured up for future use.   When he is desirous of making an impression on any individual of his followers, he turns to the particulars of that individual's conduct and conversation, communicated by the spies, calls upon him at a convenient opportunity, and gravely informs him that he has received from the Lord a revelation respecting him.   The person thus addressed is, of course, not a little startled by this extraordinary announcement, and earnestly requests to be informed of the nature of the facts so graciously communicated by the Lord.   Joe then, with all due solemnity, proceeds to state that the Angel of the Lord had come down and told him, that on such and such a day, brother Johnson, or Thompson, or whatever the name may be, had, at such or such a place, done and said so and so.   Brother Johnson of course opens his eyes very wide, at this revelation, and is more firmly than ever convinced that Smith is the Prophet of the Lord!   " For how else," reasons he, " could he know so particularly what I have been doing, when I am quite sure he was not within a mile of me ?" Thus deluded, brother Johnson takes good care to communicate his extraordinary case to his cronies, and the result is a general persuasion among the mass of the Mormons, that Joe Smith is not far from omniscient, and that it is safest to be very careful of their sayings and doings, for there is no telling whether or not the Angel of the Lord is watching them, in order to communicate to the Prophet their proceedings.

ORDER LODGE.

This is a secret lodge or society, established by Joe Smith, in consequence of a special revelation from Heaven, which he pretended to have received respecting it.   It was intended to enable him more effectually to execute his clandestine purposes.   None but the very *élite* of the Mor-

ORDER LODGE.

1. Joe Smith.　　2. Hyrum Smith.　　3. George Miller.　　4. Willard Richards.

mons are admitted into this lodge, as the mysteries of the Holy Priesthood are there, more fully than elsewhere, explained to the members, who are initiated only after they have bound themselves, by a most solemn oath, to profound and inviolate secrecy.

"Order is *Heaven's* first law; and, that confessed,
Some are, and must be, greater than the rest."

The ceremonies of initiation are in perfect keeping with the general absurdity of the new dispensation, and with the Holy Joe's mission for the "restoration of the ancient order of things."

The lodge-room is carefully prepared and consecrated; and from twelve to twenty-four sprigs of cassia, olive branches, cedar boughs, or other evergreens, are tastefully arranged about it. These are intended to represent the eternal life and unmingled bliss, which, in the celestial kingdom, will be enjoyed by all who continue in full fellowship with "Order Lodge."

The aspiring candidate for "Holy Orders" obtains admission into this sanctified body in the following manner: He is stripped naked, and blindfolded; he is then brought into the lodge-room, and in that state is conducted round, so that all the members of the lodge may be satisfied, by personal inspection, that he is a fit subject for their august association, and that he possesses the qualifications required in Deuteronomy, twenty-third chapter and first verse. While the candidate is passing round the room, in this ridiculous and degrading condition, the most excellent Grand Master is repeating, "I will bring the blind by a way that they knew not; I will lead them in paths that they have not known; I will make darkness light before them, and crooked things straight. These things will I do unto them, and not forsake them."

When the candidate has passed satisfactorily this queer examination, he is brought to the altar, before which he is made to kneel. While in this posture, the following oath or obligation is solemnly administered to him, by the Grand Master or his representative: —

" In the name of Jesus Christ, the Son of God, I now promise and swear, truly, faithfully, and without reserve, that I will serve the

Lord with a perfect heart and a willing mind, dedicating myself, wholly and unreservedly, in my person and effects, to the upbuilding of his kingdom on earth, according to his revealed will. I furthermore promise and swear that I will regard the First President of the Church of Jesus Christ of Latter Day Saints, as the supreme head of the Church on earth, and obey him the same as the Supreme God, in all written revelations, given under the solemnities of a 'Thus saith the Lord,' and that I will always uphold the Presidency, right or wrong. I furthermore promise and swear *that I will never touch a daughter of Adam,* UNLESS SHE IS GIVEN ME OF THE LORD. I furthermore promise and swear that no Gentile shall ever be admitted to the secrets of this holy institution, or participate in its blessings. I furthermore promise and swear that I will assist the *Daughter of Zion* in the utter destruction of apostates, and that I will assist in setting up the Kingdom of Daniel in these last days, by the power of the Highest and the sword of his might. I furthermore promise and swear that I will never communicate the secrets of this degree to any person in the known world, except it be to a true and lawful brother, binding myself under no less a penalty than that of having melted lead poured into my ear. So help me God, and keep me faithful."

Joe pretends that God has revealed to him the *real Master's word* which is here given to the candidate.

This obligation is varied in some cases, to suit the convenience or caprice of the Prophet; but the foregoing is the standard and usual form. It will be seen that it is both blasphemous and treasonable, in the highest degree. The candidate swears to obey the First President of the Mormon Hierarchy, as the "*Supreme God, in all written revelations;*" that is, if Joe Smith should have a "revelation," commanding him to massacre the "Gentile" citizens of Illinois, for example, or to overturn the Constitution of the United States, the members of this precious "Order Lodge" are bound and pledged, under the most heavy penalties, to assist him in so doing! If the contemptible mummery of the affair did not render it a ridiculous farce, it would merit, for its atrocity, the deepest execration of all good men and patriotic citizens. Yet, silly as are its ceremonies, this Order Lodge is not without a very strong pernicious influence. Many of the members consider themselves solemnly bound, in the presence and by the sanction of the Most High God, communicated to them by direct inspiration through his Prophet and representative, Holy Joe Smith, to execute, to the letter, whatever that inspired genius may take it into his head to command, whether it be treason, murder, arson, or robbery.

When the oath has been administered, the candidate is clothed with the robe of the order, and the precious ointment, or consecrated oil, poured upon his head, till it runs down upon his beard and the skirts of his garment. Then the nature, authority, and privileges, of the Holy Priesthood are explained to the candidate, together with the ultimate fate of all Gentiles, (as they term those who are not Mormons,) sectarian priests, apostates, and dissenters.

One of the most curious and ludicrous ceremonies, connected with the initiation into Order Lodge, is this: After the precious ointment has been poured upon the candidate, a hole is cut in the bosom of his shirt. (See plate.) This shirt must never, on any account, be worn again, but must be sacredly preserved, to keep the Destroying Angel from them and their families. These shirts are committed to the care of the wives of the members, and none but them must touch them, or know of their existence. They believe that these shirts will preserve them from death, and secure to them an earthly immortality; but Bishop Vinson Knight, one of the members, has recently died, so that it is evident the hole in his shirt could not save him. Joe will probably, however, say that a spiritual immortality only was promised.

The members of this lodge, in obedience to the above obligation, have no scruple whatever in perjuring themselves, when required to do so by the Prophet, or when it will conduce to the interest or advancement of the Holy Mormon Church; consequently they are the readiest and most dangerous tools of the Impostor.

The Mormon system of theology recognizes three Gods; the first of which is God the Father; the second is God the Son, or Jesus Christ; the third is God the Holy Ghost. In Order Lodge these are all represented; God the Father, by Joe Smith; God the Son, or Jesus Christ, by Hyrum Smith; and God the Holy Ghost, by George Miller. By these precious divinities the candidate is initiated into the higher mysteries of the Mormon Priesthood, of which all that need here be said is, that they fit him admirably for his holy work.

24

Order Lodge is of comparatively recent institution, and embraces a considerable number of members.

---◆---

MILKING THE GENTILES.

Milking the Gentiles is a kind of vernacular term of the Mormons, and signifies the obtaining of money or property from those who are not members of the Mormon Church, (or are not attached to the Mormon confederation, or government, as Jack Mormons,) by humbuggery, cajoling, and false pretences, the levying of contributions, etc. etc. Thus, when Joe is in want of funds for the Temple, Nauvoo House, or *private use*, he commissions some of his satellites of the illuminati, arms them with the parapegm of the Church, instructs them in the various ramifications of the fiscality, polity, and policy, of the confederation, and sends them out, all panoplied with Mormon glory, to *milk the Gentiles!* Money is wanted to send out missionaries to *convert the heathen* in New England, Europe, or the Holy Land of Palestine ; the Gentiles must be milked, and the needful procured ! Funds are required to sustain the Imperial Mormon Pontiff, and his Cabinet, in princely magnificence and Oriental splendor ; to keep up the excellence and surpassing beauty of the harem and the upper sanctuary; and to liquidate the pressing claims on the government of the Empire ; — to milk the Gentiles is the first expedient and the last resort, the Alpha and the Omega of Mormon financiering. Sometimes they get into tall clover, and the milk flows profusely ; at others, the fare is but middling, — Pharaoh's lean kine eat up the fatlings of the flock. Many of the poor Gentiles, however, are soaped over, and swallowed so quick that salt can't save them. They go to Nauvoo, Babylon and Mother of Harlots, but the GOLDEN CALF is not to be found there ! Joseph has fled, Orin has gone, and Willard, and Robert, and Hosea, and Dimick, and Hyrum, have hung their harps upon the willows, and refused to dance before the Lord on the holy mount ! *Sic transit gloria mundi !* For a more perfect, graphic, and interesting account of the *milking of the Gentiles*, I beg leave to refer the reader to the sermon on the *milking of the goats*, from the text, " *And thou shalt have goats' milk enough for thy food, for the food of thy household, and for the maintenance of thy maidens*," (Prov. xxvii. 27,) by BISHOP ALEXANDER CAMPBELL, of Virginia. He does it up in that inimitable style, *à la Campbell*, that rivets the attention upon any thing falling from the lips or pen of that great man. Now, if the Gentiles desire to be milked, the Mormon Elders are the chaps that can do it, until they get goats' milk a plenty. " He that hath ears to hear, let him hear."

ASSASSINATION AND ATTEMPTED ASSASSINATIONS.

MURDER OF MR. JOHN STEPHENSON.

From the Sangamo Journal of July 15, 1842.

"THE DANITES — FOUL MURDER!

" We copy the following from the Kaskaskia Republican. It has long been understood that committees were sent about the country from the establishment at Nauvoo, requiring the members of Joe Smith's Church to pay ' tithes and offerings ' for the purpose of building the Temple or Fortification at that place. The commands of Joe in this particular are, we suppose, to be implicitly obeyed. In the case before us, the individual who declined the order of Joe's servants, paid the penalty of the refusal. His house was robbed, and himself shot dead in his field !

" *From the Kaskaskia Republican.*

" ' $200 REWARD.

" ' *Murder most horrible!* — One of the most horrid and atrocious murders was committed on the person of my brother, John Stephenson, in Jackson county, Illinois, on the 2d day of June, 1842, perhaps, in the whole catalogue or annals of crime. All that is known of the circumstances attending the perpetration of the dark and hellish deed is, that my brother was ploughing in the field, his wife from home, and, no person being at the house, the foul fiend entered the house, broke open his trunk in search of money, as is supposed ; but as my brother had, but four or five days previously, been to the land-office and purchased land, there were but three dollars in the trunk. The wretch then took the gun of the deceased, and, from every appearance, concealed himself near the fence, and awaited the approach of the deceased, and as he was turning round, shot him down with his own gun.

" ' The deceased was as harmless and quiet a man as ever lived ; it is not known or believed that he had an enemy upon the earth.

" ' Myself and deceased brother joined the *Mormons* some two years since. On the 27th day of May, 1842, but six days before my brother was murdered, Brown and Abbott, two Mormons, called upon us for contributions of property and money to aid in building the Temple at *Nauvoo ;* and, upon our refusal to give up to them the amount demanded, the said two Mormons, by way of threatening us, said, *we might think ourselves well off if we had our property long.* They, the said Mormons, further told us, that they had stock to drive, and had but one dollar and twenty-five cents, and money they must have, let it come from where it would ; and they did not care where it came from ; they also said if we would take our money to Crow's, in the six mile prairie, in Perry county, on the Saturday following, they would receive it, and all should be right.

" ' It is impossible for suspicion to attach to any person not a Mormon, in the neighborhood, as being concerned in the horrid deed ; and it is believed, from all the circumstances, that the said two Mormons are connected with the bloody and foul transaction.

" ' The gun taken is a rifle, with a plain walnut stock, iron guard and thimbles ; no other mounting ; the shot-bag is of wolf-skin ; and the powder-horn had the name of Stephenson cut on it. There was a large butcher-knife in the scabbard attached to the strap of the shot-bag. The gun carries about sixty-five balls to the pound. The murderers took from the trunk a large red morocco pocket-book, with three dollars in specie ; one a Mexican dollar, which had been tried at the land-office with aquafortis, and which made a black spot on the impress of the head ; the rest of the money was in bits and quarters, with a hole in each piece.

" ' A reward of two hundred dollars will be given for the apprehension of the murderer or murderers.

" ' All papers friendly to the cause of right and justice will please give the above one insertion in their columns.

" ' EDWARD STEPHENSON.

" ' JACKSON COUNTY, Illinois, *June* 4, 1842.'

" We understand that this murder has produced great excitement in the south part of the State. A fellow-citizen murdered because he would not give up his property to a Mormon for the purpose of building the Temple and Fort at Nauvoo ! What think you of this, citizens of Illinois ? "

Will not the people of the west open their eyes to their imminent peril ? Will they suffer a community of murderers to congregate their forces, and immolate those nearest allied and most endeared to them by the ties of humanity and consanguinity, without a murmur ? Citizens, be ready to put your armor on, and spread your banners on the air! for if the battle MUST *be fought*, I will lead you on to glorious victory in this great moral struggle, where the cause of morality and true religion is bleeding at every pore. Arise in the plenitude of your strength, and assert your rights, and, in the name of the Lord God of Israel, lay the rebels low! *Vox populi vox Dei.*

THE ATTEMPTED MURDER OF GOVERNOR BOGGS.

Joseph Smith, the Mormon Prophet, in a public congregation in the city of Nauvoo, in the year 1841, PROPHESIED that Lilburn W. Boggs, Ex-Governor of Missouri, should die by *violent hands* within a year. Mr. C. S. Hamilton, of Carthage, Illinois, stated in my presence, and in the presence of several other gentlemen, at the tavern-house of Mr. R. L. Robertson, in Warsaw, Illinois, on Sunday, the 10th day of July, 1842, that he was present, and heard Smith make this prophecy. I was likewise present, and heard it. Smith was speaking of the Missouri difficulties at the time, and said that the *exterminator* should be *exterminated*, and that the DESTROYING ANGEL should do it *by the right hand of his power.* "I say it," said he, "in the name of the Lord God!"

In the spring of the year 1842, Smith offered a reward of five hundred dollars to any man that would secretly assassinate Governor Boggs. I heard the offer made at a meeting of the DAUGHTER OF ZION, (*Danites,*) in the Nauvoo lodge-room, at which meeting several of the members of the DESTROYING ANGEL (*Destructives*) were present. As a member of the *First Presidency*, I had a right to be present at all meetings of the various departments of the Church, and witness their operations; and, in this matter, as one of his councillors, I advised the Prophet to desist, and abandon his purposes in relation to Governor Boggs and the Missourians. His reply was, "*The Destroying Angel will do the work; when God speaks, his voice must be obeyed.*" Mr. Jotham Clark, of Hancock county, Illi-

24 *

nois, stated in Carthage, on the 6th of July, 1842, in the presence of Dr. Thomas L. Barnes, Jonas Hobart, myself, and others, that a Mr. Taylor, an English emigrant, told him that he heard Smith make the same offer, (five hundred dollars for any man who would kill Governor Boggs,) and that he (Taylor) had, in consequence thereof, *apostatized* from the Mormon faith, and written home to his friends in Europe, detailing the horrible facts. This was in the early part of the spring of 1842.

Mr. O. P. Rockwell left Nauvoo from one to two months prior to the attempted assassination of Governor Boggs, and returned the day before the report reached there. Colonel Francis M. Higbee told me, in Carthage, in the presence of General George W. Robinson, that Professor Orson Pratt, and his wife, Sarah M. Pratt, told him, that Mr. O. P. Rockwell, in a conversation with them, at Mr. Pratt's residence, in Nauvoo, stated that he (Rockwell) had been in Governor Boggs's neighborhood, in Missouri, and had had the honor of standing on the corner of the *Temple lot* in *Independence*. Mrs. Pratt told me the same before I left Nauvoo, and that he (Rockwell) stated that he came down the Missouri River to the Mississippi, thence down to St. Louis, Missouri, thence up to Nauvoo, Illinois.

"The (Nauvoo) Wasp," of May 28, A. D. 1842, a paper edited by William Smith, one of the Twelve Mormon Apostles, and brother of the Prophet, declared, "Who did the NOBLE DEED *remains* to be FOUND OUT."

Some weeks after Rockwell left Nauvoo, I asked Smith where he had gone. "*Gone?*" said he; "*gone to fulfil* PROPHECY," with a significant nod, giving me to understand that he had gone to fulfil his prediction in relation to the violent death of Governor Boggs. Soon after Rockwell's return, Smith said to me, speaking of Governor Boggs, "The *Destroying Angel* has done the work, as I predicted, but Rockwell was not the man who shot; THE ANGEL DID IT." Rockwell is one of the *Daughter of Zion*, (a Danite,) but I do not think that he belongs to the *Destroying Angel*.

On Friday, the 1st of July, 1842, I went to Carthage, and on the 5th, I had a call from Mr. O. P. Rockwell, the result of which is detailed in the following affidavits, to wit: —

" STATE OF ILLINOIS, }
  Hancock County, } ss.

" Personally appeared before me, Samuel Marshall, a Justice of
the Peace in and for said county, John C. Bennett, who, being duly
sworn according to law, deposeth and saith, That on the 5th of July,
1842, at the house of Mr. Hamilton, in Carthage, Mr. O. P. Rockwell came to him and desired a private interview, to which deponent replied, that if he (Rockwell) had any thing to say, he could
speak it out before the gentlemen present. Rockwell said it was a
private matter which interested them only. Deponent then went
out with him. Rockwell said, ' Doctor, you do not know your
friends; I am not your enemy, and I do not wish you to make use
of my name in your publications.' Deponent replied, that he recognized Joe Smith and all his friends as his personal enemies; to
which Rockwell replied, ' I have been informed by Warner and
Davis that you said Smith gave me fifty dollars and a wagon for
shooting Boggs, and I can and will whip any man that will tell such
a cursed lie; did you say so or not? ' After looking at him for a
moment or two, deponent said, ' I never said so, sir; but I did say,
and I now say it to your face, that you left Nauvoo about two
months before the attempted assassination of Ex-Governor Boggs,
of Missouri, and returned the day before the report of his assassination reached there; and that two persons, in Nauvoo, told me that
you told them that you had been over the upper part of Missouri,
and in Boggs's neighborhood;' to which Rockwell replied, ' Well,
I was there; and if I shot Boggs, they have got to prove it. I never
did an act in my life that I was ashamed of, and I do not fear to
go any where that I have ever been, for I have done nothing criminal.' Deponent replied, ' Certainly they have got to prove it on
you, if you did shoot him; I know nothing of what you *did*, as I
was not there. I only know the *circumstances*, and from them I draw
my own *inferences*, and the public will theirs; and now, sir, if either
you, or Joe Smith, think you can intimidate me by your threats,
you are mistaken in your man, and I wish you to understand, distinctly, that I am opposed to Joe and his holy host. I shall tell the
truth fearlessly, and regardless of consequences.' Rockwell replied,
' If you say that Joe Smith gave me fifty dollars and a wagon to
shoot Boggs, I can whip you, and will do it in any crowd.' Deponent then said, ' Why are you harping on what I have *not* said? I
have told you what I *have* said, to your face, and in the presence of
these gentlemen, and you have acknowledged the truth of all I have
said, and I shall say it again; and if you wish to fight, I am ready
for you.' The conversation then ceased on that subject. Rockwell
told deponent that he had been accused wrongfully of wishing to
assassinate him, or of being ordered by Smith to do so; but deponent said, ' I believe that Joe ordered you to do it. I know that
orders went from him to the Danites for that purpose.' Rockwell
said that Smith had never given him any such orders, neither was it
his intention; and further this deponent saith not.
                 —   " JOHN C. BENNETT.
" Sworn to, and subscribed, this 7th day of July, 1842, before me,
at my office, in Carthage.
            " SAMUEL MARSHALL, *Justice of the Peace.*"

"STATE OF ILLINOIS, } ss.
     Hancock County, }

"Personally appeared before me, Samuel Marshall, a Justice of the Peace in and for said county, Clayton Tweed, who, being duly sworn according to law, deposeth and saith, That on the 5th day of July, 1842, at the house of Mr. Hamilton, in Carthage, Mr. O. P. Rockwell came up to General John C. Bennett, and said to him, 'I wish to have some private conversation with you; will you come out of doors with me?' To which Bennett replied, 'No, sir; if you have any thing to say to me, speak it out before these gentlemen.' Rockwell then observed, 'It is a matter which interests you and myself alone, and I should like much to see you a few minutes by ourselves.' They then went out, and were some time in conversation, when loud words ensued, and deponent came up, much agitated, fearing there would be a fight, and heard Bennett say, 'I now say to your face what I said behind your back,—that you left Nauvoo about two months before the attempted assassination of Ex-Governor Boggs, of Missouri, and returned the day before the report of his assassination reached there, and that two persons in Nauvoo told me that you told them, that you had been over to the upper part of Missouri, and in Boggs's neighborhood;' to which Rockwell replied, 'If I shot Boggs, they have got to prove it.' Bennett said, 'Certainly, they have got to prove it on you if you did shoot him. I know nothing of what you *did*, as I was not there. I only know the *circumstances*, and from them I draw my own *inferences*, and the public will theirs. And now, sir, if either you or Joe Smith think you can intimidate me by your threats, you are mistaken in your man; and I wish you to understand, distinctly, that I am opposed to Joe and his holy host. I shall tell the truth fearlessly, and regardless of consequences.' Bennett further remarked, 'Why are you harping about what I have *not* said? I have told you what I *have* said, to your face, and you have acknowledged the truth of it, and I will say it again; and if you wish to fight, I am now ready for you; you will never have a better time.' The conversation then ceased, and the parties separated; and further this deponent saith not.   CLAYTON TWEED.

"Sworn to, and subscribed, before me, this 7th day of July, 1842, at my office, in Carthage.
                    "SAMUEL MARSHALL, *Justice of the Peace.*"

"STATE OF ILLINOIS, } ss.
     Hancock County, }

"Personally appeared before me, Samuel Marshall, a Justice of the Peace in and for said county, Jonas Hobart, who, being duly sworn according to law, deposeth and saith, That on the 5th day of July, 1842, at the tavern-house of Mr. Hamilton, in Carthage, he came up to where General John C. Bennett and Mr. O. P. Rockwell were in angry conversation, when he heard Rockwell say, that if any man said that Joe Smith hired him to shoot Boggs, he stated what was false. There was then some warm talk about fighting,

and Bennett said, ' I tell you, sir, to your face, what I have said behind your back, and if you are for fight, now is as good a time as
you will have.' Rockwell said he had been up into Boggs's
neighborhood, in Missouri; and said he, ' If I shot Boggs, they
have got to prove it.' Bennett said, ' Certainly they have; I do
not know what you *did*; I only know the *circumstances*. I have
told them, and I have now told them to your face, and you have
acknowledged them; and I shall tell them again, fearless of consequences;' and further deponent saith not.

" JONAS HOBART.

—

" Sworn to, and subscribed, this 9th day of July, 1842, before me,
at my office, in Carthage.

" SAMUEL MARSHALL, *Justice of the Peace.*"

" STATE OF ILLINOIS, }
  Hancock County, } ss.

" Personally appeared before me, Samuel Marshall, Justice of the
Peace in and for said county, John H. Lawton, who, being duly
sworn according to law, deposeth and saith, That on the 5th day of
July, 1842, he came up to where General John C. Bennett and O.
P. Rockwell were in conversation, at the house of Mr. Hamilton, in
Carthage, and heard Rockwell say that he had been up in Boggs's
neighborhood, in Missouri, and that if he had shot Boggs, they had
to prove it; and then began to talk of whipping Bennett, whereupon
Bennett replied, ' I have said nothing behind your back but what I
now say to your face, and if you wish to fight now, I am ready
for you.' The conversation then ceased, and the parties separated;
and further this deponent saith not.   JOHN H. LAWTON.

—

" Sworn to, and subscribed, this 6th day of July, 1842, before me,
at my office, in Carthage.   SAMUEL MARSHALL,
Justice of the Peace."

I would further say, that before Rockwell left Nauvoo,
he was abjectly poor; but since his return, he left his
family in the lower part of the city, and took up his residence at the tavern of Captain Amos Davis; has an elegant carriage and horses at his disposal, and his pockets
filled with gold. Captain Davis can testify about this
matter. These horses and carriage belonged to Smith,
and the gold was furnished by him. Smith told me that
he furnished the carriage, horses, and gold sovereigns, to
Rockwell. But said he, " It is to enable him to convey passengers from the steamboats to the Temple and
back again!" Bah! My opinion is, that Smith *procured*

the attempted assassination, (and of this I entertain no doubt whatever; I feel as certain of it as I do that I am a living man;) that Rockwell, as a member of the Daughter of Zion, acted as the *conductor* or *guide;* and that one of the twelve composing the Destroying Angel, ASSISTED BY ROCKWELL, *did the deed.* This is the amount of what I know in relation to this unfortunate transaction. JOSEPH SMITH IS THE MAN WHO SHOULD ATONE FOR THE ACT — " *Nam scelus intra se tacitum qui cogitat ullum, facti crimen habet.*" " For he who silently intends a crime, has all the guilt of the deed." There are cases in which, to resolve upon, and to commit a guilty act, are equal in point of criminality, AND THIS IS ONE. From what he said to me, it is evident that Smith knows both of the actual *perpetrators* as well as the *guide,* and that HE DIRECTED THE ACT, as in the case of Mr. Grandison Newell, of Ohio, pretending it was the will of God. As accessory before the fact, Smith had great fears of an arrest; but said he, " If Governor Reynolds demands, and Governor Carlin delivers me up, *they shall be smitten by the Destroying Angel of the Lord, like Herod, and die of the scab.*" He said God intended to save him to chastise this generation; and that, like Mahomet, he would sway an imperial sceptre over the nations of the earth, and that Missouri should bow first to the rod of his power; for said he, " *Thus saith the LORD GOD.*"

I have just received a letter from Joseph O. Boggs, M. D., a very worthy and talented brother of Governor Lilburn W. Boggs, from which I make the following extract: —

"INDEPENDENCE, Mo., *September* 12, 1842.

" GENERAL JOHN C. BENNETT:
  " Dear Sir, —
        *   *   *   *   *   *   *   *

" We have now no doubt of the guilt of Smith and Rockwell. Rockwell is known here, and was seen in Platte county for several days preceding the shooting of my brother. When he was arrested, he told the messenger that he could prove that he was seven miles north of Independence on the night that Governor Boggs was shot. This only confirms the suspicions against him.

        *   *   *   *   *   *   *   *

          " Yours, respectfully,
                    " JOSEPH O. BOGGS. '

Doctor Boggs judges correctly; there can be no reasonable doubt of their guilt. I am fully persuaded that there were three men concerned in the murderous plot — Joseph Smith, the instigator, and Orin Porter Rockwell, of the Danites, and some one of the Destructives unknown to me. That trio planned and executed that fell deed, as far as it was consummated; and nothing but fortuitous circumstances, or the interposition of Divine Providence, prevented the death of that worthy public functionary. In obedience to the requisition made upon me, I shall immediately repair to Independence, in the western confines of Missouri, in order to bring the claims of the Mormon Mahomet to public distinction to a speedy issue.

THE DURESS AND ATTEMPTED MURDER OF THE AUTHOR.

THE DURESS.

" On the 17th day of May, A. D. 1842, Joe Smith requested to see me *alone* in the preparation room of Nauvoo Lodge, U. D., on some important business. We entered, and *he locked the door, put the key in his pocket,* DREW A PISTOL ON ME, and said, ' The peace of my family requires that you should sign an affidavit, and make a statement before the next City Council, on the 19th, exonerating me from all participation whatever, either directly or indirectly, in word or deed, in the SPIRITUAL WIFE DOCTRINE, or *private intercourse with females in general;* and if you do not do it *with apparent cheerfulness,* I will make CAT-FISH BAIT of you, or deliver you over to the Danites for execution to-night; *for my dignity and purity must and shall be maintained before the public,* EVEN AT THE EXPENSE OF LIFE. Will you do it, or die ? ' I replied that he had better procure some other person or persons to do so, as there were a plenty who could do it *in truth.* ' No,' said he, ' that will not do; for it is known that you are well acquainted with all my private acts, *better than any other man;* and it is in your power to save me or damn me; and as you have now *with-*

drawn from the Church IN AN HONORABLE MANNER, OVER MY OWN SIGNATURE, — a privilege never granted to any other person, — *you must and shall* place it out of your power to injure me or the Church. Do it, or the Mississippi is your portion. Will you do it ? ' I remarked that it was a hard case, and that I would leave peaceably, and without any public exposition, if he would excuse me. He replied, ' I tell you as I was once told, " *Your die is cast!* YOUR FATE IS FIXED !! YOUR DOOM IS SEALED !!!" if you refuse. Will you do it, or die ? ' I remarked that I would, *under the circumstances*, but that it was hard to take the advantage of an *unarmed man.* ' If you tell *that* publicly,' said he, ' death is your portion ; *remember the Danites !* ' He then unlocked the door ; we went into the room below, and I gave the affidavit as subscribed before General Daniel H. Wells, an Alderman of the city, A JACK MORMON, ' WHO SOLD HIS BIRTHRIGHT TO JOE FOR A MESS OF POTTAGE,' (who was then doing business for the Saints in the lower room,) and made the statement required before the City Council on the 19th. I was not aware, until the Sunday after my return from Springfield, that any other person was apprized of the fact of the *threat of* MURDER !! But on that day, Colonel Francis M. Higbee told me, in the presence of General George W. Robinson, that HE WAS IN POSSESSION OF A SECRET THAT WOULD OPEN THE EYES OF THE PEOPLE, and that, *if it came to the worst,* he would file his affidavit ; but he would not *then* tell me what that *secret* was. General Robinson, however, informed me afterwards that *it was a knowledge of Joe's threats of murder and the duress.* Accordingly, on the 30th of June, 1842, I called upon Colonel Higbee for his affidavit, which was taken before General Hiram Kimball, an Alderman of the city, and is in the words and figures following, to wit : —

" ' STATE OF ILLINOIS, ⎰ ss.
         Hancock County, ⎱

" ' Personally appeared before me, Hiram Kimball, an Alderman of the city of Nauvoo, Francis M. Higbee, who, being duly sworn according to law, deposeth and saith, That Joseph Smith told him that *John C. Bennett could be easily put aside,* OR DROWNED, *and no person would be the wiser for it,* AND THAT IT OUGHT TO BE ATTENDED TO ; and he further remarked that THE SOONER THIS WAS DONE THE BETTER FOR THE CHURCH, *fearing, as he said, that Bennett would make some disclosures preju-*

dicial to said Smith. This was about the time of *Bennett's with-drawal from the Church,* or a short time before; and further this deponent saith not.   FRANCIS M. HIGBEE.

"'Sworn to, and subscribed, this 30th day of June, A. D. 1842.

"'HIRAM KIMBALL, *Alderman.*"

"I now declare the foregoing statement to be true to the letter; and that my affidavit, taken before Daniel H. Wells, Esq., on the 17th of May, and my statement before the City Council of Nauvoo, on the 19th, as published in 'The Wasp' of the 25th of June, 1842, and in the 'Times and Seasons,' ARE FALSE, and were taken under DURESS as above stated, and are, therefore, *destitute of moral or legal obligation.*   JOHN C. BENNETT."

"SUFFOLK, } ss.
September 13, 1842. }

"Then personally appeared the above-named John C. Bennett, and made oath that the foregoing affidavit, by him subscribed, is true.

"Before me,   BRADFORD SUMNER, *Justice of the Peace.*"

Thomas C. Sharp, Esq., editor of the "Warsaw Signal," (a paper published in Hancock, the county of Smith's residence,) in his paper of August 6, 1842, in speaking on this subject, remarks—

"The testimony of General Bennett, then, has force and effect, when taken in connection with that of Dr. Avard, W. W. Phelps, and others, as given before the Court of Inquiry in Missouri, and the direct corroborations of Colonel Higbee and Miss Martha H. Brotherton. All go to show the point arrived at, viz., that Joe Smith is a most consummate *villain* and *knave.*

"The second reason why we believe that Bennett does not speak without reason, is the fear of exposure which Joe himself seemed to manifest, on the withdrawal of Bennett from the Church. It appears that he procured an affidavit from Bennett, stating that he (Smith) had never taught any thing wrong, either by word or act. Now, we ask, why did he want this affidavit? If he was conscious of having never taught nor acted contrary to the principles of honor, honesty, and righteousness, where was the necessity of procuring from Bennett an assurance of his purity? The truth is, no explanation can be given, other than this,—that Joe was fully aware that Bennett was in possession of facts, which, if made public, would bring infamy on himself and the Church. Hence his anxiety to deprive Bennett of the power of doing injury, by procuring his affidavit, and publishing it, together with a statement of Bennett's character, before the latter had made any charge against him to the world. His object, in this, evidently was to forestall public opinion, by destroying the character of a man whose knowledge of his baseness, he knew, would render him dangerous. Now, we ask, if Joe was conscious of rectitude, why this anxiety to discredit Bennett, before he had uttered a word to the public against him? Innocent men do not generally attempt to justify themselves before they are accused; but Smith was industrious to stop the mouth of a witness who, he alleged, knew nothing against him!'"

THE ATTEMPTED MURDER.

In my communication to the Sangamo Journal of the 27th June, 1842, I stated that I had been threatened with death by the Holy Joe and his Danite band of murderers, in case I *dare make any disclosures* prejudicial to that polluted mass of corruption, iniquity, and fraud, — that King of Impostors, the holy and immaculate Joe Smith; — and in my communication of July 2d, I stated that, when on my journey to Springfield, on my arrival in Carthage, I found, as all the citizens well know, that I was followed by Mr. O. P. Rockwell, a Danite, who, on his arrival late in the night, made strict inquiries as to where I was. His ostensible business was to *put a letter in the post-office!* Bah!! I was prepared for the gentleman, and he approached me not; but another swift rider, Captain John D. Parker, another Danite, followed me to Springfield, to *carry a letter to Dr. Helm! Ah! Ha!! BAH!!!* I told Captain Parker that I was aware of his object, but I feared him not. At Virginia, in Cass county, on my return, Parker met me again, and I called the attention of the stage-driver to him, who, thereupon, put two additional balls into his pistol, and observed to me that he was then ready for him or any other person having the same object in view. On the 23d of June, 1842, the Holy Prophet, in an article over his own name, published in "The (Nauvoo) Wasp" of June 25th, threatened me with the VENGEANCE OF THE LORD, in the following language: "Unless he [Bennett] is determined to bring SUDDEN DESTRUCTION upon himself FROM THE HAND OF THE ALMIGHTY, [the *Destroying Angel*,] he will be *silent.*"

In order to *fulfil this prediction*, on the evening of the 29th of June, the DESTROYING ANGEL approached my boarding-house, (General Robinson's,) in Nauvoo, with their carriage wheels wrapped with blankets, and their horses' feet muffled with cloths, to prevent noise, about ten o'clock, for the purpose of conveying me off for " *sudden destruction*," or assassination, so as to make me " *silent*," and thus prevent disclosures. Dead men tell no tales! But, as I had an intimation of the matter in the afternoon, I borrowed two pistols of General Robinson, and one of Mr. Hunter, a merchant, and loaded them with slugs. Besides these, I had two good Bowie-knives, and some of my friends were, likewise, well armed, — well prepared to give the ANGEL a warm reception. So, after prowling around the house (the lights in which were extinguished) for some time, the " *hand of the Almighty*" withdrew! On the 6th of July, Mr. Jotham Clark told me in Carthage, in the presence of Dr. Thomas L. Barnes and Mr. Jonas Hobart, that he, having business near there, came into town to tell me that the Mormons had *threatened my life*, and warned me to be on my guard. This is the treatment dissenters receive when they come out of the *modern Babylon*, the *mother of harlots*, by the SAINTS OF THE LAST DAYS. " *Dii, talem avertite casum!* " " May the gods avert so great a misfortune! " General Wilson Law, and another Danite, went on to Jefferson City in order to blast my reputation, and prevent, if possible, the issuing of a state writ by forestalling public opinion ; but they were treated with that contempt which they so richly merited at the hands of high-minded Missourians. Dr. Foster, and five other Danites, followed me to New York City, evidently for the purpose of assassination, as the following affidavit will abundantly show : —

" BOSTON, *September* 12, 1842.

" TO WHOM IT MAY CONCERN : —

" On Wednesday evening, August 31st, I attended the lectures of General John C. Bennett, and Origen Bacheler, Esq., against Mormonism, (in the church, corner of Delancy and Christie Streets, New York,) at the close of which the General was maliciously attacked by a ruffian calling himself Dr. Robert D. Foster, a Danite from Nauvoo, in company with some others of that band. After learning that Foster and his companions were from Nauvoo, I watched their movements ; and after the lights were extinguished, and they had retired by themselves, I heard Foster say that he had found Bennett by means of the New York Herald. One of the company then asked Foster when he intended to return to Nauvoo ; to which he replied, as soon as he had SETTLED *Bennett!* Foster had a bold and unblushing female with him, whom I judged, from appearances, to be one of his *spiritual wives.*

"J. W. HALLENBECK.

" Sworn to, September 12th, 1842, before me,

" B. SUMNER, *Justice of the Peace.*

Thus it is plain to be seen that as unprincipled a set of ruffians as ever disgraced the earth, calling themselves *Saints*, are in hot pursuit of me continually, FOR THE PURPOSE OF SECRET MURDER ! ! In my public lectures in New York, I was assisted by Origen Bacheler, Esq., one of the great champions of the Christian faith, by whom I was probably saved from the assassin's steel. They seek my life in order to save their Prophet — that Grand Tartarean Hydra, whose face and hands are yet dripping with the blood of murder — from reaping the reward of his iniquity, the just penalty of violated laws; but they shall yet " tremble at the hand-writing on the wall," and shout EUREKA from the *port-holes* of their holy Temple, on their consecrated mount, within the confines of their delectable city. For vengeance shall come like a rushing torrent and a furious, beating tempest, and none shall be able to deliver from under the arm of legal power; for they shall be driven like chaff before the wind, and consumed like stubble before the devouring flame. Should I be sacrificed or slain in the conflict, my blood would be avenged by God and my country. I never feared to die, but I did not intend to sell my life cheaply until the world had the truth of the Mormon organization before them in bold relief. The issue is now made up; " their die is cast, their fate is fixed, their doom is sealed : " their temple will be profaned, their altars desecrated, their city devastated, their possessions confiscated, and their idols immolated ; and reason, sober reason, will once more resume its empire in the minds of the people, and folly, fraud, and imposture, hide their hydra head. All *honest* individuals, who have the requisite MORAL COURAGE, will now cease to worship the Mormon BAAL, in the modern *Babylon*, and will bow submissively before the Lord God of the Universe, renounce *heathenism*, and espouse *Christianity.*

CONTEMPLATED MORMON EMPIRE.

In illustration of the plans and proceedings of Joe Smith and the Mormons, it may not be amiss to give some descriptive remarks upon the states which he designed as the seat of his empire and dominion, and where he had begun to establish his deluded followers, the destined instruments of his treason and ambition.

According to the Mormon prophets, the whole region of country between the Rocky Mountains and the Alleghanies was, at a period about thirteen hundred years ago, densely peopled by nations descended from a Jewish family, who emigrated from Jerusalem in the time of the prophet Jeremiah, some six or seven hundred years before Christ. Immense cities were founded, and sumptuous edifices reared, and the whole land overspread with the results of a high and extensive civilization. The Book of Mormon speaks of cities with stupendous stone walls, and of battles in which hundreds of thousands of men were slain ! The land afterwards became a waste, howling wilderness, traversed by a few straggling bands or tribes of savages, descended from a branch of the aforesaid Jewish family, who, in consequence of their wickedness, had their complexion changed from white to black, or rather dark red ; but the emigrants from Europe, and their descendants, having filled the land, and God having been pleased to grant a revelation by which is made known the true history of the past in America, and the events which are about to take place, he had also commanded the Saints of the Latter Day to assemble themselves together there, and occupy the land which was once held by the members of the true church. The States of Missouri, and Illinois, and the Territory of Iowa, are the regions to which the Prophet has hitherto chiefly directed his schemes of aggrandizement, and which were to form the NUCLEUS of the great MORMON EMPIRE. The remaining states were to be licked up like salt, and fall into the immense labyrinth of glorious prophetic dominion, like the defenceless lamb before the mighty king of the forest !

25 *

MISSOURI. *Boundaries and Extent.* I shall here
quote from Bradford's Atlas, pp. 152—155.

" Missouri, in point of dimensions, is the second State in the
Union, being inferior in extent only to Virginia; it extends from
36° to 40° 35′ N. Lat., and from 89° 20′ to 95° W. Lon., having an
area of about 68,500 square miles. Its boundaries, as fixed by the
Constitution, are a line drawn from a point in the middle of the Mississippi, in 36° N. Lat., to the St. François, then up that river to 36°
30′, and along that parallel west to its intersection by a meridian line
passing through the mouth of the Kanzas; thence the western boundary was originally that meridian, but by act of Congress, in 1836,
the triangular tract between it and the Missouri, above the mouth
of the Kanzas, was annexed to the State; on the north, the parallel
of latitude which passes through the rapids of the River Desmoines,
forms the boundary between that river and the Missouri; thence the
Desmoines and the Mississippi make the eastern boundary. The
corner between the Desmoines and the Mississippi, now in Wisconsin, will also, in all probability, be added to Missouri, as provision
has been made by the State for its annexation, whenever the consent
of Congress shall be obtained.

" *Face of the Country. Soil.* The surface of that portion of the
State which lies north of the Missouri is generally moderately undulating, consisting of an agreeable interchange of gentle swells and
broad valleys, and rarely, though occasionally, rugged, or rising into
hills of much elevation. With the exception of narrow strips of
woodland along the watercourses, almost the whole of this region is
prairie, at least nine tenths being wholly destitute of trees. The
alluvial patches or river-bottoms are extensive, particularly on the
Missouri, and generally of prodigious fertility, and the soil of the
upland is equal, if not superior, to that of any other upland tract of
equal extent in the United States. (Long's *Expedition.*) The
region south of the Missouri and west of the Osage, is of the same
description; [the Northern and Western Missouri country is most
felicitous and delightful, with a soil of inexhaustible fertility, and
a salubrious climate, rendering it a most desirable and pleasant residence;] but south-east of the latter river, the State is traversed
by numerous ridges of the Ozark Mountains, and the surface is here
highly broken and rugged. This mountainous tract has a breadth
of from 100 to 150 miles, but although it often shoots up into precip-
itous peaks, it is believed that they rarely exceed 2000 feet in height.
No accurate measurements of their elevation have, however, been
made, and little is known of the course and mutual relations of the
chains. The growth here is pitch pine, shrub oaks, cedar, &c., in-
dicative of the poverty of the soil; in the uplands of the rest of the
State, hickory, post-oak, and white-oak, &c., are the prevailing
growth, and in the river-bottoms, the cotton-tree, sycamore or but-
ton-wood, maple, ash, walnut, &c., predominate. The south-east-
ern corner of the State, below Cape Girardeau, and east of the
Black River, is a part of that great inundated region of which some
general account has already been given under the head of Arkansas;

a considerable proportion of this tract is, indeed, above the reach of the floods, but these patches are isolated and inaccessible except by boats, during the high stages of the water. It is asserted on the authority of intelligent residents, that the bottoms of the St. Francis were not subject to be overflowed previous to the earthquakes of 1811 and 1812, when an extensive tract in the valley of that river sunk to a considerable depth. According to Stoddard, who knew nothing of the shocks of 1811, earthquakes have been common here from the first settlement of the country; he himself experienced several shocks at Kaskaskia in 1804, by which the soldiers stationed there were aroused from sleep, and the buildings were much shaken and disjointed; and oscillations still occur with such frequency as to be regarded with indifference by the inhabitants, who familiarly call them *shakes*. But the agitations of December, January, and February, 1811 and 1812, which were felt from New England to New Orleans, are the only ones known to have left permanent traces on the face of the earth, although there is every probability that this part of the valley of the Mississippi has been much convulsed at former periods. In 1812, the earth here opened in wide chasms, from which columns of water and sand burst forth; hills disappeared, and their places were occupied by lakes; the beds of lakes were raised, and their waters flowed off, leaving them dry; the courses of the streams were changed by the elevation of their beds and the falling in of their banks; for one whole hour the current of the Mississippi was turned backwards towards its source, until its accumulated waters were able to break through the barrier that had dammed them back; boats were dashed on the banks, or suddenly left high and dry in the deserted channel, or hurried backwards and forwards with the eddying surges, while in the midst of these awful changes, electric fires, accompanied by loud rumblings, flashed through the air, which was darkened by clouds of vapor. In some places, submerged forests and cane-brakes are still visible at a great depth on the bottom of lakes, which were then formed. That the cause of these convulsions was not local, as some have imagined, is evident enough from the fact, that the Azores, the West India Islands, and the northern coast of South America, were unusually agitated at the same time, and the cities of Caraccas, Laguayra, and others on the last, were totally destroyed. (*Memoirs of Am. Acad.* Vol. III. *Ex. Doc. 1st Sess. 24th Cong.* Vol. I. Doc. 11. *Sen. Doc. same Session, Doc.* 113. Long's *Expedition to the Rocky Mountains,* Vol. II. 325.)

"*Rivers.* Missouri is abundantly supplied with navigable channels, affording easy access to all parts of the State. The Mississippi washes the eastern border, through a distance of about 470 miles by the windings of the stream. Above St. Genevieve, it flows for the most part between high and abrupt cliffs of limestone, rising to an elevation of from 100 to 400 feet above the surface of the river, sometimes separated from it by bottoms of greater or less width, and at others springing up abruptly from the water's edge. A few miles below Cape Girardeau, and about 35 miles above the mouth of the Ohio, are the rocky ledges called the Little and Grand Chain, and about half way between that point and St. Genevieve, is the Grand Tower, one of the wonders of the Mississippi; it is a stupendous pile

of rocks of a conical form, about 150 feet high and 100 feet in circumference at its base, rising up out of the bed of the river. ' It seems,
in connection with the rocky shores on either side, to have opposed,
at some former period, a barrier to the progress of the Mississippi,
which must here have had a perpendicular fall of more than 100
feet.' (Schoolcraft, *Lead Mines*.)   Colonel Long refers the position of this now obliterated cataract to the Grand Chain.   The
principal tributaries of the Mississippi, with the exception of the
Missouri, are the Desmoines, Wyaconda, Fabius, Salt, and Copper
River, above that great stream, and the Merrimac, St. Francis, and
White River below, the two last passing into Arkansas.   Desmoines,
which is only a boundary stream, is navigable 170 miles, and Salt
River, whose northern sources are in Wisconsin, and southern in
Boone county, and which takes its name from the salt licks or salines
on its borders, may be navigated by small steamboats to Flor-
ida, 85 miles.   The Rivière au Cuivre, or Copper River, is also a
navigable stream, but the navigation of all these rivers is interrupted
by ice in winter, and by shoals and bars in the dry season.   The
Merrimac, or Merameg, has a course of 250 miles, but is navigable
only about 50 miles, except in the highest stages of the water.   The
Bourbeuse, or Muddy River, Big River, and Fourche à Courtois, are
its tributaries.   The St. François, or Francis, is a much more considerable river, but its navigation is interrupted by several rafts or jams
of drift-wood, and at the *Spread* its waters are dissipated into so many
channels, that it is difficult to find one which may be navigated; but
these obstructions will soon be removed, and the river will then be
navigable by steamboats to Greenville.   The Black River, after
having received the Current, Eleven Points, and Spring Rivers,
enters the White River in Arkansas.   That great stream sweeps
round into the south-western part of this State, from which it receives
several large streams, and further west are the tributaries of the
Neosho.

   " The Missouri flows through the State for a distance of about 600
miles, but although steamboats have ascended it 2500 miles from its
mouth, its navigation is rendered difficult and dangerous by sand-
bars, falling banks, snags, and a shifting channel, and is only practicable about four months in the year, being interrupted by ice in
winter and by the shoals in summer.   It is below the mouth of the
Platte, not far above the northern line of Missouri, that it assumes
the turbulent and turbid character which it imparts to the Mississippi.   To the distance of about 400 miles from its mouth its banks
are clothed with trees, but beyond this the country is almost entirely
unwooded, even on its borders.   The Nishnabottana, Nodawa, Little
Platte, Grand River, and Chariton, considerable streams rising in
Wisconsin, are the principal tributaries from the north, and the
Lamine, Osage, and Gasconade, from the south.   The Osage is the
most important of these rivers; it rises in the Indian Territory, and
flows through some of the most fertile lands in Missouri for a distance, by its windings, of nearly 600 miles; it is navigable for
steamboats to the mouth of the Sac, about 200 miles, and to the
western frontier by large keel boats.   The Sac, Pomme de Terre,
Niangua, and Grand River, its tributaries, are navigable streams.

The Gasconade rises in the mountainous tract near the heads of the tributaries of White River, and has a course of about 250 miles ; it is navigable upwards of 100 miles.

"*Minerals.* Perhaps no region in the world surpasses Missouri in the variety and abundance of its mineral resources; to inexhaustible stores of lead and iron, coal and salt, are to be added zinc, manganese, antimony, plumbago, iron pyrites, arsenic, and copper, nitrous and aluminous earth, potter's clay, marble, freestone, and granite, sulphuretted and thermal waters, &c., and according to some accounts, indications of silver and cobalt occur. The geological features of the country, notwithstanding several partial explorations, have been imperfectly examined ; but generally speaking, the prevailing rocks are carboniferous limestones and saliferous sandstones; the Ozark Mountains appear to consist mainly of masses of intrusive rocks, granite, sienite, porphyry, &c., and of altered limestones and sandstones. The repository of the lead-ore, which is galena or sulphuret of lead, is magnesian limestone, but the limits and extent of the galeniferous region have never been ascertained ; the ore is known to be abundant, not only in the counties of Washington, Jefferson, St. Francis, St. Genevieve, Madison, and the contiguous districts, usually called the lead region, and the seat of the oldest and most extensive diggings, but also in several counties west of the Osage, as Morgan and Cole, and in several north of the Missouri; and the Wisconsin mines are in the same rock. Operations were commenced here by the French as early as 1720, but were suspended about twenty years later, and were not again carried on with much activity until after the cession of Louisiana to the United States. The processes have been of the rudest sort; wherever indications of the mineral, as the galena is called by the miners, appear on the surface, an excavation has been commenced, and the whole surface of the ground has been cut out into pits of various sizes, from three or four to twenty feet in diameter, and from ten to fifteen feet in depth, the digging being abandoned as soon as the depth renders it inconvenient to throw out the earth, or to hoist out the mineral by a simple windlass and bucket ; blasting is also resorted to when a rich vein is struck in the metalliferous rock, but much of the ore is found loose in alluvial deposits, in lumps of various sizes. In a large way, it yields from 80 to 85 per cent. of pure metal, but by more careful processes might be made to give considerably more. The annual produce of the Missouri diggings is at present about 7,000,000 pounds, a portion of which is manufactured into shot and sheet lead. Previous to 1836, the land was the property of the United States, and was leased to individuals for short terms of time, which led to wasteful and extravagant modes of working the mines ; but in that year the mineral lands were sold, and some attempts have already been made, by some of the proprietors, to introduce the scientific processes practised in Europe. (Schoolcraft, *Lead Mines of Missouri.* Featherstonhaugh, *Geological Report on the Elevated Country between the Missouri and Red Rivers. Franklin Journal*, Vol. XXI. Wetmore, *Gazetteer of Missouri.*)

" Iron-ore is found in numerous localities, but we have no particular account of its character and quantity, except in the case of the enormous masses in Madison and Washington counties. The Iron Mountains of this district, which have lately attracted the attention of capitalists, are thus described by Professor Shepard, who visited them in 1837 : 'The Pilot Knob and the Iron Mountain are lofty peaks in this hilly range, the former about 600 feet high and three miles in circuit, and the latter 350 feet in height with a circuit of about two miles. The Pilot Knob may be denominated a ferruginous porphyry, or an aggregate of feldspar and specular iron, the latter occurring of a fine (steel-grained) granular structure, and containing imbedded crystals and round grains of feldspar, while the Iron Mountain is a homogeneous deposit of pure, massive specular iron, containing only in a few exceedingly rare cases single crystals of feldspar. We have, then, in this extraordinary region, in the first place, hills many hundred feet high, composed entirely of a compact, cherry-red feldspar, variegated with veins of black by oxide of iron ; in the second place, the Pilot Knob, a mountain made up in large proportion of specular iron, the feldspar often scarcely exceeding the ore with which it is mixed ; and lastly, the Iron Mountain, in which the whole mass is so nearly pure ore, that the observer is forced to search with the closest scrutiny to detect in it even a few solitary crystals of feldspar. In offering a statement respecting the extent and richness of the ore, I hesitate not to say, that it surpasses, for quantity and quality, every thing before known in the metallic history of our earth.' (Shepard, *Report on the Missouri Iron Mountains*, 1838. *Prospectus of the Missouri Iron Company.*) Although copper and silver are known to exist, and have been successfully worked, we have no definite account of the situation and extent of the ores. Bituminous coal is found in almost every county, except in the mineral district, and the beds are said to be of great extent and of easy access. Salt-springs are numerous, but little attention is paid to the manufacture of salt."

COUNTIES, POPULATION, AND COUNTY TOWNS.

Counties.	Census of 1840.				County Towns.
	Whites.	Free Col'd.	Slaves.	Total Pop.	
Audrain,........	1,752	2	195	1,949	
Barry,..........	4,518	8	269	4,795	
Benton,.........	3,933		261	4,205	Benton C. H.
Boone,..........	10,529	24	3,008	13,561	Columbia.
Buchanan,.......	6,004	6	227	6,237	
Caldwell,........	1,397		61	1,458	
Callaway,.......	8,601	22	3,142	11,765	Fulton.
Cape Girardeau,..	8,020	14	1,325	9,359	Jackson.
Carroll, ...	2,155		268	2,423	Carrollton.
Chariton,........	3,709	20	1,017	4,746	Keytesville.
Clark,..........	2,423	3	420	2,846	
Clay, ...	6,373	34	1,875	8,282	Liberty.
Clinton,.........	2,530	3	191	2,724	Plattsburg.
Cole,...........	8,073	34	1,179	9,286	JEFFERSON CITY.
Cooper, ...	8,312	15	2,157	10,484	Booneville.

Counties.	Census of 1840.				County Towns.
	Whites.	Free Col'd.	Slaves.	Total Pop.	
Crawford,........	3,377		184	3,561	Little Piney.
Daviess,.........	2,600	2	134	2,736	
Franklin,........	6,447	14	1,054	7,515	Newport.
Gasconade,......	4,987	1	342	5,330	Mount Sterling.
Greene,.........	4,693	2	677	5,372	Springfield.
Howard,.........	9,381	44	3,683	13,108	Fayette.
Jackson,.........	6,245	6	1,361	7,612	Independence.
Jefferson,........	3,960	12	324	4,296	Herculaneum.
Johnson,........	3,911	4	556	4,471	
Lafayette,.......	4,799	26	1,990	6,815	Lexington.
Lewis,..........	4,966	9	1,065	6,040	Monticello.
Lincoln,.........	5,873	4	1,572	7,449	Troy.
Linn,...........	2,102		143	2,245	
Livingston,......	4,082	2	241	4,325	
Macon,..........	5,808	1	225	6,034	
Madison,........	2,762	22	611	3,395	Fredericktown.
Marion,.........	7,239	42	2,342	9,623	Palmyra.
Miller,..........	2,170	1	111	2,282	
Monroe,.........	7,813	5	1,687	9,505	Monroe C. H.
Morgan,.........	3,891	4	512	4,407	Versailles.
Montgomery,....	3,524	20	827	4,371	Danville.
New Madrid,.....	3,748	5	801	4,554	New Madrid.
Newton,.........	3,616	5	169	3,790	
Perry,..........	4,968	14	778	5,760	Perrysville.
Pettis,..........	2,377	1	552	2,930	Georgetown.
Platte,..........	8,049	6	858	8,913	
Pike,...........	8,157	17	2,472	10,646	Bowling Green.
Polk,...........	7,978	9	462	8,449	
Pulaski,.........	6,338	1	190	6,529	Waynesville.
Ralls,...........	4,450	11	1,209	5,670	New London.
Randolph,.......	5,749	12	1,437	7,198	Randolph.
Ray,............	5,714	5	834	6,553	Richmond.
Ripley,..........	2,777	2	77	2,856	Van Buren.
Rives,...........	4,086	4	636	4,726	
St. Charles,.....	6,286	28	1,597	7,911	St. Charles.
St. François,.....	2,694	16	501	3,211	Farmington.
St. Genevieve,...	2,563	37	548	3,148	St. Genevieve.
St. Louis, ...	30,505	858	4,616	35,979	St. Louis.
Saline,..........	3,635	8	1,615	5,258	Walnut Farm.
Scott,..........	5,028	18	928	5,974	Benton.
Shelby,.........	2,587	11	458	3,056	
Stoddard,.......	3,081	1	71	3,153	
Taney,..........	3,212	12	40	3,264	
Van Buren..,....	4,448	31	214	4,693	
Warren,.........	3,555	2	696	4,253	
Washington,.....	6,248	42	923	7,213	Potosi.
Wayne,.........	3,069	12	322	3,403	Greenville.
Total,	323,888	1,574	58,240	383,702	

JEFFERSON CITY, (a beautiful and commanding place,) the seat of government, is situated near the geographical centre of the State, and is destined for future greatness.

INDEPENDENCE, in Jackson county, as remarked else-where, which is situated in the very heart of this delightful, fertile, and healthy country, is considered their ZION, or *haven of ultimate repose;* but as it is not a commercial mart, ST. LOUIS has been designated as their great empo-rium — *the Joppa to their Jerusalem.* St. Louis is situated on the west bank of the Mississippi, " 17 miles below the mouth of the Missouri, 175 miles above the mouth of the Ohio, 1350 from the Gulf of Mexico, 860 below the Falls of St. Anthony, 850 by the post routes from Washington, and 1200 from Santa Fé by way of Independence." The advantages of this situation are but beginning to be appreciated. From its position, St. Louis commands the internal trade of one half the North American continent, and will, undoubtedly, at no distant period, be one of the largest cities of the world; placed as it is in the centre of a most fertile, salubrious, and delightful country, with the mighty Mississippi stretching hundreds of miles upon each side of it, and the no less colossal Missouri emptying its thousand leagues of waters at the very doors of its citizens, and with two other great rivers, the Ohio and the Illinois, bringing it the tribute of their navigable waters. The lat-ter river will, also, by its union with Lake Michigan by a canal, bring to St. Louis the commerce of the vast coun-tries which stretch north of the great lakes, and also that of a large portion of their shores. I cannot but admire the judgment with which the Mormon leaders selected this, the very heart of North America, as the chief seat of their vast empire. Could they have succeeded in erecting there an independent military organization, they would have been able to control, in time, almost the whole continent. But Providence, which, for its own wise, though inscruta-ble purposes, permitted them to proceed, for a season, un-checked in their audacious career, has at length interposed, and will scatter them and their wild, Utopian schemes, like the sand of the desert before the blast of the furious tornado.

" *Productive Industry.* The vast prairies of which the greater part of Missouri is composed, furnish admirable natural pastures for the live stock of the new comers, and grazing has, therefore, formed an important branch of agricultural industry in this State. Black cattle, horses, and hogs, are raised in great numbers for exportation. ' The business of rearing cattle is almost reduced to the simple operation of turning them out upon the prairies, and letting them fatten until the owners think proper to claim the tribute of their flesh.' Salted beef, tallow, hides, pork, and live stock, are important articles of export; the number of hogs slaughtered for exportation in 1836, is stated at nearly 100,000. (*Western Address Directory.*) Cotton is raised in the southern part of the State, but not in considerable quantities; tobacco is more extensively grown, and hemp, wheat, Indian corn, and other cereals are cultivated with success. The only mineral which has been much worked is lead, which is in part exported in pigs, and in part manufactured into sheet lead and shot. But the beds of coal and lime, the profusion and good quality of the iron-ore, and the heavy cost of transporting iron from the sea to these remote regions, will soon make that metal one of the most valuable products of the State. Some lumber, furs, and skins, are procured from Missouri, but most of the last-named are now brought from beyond her borders. The Santa Fé trade employs several hundred men, with 40 or 50 wagons, and the caravans bring home specie, wool, and mules, in return for powder, rifles, knives, cotton and woollen goods, &c."

Hygiene. — Persons removing to the west should, particularly during their acclimatement, wear flannel next the skin, avoid the heavy dews and fogs, and make free use of the TOMATO, (which is one of the very best alteratives and deobstruents known to the *Materia Medica* — possessing, in an eminent degree, the virtues of calomel divested of the deleterious qualities,) by which they will, in most cases, avoid all those harassing bilious affections, and obstructions, to which unacclimated persons are so frequently subjected. The west, in many parts, is as healthy as any other portion of the globe; but in all migratory operations, a certain acclimation has to be passed through, in which, however, with proper care, *there is no danger whatever.* In the GREAT WEST, the seat of this contemplated vast Western Empire, *the water is pure, the land fertile, the climate salubrious, and the beauty of the scenery unsurpassed* — presenting at once the NE PLUS ULTRA of an earthly *Elysium.*

ILLINOIS AND IOWA. These extensive regions of country, of superior excellence and surpassing beauty, are not very dissimilar to the State already described, and were to form the remaining portion of the vast domain of the nu-

26

cleus before which nations, kingdoms, and empires, were to fall. As the GREAT PLOT AND LEAGUE is now fully before the nation, and as my limits will not allow me to prosecute the subject further in this Exposé, I will close this chapter with the single remark, that the public weal requires the vigilant eye of the body politic to LOOK WELL TO THE WEST!

------------------◆------------------

AN APPEAL TO THE PUBLIC.

I have elsewhere shown the danger that menaces our civil and political institutions from the machinations of the Mormon Impostor, and I now wish to appeal to the feelings and the fears of the Christian community, and to urge all good and religious men to unite their efforts for the purpose of checking and suppressing this Monster in his career of wickedness and blasphemy. The developments I have made, and the documents I have produced, are surely sufficient to convince every man of sense and foresight, that Joe Smith meditates the total overthrow, not only of our government and of our social fabric, but of all creeds and religions that are not in perfect accordance with his own bloody and stupid imposture. The course he has hitherto pursued, particularly in Missouri, shows clearly as the noonday sun, that, had he but the power, he does not lack the will, to propagate his doctrines by the cannon and the bayonet. The Mormons, as soon as they acquired a majority, would proceed to exterminate, or convert forcibly, all those, whether Christians or Heathens, whom they style Gentiles, in distinction from their saintly selves. Even were this not to be inferred from their present conduct, we could readily foretell it from the experience of the course of such fanatics afforded us by history.

The dreadful atrocities perpetrated by the Jews when they rose to follow the numerous pretended Messiahs who have appeared since Christ, are well known to every reader, as also are the miserable calamities which befell the Hebrew nation in consequence of their infatuation after these villanous impostors.

When Barchochebas, or, as he styled himself, the Son of a Star, had caused an insurrection against the Romans, the Jews, believing him to be their long-promised Savior, flocked to his standard in immense numbers, and for a long time defied the whole power of the Roman empire, and treated with the most abominable cruelty those of the Gentiles who fell into their hands. They slaughtered, in the course of their rebellion, not less than one hundred thousand Roman citizens, and they were themselves finally subdued only by the sacrifice of more than half a million of lives.

In the fifth century appeared another of these pretenders to the Messiahship, who, in the Island of Candia, so grossly deluded his countrymen, that hundreds threw themselves, at his command, into the sea, because he had promised to conduct them safely through it to the Promised Land.

In the sixth century appeared one named Julian, who, after a long and bloody war, was captured by the generals of Justinian, and put to death, together with his chief adherents.

In 1157, Spain was very much disturbed by another, who so excited against himself the anger of the Mohammedans, that nearly all the Jews in Granada were massacred for supporting him in his insane pretensions.

Towards the close of the twelfth century, also, there arose, in the province of Hamadan, in Persia, an impostor of no common quality, the famous David El David, or, as he is often termed, David Alroy. He defeated, in several sanguinary battles, the sultans of Roum and of Persia, overthrew the army of the caliph, and even captured Bagdad, the capital of the Mohammedan empire, where he reigned for some time in great splendor, and was finally captured and killed by Alp Arslan, king of Karasme. His career, which caused the almost entire destruction of the flourishing Jewish communities in the neighborhood of the Tigris and Euphrates, has been made the subject of a most splendid and eloquent work, by the younger D'Israeli.

It is worthy of remark that all these, and scores of other

Jewish impostors, pretended, as Joe Smith now does, that they were raised up of God to fulfil the ancient prophecies, and restore the Jews to their Promised Land. Like Smith, they based their claims on a literal interpretation of prophecy, found manifold texts as explicit as the Mormon wall, the stick of Ephraim, the flying angel, and the others alleged in favor of the Mormon pretended revelation. They added miracles and prodigies wherever they were wanted, and found dupes enough to believe and run after them, and sacrifice all earthly good to their preposterous claims, as the Mormons now do to the claims of Smith.*

But the most striking historical parallel to the course of the Mormons, and one, too, from which Smith and his comrades have derived the ideas of many of their proceedings, is contained in the career of the Anabaptists.

They appeared in the year 1525, in Germany, during the religious excitement and confusion produced by the attempts of Luther and his coadjutors to reform the Papacy. They so remarkably resembled the Mormons, that it is quite evident the latter have taken them for models, and have copied their doings with as much accuracy as the spirit of the age would permit. The first leader of the Anabaptists was a low, ignorant fellow, named Thomas Munster, who, like Joe Smith, was at the same time their prophet and military commander. They, precisely again like the Mormons, gave themselves out for " *Latter Day Saints*," and professed to be chosen by the Almighty as instruments to produce the promised millennium reign of Christ on earth. They believed, likewise, that they were especial favorites of Heaven in every respect, and that they were, when they wished it, favored with familiar personal intercourse with the Deity, and from him constantly received revelations and instructions. They also believed that their faith rendered them invulnerable to the assaults of their enemies, and that, like the Hebrew leaders of old, they were empowered to confound and to overthrow, by the most stupendous miracles, the adversaries of the Lord and of his church. They also pretended to have frequent visions of all kinds, and related most wonderful tales of their interviews and combats with evil spirits. They also,

* Prof. Turner.

like the Mormons, indulged their fancies in prophesying the most horrid calamities to their enemies, and the greatest convulsions in the natural and political world. Such was their enthusiastic zeal, that they soon excited the peasants and ignorant classes of Germany to a pitch of fanaticism unequalled in human history since the days of Mahomet. Their leader, Munster, at length asserted that God had commanded him to resort to arms, in order more speedily to bring about the millennium and the reign of Christ and his saints on the earth!

Accordingly he armed and assembled a vast multitude of his followers, composed altogether of the brutalized peasants of Germany, in whom ages of political and religious oppression had almost extinguished the last vestige of resemblance to Him in whose image they were created at the beginning, and proclaiming himself King of Zion, began to plunder and devastate the towns and castles of Germany, and to slaughter, in the most cruel manner, the classes who, still retaining their senses, endeavored to check his enormities. At length he was met in battle by the imperial forces, and was defeated and captured, after five thousand of his deluded followers had been slain, and the rest routed. Munster was, as he richly deserved, publicly executed soon after he was taken prisoner.

This defeat, and the death of their prophet and general, though it checked for a time the career of these fanatics, did not entirely suppress their zeal or their outrages. A few years afterwards, they, by divine revelation, as they pretended, placed John Matthias at their head, who, bent on following out the plans of the martyred Munster, issued a proclamation in the style of those so profusely given to the world by Joe Smith, commanding the saints to assemble at the New Zion, which Matthias declared was the city of Munster. He pretended that God would from thence enable them so to extend their power, that all the kings of the earth would submit to the dominion of the prophet, and the whole world be conquered by his holy legions. They proceeded in good earnest to carry their insane plans into effect, and, after committing numberless atrocities, were besieged by the civil authorities, and, after a long and terrible siege, during which they defended them-

26 *

selves with the greatest resolution, Mount Zion was taken by storm, and the German Joe Smith, with upwards of a hundred thousand of his adherents, was put to the sword. It is unnecessary to do more than to allude to the well-known history of Mahomet, who, fatally for mankind, was enabled to carry out, to the fullest extent, schemes similar to those attempted by the persons I have mentioned above. There is no doubt that Joe Smith would, if he possessed the capacity, imitate the great Arabian impostor, even in his wars and conquests.

And now, my fellow-citizens, permit me to appeal to you again and again, on this most momentous subject, and urge you, in the name of all that you hold dear and sacred, to spare no efforts to put down this hydra-headed monster of Mormonism, before it swallows up all that is valuable to you in this life or in the next. Unite yourselves, and stand not idly by, suffering a few zealous individuals to fight, single-handed, the battles of humanity and religion.

If this Mormon villain is suffered to carry out his plans, I warn the people of these United States, that less than twenty years will see them involved in a civil war of the most formidable character. They will have to encounter a numerous and ferocious enemy, excited to the utmost by fanaticism and by pretended revelations from God, and led on by reckless, ambitious, and, in some respects, able scoundrels, who will not pause in the execution of their projects, even though to accomplish them they should deluge this fair land with the blood of her sons, and exterminate the results of the toil and the civilization of more than two centuries. I *know* that these things are so. I *know* that the Mormon leaders entertain these designs, and I know the strength and the force that a few more years of impunity will enable them to bring to the accomplishment of their treasonable projects. In proof of what I now assert, I appeal with confidence to the documents and testimony contained in this volume, and I ask every patriotic and religious citizen to examine it carefully and dispassionately, and then say if my statements are not supported as strongly as those of any man need be. And yet what I have given is not a tithe of what might be brought forward upon the subject, had I but the time to gather it. What I here present has been collected in haste, and in a part of the Union distant from that in which knowledge relating to Mormonism can be most readily obtained. Many persons, upon whom I relied for evidence, and who live in the Holy City, have been deterred by threats and apprehensions from testifying, though, as this work will show, many others have nobly come forward, and with great moral courage have stated what they know.

It is to vigorous and united effort that we must look for the final suppression of Mormonism; and the citizen and the Christian is highly culpable, who stands by in apathy, and, with folded arms, coolly looks upon the progress of a system that will eventually destroy, if not timely checked, our religion and our liberties, and involve us and our country in the most direful and irretrievable calamities.

The Mormons, strong already in their numbers and their zeal, are increasing like the rolling snowball, and will eventually fall with the force of an avalanche upon the fair fabric of our institutions, unless the people, roused to resist their villany, quit the forum for the field, and, meeting the Mormons with their own arms, crush the reptile before it has grown powerful enough to sting them to the death.

EXTRACTS FROM A DOCUMENT

PUBLISHED BY ORDER OF THE GENERAL ASSEMBLY
OF MISSOURI.

EXTRACT FROM GOVERNOR BOGGS'S MESSAGE OF 1840.

" Since your last session, the unpleasant difficulties between a portion of the citizens of our State and the Mormons have entirely subsided, with the exception of some slight interruptions on our northeastern border. After that infatuated and deluded sect had left our State, they industriously propagated throughout the Union the most exaggerated details of our difficulties, and the foulest calumnies against our citizens. In some of our eastern cities, missionaries of their creed were employed, daily making converts to their cause by proclaiming the cruelties which they alleged they had endured at the hands of our authorities. The report of our alleged barbarities has not been confined to our Union, but even at this day in Europe they are made the groundwork of proselyting, and their orators find it to their interest to distort the acts into a persecution, which, in every religious excitement that has marked the history of the earth, has always been found the most effectual weapon of conversion.

"In all intestine commotions, particularly when mingled with religious fervor, it frequently happens that cases occur of peculiar hardship and unusual distress, and when public sympathy is excited in their behalf, these unavoidable consequences of civil dissension may easily be magnified into barbarous cruelty. That such cases arose in the course of the difficulty, I do not doubt. But they must be attributed to the excited nature of the contest of the parties, and not to any desire, on the part of our constituted authorities, to wilfully or cruelly oppress them.

"These people had violated the laws of the land by open and avowed resistance to them; they had undertaken, without the aid of the civil authority, to redress their real or fancied grievances; they had instituted among themselves a government of their own, independent of and in opposition to the government of this State; they had, at an inclement season of the year, driven the inhabitants of an entire county from their homes, ravaged their crops, and destroyed their dwellings. Under these circumstances, it became the imperious duty of the Executive to interpose and exercise the powers with which he was invested, to protect the lives and property of our citizens, to restore order and tranquillity to the country, and maintain the supremacy of our laws.

"We owe to our reputation, both at home and abroad, the duty of cleansing every aspersion that may rest upon it. Our State character should be held equally as dear as our individual reputation, and we should use the same exertion in maintaining the one as spotless as the other. Full testimony as to all the necessary facts of that controversy has been preserved or can easily be procured. Written evidence, on both sides, has been filed among the papers of your last session, and forms part also of the records of several of your courts. The facts, as they occurred, can be presented to the world upon proof perfectly conclusive, and the reputation of our State can be rescued from reproach by an exposition of the true causes and events of these difficulties.

"In recommending the publication of this testimony, I have no care about its effect upon the principles of that sect. Our constitution has given us the high privilege of religious independence, and left the worship of the Supreme to the unfettered will of every member of the community. If true, the creed of that sect will ultimately triumph; if false, it will 'die amidst its worshippers.' To explain the attitude which we have been made to assume, I would recommend the publication of all the evidence relating to the occurrence, and distributing the same to the chief authorities of each State "

TESTIMONY ACCOMPANYING THE MESSAGE.

Affidavit of Adam Black.

" STATE OF MISSOURI, ⎱ ss.
County of Daviess, ⎰

" Before me, William Dryden, one of the Justices of the Peace of said county, personally came Adam Black, who, being duly sworn according to law, deposeth and saith, that on or about the 8th day of August, 1838, in the county of Daviess, there came an armed force of men, said to be 154, to the best of my information, and surrounded his house and family, and threatened him with *instant death* if he did not sign a certain instrument of writing, binding himself, as a Justice of the Peace for said county of Daviess, not to molest the people called Mormons, and threatened the lives of myself and other individuals, and did say they intended to make every citizen sign such obligation, and further said they intended to have satisfaction for abuse they had received on Monday previous, and they would not submit to the laws.   *   *   *

         " ADAM BLACK.

" Sworn to and subscribed this 28th day of August, 1838.

         " W. DRYDEN, *Justice of the Peace*

D. Ashby and Others to the Governor.

" BRUNSWICK, *September* 1, 1838.

       " His Excellency LILBURN W. BOGGS :

" Dear Sir,—

" Our country is in a complete ferment, and our families are rendered daily unhappy in consequence of the reports which are constantly coming in concerning the hostile intentions of the Mormons and their allies, as it is currently reported and believed that they have ingratiated themselves with the Indians, and indeed they say so, to assist them in *their diabolical career.*

" The fears of the people are greatly excited, and nothing is now talked of but the contemplated struggle, and plans seem to be devising all around us for the most efficient protection against their encroachments. A deadly hostility is kept constantly alive on their borders, and our old neighbors and friends are petitioning help from abroad to relieve them in their present difficulties. Being remote from the immediate vicinity of the Mormon troubles, we can give but little of authentic data on which to act; but we are strongly of opinion that there is a *deeply-laid scheme* existing among these fanatics, that will be *highly destructive to character*, and at once *subversive of the rights and liberties of the people.*

" We have the best authority for believing that, in their public teachings, their people are taught to believe and expect that immense numbers of Indians, of various tribes, are only waiting the signal for a general rise, when, as they state it, the ' *Flying or Destroying Angel* ' will go through the land, and work the general destruction of *all that are not Mormons.* It is not our object at the present to trouble you with a detail of all the reports in reference to this affair ; but we will state a case within our own knowledge, com. ing from a man who left this neighborhood to join the Mormons, and who has the reputation, among the citizens of Chariton county, for a number of years, of being a man of strict veracity. He has returned perfectly satisfied that their object is every thing opposite to Christian feeling and principle. The following statement which he makes, is given at his own request, and under his own hand : — ' I have resided among the people called Mormons about five months, during which time I have had frequent opportunities of meeting with them, both in their public and *private* associations, and have sought every possible opportunity of acquiring information. I distinctly recollect hearing Joseph Smith, the Prophet, state, in a public discourse, that he had *fourteen thousand men,* not belonging to the Church, ready at a moment's warning, which was generally understood to mean *Indians.* It was a very common source of rejoicing among all classes, even the women and children participating, that the time had arrived when all the wicked should be destroyed from the face of the earth, and that the Indians should be the principal means by which this object should be accomplished. There is a common feeling amongst them, amounting to *a conspiracy to protect one another against the civil officers of the country,* EVEN IF IT SHOULD BE ATTENDED WITH DEATH. The public teachers have recently been very urgent in soliciting the people to fly to their towns for protection, as the time had arrived when the ' *Flying Angel* ' should pass through the land, accompanied by the *Indians,* to accomplish the work of destruction, and furthermore stating that they will have enough to do to protect themselves while this work is going on.   NATHAN MARSH.'

" From the above facts, added to the general reports, we have, with all due consideration, thought proper to suggest to your Excellency the propriety of issuing orders to the militia, so that in case of necessity they may be called on according to the exigency of circumstances.

             " Your obedient servants,   DANIEL ASHBY,
                                                JAMES KEYTE,
                                                STERLING PRICE."

The Clerk of the Circuit Court of Carroll County to the Governor.

" CARROLLTON, Missouri, *September* 6, 1838.

" HON. L. W. BOGGS, Governor of Missouri.
    " Sir, —
       " I am requested by the Committee of Safety appointed for Carroll county, to forward to your Honor a copy of an affidavit made by John N. Sapp, the contents of which, they have every rea-

son to believe, are true; they wish your Honor, if you should consider the same advisable, to acquaint the Indian agents on our frontier with that part of the affidavit which relates to the Indians.

" I have the honor to be,
" With great respect,
" Your obedient servant,
" JOSEPH DICKSON.

" ' STATE OF MISSOURI, }
County of Carroll. }

" ' I, John N. Sapp, do solemnly swear that I resided in Daviess county, State aforesaid, for about the space of five months, and was a member of the Church of the people styled Mormons, and that I left them about the 15th day of August last by stealth. When I left them, they (said people styled Mormons) were building blockhouses, and calculated this fall to build fortifications for the protection of themselves and families in time of war, for which they were making every arrangement; and the understanding is, that each man has to cultivate one acre of land, and if the produce raised on said acre is not sufficient for their mainteinance, and that of their families, they are to take the balance from the Missourians, (thereby meaning the people of other denominations;) and I do further say there are betwixt eight and ten hundred men, well armed and equipped, who have taken an oath to support Joseph Smith and Lyman Wight, in opposition to the laws of the State of Missouri, or otherwise, which said men are called Danites; and I was a member of said body of Danites, and have taken the above oath; and I do further say, I have heard Lyman Wight say, they had TWELVE MEN, [THE DESTROYING ANGEL,] of their Church, among the Indians, and that their object was to induce the Indians to join them (the said Mormons) in making war upon the Missourians, and they expected to be fully prepared to commence war this fall, or next spring at furthest. And I also say, the Danites aforesaid *are sworn to cowhide any person or persons who may say aught against Joseph Smith and Lyman Wight*, and if that will not prevent them from speaking about said Smith and Wight, then they are to ASSASSINATE THEM.
his
" ' JOHN N. ⋈ SAPP.
mark.

" ' Subscribed and sworn to before me, JOSEPH DICKSON, Clerk of the County Court, within and for the county of Carroll, State of Missouri, on the 4th of September, 1838,
" ' JOSEPH DICKSON, *Clerk.*' "

Statement of William Dryden.

" To His Excellency L. W. BOGGS,
Governor of the State of Missouri:

" Your petitioner, William Dryden, an acting Justice of the Peace, within and for Daviess county, would respectfully represent, that the counties of Daviess, Caldwell, and Livingston, are settled, in part, by a denomination of people called Mormons. These Mormons, to the number of about fifteen hundred men, have associated themselves together, and have resisted, and do resist with force of arms, legal process against persons belonging to their denomination. Your petitioner further states, that on the 29th day of August last past, Adam Black appeared before me, and made oath, that A. Ripley, G. A. Smith, and others, had been guilty of a high offence, known to the law, in substance, as follows, to wit: That on or about the 8th day of August, 1838, in Daviess county, there came an armed force to his (Black's) house, in said county, among whom, the said Ripley, Smith, and other persons named in said affidavit, were a part, and then and there, with deadly weapons, made an assault upon him, (the said Black,) and then and there threatened him (Black, who was then an acting Justice of the Peace, within and for Daviess county aforesaid) with *instant death*, if he did not sign a certain instrument of writing, binding himself, as a Justice of the Peace of said county of Daviess, not to molest the people called Mormons, and threatened the lives of himself (the said Black) and others, and said they intended to make every citizen of said county sign such obligation, &c.

"Your petitioner further states, that he immediately issued a writ, pursuant to law, for the arrest of the said A. Ripley, G. A. Smith, and others, commanding the officer, intrusted with the execution of said writ, after the arrest, to bring the bodies of the persons therein named forthwith before your petitioner, to answer the complaint, and further to be dealt with according to law. There being no constable within the township of which I am justice, he having been driven from the county by and through fear of the Mormons, and your petitioner believing that said writ would not be executed, unless a special deputy was made for that purpose, your petitioner, then and there, appointed Nathaniel H. Blakely a special deputy, to serve said writ, and said appointment was endorsed on said writ, and signed by myself officially, and then and there delivered to the said Blakely. Your petitioner further states that the said Blakely took the said writ, and summoned a guard, consisting of ten men, who went in search of the persons named in said writ, for the purpose of executing said writ; but the said constable returned, that the persons named in said writ were not found in said county, by reason of himself and guard having been driven, by force, from the town, in said county, in which the offenders were supposed there to be. The said affidavit, writ, and return, are herewith respectfully submitted to your Excellency.

"Your petitioner further believes and represents, that the Mormons are so numerous, and so well armed, within the limits of the counties of Caldwell and Daviess, that the judicial power of the counties is wholly unable to execute any *civil* or *criminal* process within the limits of either of said counties, *against a Mormon or Mormons*, as they, each and every one of them, act in concert, and outnumber the other citizens. They also declare that *they are independent*, and your petitioner verily believes that the Mormons hold in utter contempt the institutions of the country in which they live.

" Your petitioner further represents, some time about the 8th of September last, that three individuals were arrested by the said Mormons, in Caldwell county, and held in custody, and your petitioner represents that he believes they are still in confinement, without any warrant of law. Your petitioner further represents that he verily believes that no civil officer of the State could cause to be executed any legal process within either of said counties of Caldwell or Daviess.

" Your petitioner, therefore, respectfully prays your Excellency to furnish the civil officers, within and for the counties of Daviess and Caldwell, a sufficient number of troops to enable them to execute the laws of the land, and bring the offenders, aforesaid, to justice. To this end your petitioner will ever pray, &c.

" WILLIAM DRYDEN,
" Justice of the Peace, Daviess County.

" September 15, 1838. "

Statement of C. Jackson and Others.

" CAMP NEAR DE WITT, October 7, 1838.

" To the Citizens of Howard County:

" Gentlemen, —

" This county is the theatre of a civil war, and will soon be one of desolation, unless the citizens of the adjoining counties lend immediate assistance. The infatuated Mormons have assembled in large numbers in De Witt, prepared for war, and are continually pouring in from all quarters where these detestable fanatics reside.

" The war is commenced! blood has been shed — they shed it; they waylaid and fired upon a body of the citizens of Carroll county, and wounded some. They are the aggressors — they have been guilty of high treason; they have violated the laws, and shed the blood of our citizens; and we think this one of the cases of emergency in which the people ought to take the execution of justice in their own hands. Speedy action is necessary; the progress of their imposition, insult, and oppression, ought to be checked in the beginning. The people must act together — they must act energetically.

" It is now 12 o'clock at night — the Mormons are lurking around our camp, and making preparations to attack us before day. Our numbers are much less than theirs, and we will have to act on the defensive, until we procure more assistance. About two hours ago, the Mormons were reënforced by sixty-two mounted men, well armed, from Far West; they are arriving every night; two nights ago, it is thought one hundred came to De Witt, for the purpose of making war upon the people of this county.

" Under such circumstances, you cannot fail to come forward immediately. Can you not be here by Sunday or Monday at furthest? Come by fives and tens, if you cannot come by companies; bring all you can. This is no false excitement or idle rumor — it is the cold reality, too real. We will anticipate you immediately, and shall expect your coöperation and assistance in expelling the fanatics, who are mostly aliens by birth, and aliens in principle from the county. We must be enemies to the common enemies of our laws, religion, and country.

"Your friends and fellow-citizens,

"CONGRAVE JACKSON,	JOHN L. TOMLIN,
"LARKIN K. WOODS,	SIDNEY S. WOODS,
"THOMAS JACKSON,	GEO. CRIGLER,
"ROLLA M. DAVIESS,	WM. L. BANKS,
"JAMES JACKSON, JR.,	WHITFIELD DICKEN.
"JOHNSON JACKSON,	

"P. S. Our guard was just now fired upon by the Mormons. They have become imboldened by their recent reënforcements, and we will have to act on the defensive, until assistance arrives."

Affidavit of Philip Covington.

"STATE OF MISSOURI, } ss.
County of Daviess, }

"I, Philip Covington, an acting Justice of the Peace within and for said county, do certify, that on the 18th inst., one hundred or more Mormons marched to Gallatin, and drove the citizens from said place, then robbed the store and post-office, and burned said store and office. On the 20th of this inst., twenty-five armed Mormons came to my house, and gave me orders to leave the county against next morning, or they would be upon me and my family. Myself, with many other citizens, have left the county. They are now robbing and burning the dwellings of the defenceless citizens.

'Given under my hand, this 22d day of September, 1838.

"PHILIP COVINGTON, *J. P.*"

Colonel Peniston to the Governor.

"DAVIESS COUNTY, Missouri, *October* 21, 1838.

To His Excellency the Governor of Missouri:

"Sir, —

"I deem it my duty, made so not only from the law as an officer, but also as an individual, to report and make known to your Excellency the unheard-of and unprecedented conduct and high-handed proceedings of the Mormons of this and Caldwell counties, towards the other citizens of this county, being myself one of the sufferers.

"On Monday, the 15th inst., we learned that the Mormons were collecting in Far West, for the purpose of driving what they term the mob from this county, by which we understand the citizens that were not Mormons; and accordingly they have come, and our worst apprehensions have been already fulfilled. They have plundered or robbed and burned every house in Gallatin, our county seat, among the rest our post-office; have driven almost every individual from the county, who are now flying before them with their families, many of whom have been forced out *without necessary clothing;* THEIR WIVES AND LITTLE CHILDREN WADING, IN MANY INSTANCES, THROUGH THE SNOW WITHOUT A SHOE!!! When the miserable families are thus forced out, their houses are *plundered* and *burned;* they are making this universal throughout the county. They have burned for me two houses; and, sir, think this not exaggeration, *for all is not told;* and for the truth of all and every statement here made, I pledge the honor of an officer and gentleman.

" These facts are made known to you, sir, hoping that your authority will be used to stop the course of this banditti of Canadian refugees, and restore us to our lost homes. I neglected to state that, among the rest, our County Treasurer's office has been also burned. I will only ask, in conclusion, can such proceedings be submitted to in a government of laws ? I think not, and must answer my interrogatory — No, notwithstanding the *political juggling* of such men as ——————————— and some others, whose reports and circulations, setting the conduct and character of the Mormons favorably before the community, are believed by the people of this county to be prompted by the hope of interest or emolument.

" I am yours, sir,
" With due regard,
" WM. P. PENISTON,
Col. 60th Reg. 2d Brig. 3d Div. Mo. Mi.

" P. S. Since writing the above, I have procured the testimony, on oath, of some six or eight persons, corroborating my statement, which accompanies this.

" W. P. P."

Affidavit of Samuel Venable.

" This is to certify that I was called upon last night to wait upon a lady who was about to increase her family; she had travelled, as she told me, about *eight miles* IN LABOR, to get from the Mormons, who were engaged in driving off the people from their homes, giving them only about three days' notice, *plundering* and *robbing* their houses. The lady alluded to above, Mrs. Smith by name, stopped on the camp ground on the east of Daviess county, where she increased her family. There was another lady who stopped on the camp ground, *whose baby was but four days old.*

" I was also at Mr. White's this morning, who lives in Livingston county, who was on yesterday very much injured in property by the Mormons. I saw a good deal of the mischief by them done, and was told by Mrs. White that, in addition to the above, she received from them invectives; that they had plundered the house, *taken cloths,* and other articles; destroyed all their *bee-stands;* taken off *drawing chains, log chains,* &c. The quantity of *oats, fodder,* and *corn* taken from White's must have been considerable, as they fed about *two hundred horses,* leaving on the ground where they fed a great deal of oats, &c. Given under my hand, this 22d October, 1838.   SAMUEL VENABLE.

" I certify that the above is a true copy of the instrument given, sworn, to, and subscribed before me on 22d of this instant, this 22d October, 1838.   Levi F. Gaben, *J. P.*"

Citizens of Ray County to the Governor.

" Richmond, Missouri, *October* 23, 1838.

" To the Governor of the State of Missouri :

" Sir, —

" The alarming state of Daviess county, and the panic produced by the late movements of the Mormons in that county, have produced a degree of excitement and alarm here, that has not been heretofore witnessed. The latest accounts from Daviess county that have reached us, say that all the inhabitants of Daviess county have left, and sought refuge in Livingston or this county. The storehouse of Jacob Stollings, in Gallatin, was robbed and burned by the Mormons ; the post-office kept there was also destroyed, and we believe that the houses of five or six of the inhabitants of Daviess have been destroyed by fire, the property taken away, and the women and children obliged to flee. The arms of all the citizens in Daviess, they could find, have been taken by them forcibly ; they have carried away the cannon from Livingston county, and have it now in their possession.

" The Mormons have robbed George Worthington, post-master, at Gallatin, of his notes and property, *to the amount of nearly* $2000. In short, the news from them reaches us hourly, that they are destroying the property of the citizens they cannot carry away, and all that they can carry away, they take. *Blood* and *plunder* appear to be their object, and those who do not join with them in their incendiary conduct, are *banished* from Caldwell, and all those of other counties who are opposed to them, are *threatened*. It is the desire of the citizens that his Excellency would visit this section of country, and call out a sufficient number of troops to put a stop to the further ravages of these fanatics. If some such measures are not taken shortly, the whole country will be overrun. We now firmly believe *they are aggressors,* and say they will indemnify themselves for losses in Jackson and Carroll. We are not alarmists, and have had no fears, until lately, that these fanatics would have dared to behave as they have lately. There seems to be but one opinion here on the subject, and that is, unless a military force is brought to act against them, and that shortly, they will destroy as far as they are able. We think it our duty to advise you of these things.

" Very respectfully,

" R. S. Mitchell,	M. P. Long,
" John N. Hughes,	James S. Bell,
" Thos. McKinney,	B. J. Brown, *Sheriff,*
" Jesse Comer,	George Woodward,
" T. L. D. W. Shaw,	Lewis S. Jacobs,
" G. Lenhart,	Berry Huges,
" John C. Richardson,	Wm. Hudgins, P. M.

" We are deficient in arms; if there are any to spare, we wish them brought up here.   WM. HUDGINS."

T. C. Burch to the Governor.

"RICHMOND, Missouri, October 23, 1838.

" To His Excellency the Governor of Missouri:

" The Mormon difficulties are arising, and have arisen here to an alarming height. It is said (and I believe truly) that they have recently robbed and burned the storehouse of Mr. J. Stollings, in Gallatin, Daviess county, and that they have burned several dwelling-houses of the citizens of Daviess, taken their arms from them, and have taken some provisions.

" Mormon dissenters are daily flying to this county for refuge from the ferocity of the Prophet Joe Smith, who, they say, threatens the lives of all Mormons who refuse to take up arms at his bidding, or to do his commands. Those dissenters (and they are numerous) all confirm the reports concerning the *Danite Band*, of which you have doubtless heard much, and say that Joe infuses into the minds of his followers *a spirit of insubordination to the laws of the land*, telling them that the *kingdom of the Lord* is come, which is superior to the institutions of the earth, and encourages them to fight, and promises them the spoils of the battles.

" A respectable gentleman of my acquaintance, from Livingston, is here now, who informs me that the Mormons are robbing the citizens of Livingston, on the borders of Caldwell, of their corn and whatever else they want; that they have taken a cannon from Livingston county, and are prowling about the country, a regularly-formed *banditti*. That the Prophet Joe Smith has persuaded his Church, that they are not, and ought not to be, amenable to the laws of the land, and is still doing it, I have no doubt. The Danite Band, as I am informed by numbers of the most respectable of the Mormons, (who are now dissenters,) binds them to support the High Council of the Mormon Church and one another in all things, *whether right or wrong*, and that even by *false swearing*. I have taken much pains to be informed correctly about this Danite Band, and I am well satisfied that my information, as above stated, is correct. I have no doubt but that Joe Smith is as lawless and consummate a scoundrel, as ever was the Veiled Prophet of Khorassan. I believe the criminal law in Caldwell county cannot be enforced upon a Mormon. Grand juries there will not indict. Joe declares, in his public addresses, that he can revolutionize the United States, and that if provoked he will do it. This declaration has been heard by Colonel Williams of this place, and other gentlemen of equal veracity. I have hoped that the civil authority would prove sufficient for the exigency of the case, but I am now convinced that it is not, so long as indictments have to be found by a jury of the county in which the offence may be committed.

" I do not pretend to have wisdom enough to make a suggestion as to what your Excellency should do. The evil is alarming,

27 *

beyond all doubt. I suggest the foregoing facts for your consideration.

> "I am, very respectfully,
>
> "Your obedient servant,
>
> "THos. C. BURCH.

"P. S.   Judge King will give you some information by the next mail.   T. C. B."

Hon. A. A. King to the Governor.

"RICHMOND, *October* 24, 1838.

"Dear Sir,—

"As Mr. Williams will be to see you in reference to our Mormon difficulties, and will be able to say all to you, perhaps, that can be said, I deem it a duty, notwithstanding, to give you such information as I have sought and obtained, and it is such that I assure you may be relied on.

"Our relations with the Mormons are such that I am perfectly satisfied the arm of the civil authority is too weak to give peace to the country.   Until lately, I thought the Mormons were disposed to act only on the defensive; but their recent conduct shows that THEY ARE THE AGGRESSORS, and that they intend to take the law into their own hands.   Of their recent outrages in Daviess county, you have doubtlessly heard much already; of their course of conduct in Daviess, I will give you the general facts, for to give particulars would far transcend the limits of a letter.

"On Sunday, before they marched to Daviess, Joe Smith made known his views to the people, and declared the time had come when they would avenge their own wrongs, and that all who was not for them, and take up arms with them, should be considered against them; that their property should be confiscated, and their lives also be forfeited.   With this declaration, and much else said by Smith, calculated to excite the people present, the next day was set to meet and see who was for them and who against them, and under such severe penalties there was none, that I learn, who did not turn out, and about three or four hundred men, with Smith at their head, marched to Daviess; this was on Tuesday; the next day was the snow-storm, and upon Thursday they commenced their ravages upon the citizens, *driving them from their houses and taking their property.*   Between eighty and one hundred men went to Gallatin, pillaged houses, and the store of Mr. Stollings, and the post-office, and then burned the houses; they carried off the spoils on horseback and in wagons, and now have them, I understand, in a storehouse near their camp.   Houses have been robbed of their contents, beds, clothing, furniture, &c., and all deposited, and they term it a *consecration to the Lord.*   At this time there is not a citizen in Daviess except Mormons.   Many have been driven without warning; others have been allowed a few hours to start.   The stock of the citizens have been seized upon, *killed and salted up by hundreds.* From fifty to *one hundred wagons* are now employed in *hauling in the corn from the surrounding country.*   They look for a force against them, and are consequently preparing for a siege, building block-houses, &c. They have lately organized themselves into a band, of what they call *Danites*, and sworn to support their leading men in all they say and do, *right or wrong*, and further to *put to instant death* those who will betray them. There is another band, of *twelve*, called the DESTRUCTIVES, whose duty it is to watch the movements of men, and of committees, and to avenge themselves for supposed wrongful movements against them, by privately burning houses, property, and even laying in ashes towns, &c.

"I find I am running out my letter too much in detail; I do not deem it necessary to give you a minute detail of all the facts of which I am possessed, but I give you the above in order that you may form some idea of the disposition of these people. The Mormons expect to settle the affair at the point of the sword, and I am well warranted in saying to you that the people in this quarter of the State look to you for that protection which they believe you will afford when you have learned the facts. I do not pretend to advise your course, nor make any suggestions other than what I have stated, — that it is utterly useless for the civil authorities to pretend to interpose. The country is in great commotion, and I can assure you that, either with or without authority, something will shortly have to be done.

"I hope you will let me hear from you by the return of Mr. Williams, and if you should come up the country shortly, it will give me pleasure to take the trouble to see you.

"I am, very respectfully,

"AUSTIN A. KING."

Affidavit of Thomas B. March.

"At the request of a committee of the citizens of Ray county, I make the following statement in relation to the recent movements, plans, and intentions, of the Mormons in the counties of Caldwell and Daviess : —

"Shortly after the settlement of the difficulties at De Witt, in Carroll county, a call was made by the Mormons at Far West, in Caldwell county, for volunteers to go to Daviess county to disperse the mob, as they said. On the day before this, Joseph Smith, the Prophet, had preached, in which he said, that all the Mormons who refused to take up arms, if necessary, in difficulties with the citizens, *should be shot, or otherwise put to death ;* and as I was there with my family, I thought it most prudent to go, and did go, with my wagon, as the driver. We marched to Adam-on-diahmon, and found no troops or mob in Daviess county. Scouting parties frequently went out, and brought in intelligence that they had seen from three to five hundred men. We got to 'Diahmon on Tuesday evening, and on the next day a company of about eighty of the Mormons, commanded by a man fictitiously named Captain Fearnought, marched to Gallatin. They returned, and said they had run off from Gallatin twenty or thirty men, and had taken Gallatin, — had taken one prisoner, and another had joined the company. I afterwards learned from the Mormons that they had burnt Gallatin, and that it was done by the aforesaid company that marched there. The Mormons informed me that they had hauled away all the goods from the store in Gallatin, and deposited them at the Bishop's storehouses at 'Diahmon. On the same day, Lyman Wight marched about eighty horsemen for Millport. He returned before night, and called for Joseph Smith and Hyrum Smith, to report to them, (said Hyrum being counsellor of said Joseph the Prophet,) and said Wight reported that he had been in sight of Millport — saw no one to fight — but that the people generally had gone and left their houses and property. The Prophet, on hearing the property was left, commenced a reply, and said, ' We had better see to it,' when Wight stopped him by saying, ' Never mind, we will have a private council; ' and Smith replied, ' Very well.' The private council I did not hear. The men were determined to go to their camps. The same evening, a number of footmen came up from the direction of Millport, laden with property, which I was informed consisted of beds, clocks, and other household furniture. The same night, I think, about three wagons were despatched for about *forty bee-gums*, and the next day I saw several gums, when they were splitting them up, and taking the honey and burning the gums, in which business of taking out the honey, but few were engaged, for fear, as they said, they would be called on as witnesses against them. When Wight returned from Millport, and informed Smith that the people were gone and the property left, Smith asked him if they had left any of the *negroes* for them, and Wight replied, ' No; ' upon which some one laughed, and said to Smith, ' *You have lost your negro then.*' During the same time, a company, called the Fur Company, were sent out to bring in *fat hogs* and *cattle*, calling the *hogs* BEARS, and the *cattle* BUFFALOES, [and the *honey* SWEET OIL — BEAR MEAT, BUFFALO, and SWEET OIL — pretty good living !] They brought in at one time seven cattle, and at another time, four or five, belonging to the people of Daviess. Hogs were brought in dead, but I know not how many; I saw only two. They have among them a company consisting of all that are considered *true Mormons*, called the Danites, who have taken an oath to support the heads of the Church *in all things, that they say or do*, WHETHER RIGHT OR WRONG. Many, however, of this band are much dissatisfied with this oath, as being against moral and religious principles. On Saturday last, I am informed by the Mormons that they had a meeting at Far West, at which they appointed a company of *twelve*, by the name of the Destruction Company, for the purpose of burning and destroying ; and that if the people of Buncombe came to do mischief upon the people of Caldwell, and committed depredations upon the Mormons, they were to burn Buncombe ; and if the people of Clay and Ray made any movements against them, this destroying company were to burn Liberty and Richmond. This burning was to be done secretly, by going as incendiaries. At the same meeting, I was informed, they passed a decree that no Mormon dissenter should leave Caldwell county alive ; and that such as attempted to do it, should be *shot down*, and *sent to tell their tale in eternity.* In a conversation between Dr. Avard and other Mormons, said Avard proposed to *start a pestilence* among the Gentiles, as he called them, by *poisoning their corn, fruit*, &c., and saying it was the work of the

Lord ; and said Avard advocated LYING for the support of their religion, and SAID IT WAS NO HARM TO LIE FOR THE LORD ! ! The plan of said Smith, the Prophet, is to take this State ; and he professes to his people to intend taking the United States, and ultimately the whole world. *This is the belief of the Church*, and my own opinion of the Prophet's plans and intentions. It is my opinion that neither said Joseph Smith, the Prophet, nor any one of the principal men, who is firm in the faith, could be indicted for any offence in the county of Caldwell. The Prophet inculcates the notion, and it is believed by every true Mormon, that *Smith's prophecies are superior to the law of the land.* I have heard the Prophet say that he should yet *tread down his enemies*, and *walk over their dead bodies ;* that if he was not let alone, he would be a *second Mahomet* to this generation, and that *he would make it one gore of blood from the Rocky Mountains to the Atlantic Ocean ;* that *like Mahomet,* whose motto, in treating for peace, was ' *the Alcoran or the Sword,*' so should it be eventually with us, ' JOSEPH SMITH OR THE SWORD.' These last statements were made during the last summer. The number of armed men at Adam-on-diahmon was between three and four hundred.   THOMAS B. MARCH.

" Sworn to and subscribed before me, the day herein written.
                          " HENRY JACOBS, *J. P., Ray County, Missouri.*
" RICHMOND, Missouri, *October* 24, 1838."

Affidavit of Orson Hyde.

" The most of the statements in the foregoing disclosure of Thomas B. March *I know to be true ;* the remainder *I believe to be true.*   ORSON HYDE.
" RICHMOND, *October* 24, 1838.

" Sworn to and subscribed before me, on the day above written.
                          " HENRY JACOBS, *J. P.*"

Certificate of Thomas C. Burch and Others.

" The undersigned committee, on the part of the citizens of Ray county, have no doubt but Thomas B. March and Orson Hyde, whose names are signed to the foregoing certificates, have been members of the Mormon Church in full fellowship until very recently, when they voluntarily abandoned the Mormon Church and faith, and that said March was, at the time of his dissenting, the president of the twelve Apostles, and president of the Church at Far West, and that said Hyde was at that time one of the twelve Apostles, and that they left the Church, and abandoned the faith of the Mormons, from a conviction of their *immorality* and *impiety.*

" THOS. C. BURCH,	J. R. HENDLEY,
" WILLIAM HUDGINS,	C. R. MOREHEAD,
" HENRY JACOBS,	O. H. SEARCY.
" GEORGE WOODWARD,	

" RICHMOND, *October* 24, 1838."

General Clark to the Governor.

" To His Excellency L. W. BOGGS:

" Sir, —

* * * * * * * * * *

" I find, by inquiry, that with all the enormities we have heard charged against these people, [the Mormons,] many of which charges we looked upon as the offspring of prejudice on the part of our citizens, THE HALF HAS NOT YET BEEN TOLD !! *There is no crime, from* TREASON *down to the most* PETTY LARCENY, *but these people, or a majority of them, have been guilty of, all, too, under the counsel of Joseph Smith, Jr., the Prophet!* They have committed TREASON, MURDER, ARSON, BURGLARY, ROBBERY, LARCENY, AND PERJURY!!! They have societies formed under the most binding covenants in form, and the *most horrid oaths,* to circumvent the laws, and *put them at defiance,* and to *plunder,* and *burn,* and *murder,* and divide the spoils for the use of the Church. This is what they call the Danite Society.   *   *   *   *

" Under this horrid system many of the citizens of Daviess county, who went to that frontier *poor,* and who, by their industry and economy, had acquired a *good living,* have been *robbed of every article of property they have, their homes burnt before their eyes, and they and their wives and children driven out of the county, without any kind of shelter!* In one instance I have been informed that a family was ordered off, and their houses burnt in their sight, and a woman driven out *while it was snowing, with a child only four days old;* in another case, I was informed the family was driven away, and *the woman was compelled to ask protection in a few miles, where she was delivered of a child a short time after she was thus treated!* These, sir, are SOME of the offences of these people.   *   *   *

" I am, sir,

" Your obedient servant,

" JOHN B. CLARK,

" *Major-General Commanding.*"

The Governor to General Clark.

" Major-General JOHN B. CLARK:

" Sir, —

" Your communication, by express, of October 30, enclosing one from Major-General Atchison and Lucas, of the 28th October, has been received. It is impossible for me to leave here; the near approach of the meeting of the legislature renders it necessary that every moment of my time be employed in preparation to meet them. It was considered by me that full and ample powers were vested in you to carry into effect my former orders. The case is now a very plain one; *the Mormons must be subdued, and* PEACE *restored to the community.* You will, therefore, proceed without delay to execute the former orders. Full confidence is reposed in your ability to do so; your force will be amply sufficient to accomplish the object. Should you need the aid of artillery, I would suggest that an application be made to the commanding officer of Fort Leavenworth, for such as you may need. You are authorized to request the loan of it in the name of the State of Missouri. My presence then could effect nothing. I therefore again repeat that you are authorized, and full power is given you, to take whatever steps you deem necessary, and such as the circumstances of the case may seem to demand, to subdue the insurgents, and give peace and quiet to the country. The ringleaders of this rebellion should be made an example of; and, IF IT SHOULD BECOME NECESSARY FOR THE PUBLIC PEACE, the Mormons should be exterminated or expelled from the State. In order that no difficulty may arise in relation to the command, I must inform you that neither General Atchison nor Lucas have been called into service under the late order, (except General Lucas was directed to raise four hundred men in his division, and to place them under the command of a Brigadier-General.) The privilege was offered him of commanding the troops from his own division, though subject to your orders. All the troops now under arms, and those that may arrive at the seat of war, are placed under your command.

" You will report to me by express, and keep me regularly informed of any thing of importance which may occur. The near approach of winter requires that your operations should be hastened. After having restored quiet, you will cause the people of Daviess county, who have been driven from their homes, to be reinstated.

" I am, respectfully,
" Your obedient servant,
" L. W. BOGGS,
" *Commander-in-Chief.*"

Certificate of Mormons as to the Conduct of General Clark and his Troops.

" RICHMOND, *November* 23, 1838.

" Understanding that Major-General Clark is about to return with the whole of his command from the scene of difficulty, we avail ourselves of this occasion to state that we were present when the Mormons surrendered to Major-General Lucas at Far West, and remained there until Major-General Clark arrived ; and we are happy to have an opportunity, as well as the satisfaction, of stating that the course of him and his troops, while at Far West, was of the most respectful, kind, and obliging character towards the said Mormons; and that the destitute among that people are much indebted to him for sustenance during his stay. The modification of the terms upon which the Mormons surrendered, by permitting them to remain until they could safely go in the spring, was also an act that gave general satisfaction to the Mormons. We have no hesitation in saying that the course taken by General Clark with the Mormons was necessary for the public peace; and that the Mormons are generally satisfied with his course, and feel in duty bound to say that the conduct of the General, his staff officers, and troops, was highly honorable as soldiers and citizens, so far as our knowledge extends; and we have heard of nothing derogatory to the dignity of the State in the treatment of the prisoners.

                    " Respectfully, &c.,
                        " W. W. PHELPS,
                        " GEO. WALTER,
                        " JOHN CLEMINSON,
                        " G. M. HINKLE,
                        " JOHN CORRILL."

EVIDENCE

GIVEN BEFORE THE HON. AUSTIN A. KING,

JUDGE OF THE FIFTH JUDICIAL CIRCUIT IN THE STATE OF MISSOURI,

At the Court-House in Richmond, in a Criminal Court of Inquiry, begun November 12, A. D. 1838, on the Trial of Joseph Smith, Jr., and Others, for High Treason, and other Crimes against the State.

" STATE OF MISSOURI *vs.* JOSEPH SMITH, JR., HYRUM SMITH, LYMAN WIGHT, EBENEZER ROBINSON, ALANSON RIPLEY, and others; who were charged with the several crimes of HIGH TREASON AGAINST THE STATE, MURDER, BURGLARY, ARSON, ROBBERY, AND LARCENY.

" *Sampson Avard*, a witness produced, sworn, and examined on behalf of the State, deposeth and saith : ' That about four months ago, a band, called the *Daughter of Zion*, (since called the *Danite Band*,) was formed of the members of the Mormon Church, the original object of which was to *drive* from the county of Caldwell all those who dissented from the Mormon Church; in which they succeeded admirably, and to the satisfaction of those concerned. *I consider Joseph Smith, Jr., as the prime mover and organizer of this Danite Band.* The officers of the band, according to their grades, were brought before him, at a school-house, together with Hyrum Smith and Sidney Rigdon; the three composing the First Presidency of the whole Church. Joseph Smith, Jr., *blessed them,* and *prophesied over them;* declaring that they should be the means, in the hands of God, of bringing forth the millennial kingdom. It was stated by Joseph Smith, Jr., that it was necessary that this band should be bound together, by a covenant, that *those who revealed the secrets of the Society should be* PUT TO DEATH. The covenant taken by the

Danite Band was as follows, to wit : They declared, holding up their right hands, " In the name of Jesus Christ, the Son of God, I do solemnly obligate myself ever to conceal, and never to reveal, the secret purposes of this society, called the Daughter of Zion. Should I ever do the same, I hold my life as the forfeiture." The Prophet, Joseph Smith, Jr., together with his two councillors, (Hyrum Smith and Sidney Rigdon,) were considered as *the supreme head of the Church; and the Danite Band felt themselves as much bound to obey them, as to obey the* SUPREME GOD. Instruction was given by Joseph Smith, Jr., that if any of them should get into a difficulty, the rest should help him out; and that they should stand by each other, RIGHT OR WRONG. This instruction was given at a Danite meeting in a public address. * * *

" ' At the election last August, a report came to Far West, that some of the brethren in Daviess county were killed. I called for twenty volunteers to accompany me to Daviess to see into this matter. I went, and about one hundred Mormons accompanied me to *Adam-on-diahmon* — Mr. Joseph Smith, Jr., in company. When I arrived there, I found the report exaggerated. *None were killed.* We visited Mr. Adam Black — about 150 or 200 men of us armed. Joseph Smith, Jr., was commander; and if Black had not *signed the paper* he did, it was the common understanding, and belief, that *he would have shared the fate of the dissenters!* * * *

" ' Joseph Smith, Jr., the Sunday before the late disturbances in Daviess, at a church meeting, gave notice that he wished the whole county collected on the next day (Monday) at Far West. He declared (on Sunday or Monday — I don't recollect which) that *all who did not take up arms in defence of the Mormons of Daviess should be considered as tories, and should take their exit from the county.*

" ' At the meeting on Monday, when persons met from all parts of the county of Caldwell, Joseph Smith, Jr., took the pulpit, and delivered an address.

* * * * * * * * * *

" ' In the address, he related an anecdote about a captain who applied to a Dutchman to purchase potatoes, who refused to sell. The captain then charged his company several different times, not to touch the Dutchman's potatoes. In the morning, the Dutchman had not a potatoe left in his whole patch ! This was in reference to touching no property in our expedition to Daviess county that did not belong to us, but he told us that *the children of God did not go to war at their own expense.* * * * * * * *

" ' Lyman Wight observed that, before the winter was over, he thought we would be in ST. LOUIS, *and take it.* Smith charged them that they should be united in supporting each other. Smith said, on some occasions, that one should chase a thousand, and two put ten thousand to flight; that he considered the United States rotten. He compared the *Mormon Church to the little stone spoken of by the prophet Daniel, and the dissenters first, and the State next, was part of the image that should be* DESTROYED *by this* LITTLE STONE ! ! The council was called on to vote the measures of Smith, which they did unanimously. On the next day Captain Patten (who was called by the Prophet, Captain Fearnought) took command of about one

28

hundred armed men, and told them that he had *a job* for them to do, and that the work of the Lord was rolling on, and they must be united. He then led the troops to Gallatin, saying he was going to attack the mob there. He made a rush into Gallatin, dispersing the few men there, and *took the goods out of Stolling's store, and carried them to 'Diahmon, and I afterwards saw the storehouse on fire.* When we returned to 'Diahmon, *the goods were deposited in the Lord's storehouse,* UNDER THE CARE OF BISHOP VINSON KNIGHT!!! Orders were strictly given that all the goods should be deposited in the Lord's storehouse. No individuals were to appropriate any thing to themselves *until a* GENERAL DISTRIBUTION should be made. Joseph Smith, Jr., was at Adam-on-diahmon, giving directions about things in general connected with the war. When Patten returned from Gallatin to Adam-on-diahmon, the goods were *divided,* or *apportioned out, among those engaged;* and *these affairs were conducted under the superintendence of the* FIRST PRESIDENCY! * * *

" ' Some months ago, I received orders to destroy the paper concerning the Danite Society; which order was issued by the First Presidency, and which paper, being the *Constitution* for the government of the Danite Society, was in my custody, but which I did not destroy. It is now in General Clark's possession. I gave the paper up to General Clark after I was taken prisoner. I found it in my purse, where I had previously deposited it, and believe it never had been in any person's possession after I first received it. This paper was taken into President Rigdon's house, and read to the Prophet and his Councillors, and was unanimously adopted by them *as their rule and guide in future.* After it was thus adopted, I was instructed by the Council to destroy it, as, if it should be discovered, it would be considered TREASONABLE. This Constitution, after it was approved by the First Presidency, was read, article by article, to the Danite Band, and unanimously adopted by them. This paper was drawn up about the time the Danite Band was formed. Since the drawing up of the paper against the dissenters, it was that this Constitution of the Danite Band was draughted; but I have no minutes of the time, as we were directed not to keep written minutes; which Constitution, above referred to, is as follows : —

" ' Whereas, in all bodies, laws are necessary for the permanency, safety, and well-being of society, we, the members of the society of the Daughter of Zion, do agree to regulate ourselves under such laws as, in righteousness, shall be deemed necessary for the preservation of our holy religion, and of our most sacred rights, and of the rights of our wives and children. But, to be explicit on the subject, it is especially our object to support and defend the rights conferred on us by our venerable sires, who purchased them with the pledges of their lives, their fortunes, and their sacred honors. And now, to prove ourselves worthy of the liberty conferred on us by them, in the providence of God, we do agree to be governed by such laws as shall perpetuate these high privileges, of which we know ourselves to be the rightful possessors, and of which privileges wicked and designing men have tried to deprive us, by all manner of evil, and that purely in consequence of the tenacity we have manifested in the discharge of our duty towards our God, who had given us those rights and privileges, and a right, in common with others, to dwell on this land. But we, not having the privileges of others allowed unto us, have determined, like unto our fathers, to resist tyranny, whether it be in kings or in the people. It is all alike unto us. Our rights we must have, and our rights we shall have, in the name of Israel's God.

"' Art. 1. All power belongs originally and legitimately to the people, and they have a right to dispose of it as they shall deem fit; but, as it is inconvenient and impossible to convene the people in all cases, the legislative powers have been given by them, from time to time, into the hands of a representation composed of delegates from the people themselves. This is and has been the law, both in civil and religious bodies, and is the true principle.

"' Art. 2. The executive power shall be vested in the PRESIDENT *of the whole Church,* and *his Councillors.*

"' Art. 3. The legislative powers shall reside in the PRESIDENT and *his Councillors* together, and with the *Generals* and *Colonels* of the society. By them all laws shall be made regulating the society.

"' Art. 4. All offices shall be during life and good behavior, or to be regulated by the law of God.

"' Art. 5. The society reserves the power of electing its own officers, with the exception of the Aids and Clerks which the officers may need in their various stations; the nomination to go from the Presidency to his second, and from the second to the third in rank, and so down through all the various grades. Each branch or department retains the power of electing its own particular officers.

"' Art. 6. Punishments shall be administered to the guilty in accordance to the offence; and no member shall be punished without law, or by any others than those appointed by law for that purpose. The *legislature* shall have power to make laws *regulating punishments,* as IN THEIR JUDGMENT shall be wisdom and righteousness.

"' Art. 7. There shall be a Secretary, whose business it shall be to keep all the legislative records of the society; also to keep a register of the names of every member of the society; also the rank of the officers. He shall also communicate the laws to the Generals, as directed by laws made for the regulation of such business by the legislature.

"' Art. 8. All officers shall be subject to the commands of the Captain-General, given through the Secretary of War; and so all officers shall be subject to their superiors in rank, according to laws made for that purpose.

"' In connection with the *grand scheme* of the Prophet, his Preachers and Apostles were instructed to preach to and instruct their followers, (who are estimated in Europe and America at about 40,000,) that it was their duty to come up to the STATE *called* FAR WEST, and to *possess* the KINGDOM; *that it was the will of God they should do so;* and *that the Lord would give them power to* POSSESS THE KINGDOM. There was another writing drawn up, in June last, which had for its object to get rid of the dissenters, and which had the desired effect; (this is the paper drawn up against the dissenters referred to by the witness.)   Since that time, and since the introduction of the *scheme of the Prophet*, made known in the above Constitution, I have heard the Prophet say that it was a fortunate thing that we got rid of the dissenters, as they would have endangered the rolling on of the *Kingdom of God* AS INTRODUCED, and *to be carried into effect*, BY THE DANITE BAND; that they, the dissenters, were great obstacles in their way; and that, unless they were *removed*, the aforesaid Kingdom could not roll on. [This paper against the dissenters is as follows:—]

"'FAR WEST, *June*, 1838.

"'To OLIVER COWDERY, DAVID WHITMER, JOHN WHITMER, WILLIAM W. PHELPS, and LYMAN E. JOHNSON, greeting:

"' Whereas the citizens of Caldwell county have borne with the abuse received from you, at different times, and on different occasions, until it is no longer to be endured; neither will they endure it any longer, having exhausted all the patience they have, and conceive that to bear any longer is a vice instead of a virtue.   We have borne long, and suffered incredibly; but we will neither bear nor suffer any longer; and the decree has gone forth from our hearts, and shall not return to us void.   Neither think, gentlemen, that, in so saying, we are trifling with either you or ourselves; for we are not.   There are no threats from you—no fear of losing our lives by you, or by any thing you can say or do, will restrain us; for *out of the county you shall go*, and NO POWER SHALL SAVE YOU.   And you shall have three days after you receive this communication *to you*, including twenty-four hours in each day, for you to depart with your families, peaceably; which you may do, undisturbed by any person; but in that time, if you do not depart, we will use the *means* in our power to *cause you to depart;* for GO YOU SHALL.   We will have no more promises to reform, as you have already done, and in every instance violated your promise, and regarded not the covenant which you had made, but put both it and us at defiance.   We have solemnly warned you, and that in the most determined manner, that if you did not cease that course of wanton abuse of the citizens of this county, that vengeance would overtake you, sooner or later, and that when it did come it would be *as furious as the mountain torrent*, and *as terrible as the beating tempest;* but you have affected to despise our warnings, and pass them off with a sneer, or a grin, or a threat, and pursued your former course; and *vengeance* sleepeth not, neither does it slumber; and unless you heed us this time, and attend to our request, it will overtake you *at an hour when you do not expect*, and *at a day when you do not look for it;* and FOR YOU THERE SHALL BE NO ESCAPE; for there is but one decree for you, which is, Depart, depart, or a more fatal calamity shall befall you.

*   *   *   *   *   *   *   *   *   *   *

"'The above was signed by some 83 Mormons.

*   *   *   *   *   *   *   *   *   *   *

*   *   *   "'I have looked upon him [HYRUM SMITH] as one composing the First Presidency; acting in concert with *Joseph Smith, Jr.*, approving, by his *presence, acts*, and *conversations*, the *unlawful schemes* of the PRESIDENCY. * * *

"'I was continually in the society of the Presidency, receiving instructions from them as to the teachings of the Danite Band; and I continually informed them of my teachings; and they were well apprized of my course and teachings in the Danite Society.

* * * * * * * * * * *

"'And further this deponent saith not.

"'SAMPSON AVARD.'"

"*Maurice Phelps*, a witness produced, sworn, and examined, for the State, deposeth and saith: 'That * * * * * *

"'On our return from the battle-ground, near Log Creek timber, in Caldwell county, we met Joseph Smith, Jr., Lyman Wight, and others, who went to the wounded and pronounced blessings on them, and prayed for them to be healed and saved. When we started from McDaniel's field fence, the only command given, that I heard, was, "Boys, follow me!" given by the commander. I have been in two Danite meetings. The first, I did not make any exception to; but, in the second, the following exceptionable doctrine was inculcated: "*that we should take spoil, or plunder*, IN SOME CASES."

* * * * * * * * * * *

"'The day before the Mormons went to *Adam-on-Diahmon*, J. Smith, Jr., in an address, told an anecdote of a Dutchman who had been applied to by a captain to purchase potatoes, &c.

* * * * * * * * * * *

"'And further this deponent saith not. MAURICE PHELPS.'"

"*John Corrill*, a witness produced, sworn, and examined, in behalf of the State, deposeth and saith: 'That about last June I was invited to a *private meeting*, in which an effort was made to adopt some plan to *get rid of the dissenters*. There were some things I did not like, and opposed it, with others, and failed. After that, I met PRESIDENT RIGDON, and *he told me I ought not to have any thing to do with it ;* that they would do as they pleased. *I took his advice.* I learned afterwards that they had secret meetings; but I was never invited. * * *

"'In a few days, there seemed considerable excitement among the people, and the dissenters left, as I advised them *they were in danger.* I was afterwards invited to one of these meetings, where an oath, in substance the same as testified to by Doctor Avard, was administered. The society was ultimately organized into companies, and captains of tens and fifties were appointed. I took exceptions only to the teachings as to the duties of that society, wherein it was said, *if one brother got into any kind of a difficulty, it was the duty of the rest to help him out*, RIGHT OR WRONG.

* * * * * * * * * * *

"'In the last, or in some public meeting, Joseph Smith, Jr., said, if the people would let us alone, we would preach the gospel to them in peace ; but, if they came on us to molest us, *we would estab-*

28 *

lish our religion by the sword; and THAT HE WOULD BECOME TO THIS GENERATION A SECOND MAHOMET.

* * * * * * * * * * *

" ' This *Mormon Church* has been represented as being the *little stone* spoken of by Daniel, which should roll on and CRUSH ALL OPPOSITION TO IT, and ultimately should be established as a TEMPO-RAL as well as a *spiritual* KINGDOM. These things were to be carried on through the instrumentality of the *Danite Band*, as far as *force* was necessary, if necessary, they being organized into bands of tens, fifties, &c., READY FOR WAR. The teachings of that society led them to *prohibit the talkings of any persons against the* PRESI-DENCY; so much so, that *it was dangerous for any man to set up opposition to any thing that might be set on foot, and I became afraid to speak my own mind.* * * * * * * *

" ' On Sunday, Joseph Smith, Jr., in his discourse, spoke of persons' TAKING, at some times, what, at other times, it would be wrong to take; and gave, as an example, the case of David eating the shewbread, and also of the Savior and his Apostles plucking the ears of corn and eating, as they passed through the cornfield.

* * * * * * * * * * *

" ' No persons were suffered to leave the county in this extreme time, and I met with Phelps to consult as to what we ought to do. After the troops got to 'Diahmon, in all about four or five hundred men, I heard Lyman Wight addressing a portion of the men who were there, — " that the earth was the Lord's, and the fulness thereof, with the cattle upon a thousand hills; and if I was a hungry, I would not tell you; " that the *Saints* of the Lord had the same privilege or rights. After that, or perhaps the next day, I saw a drove of some four or five cattle pass along, and asked what cattle these were; and was answered that they were a drove of *buffalo;* others observed, they were cattle a *Methodist priest* had CONSECRATED!

* * * * * * * * * * *

" ' Smith, the Prophet, here asked him [Wight] if they had taken the *negroes.* He said, " Yes." Some one then laughingly observed, " Smith, *you have lost your negro.*" * * * *

" ' I think the original object of the Danite Band was to *operate* on the dissenters; but afterwards it grew into a system to *carry out the designs of the* PRESIDENCY; and, if necessary, to use PHYSICAL FORCE to upbuild the Kingdom of God; *it was to be done by* THEM.

* * * * * * * * * * *

" ' And further this deponent saith not.

" ' JOHN CORRILL.' "

———

" *James C. Owens*, a witness produced, sworn, and examined, on behalf of the State, deposeth and saith: ' In the morning of the day that the militia arrived at Far West, I heard Joseph Smith, Jr., in a speech to the Mormon troops, say that he did not care any thing about the coming of the troops, *nor about the laws;* ' * * and that *he did not intend to try to keep the laws,* or please them any

longer; — that they were a DAMNED SET, and God should damn them, *so help him Jesus Christ;* that he meant to go on them as he had begun, and take his own course, and KILL AND DESTROY, and told the men to fight like *angels;* that heretofore he told them to fight like *devils,* but now he told them to fight like *angels;* that *angels* could whip *devils.*   *   *   *   *   *   *   *   *
He swore considerably, and observed that they might think that he was *swearing;* but that God Almighty would not take notice of him in cursing such a *damned set as they were.*   *   *   *   *   *
He stated, at that or some other time, that as they had commenced *consecrating* in Daviess county, that *he intended to have the surrounding counties consecrated* TO HIM; that *the time had come when the riches of the Gentiles should be consecrated to the Saints! !*

    *   *   *   *   *   *   *   *   *   *   *

" ' And further this deponent saith not.

" ' JAMES C. OWENS.' "

" *John Cleminson,* a witness produced, sworn, and examined, in behalf of the State, deposeth and saith: 'Some time in June, I attended two or three Danite meetings; and it was taught there, as a part of the duty of the band, that they should support the PRESIDENCY *in all their designs,* RIGHT OR WRONG; that whatever they said was to be obeyed, and whoever opposed the Presidency in what they said, or desired done, should be expelled the county, or *have their lives taken.* The three composing the Presidency were at one of those meetings; and, to satisfy the people, Doctor Avard called on Joseph Smith, Jr., who gave them a pledge, that if they led them into difficulty, he would give them his head for a foot-ball, and that it was the will of God these things should be so. The teacher and active agent of the society was Doctor Avard, and *his teachings were approved of by the Presidency.* Doctor Avard further taught, as a part of their obligation, that if any one betrayed the secret designs of the society, *he should be killed* and laid aside, and nothing said about it!   *   *   *   *   *   *   *

    *   *   *   *   *   *   *   *   *   *   *

" ' A great deal of other property was brought into the Mormon camps; but I do not know where it came from, but understood it to be consecrated property. It was frequently observed among the troops, that the time had come when the riches of the Gentiles should be consecrated to the Saints.

    *   *   *   *   *   *   *   *   *   *   *

" ' And further this deponent saith not.

" ' JOHN CLEMINSON.' "

" *Reed Peck,* a witness produced, sworn, and examined, on behalf of the State, deposeth and saith: ' A short time after Cowdery and the Whitmers left Far West, (some time in June,) ————— and Philo Dibble invited me to a Danite meeting. I went; and the only speaker was Doctor Avard, who explained the object of the meeting, and said that its object was, that we might be perfectly organized to defend ourselves   *   *   ; that we were all to be governed by the Presidency, and do whatever they required, and uphold them; that *we were not to judge for ourselves whether it were right or wrong;* that God had raised up a PROPHET *who would judge for us;* and that it was proper we should stand by each other *in all cases;* and he gave us an example : If we found one of the Danites in a difficulty, in Ray or Clay, for instance, we should rescue him, if we had to do with his adversary as Moses did with the Egyptian — PUT HIM IN THE SAND ! ! ! It made no difference whether the Danite was to blame, or not; they would pack to Far West, and there be taken care of.

*   *   *   *   *   *   *   *   *   *   *

" ' I was present at one meeting when the officers of the society were presented and introduced to the Presidency, each officer receiving a blessing from them.   *   *   *

" ' I heard Avard, on one occasion, say that the Danites were to consecrate their surplus property, and to come in by tens to do so ; and if they lied about it — *he said Peter killed Ananias and Sapphira, and that would be an example for us.*   *   *   *

" ' On the day before the last expedition to Daviess, I heard Joseph Smith, Jr., in a speech, say, in reference to STEALING, that in a *general* way he did not approve of it; BUT that, on one occasion, our Savior and his disciples *stole corn* in passing through the cornfields, for the reason that they could not otherwise procure any thing to eat.   He told an anecdote of a Dutchman's potatoes, and said, in substance, that a colonel or captain was quartered near a Dutchman, from whom he wished to purchase some potatoes, who refused to sell them.   The officer then charged his men not to be caught stealing the Dutchman's potatoes; but *next morning he found his potatoes all dug.*   *   *   *

" ' When the troops arrived at 'Diahmon, they were divided into companies of twenty, forty, fifty, &c., just as they might be called for.   These companies were sent out in different parts of the country, as I saw them thus occasionally going out and coming in.   I saw a company of about fifty, called a FUR COMPANY, come once. Some had one thing and some another; one I saw with a feather bed; another had some spun yarn.   I understood from some of those who were bringing property, that they were to take it to the BISHOP'S STORE, and deposit it; and if they failed to do so, it would be considered *stealing !*   *   *   *

" ' I heard Perry Keyes, one who was engaged in the depredations in Daviess, say that Joseph Smith, Jr., remarked, in his presence, that it was his intention, after they got through in Daviess, to go down and take the store in Carrollton.   This remark Smith made while in Daviess.   After the Mormon troops returned to Far West from Daviess, I saw several of the captains of tens, who had been in that expedition, making out a list of their men, for the purpose, as they said, of being handed in, that they might receive *their portion* of the SPOILS.

*   *   *   *   *   *   *   *   *   *   *

" ' Some time previous to the difficulties in Daviess, the first time when the militia went out there for the purpose of keeping the peace, I heard Joseph Smith, Jr., in a public address, say that he had a reverence for the Constitution of the United States and of this State ; but, *as for the* LAWS *of this State, he did not intend to regard them, nor to care any thing about them, as they were made by lawyers and blacklegs.*

*   *   *   *   *   *   *   *   *   *   *

" ' In that council Avard said, an arrangement was made to dispose of the dissenters, to wit: that all the head officers of the Danite Band should have a list of the dissenters, both here and in Kirtland; " and," said he, " I will tell you how I will do them: when I meet one damning the Presidency, I can damn them as well as he ; " and, if he wanted to drink, he would get a bowl of *brandy,* and get him *half-drunk,* and, taking him by the arm, he would take him to the woods or brush, " and," said he, " would *be into their guts in a minute,* and PUT THEM UNDER THE SOD "!!!

*   *   *   *   *   *   *   *   *   *   *

' ' And further this deponent saith not.

" ' REED PECK.' "

" *William W. Phelps,* a witness on the part of the State, produced, sworn, and examined, deposeth and saith : ' That——

*   *   *   *   *   *   *   *   *   *   *

" ' It was observed in the meeting, that if any person spoke against the Presidency, they would hand him over to the hands of the *Brother of Gideon.*

*   *   *   *   *   *   *   *   *   *   *

" ' The object of the meeting seemed to be to make persons *confess* and repent of their sins to God and *the Presidency;* and arraigned them for giving false accounts of their *money* and *effects* they had on hand ; and they said, whenever they found one guilty of these things, they were to be handed over to the *Brother of Gideon.* Several were found guilty, and handed over as they said. I yet did not know what was meant by this expression, the ' Brother of Gideon.' Not a great while after this, secret or private meetings were held ; I endeavored to find out what they were, and I learned, from John Corrill and others, they were forming a secret society, called *Danites,* formerly called the Brother of Gideon.

*   *   *   *   *   *   *   *   *   *   *

" ' I remarked to him, I thought such a thing treasonable — *to set up a government within a government.* He [D. W. Patten] answered, it would not be treasonable if they would maintain it, or *fight till they died.* Dimick B. Huntington, and some others, made about the same remark.

*   *   *   *   *   *   *   *   *   *   *

" ' There was a short speech made then, by Joseph Smith, Jr., about carrying on the war; in which he said, it was necessary to have something to live on ; and, when they went out to war, it was necessary to *take spoils* to live on. This was in reference to the dissenters, as well as to the people of Daviess, where they were going. In this speech he told the anecdote of the Dutchman's potatoes.

*   *   *   *   *   *   *   *   *   *   *

" ' Wight asked J. Smith, Jr., twice, if he had come to the point now to *resist the law;* that he wanted this matter now distinctly understood. He said he had succeeded in smoothing the matter over with Judge King, when he was out; and that he defied the United States to take him; but that he had submitted to be taken, because he (Smith) had done so. This was in reference to the examination for the offence for which he and Smith had been brought before Judge King in Daviess. Smith replied, *the time had come when* HE SHOULD RESIST ALL LAW ! ! !

*   *   *   *   *   *   *   *   *   *

" ' And further this deponent saith not.

" ' W. W PHELPS.' "

" *George M. Hinkle*, a witness for the State, produced, sworn, and examined, deposeth and saith:

*   *   *   *   *   *   *   *   *   *   *

" ' There was much mysterious conversation in camps, as to *plundering* and *house-burning;* so much so, that I had my own notions about it; and, on one occasion, I spoke to Mr. Smith, Jr., in the house, and told him that this course of burning houses and plundering, by the Mormon troops, would ruin us; that it could not be kept hid, and would bring the force of the State upon us; that houses would be searched, and STOLEN PROPERTY *found.* Smith replied to me, in a pretty rough manner, to *keep still;* that I should *say nothing about it;* that it would discourage the men, and *he would not suffer me to say any thing* about it. Again, in a private conversation, I said to him I would not raise a mutiny by saying any thing publicly; but I wished to talk to him *privately*, not wishing, however, to set myself up above him in the matter, but that I wished to do it for the good of the Church. I knew this was the way I could get to talk with him. I explained myself more fully than when in the house; and told him I thought things were running to a dangerous extreme, and he ought to exercise his influence to stop it, as this course of things would ruin his people. He answered that I was mistaken, and that *I was scared*, and that *this was the only way to gain our liberty and our* POINT ! ! !   *   *   *   *   *

" ' I saw a *great deal* of PLUNDER and BEE-STANDS brought into camp; and I saw many persons, for many days, taking the *honey* out of them; I understood this property and plunder were placed into the hands of the Bishop at 'Diahmon, named VINSON KNIGHT, to be divided out among them, as their wants might require. There were a number of *horses* and *cattle* drove in, also *hogs* hauled in dead with the hair on; but whose they were, I know not. *They were generally called* CONSECRATED PROPERTY !

*   *   *   *   *   *   *   *   *   *   *

" ' I have heard Joseph Smith, Jr., say that he believed MAHOMET was a *good man;* that the Koran was not a true thing, but *the world belied Mahomet, as they had belied him,* and that MAHOMET WAS A TRUE PROPHET!! The general teachings of the Presidency were, that the *Kingdom* they were setting up was a TEMPORAL as well as a spiritual kingdom; that *it was the little stone spoken of by Daniel.*

* * * * * * * * * * *

" ' It was taught, that *the time had come when the riches of the Gentiles were to be consecrated to the true Israel. This thing of taking property was considered a fulfilment of the above prophecy.*

* * * * * * * * * * *

" ' After we came in from 'Diahmon to Far West, from the last expedition to Daviess, Joseph Smith, Jr., said he intended to *hoist a war flag, or standard,* on the square in Far West, on which he intended to write, " *Religion aside, and free toleration to all religions, and to all people that would flock to it;* and that he believed thousands in the surrounding country would flock to it, and give him force sufficient to accomplish his designs in maintaining his flag and in carrying on the war. The morning that I marched to Far West, to meet the militia to confer with them, as above referred to, Joseph Smith, Jr., made a speech to the troops who were called together, in which he said that the troops which were gathering through the country were a *damned mob;* that he had tried to please them long enough; that he had tried to *keep the law* LONG ENOUGH; but, *as to keeping the law of Missouri any longer, he did not intend to try to do so.* That the whole State was a mob set; and that, if they came to fight him, HE WOULD PLAY HELL WITH THEIR APPLE-CARTS!!! He told his people that they heretofore had the character of fighting *like devils,* but they should now fight *like angels,* for *angels* could whip *devils!* While in Daviess, on the last expedition, I mentioned the great difficulties the course they were pursuing would likely get them into; the reply was, *by a number of them,* that, as the *citizens* had *all fled,* there would be none to prove it by but *themselves,* and THEY COULD SWEAR AS THEY PLEASED IN THE MATTER!!! These, I believe, were of the *Danite order!* And I understood from them that THEY COULD SWEAR EACH OTHER CLEAR, IF IT SHOULD BECOME NECESSARY!!

* * * * * * * * * * *

" ' In that conversation, while many were present, I heard Lyman Wight say, that *the sword had now been drawn, and should not be sheathed* until he had marched to De Witt, in Carroll county, into Jackson county, and into many other places in the State, and *swore that he was able to accomplish it.*

* * * * * * * * * * *

" ' And further this deponent saith not.

" ' G. M. HINKLE.' "

———

" *Thomas M. Odle,* a witness for the State, produced, sworn, and examined, deposeth and saith : ' On the Saturday after *Gallatin was burnt*, an armed company of TWELVE MEN [*Mormons*] rode up to Mr. Raglin's house, in Daviess county, where I resided. They inquired for John Raglin. I told them where he had gone. They said their object was to drive the mob [the citizens] from the county, and that I must go. I replied that I could not; that I had no way to get off, and that my family were barefooted. They replied, that made no difference, *I must go;* and said, if I was not gone by next morning's sun-rising, *they would take my life!* They told Mrs. Raglin she must put out; that there she could not stay, and that Raglin had better never show himself there; that *they would take his life* if they ever set their eyes on him. Next morning, by the assistance of friends, we did start, leaving most of our property there. Since then I have returned, and found the *houses burnt*, and the *property gone*, consisting of *household stuff* and TWENTY-NINE BEE-GUMS.

*   *   *   *   *   *   *   *   *   *   *

" ' They further said that they were at the defiance of any set of men that could come against them; and that *they now intended to make it* A WAR OF EXTERMINATION!!'

*   *   *   *   *   *   *   *   *   *   *

" ' And further this deponent saith not.

his
" 'THOMAS M. ⋈ ODLE.' "
mark.

———

"*Allen Rathbun*, a witness for the State, produced, sworn, and examined, deposeth and saith : ' On the day before the battle with Bogart, I was in Far West; and early in the morning, Daniel Carn, one of the defendants here, asked me to help him grease his wagon. I did so, and asked him where he was going. He said he was going out to Mr. Raglin's, in Daviess county; that THERE WERE ABOUT FORTY BEE-STANDS THERE, *that they were going for.* Directly after, I was at Morrison's store, in Far West. There was a company of ten or a dozen men there, with two or three wagons. I heard Mr. Huntington ask for brimstone. Some of the company said they had two pounds. Huntington answered that would do. Mr. Hunter, of the defendants, here gave the word of command, and they marched off, — Mr. Daniel Carn with his wagon with them. Late that evening, I saw Mr. Carn's wagon at his grocery door, in Far West. I saw Carn and Huntington unloading it. It was loaded with *one bee-gum* and *household stuff*, consisting of *beds* or *bed-clothes*, KINDER tied up; also there were *onions* in the wagon. Mr. Carn, that evening, remarked, that there would be in, that night, a considerable number of *sheep* and *cattle;* and further remarked, that it looked to him sometimes that it was not right to *take plunder*, but *that it was according to the directions of Joseph Smith, Jr., and that was the reason why he did it.* The next morning, I saw a considerable number of *sheep* on the square in Far West, — near about *one hundred!* I then left Far West, and returned home, (in the east part of

Caldwell county,) having been summoned to Far West by my militia captain, but performed no military duties while there.

"'And further this deponent saith not.   ALLEN RATHBUN.'"

"*Andrew J. Job*, a witness for the State, produced, sworn, and examined, deposeth and saith : ' While the Mormon troops were in Daviess county, in the last expedition, I was taken prisoner by Captain Fearnought, (as he was called,) who, I have since learned, was a Mr. Patten. While they were getting me into 'Diahmon about midnight, I passed on between Millport and that place, and counted ten houses on fire.

* * * * * * * * * * *

" 'After I left 'Diahmon, I went to my step-mother's, and made efforts to get out of the county. After the Mormons surrendered at 'Diahmon to the militia, I went with my step-mother to 'Diahmon, to hunt for her property, which had been left at the house when she moved, and which was missing on her return, — such as *beds, bedclothing, knives and forks, a trunk,* &c. On examination, we found at the house of LYMAN WIGHT, and upon *his bedstead,* a *feather bed,* which I KNEW to be the one left by her at the time she fled from the Mormons. I knew the bed from its appearance ; the tick was striped and pieced at the end, and the stripes of the piece turned crosswise ; also, we found *in Wight's house* a set of *knives and forks,* which *I knew* were the same left at her house, as above stated. My step-mother left her residence, (in two miles of 'Diahmon,) where she left the above articles, on Wednesday before I was taken prisoner, which was on the Sunday night after ; and when at 'Diahmon, the night I was a prisoner, I slept on that same bed, as I believed it to be, at one *Sloan's,* as I understood his name to be. When my step-mother left her home near 'Diahmon, where the above articles were left, she went into the lower part of Daviess ; to which place 1 went when turned loose as a prisoner. My father's name is Robert Job.

" 'And further this deponent saith not.   his

" ' ANDREW J. ⋈ JOB.' "

mark.

"*Burr Riggs*, a witness for the State, produced, sworn, and examined, deposeth and saith :

*   *   *   " ' While in 'Diahmon, I saw a great deal of plunder brought in, consisting of *beds and bed-clothes ;* I also saw one clock, and I saw *thirty-six head of cattle* drove in, and put into a pen. All the above property was called *consecrated property* ; and I heard John L. Butler, one of the Mormons who was engaged in assisting to drive the cattle in, say that they had taken the cattle from the citizens of the Grindstone Fork ; and said he had made a valuable expedition. I saw Ebenezer Robinson there, who had a gun-barrel in his hand. I asked him where he got it, and he told me that the evening before *he had set a barn on fire*, and that he heard the gun go off while the house was burning, and he went back and got the barrel out of the ruins of the barn.

* * * * * * * * * *

" Two or three days before the surrender of the Mormons to the militia at Far West, I heard Joseph Smith, Jr., say that the sword was now unsheathed, and should not again be sheathed until he could go through these United States, and live in any county he pleased, peaceably. I heard this from him, also, before the last expedition to Daviess, when Gallatin and Millport were burnt, as well as afterwards, and I heard it on several occasions.

* * * * * * * * * *

" 'And further this deponent saith not.   BURR RIGGS.' "

———

" *John Whitmer*, a witness for the State, produced, sworn, and examined, deposeth and saith : 'About the 17th of April last, at a meeting of perhaps fifteen or twenty-five, in Far West, Joseph Smith, Jr., spoke in reference to difficulties they had, and their persecutions, &c., in and out of the church. Mr. Smith said, he did not intend in future to have any process served on him, and the officer who attempted it *should die;* that any person who *spoke* or *acted* against the *Presidency* or the *Church* should leave the country *or die;* that he would suffer no such to remain there ; that they should *lose their head.*

* * * * * * * * * * *

" 'Among others, I conversed with Alanson Ripley. I spoke of the supremacy of the laws of the land, and the necessity of, at all times, being governed by them. He replied that, as to the technical niceties of the law of the land, *he did not intend to regard them;* that the kingdom spoken of by the prophet Daniel had been set up, and that it was necessary every kingdom should be governed by its own laws. I also conversed with ————, on the same subject, who answered, (when I spoke of being governed by the laws, and their supremacy,) " When God spoke, he must be obeyed," whether his word came in contact with the laws of the land or not; and that, as the kingdom spoken of by Daniel had been set up, its laws must be obeyed. I told him I thought it was contrary to the laws of the land to drive men from their homes ; to which he replied, such things had been done of old, and that the gathering of the Saints must continue, and that dissenters could not live among them in peace.

" 'I also conversed with Mr. J. Smith, Jr., on this subject. I told him I wished to allay the (then) excitement, as far as I could do it. He said, the excitement was very high, and he did not know what would allay it ; but remarked, he would give me his opinion, which was, that if I would put my *property* into the hands of the *Bishop and High Council*, to be disposed of according to the *laws of the Church*, he thought that would allay it, and that the Church, after a while, might have confidence in me. I replied to him, I wished to control my own property. In telling Mr. Smith that I wished to be governed by the laws of the land, he answered, " Now, you wish to pin me down to the law."

" ' And further this deponent saith not.

" ' JOHN WHITMER.' "

" *George W. Worthington,* a witness on behalf of the State, produced, sworn, and examined, deposeth and saith : ' It was on Thursday, about the 18th day of October last, that Gallatin was taken by the Mormons. I reside in about a quarter of a mile of town. About one hundred Mormons, commanded by Captain Patten, as I have since learned, rushed into town ; seven or eight of the citizens were there, who immediately fled. A portion of the Mormons (about fifty) surrounded my house. They took a horse, saddle, and bridle out of my yard, belonging to John A. Williams, of Daviess county. They attempted to take my mare also, but ultimately agreed to let me have her ; but they took my gun. I wished to know the name of the man who got it, so that I might get it at some future day. The captain told me I need not ask for names ; for they would not be given ; they then all went up into town, as they said, to attend to *that store ;* shortly after, three or four of them returned to my house again ; and one of them was Joel S. Miles, one of the defendants here ; they came after a Mormon girl, who was at my house ; and they told me that, if I belonged to neither party, I had better put off, and take the best of my property with me. After they left, I went up into town, to see after some books, notes, and accounts, I had up in town ; but could not get hold of them, as *they had been taken.* I met with one of the company, some distance from Stolling's store, who told me if I would go to 'Diahmon, I could get them, as well as a coat-pattern, which had also been taken. This person advised me to go to 'Diahmon or Far West for protection. I turned off from him to return home. I looked towards the storehouse, and saw the smoke in the roof; and in a short time the flames burst out of the top of the house. I thought it best then for me to put out, seeing they were burning. It alarmed me, and I fixed, and did start, that evening, leaving something like $700 *worth of property in my house.* After I left, *my house was burnt, and the property gone.* Since then, I have seen some of my property in a vacant house in 'Diahmon ; some in a storehouse ; *some in a house said to be Bishop Knight's ;* all in 'Diahmon. These articles consisted of a clock, two glass jars, a box-coat, a paper of screws, some paints, a canister of turpentine, and some planes, chisels, squares, &c.   *   *   *

" ' And further this deponent saith not.

" ' GEO. W. WORTHINGTON.' "

" *Patrick Lynch,* a witness for the State, produced, sworn, and examined, deposeth and saith : ' I was living in Gallatin, a clerk in Stolling's store, when the Mormons took that place, which was about the middle of October last. When the Mormons had approached to within fifty or one hundred yards of the storehouse, I left, having first locked the door, and deposited the key in my pocket. I ran into the brush, between one hundred and two hundred yards of the storehouse, where I saw them taking the goods from the house; some were packed off on horses; and after that, when near half a mile off, I saw wagons, apparently loaded, which I believed to be goods from the store. I have found a number of articles taken from the store in 'Diahmon, since the surrender of arms there by the Mormons — such as tin-ware, painted muslin, a piece of bleached domestic, a piece of brown cloth, a lady's cloak, three pair of scales, and a part of two sets of weights, a leger and three day-books, and the notes of hand to the amount of perhaps $300, were taken from the store. The books have not been recovered, but *the notes I found in the house of Bishop Knight*, at 'Diahmon, in the possession of his wife, except such notes as were on Mormons; these we have not recovered. In about three hours after the Mormons took Gallatin, I returned, and found the storehouse burnt. The post-office and treasurer's office were kept in the storehouse, and the records, papers, &c., belonging to each, were either taken off by the Mormons or consumed by the fire.

" ' And further this deponent saith not.

" ' PATRICK LYNCH.' "

REMARKS BY WAY OF ADDENDUM.

The moiety of testimony now in my possession is here closed, and I rest the case with the public. The evidence is conclusive on all points, and the facts are sustained by unimpeachable witnesses. The reliance of the Mormons on BRIBED and PERJURED witnesses; their confidence in the falsehoods of R. D. Foster, "that notable liar, scoundrel, and villain," as General Robinson calls him; their EXCOMMUNICATION (*letters of Marque and Reprisal*) of Colonel Orson Pratt, *simply because he defended his innocent and abused wife against the calumnies of* BAAL; their heralding and trumpeting forth the wild and incoherent sayings of Miss Eliza Rigdon, uttered during her recent severe sickness, when she was perfectly delirious, — (laboring under mental hallucination at the acme of consecutive exacerbations of high febrile and cerebral excitement, consequent upon an attack of *Pneumonia Typhoides*,) knowing that by the declarations of so good and pious a young lady, made under any circumstances, they could gull and stultify the credulous portion of community, and thus for a time bolster up the Mormon imposture; their recent vile and abusive attacks, as published in "The Wasp," of September 3, 1842, on General James Gordon Bennett, the "*Napoleon*" Editor of the New York Herald, for the only reason that he had indulged in a little pleasantry in relation to their Prophet, when at the same time they are under the most marked obligations to him for past favors; their contemptible, absurd, and vituperative, publications against Moses Y. Beach, Esq., the *Lion* Editor of the New York Sun; their calumnies and slanderous bulletins against Messrs. Sharp, Bartlett, and Davis, the accomplished Editors of the Warsaw Signal, Quincy Whig, and Alton Telegraph; their attempts to wrest the Nauvoo post-office from Sidney Rigdon, Esq., the present incumbent, by false representations to the Department, in order to enable them to purloin and suppress my communications; their great umbrage at Mr. Rigdon because he will not perjure himself to relieve their Hyena Joe from his quandary in the case of Nancy; their system of duplicity, usurpation, and fraud, in the cases of Oliver H. Olney, F. G. Bishop, and others; their violent abuse of every person who has the honesty and MORAL COURAGE to expose their iniquities; with hundreds of other reasons that might be urged, — all go to show that barefaced lying, perjury, fraud, and corruption, (coupled with MURDER, according to other evidence,) are their *dernier ressort*, to save themselves from infamy and disgrace, and in relation to which they have no more scruples of conscience than the wandering Arab, or the degraded Hottentot. They have made lies their refuge, and under falsehood have they hid themselves. All I ask is a careful perusal of this Exposé, and a critical examination of the testimony. The case is now respectfully submitted.

University of Illinois Press
1325 South Oak Street
Champaign, IL 61820-6903
WWW.PRESS.UILLINOIS.EDU